NEW CENTURY BIBLE COMMENTARY

General Editors

RONALD E. CLEMENTS
(Old Testament)

MATTHEW BLACK
(New Testament)

Hebrews

THE NEW CENTURY BIBLE COMMENTARIES

*Not yet available in paperback
Other titles are in preparation

NEW CENTURY BIBLE COMMENTARY

Hebrews

R. McL. Wilson

WM. B. EERDMANS PUBL. CO., GRAND RAPIDS

MARSHALL MORGAN & SCOTT PUBL. LTD., BASINGSTOKE

CONTENTS

CONTENTS

PREFACE

Every commentator is in some measure dependent on those who have gone before him; it would be folly not to avail oneself of the contribution they have made. At the same time, every commentary is unique because (except where it is a joint venture) it represents one person's approach, one person's view and understanding of the text. I have endeavoured to make due acknowledgement of my debts, but in a commentary intended for the non-specialist have avoided extensive citation of authorities on this side and on that. Those who wish detailed references to the literature will find abundance in the commentary by Herbert Braun (*An die Hebräer*, Tübingen 1984), which appeared when this work was well advanced—and his name had already been repeatedly used to refer to his *Qumran und das Neue Testament*. Failure to mention a book does not mean that it was not known, merely that there was no opportunity for quotation, or no specific indebtedness that called for acknowledgment.

For the benefit of students who may have to use the Greek, I have made frequent reference to the Bauer-Arndt-Gingrich lexicon, less frequent to *TDNT*, largely because I have *BAG* at hand but use the German edition of the other. I have kept the use of Greek to an absolute minimum, but have endeavoured to explain the textual foot-notes to *RSV*, and also to provide some indication of the reasons for which modern English versions differ.

My chief aim has been to try to see what the author wants to say to his readers. To that end I have introduced occasional retrospective summaries in the attempt to show the continuity of the argument. I have avoided homiletics—understanding of the author's message must be the first step. Only thereafter can we begin to see and reflect on what that message may mean for us, in the changing circumstances of our own time.

Prof. Ernest Best very kindly read a large part of the typescript, and made many valuable comments. That I have not profited more from his suggestions is of course my fault, and not his.

ABBREVIATIONS

BIBLICAL

OLD TESTAMENT (*OT*)

Gen.	Jg.	1 Chr.	Ps.	Lam.	Ob.	Hag.
Exod.	Ru.	2 Chr.	Prov.	Ezek.	Jon.	Zech.
Lev.	1 Sam.	Ezr.	Ec.	Dan.	Mic.	Mal.
Num.	2 Sam.	Neh.	Ca.	Hos.	Nah.	
Dt.	1 Kg.	Est.	Isa.	Jl.	Hab.	
Jos.	2 Kg.	Job	Jer.	Am.	Zeph.	

APOCRYPHA (*Apoc.*)

1 Esd.	Tob.	Ad.Est.	Sir.	S3 Ch.	Bel	1 Mac.
2 Esd.	Jdt.	Wis.	Bar.	Sus.	Man.	2 Mac.
			Ep.Jer.			

NEW TESTAMENT (*NT*)

Mt.	Ac.	Gal.	1 Th.	Tit.	1 Pet.	3 Jn
Mk	Rom.	Eph.	2 Th.	Phm.	2 Pet.	Jude
Lk.	1 C.	Phil.	1 Tim.	Heb.	1 Jn	Rev.
Jn	2 C.	Col.	2 Tim.	Jas	2 Jn	

GENERAL

AV	*Authorised Version*
BAG	W. Bauer, W. F. Arndt, F. W. Gingrich, *Greek-English Lexicon of the New Testament*
BZNW	*Beiheft zur Zeitschrift für die Neutestamentliche Wissenschaft*
Exp.T.	*Expository Times*
LXX	Septuagint
Mss	Manuscripts
NEB	*New English Bible*
NHC	*Nag Hammadi Codex* (Codices)

NHLE	*The Nag Hammadi Library in English*
NHS	*Nag Hammadi Studies monograph series*
NTS	*New Testament Studies*
RGG	*Die Religion in Geschichte und Gegenwart*
RSV	*Revised Standard Version*
SJT	*Scottish Journal of Theology*
SNTS	*Studiorum Novi Testamenti Societas*
TDNT	*Theological Dictionary of the New Testament* (trans. by G. W. Bromiley of Kittel-Friedrich, Theologisches Wörterbuch)
UBS	United Bible Societies
WUNT	*Wissenschaftliche Untersuchungen zum Neuen Testament*

SELECT BIBLIOGRAPHY

COMMENTARIES

H. Braun (Handbuch z. NT), Tübingen 1984
F. F. Bruce (New London Commentary), London 1964
G. W. Buchanan (Anchor Bible), New York 1972
M. Dods (Expositor's Greek Testament), London 1910
J. Héring (Commentaire du Nouveau Testament), Neuchâtel 1954
E. Käsemann, *Das wandernde Gottesvolk*, Göttingen 1957 (ET Minneapolis 1984)
O. Michel (Meyer Kommentar), Göttingen 1966
J. Moffatt (ICC), Edinburgh 1924
H. W. Montefiore (Black's NT Commentaries), London 1964
C. Spicq (two vols.), Paris 1952
—(Sources bibliques), Paris 1977
B. F. Westcott, London 1909

OTHER WORKS

H. Braun, *Qumran und das Neue Testament*, Tübingen 1966
R. E. Brown, *Jesus God and Man*, London 1968
W. D. Davies and D. Daube, *The Background of the New Testament and its Eschatology* (Studies in Honour of C. H. Dodd), Cambridge 1964
B. Demarest, *A History of Interpretation of Hebrews 7, 1–10 from the Reformation to the Present*, Tübingen 1976
L. K. K. Dey, *The Intermediary World and Patterns of Perfection in Philo and Hebrews* (SBL Diss. Series 25), Missoula 1975
C. H. Dodd, *According to the Scriptures*, London 1952
—*The Bible and the Greeks*, London 1935
J. E. Fossum, *The Name of God and the Angel of the Lord* (WUNT 36), Tübingen 1985
L. Goppelt, *Typos*, ET Grand Rapids 1982
D. M. Hay, *Glory at the Right Hand* (SBL Monograph Series), Nashville and New York 1973
O. Hofius, *Katapausis* (WUNT 11), Tübingen 1970
—*Der Vorhang vor dem Thron Gottes* (WUNT 14), Tübingen 1972
F. L. Horton, *The Melchizedek Tradition*, Cambridge 1976
G. Hughes, *Hebrews and Hermeneutics*, Cambridge 1979
W. Manson, *The Epistle to the Hebrews*, London 1951
A. D. Nock, *Essays on Religion and the Ancient World*, ed. Zeph Stewart, Oxford 1972
D. Peterson, *Hebrews and Perfection*, Cambridge 1982
P. J. du Plessis, ΤΕΛΕΙΟΣ. *The Idea of Perfection in the New Testament*, Kampen 1959

E. Schürer, *The History of the Jewish People in the Age of Jesus Christ*, rev. G. Vermes, F. Millar, M. Black, Edinburgh (vol. I 1973, vol. II 1979)

S. W. Sowers, *The Hermeneutics of Philo and Hebrews*, Richmond 1965

A. Vanhoye, *La structure littéraire de l'épître aux Hébreux*, Paris 1963

G. Vermes, *The Dead Sea Scrolls in English*, London 1962

—*The Dead Sea Scrolls: Qumran in Perspective*, Cleveland 1978

R. Williamson, *Philo and the Epistle to the Hebrews*, Leiden 1970

INTRODUCTION

to

Hebrews

In matters of introduction Hebrews presents many problems for consideration, more perhaps than any other letter in the New Testament: its date, destination, character and purpose, the place of writing, the identity of the persons addressed, the situation to which the letter is directed, not to speak of its authorship—all have been subjects of discussion and debate. Nor can it be said that the discussion has yielded any final conclusions in regard to some of these questions. In the nature of the case, this is only to be expected: the resources at our disposal simply are not adequate. Much of our information has to be extracted from the letter itself, and without the necessary background information to supply clues to its interpretation, there are numerous points on which difference of opinion is possible. Over and over again we must reconcile ourselves to the fact that we do not absolutely *know* the answers; we are dealing with conjecture, with probabilities rather than with certainties. In such circumstances there is no room for dogmatism.

Where so much is in debate, the wisest course is to begin with what is reasonably well established, and work from there into the more obscure areas, using such inferences as may be possible to help us clear the ground. Such a procedure may not in the end bring us to any final results, but it will at least serve to eliminate the 'non-starters', those hypotheses for which there is no ground whatsoever.

1. INCLUSION IN THE NEW TESTAMENT CANON

Now if there is one thing certain about this letter, it is that it had rather a chequered career in the history of the development of the New Testament canon. Here we are dealing with objective facts, which can be documented from external evidence. Hebrews was known to Clement of Rome, who quotes from it in his letter to Corinth (cf. 1 Clem. 36:2–5). It therefore fulfils one at least of the criteria laid down by Eusebius, that of 'knowledge by the ancients'. Yet Hebrews was one of the seven disputed books which were latest in securing final recognition as belonging to the canonical New Testament. Some three centuries after Clement, Jerome remarks 'If the usage of the Latins does not receive it (i.e. Hebrews) among the canonical Scriptures, neither indeed by the same liberty do the Churches of the Greeks receive the Revelation of John. And yet we accept both, in that we follow by no means the habit of today, but the authority of ancient writers, who for the most part quote each of them'. Some twenty years earlier he had been rather less certain, for elsewhere he writes 'The apostle Paul writes to seven churches, for his eighth letter to the Hebrews is by many excluded from the number'. Jülicher notes that while he often uses a cautious formula of citation, the number of cases in which he adduces Hebrews as a letter of Paul grows ever greater with the passing of time (*Einleitung*, 7th edn, [1931], p. 530; cf. Westcott lxxiif.). With Augustine the converse is true: at first he quotes it as Pauline, later he is hesitant, and finally he always cites it anonymously (Souter, *Text and Canon of the NT*, 2nd edn, [1975], p. 174).

Looking back to earlier centuries, the letter was known to Irenaeus (II. 47. 2 Harvey (vol. I p. 368), alluding to Heb. 1:3), but we can say no more than that. Indeed, of the eleven references in Harvey's index to the *Adversus Haereses* three relate to passages in which Hebrews is echoing the Old Testament, and another seven are at most allusions without any close or exact quotation. In no case is the allusion introduced by a formula to suggest quotation of a canonical document. Tertullian (*de Pud.* 20) speaks of the letter as 'more widely received among the churches than that apocryphal Shepherd of the adulterers', but attributes it to Barnabas.

It was in Alexandria that Hebrews first achieved recognition, and here the evidence of Clement and Origen is both interesting and instructive. Clement according to Eusebius (*HE* VI. 14.2) said that it was Pauline, written to the Hebrews in the Hebrew language and translated by Luke for the benefit of the Greeks. He also quotes Pantaenus' attempt to explain the absence of Paul's name from the beginning of the letter: either it was prudently omitted to avoid alienating readers already prejudiced against him, or it was out of modesty, for Jesus himself was the Apostle to the Hebrews, Paul apostle to the Gentiles. Origen, in a passage also quoted by Eusebius (*HE* VI.25.11–14), observes that the style of Hebrews is not that of Paul, but a purer Greek in respect of composition. Nevertheless he maintains that the ideas of the letter are not inferior to the apostolic writings. Further on he adds his opinion that the thoughts are those of the apostle, but the language and composition belong to someone who noted down what was said by his teacher. 'Who wrote the epistle, God only knows for certain'. He mentions the suggestions that the author was either Luke or Clement of Rome, but is prepared to commend those churches which accept the letter as Paul's.

From this brief survey some conclusions may immediately be drawn: first, whoever the author was, he certainly was not Paul (for some differences cf. Kümmel, *Introd.*, p. 276f.). Quite apart from the differences of language, style and theology, there is the fact that no other letter attributed to Paul ranks among the disputed books, not even those regarding which modern scholars have expressed their doubts. Had Paul's name been attached to it from the outset, there would probably have been no debate as to its canonicity.

Secondly, the evidence affords ample justification for Westcott's conclusion (lxxi) that the difference between Alexandria and the West regarding Hebrews springs from their different estimates of canonicity and authorship. 'The Alexandrians emphasised the thought of canonicity and, convinced of the canonicity of the epistle, placed it in connection with St Paul. The Western Fathers emphasised the thought of authorship and, believing that the Epistle was not properly St Paul's, denied its canonical authority'. Indeed, it is probably not too much to suggest that the remarks of Clement and Origen are intended to support its canonical status by linking it so far as possible with Paul, short of actually affirming that he wrote the letter. They clearly valued the book, but it is no less clear that they were fully aware of the differences in language and style which set it apart from Paul's letters. If apostolicity was coming to rank among the criteria of canonicity, the only course open was to find some secondary link, as with the association of Mark with Peter and Luke with Paul in the case of the Gospels. In point of fact, the significance and authority of the book do not depend upon its authorship. Even if it was not written by Paul, it remains an important document in its own right, both as coming from the earliest days of Christianity and as the work of an author of great skill and capacity.

The reservations of the Western Fathers are probably based not only on grounds of authorship but also on reasons of doctrine. Had they *wanted* to retain the book, they would, like the Alexandrians, have found a way. The inference is that they had doctrinal reasons for rejecting it. Thus Campenhausen writes 'That the rejection of Hebrews in the West is linked with anti-Montanism seems certain' (*The Formation of the Christian Bible*, 232). Hebrews adopts the 'rigorist' position with regard to apostasy (6:4ff.; 10:26f.; 12:16f.), admitting no second opportunity for repentance. It is significant that only two Western writers prior to the end of the fourth century mention the letter, and both ascribe it to Barnabas. Tertullian's description of Barnabas as 'a man sufficiently authorised by God', (*de Pud.* 20), together with the reference to Paul in the context, suggests that this is another attempt (like Clement's suggestion of Luke) to find an 'apostolic' author if not an apostle. The identity of the author was therefore quite unknown. Campenhausen (127 n. 92; 143 n. 181) holds that the letter would be read as Paul's (cf.

the conclusion, e.g. 13:23), even that it was intended to be read as
Paul's, but the fact remains that the Pauline attribution is comparatively late and only becomes generally established from the fourth
century on. The names suggested earlier are those of Clement (of
Rome), Luke and Barnabas.

A third conclusion which may be drawn is a firm *terminus ante
quem* for the writing of the letter. If it was known to Clement of
Rome, it must have been written before he wrote, about AD 96.
Unfortunately this does not take us very far, since we have no means
of knowing what length of time should be allowed before that date.
The internal evidence of the letter suggests that it was written to
Christians of the second generation: the salvation first proclaimed
by the Lord 'was attested to us by those who heard him' (2:3); the
author can reproach his readers that 'by this time' they ought to be
teachers, instead of still requiring elementary instruction (5:12);
they have evidently had to face persecution (10:32ff.), and on one
interpretation of 13:7 this had involved the martyrdom of some of
their leaders; 13:23, if it is not just a piece of 'window dressing' to
suggest Pauline authorship, indicates that Timothy is still alive.
Again, however, this does not take us very far. Every Christian
community outside the area of Jesus' public ministry had received
the Gospel from 'those who heard', whether it was founded five
years after the Resurrection or fifty. Assessment of 5:12 depends
entirely on our judgment of what the author expected of his readers;
it does not *necessarily* imply any great length of time. The reference
to Timothy is not very helpful either, since we know neither the
date of his birth nor that of his death, nor how active he was in his
later years. If he was born about AD 20, the 'allotted span' would
take us down to about AD 90, but this is conjectural and in any case
not of much assistance. Even if he was still alive, the reference to
him does not prove Pauline authorship. The letter could have been
written by some other member of the circle of Paul's associates, or
by someone quite outside that group who knew that news of
Timothy would be of interest to the people to whom he was writing.

The reference to persecution might seem to afford a firmer basis,
if we could assume that the persecution was that of Nero and the
one which appears to be threatening, that under Domitian. But
apart from the fact that a persecution under Domitian has been
disputed, it is by no means certain that the persecution the readers
had endured was that of Nero, which appears to have been limited
to Rome itself. It would of course be different if the letter was
written to the church in Rome, but the destination is another point
in dispute. There is also the question whether we should think of
formal persecution, for example by the state authorities, or some

kind of local hostility which if less dramatic might be no less painful for those who had to endure it. Christians from the beginning were exposed to attack, simply because they were different.

Another point which calls for mention here is the Fall of Jerusalem in AD 70. On the one hand it is argued that the author shows no knowledge of this event, and that the letter must therefore be dated earlier. Certainly if he wished to demonstrate the temporary and transitory nature of the old order, it would have been a telling argument that it was in fact a thing of the past, the Temple now in ruins, the sacrificial system no longer in operation. On the other hand it is pointed out that he never mentions the Temple at all. It is with the tabernacle in the wilderness that he is concerned, and his whole argument is based upon the Old Testament, not upon contemporary history. Moreover a case can be made for the view that sacrifices continued to be offered in Jerusalem even after the destruction of the Temple (cf. K. W. Clark, 'Worship in the Jerusalem Temple after AD 70', NTS 6 [1959–60], pp. 269–280; Michel pp. 56–58). It may be added that Clement of Rome (1 Clem. 32:2) writes, well after the Fall of Jerusalem, of 'the priests and levites who minister unto the altar of God' (cf. also 40:5), with no hint that the Temple was no longer in existence. Once again what appears to be a telling argument proves on closer investigation to be indecisive.

A few points should be noted in relation to the Alexandrian tradition: first, Clement's suggestion of a Hebrew original is most improbable, nor is Origen's suggestion of a disciple's notes of his teacher's discourse any better. The language and style tell against both these ideas, and the fact that the Old Testament quotations are almost without exception from the Septuagint, even where it diverges from the Hebrew, is decisive against Clement's suggestion. A translator could of course have used LXX in making his translation, but when the point of the argument depends on a LXX reading it cannot go back to a Hebrew original. Against Origen it must be said that these are not mere notes; this is a polished and well argued discourse. Were Origen correct, the disciple would rank above his master!

On the other hand, Clement's reference to Luke is interesting, since the affinities between Luke and Hebrews have attracted the attention of modern scholars also. The question here however is whether these affinities are such as to demand common authorship, or whether we should not, with C. P. M. Jones ('The Epistle to the Hebrews and the Lucan Writings' in *Studies in the Gospels*, ed. D. E. Nineham, pp. 113–144), classify Luke and Hebrews together as forming a solid bloc in distinction from Mark and Matthew, from

Paul, and from John. This would be of some significance as isolating another strand in the manifold variety of New Testament theology.

II. AUTHORSHIP

The traditional ascription to Paul has already been ruled out, but three other candidates have been mentioned in our early sources: Clement of Rome, Luke and Barnabas. Of these Luke is perhaps the most likely, in view of the affinities referred to above, but as Montefiore pertinently notes 'Luke, unlike our author, is untouched by Alexandrian thought, and he is primarily interested in facts, and not in the kind of theological speculation with which this Epistle abounds.' As for Clement and Barnabas, the other writings under their names make it impossible to think that either of them wrote Hebrews as well. As Montefiore puts it, Hebrews was 'written by someone with a first rate mind, an economical style and a great command of language', Clement's letter to the Corinthians 'by someone with a second rate mind and an imitative style'; and again, 'it is not absolutely impossible that Barnabas could have written this letter; but it is impossible that the Epistle to the Hebrews could have been written by the author of the Epistle of Barnabas'. In addition, there is the question raised by Jülicher (p. 159): could Barnabas, a levite at home in Jerusalem, have been guilty of the errors relating to OT ordinances which appear in 9:3f. and 7:27?

In more modern times numerous suggestions have been made, the most popular among them being that the author was Apollos (first suggested by Martin Luther). According to Ac. 18:24ff., Apollos was a Jew of Alexandria, an eloquent man, well versed in the scriptures, who 'powerfully confuted the Jews in public, showing by the scriptures that the Christ was Jesus'. This description quite admirably matches the characteristics required in any candidate for consideration. Possessed of perhaps the best Greek style in the New Testament, our author was certainly eloquent, and his use of Old Testament quotations proves him 'versed in the scriptures' and well capable of confuting the Jews in public. Moreover the affinities with Philo (see below) suggest some connection with Alexandria. It is therefore not surprising that Apollos should be the most popular candidate, although it is pressing the evidence rather far to argue, with Montefiore, that Hebrews was written by Apollos *to Corinth* and thus was a factor contributory to the situation which elicited Paul's Corinthian correspondence (see C. K. Barrett, *The First Epistle to the Corinthians* [1968], pp. 8ff; for a detailed rebuttal, see L. D. Hurst in *SJT* 38 [1985], pp. 505–513). As Montefiore himself admits, the points he makes are not all equally telling. It is of course *possible*, but we can say no more than that. We simply do not know enough of the circumstances underlying the writing of 1 Corinthians and as Barrett says, paraphrasing 1 C. 4:6, 'it is better not to read too much between the lines'. It should perhaps be added that, popular though it is, the identification of Apollos as the author is still conjectural. Something depends on our estimate of the historical value of Acts, and in any case we cannot assume that the one Alexandrian Jew who happens to be named in the New Testament was the only one of many thousands who was converted in this period to Christianity. In addition there are the points made by William Manson (p. 172), that if Apollos had been the author it is difficult to think that the Alexandrian Church would not have preserved some knowledge of the fact, or that Clement of Rome would not have mentioned him in writing to the Corinthians (a point against Montefiore's theory also), and finally that we have no knowledge of any connection of Apollos with Rome, which (see below) is perhaps the most likely destination for the letter.

One other candidate calls for brief mention: Priscilla. In Ac. 18:2 she is mentioned as the wife of Aquila, but in verses 18 and 26 she is given the first place, which has led to the inference that she was the dominant partner. It has been suggested that if her name stood in the original introductory formula this would account for the suppression of that formula in a period when the prominence of women in Montanism and as mediators of esoteric tradition in some Gnostic circles had provoked suspicion of women in places of responsibility. This however is no more than conjecture. We have nothing written by Priscilla, nor do we know any more of her than is recorded in the pages of the New Testament. The same may be said of many another candidate. Indeed, it is perhaps not too much to say that the effort to identify the author is strongly reminiscent of the efforts of the writers of the *NT* Apocrypha to make good the gaps in the information supplied by the New Testament, and of much the same historical value. It should perhaps be added that the one clear pointer in this respect is indisputably masculine (see on 11:32), which would appear to rule out a woman author.

In short, the problem of authorship remains unsolved. The author certainly was not Paul, and Apollos is probably the strongest candidate. But that is all. That is not, of course, a satisfactory situation for those who must at all costs have clear-cut and definite answers for every problem, but some words of William Manson (p. 172) deserve consideration: 'It may be some compensation for our ignorance . . . to have it brought home to us that Early Christianity

was even richer in creative minds and personalities than the exiguous
surviving evidence of tradition gives us to understand'.

III. DESTINATION AND PLACE OF WRITING

These two questions may be conveniently taken together, since there
is comparatively little to be said about the second, and there are
points at which these questions inter-lock. The letter, for example,
was known in Rome by the end of the first century, and valued by
Clement and Origen in the third. Was it perhaps written from Rome
to Alexandria, or from Alexandria to Rome? If a copy was retained
by the author, this would account for its presence in both cities.
But this again is conjecture. We do not know the processes by which
the letter was circulated in the early Church, or how widely it was
circulated; nor can we assume without more ado that the author
would retain a copy. Its 'Alexandrianism' might seem to favour
Alexandria as the place of writing, but a moment's reflection will
show that this simply does not follow. Scholars influenced by
Bultmann are not confined to Germany, nor are all their books
written there! Moreover, we have no real knowledge of Christianity
in Egypt until well into the second century. Alexandria with its
large Jewish population might seem to be a very obvious and natural
field for the early Christian mission, but our oldest sources have
nothing to say. Tradition links the founding of the church in Alexandria with the name of Mark, but the fact that neither Clement nor
Origen says anything about it makes this tradition one of very
doubtful value.

One clue might seem to be provided in the closing verses, in the
words 'Those who come from Italy send you greetings' (13:24), but
again this is not conclusive. 'Those from Italy', to use a literal
translation, might mean the church in Rome together with other
Christians in Italy, but is scarcely a very natural phrase for the
church of Rome by itself; and once again, we do not know very
much about Christianity in Italy in the early period. Acts mentions
Christians in Puteoli (28:13–14) as well as in Rome, and a *Sator*
square (if it is Christian; cf. F. L. Cross, *The Early Christian Fathers*,
London [1960], p. 200f.) was found in the ruins of Pompeii, but
that is not much to go on. That there were Christians in Italy outside
of Rome at an early period is entirely possible; but it is not certain,
nor can we say how numerous they were. In any case the phrase is
open to other interpretations. If the latter was written to a church
in Italy, it could mean that Italians living abroad had asked for their
greetings to be conveyed to their homeland. This would of course

support the view that the letter was written to Rome, a theory already suggested by the fact that our earliest attention, in *1 Clement*, comes from Rome. There is however, as Montefiore points out, a third possibility: that 'those from Italy' were a group known both to the author and to the recipients. In keeping with his theory (see above) that the letter was written by Apollos to Corinth, he instances Aquila and Priscilla, the only people in the New Testament described as 'from Italy' (Ac. 18:2). They send their greetings through Paul to Corinth (1 C. 16:19), and if Apollos was writing from Ephesus to Corinth it would be only natural for them to do so here. To this extent Montefiore's theory fits, but it is not the *only* possibility: there may have been other Christians from Italy, unknown to us, in some other community of the early Church. To establish the possibility of a theory is one thing, to prove that is the complete and sufficient solution to a problem is quite another. It might equally well be suggested that 'those from Italy' are Aquila and Priscilla, who have asked for their greetings to be conveyed to friends *in Rome*. After all, they had come from Rome in the first place (Ac. 18:2); but from Rom. 16:3 (if it was addressed to Rome) they were already back in Rome when Paul wrote.

Of the three cities mentioned as possible destinations, Alexandria should probably be ruled out. Corinth is certainly possible, but we cannot say more. Rome is probably the most popular suggestion. A quarter of a century ago William Manson sought to be more specific and identify the addressees as the Jewish Christian minority in the Church at Rome. He also sought 'to integrate the Epistle afresh into the history of the world mission from its inception in Stephen', and 'to trace the connection between the doctrine of Hebrews and the theology of the world-mission as a whole'. Here again we are dealing with theories and possibilities, which have been differently assessed by different scholars; some have cordially welcomed the suggestion, where others have been more or less sceptical.

At this point the question of destination inter-locks with another problem, that of the identity of the addressees and the situation to which the letter was directed. On the traditional view, the addressees were Jewish Christians, tempted to relapse into Judaism. It was then a matter of identifying the particular locality in which they lived. Some thought of Rome, but Westcott for example argued for Jerusalem, although he frankly admitted that his conclusion was not beyond doubt.

One major difficulty for Westcott's view is the fact that the letter is written in Greek, and that its argument from the Old Testament sometimes depends on LXX readings. This is certainly hard to explain if the letter was written to Jerusalem. This theory, incidentally, provides yet another inter-lock, since Westcott goes on to argue for a date between AD 64 and 67 (see further below). A more recent theory, represented in particular by James Moffatt and E. F. Scott, challenges the traditional view and, in Manson's words (p. 16), 'detaches the Epistle altogether from its traditional Jewish-Christian moorings and floats it out into the main stream of the general life of the contemporary Church'. According to Moffatt (xvii), 'the writing, in short, might have been called *ad gentes* as aptly as First Peter, which also describes Gentile Christians ὁ λαός, the People'. Now the fact that an author was probably a Jewish Christian does not of course mean that his readers were. His argument and approach may be determined by his own background and upbringing rather than by theirs. Nevertheless it must be said that the particular type of approach which we find in Hebrews is more naturally to be understood if the author was a Jewish Christian writing to Jewish Christians and drawing upon their common background and heritage in the Old Testament scriptures. At all events Manson, in reaction against 'the modern volte-face in criticism' yet not entirely satisfied with the traditional theory, sought to develop a new theory which would more adequately meet the requirements of the situation. However, although the hypothesis of Jewish-Christian readers has been quite widely held, it is by no means the only solution offered, and probably not the majority view (cf. Kümmel, *Introd.*, p. 280, who says 'The author writes to Christians as Christians'; also Schenke-Fischer, *Einleitung* II p. 271f.).

In sum, there is little that can be said about the destination, nor can we be any more confident about the place of writing. It is conceivable that the letter was written from Rome to some unknown destination, but the reference to 'those from Italy' would perhaps be more natural if the author was outside Italy. Of the suggested destinations Rome would seem to be the most probable. The letter was certainly there by the end of the first century, when Clement wrote his First Epistle, and the most natural inference is that it was addressed to Rome in the first place. We do not really know the extent to which such documents were circulated among the Christian communities in the first century, and it would be a mistake to imagine that every book in the New Testament was immediately disseminated throughout the Church as soon as it made its appearance. But if it was Rome this might, as already noted, occasion difficulty with attribution to Apollos. We have no information to suggest that Apollos ever had any connection with that city.

One point to which attention should be drawn is the way in which the problems inter-lock. The questions of authorship, date, destination and the identity of the addressees are all to some extent

inter-related, and decisions about one may have a bearing on our conclusions about another. Equally, a false conclusion on one question
may lead us into quite erroneous inferences regarding the others.
In such a situation, unsatisfactory though it may be, we must often
reconcile ourselves to an admission of ignorance, or at most to the
recognition that a conclusion is possible, but not the only possiblity.

IV. DATE

The one fixed point we have is the *terminus ante quem* provided by
the use of Hebrews by Clement of Rome about AD 96, which leaves
a possible range of something over half a century. Attempts have
been made to narrow the gap, but without any conspicuous success.
Thus, as already noted, the absence of any reference to the Fall of
Jerusalem and the destruction of the Temple does not in fact prove
anything. Westcott (p. 42f.) argues on this basis for a date between
64 and 67, but his view that 'the destruction of Jerusalem must
have been indicated if it had occurred' is at least open to question.
Montefiore's theory that the letter was written by Apollos to Corinth
would entail an even earlier date. He suggests AD 52–54 (p. 28),
which might be considered too early. How much time should be
allowed, for example, for the development of Christological thinking
reflected in the letter? Again, if it was sent to Corinth how did
Clement come by his knowledge of it? Montefiore's suggestion that
'before he wrote this letter, he had doubtless informed himself of
any early letters which they had in their archives' perhaps assumes too
much, and may even represent an undue modernisation. In view of the
distance from Rome to Corinth and back, it must be considered
rather improbable that Clement did any such thing. It is much more
likely that he already had the letter in Rome, however it got there.
   If it was in Rome, how long had it been there before Clement
used it? One can understand one of Paul's churches preserving a
letter from him, but it is more difficult to imagine any church
preserving an anonymous letter for any length of time. That would
suggest a date not long before Clement himself wrote, but he could
equally well be quoting a book with which he had long been familiar.
He had himself found it of value, and perhaps had long mulled over
it, so that to quote it, perhaps some years later, was perfectly
natural. Once again, however, this is conjectural.

   A personal view. The discussion so far has been almost completely
negative, and deliberately so. It is important for us to recognise the

limitations of our knowledge, to distinguish between established facts and opinions or conjectures, however plausible the latter may appear. In the case of Hebrews the evidence often is quite simply not sufficient to allow the formulation of a positive answer to many of the questions we should like to raise. The reader however has a right to expect that the author of a commentary, having worked long with the text and the relevant literature, will have some opinions of his own, however tentative, and will not remain for ever halting between two opinions.

The question which lends itself most readily to an answer is probably that of destination, since as observed above a fairly strong case can be made out for Rome. Corinth is admittedly possible, but might entail too early a date. One might go even further, and adopt William Manson's case for the letter being addressed to the Jewish-Christian wing of the Church in Rome, although some other parts of his theory have weakened under criticism from such authors as Marcel Simon (*St Stephen and the Hellenists*, London [1958]). One difficulty is that the strongest candidate for authorship is undoubtedly still Apollos, and there is nothing whatever to suggest that he ever had any connection with Rome. However, as a distinguished lady scholar once remarked in conversation, there is always Priscilla! Here probably we should frankly admit our ignorance. Whoever the author was, he (or she) was certainly possessed of gifts of a very high order.

In regard to the date there are two main factors for consideration, both rather imponderable: the time required for the Christological and other development evident in the book, and the question how long it had been known to Clement of Rome before he quoted it. Paul's letters show the extent of the development by the time he wrote, but even so Montefiore's suggestion that Apollos wrote it to Corinth and that it was therefore a factor contributory to the Corinthian situation seems to put it rather too early. Between 65 and 70 the Church in Rome would still be recovering from the shock of the Neronian persecution, in which according to tradition both Peter and Paul lost their lives. It is difficult to think of Hebrews as addressed to that situation, so that it should probably be placed somewhat later. Moreover the links with Luke-Acts point to the post-Pauline period (Kümmel, *Introd.* p. 282, suggests between 80 and 90; so too Schenke-Fischer, *Einleitung* II p. 272). This however works against Manson's theory that it was addressed to Jewish Christians, since it is open to question how long a Jewish Christian group could maintain any independent identity with the passage of time (cf. Schenke-Fischer p. 271; but Manson argued not for a

Jewish Christian community but a Jewish Christian wing *within* the church at Rome).

In short, we have to reconcile ourselves to the fact that on most of these questions we have no firm knowledge, only a variety of conflicting opinions advanced by modern scholars (see for example the views discussed by Kümmel, *Introd.* pp. 279ff.). The book was certainly written before the end of the first century, by some unknown Jewish Christian, probably to Rome and possibly to other Jewish Christians. Beyond that we are reduced to speculation, but broadly the alternatives may be reduced to two: if Hebrews was addressed to Jewish Christians the probability would seem to favour an earlier date, before the Neronian persecution, which creates some difficulty with regard to its use by Clement of Rome and also with regard to the Christological and other development that is evident from its contents. On the other hand a late date would seem to entail a Gentile rather than Jewish Christian readership, while it is difficult to imagine 12:4 being written to the church in Rome after the Neronian persecution. The choice between these alternatives is by no means easy. The majority opinion today would appear to favour the later date, but there are still those (including the present writer) who are reluctant to abandon entirely the view that Hebrews is addressed to Jewish Christians (cf. the discussion in J. A. T. Robinson, *Re-dating the New Testament*, London [1976], p. 200ff., who would place the book (p. 220) in 'that uneasy interval between the deaths of Peter and Paul and that of Nero'.

Walter Schmithals (*Neues Testament und Gnosis* [1984], p. 138ff.) has recently introduced a new element into the discussion by suggesting that Hebrews be interpreted in the light of the situation of the 'Apo-synagogos', i.e. persons forced out of the synagogue as a result of the re-organisation at Jamnia following the Fall of Jerusalem. The letter is directed to 'God-fearing Gentile Christians who are now (80–100) being driven out of the synagogue. Thereby they fall under the pressure of persecution, whether from the side of the synagogue or from that of the state authorities (so 10:32ff.) or a combination of both (12:1ff.; 13:3)'. Such expulsion entailed the loss of any privileges or recognition accorded to the Jews, a breach in family and social contacts, and would leave those concerned rootless and friendless in an alien environment. Moreover the Roman authorities were always reluctant to sanction the introduction of new religions within the city boundaries. Such a situation might well account for the loss of confidence and enthusiasm to which the letter is directed, nor do we need to await the actual promulgation of the *birkath-ha-minim* for such a situation to arise.

The pressures would be felt almost as soon as the Jamnia re-organisation began.

One query relates to the identification of those concerned as 'God-fearing Gentile Christians'. Such people would obviously be under pressure: having broken off old ties to associate with the synagogue, they would find it difficult to renew their former associations, and would be constantly under suspicion. But might the group not include people of Jewish origin as well? Christianity and Judaism had been gradually drawing apart, and the Fall of Jerusalem in AD 70 marks the end of an era. The Jerusalem Church no longer provided a focal point as the headquarters of Jewish Christianity, whatever view we take of the patristic tradition of the migration to Pella (Euseb. *HE* III.5.3). But Jewish Christianity continued to survive, if in declining numbers and with tendencies increasingly adjudged heretical, at least well into the second century.

The merit of Schmithals' proposal is that it provides occasion and motive for the writing of the letter, an explanation of the situation of the addressees, and also a reason for the use of argument from the Old Testament, which would be appropriate for readers long associated with the synagogue. It also affords a date which would fit well with what is suggested by other factors, perhaps between 80 and 90 AD. On the other hand it would probably entail the abandoning of any attempt to identify the author, as this might seem too late for either Apollos or Priscilla; but as indicated above that is not too serious a problem. The one reservation necessary seems to be that the addressees need not have been solely Gentile Christians; they may have included Jewish Christians as well.

There is however another point which deserves consideration. If the book *was* written for Jewish Christians, and this is admittedly only a possibility, it was Gentile Christians who preserved and handed it down. They must therefore have found it relevant and meaningful, although perhaps with some re-interpretation in the light of a changing situation. For the modern reader, much of it appears strange and on the surface irrelevant. There are still priests in some branches of the Church, but priesthood and sacrifice on the Old Testament model are alien to our experience, and at best for us no more than metaphor. However, when we see the point of the author's message then its relevance begins to emerge. Our approach to Jewish Christianity is perhaps too much coloured by recollection of Paul's conflict with Judaisers in Romans and Galatians, of which there is nothing in Hebrews. This book is written for people who have lost their first enthusiasm, who have grown weary of well-doing, who have need of the admonition 'Stiffen your drooping arms and shaking knees, and keep your steps from wavering'

(12:12f. *NEB*). The danger is not, as the old traditional theory held, that of relapse into Judaism, it is the danger of a loss of hope and confidence, of abandoning the Christian faith in the face of pressures of one kind or another; and it is this that makes it relevant in the very different world of today. Not every part of Hebrews lends itself to modern use, but its vigorous and sturdy exhortation and encouragement to press forward with faith and hope and assurance carries a message for the Church in every age. In this connection reference may be made to two pages in Michel's commentary (pp. 90–91), on the influence of Hebrews in worship and in hymnody: 'Many a motif has passed from Hebrews into the language and hymnody of the Church, so that one must admit that it has won a greater glory in the Church than in theological research'. He refers of course to the *Kirchengesangbuch*, but the remark would hold for hymns in English as well.

One further point calls for attention here: the absence of any super-scription at the beginning. Letters in the ancient world normally began with a more or less conventional formula containing the name of the sender, the name of the addressee and a word of salutation, usually translated in the form: A to B, greeting. This can be seen from many examples in the Papyri as well as from the New Testament, although Paul in particular always expands the formula, first by adding a statement of his credentials as an apostle and also by extending the single Greek word *chairein* into a Christian greeting such as 'grace (*charis*) and peace from God our Father and the Lord Jesus Christ'. Hebrews has no such introductory formula, which raises at once the question whether it is indeed a genuine letter, written for a specific purpose and addressed to a particular group in a particular situation, or a document of some other kind. There is one other example in the New Testament, namely 1 John, which Houlden describes as not a letter but a theological tract (*The Johannine Epistles* London [1973], p. 31), and Westcott before him as a Pastoral (*The Epistles of St John* London [1902], 29f.). The difference is that Hebrews does have a formal close with personal greetings, whereas 1 John, in Westcott's words, 'is destitute of all that is local or special'.

It is entirely possible that the author has taken a homily or address, already composed, which he felt to be appropriate to the situation, and sent it as a letter, adding a few lines of admonition, commendation and greeting at the end; but in that case we should still have expected some indication of the address to which it was sent. Alternatively, copies might have been sent to several churches, which would make it more of a circular than a letter written to a particular church for a specific purpose. In this case the letter might not be specifically directed to any special situation, but more to a situation facing the church in general in this period. Against this, there are indications to suggest that the readers are personally known to the author, and that he does have a specific situation in view when he writes. A further question here is that of probability: it is possible that the author acted in this way, but how likely is it? What could have led him to take this course? In regard to such questions we can only speculate.

If there was a formula at the beginning, what has become of it? Here there seem to be two possibilities, accidental loss or deliberate suppression. The first must be viewed as unlikely, since in that case we should expect the damage to be more extensive; but the letter does not seem to have anything missing. It begins with a polished and elaborate period containing words and phrases which are known to have been popular at the beginning of a speech, and marked (in the Greek) by alliteration and assonance. Manuscripts damaged at the beginning usually lack a few of the opening lines, and it would be strange if the loss was limited to the superscription alone.

Deliberate removal would imply that there was something in the introductory formula which caused reservations to the mind of later scribes and copyists. For example, if the name of the sender was not that of Paul, the formula might have been suppressed at a time when attempts were being made to claim the letter as Paul's; but in that case, why not simply substitute Paul's name? Again, Priscilla has been suggested as a possible author. It might be that the name was suppressed when the Church began to have reservations about the role of women in places of authority and responsibility; but once again, why not simply substitute Paul's name? Against both these suggestions it must be said that no trace of any formula, or the name of the sender, has survived. If there was a formula, it must have been lost at a very early date, to leave no trace in the manuscript tradition. But these suggestions would imply removal at a rather later stage, since these questions did not arise in the earliest days of the Church's history.

On the whole, despite the reservations expressed above, there is something to be said for the view that originally there was no superscription, and that Hebrews is not strictly a letter. The best description is the author's own, a λόγος παρακλήσεως (13:22), a word of exhortation, or perhaps better, of encouragement.

v. THE BACKGROUND OF THOUGHT AND IDEAS

The results of the preceding sections have been comparatively meagre: almost all that can be said with any confidence is a) that Hebrews was not written by Paul, on grounds of language, style and theology; and b) that it nevertheless belongs to the first Christian century, somewhere before AD 96, when it is quoted by Clement of Rome. The evidence at our disposal does not allow firm conclusions in regard to the other questions. As already noted, this is of course unsatisfactory for those who must at all costs have definite and clear-cut answers to every question, but it is a simple matter of fact: on many of these points we are reduced to conjecture. Now it is legitimate to speculate, to try out various hypotheses in order to see which are the more probable; but we have to recognise first that the hypothesis which to one scholar appears very probable may to another be no more than a possibility, and sometimes a remote possibility; and second that there is danger in building hypothesis upon hypothesis. The result may be no more substantial than a house of cards.

1. Parallels

When we turn to the question of the background of the letter, the sources of the author's thought and ideas, the influences which may have affected him, we are on somewhat firmer ground, since here we are dealing with known quantities, in the works of other authors or the literature of various groups, which we can compare with the text of Hebrews. Here again however a word of caution is in order: we may note parallels, but what do these parallels signify? Are they such as might occur in two authors writing independently, authors with to some extent a similar background, or facing similar problems, similar situations; or are they such as to suggest that one writer has been influenced by the other, or by the group which he represents: or finally are they enough to show that the one author has served as a source for the other, who has drawn upon his work, quoted him, used his ideas? These are in fact three different possibilities, difficult as it may sometimes be to decide between them. Moreover, we must beware of the lure of fashion. It is both natural and proper that when any new discovery is made, any new method of approach developed, the new evidence should be compared with our existing sources to see if it sheds any new light on long-standing problems, the new method applied to see if it yields any fresh results; but we must avoid the temptation to assume that the new method, the new discovery, provides the complete and final answer to our questions. Sometimes it does no more than add a further factor for consideration.

At one time it was more or less taken for granted that parallels to Paul's letters in other parts of the New Testament were evidence of Pauline influence, a view later criticised as talk of 'an all-pervasive Paulinism'. It is now recognised that Paul for all his originality was indebted to his predecessors and draws upon the common early Christian tradition. Parallels between Paul and Hebrews may therefore reflect not Pauline influence on Hebrews but their common dependence upon that early Christian tradition. Again, parallels have been noted with the voluminous writings of Philo of Alexandria, and the author of Hebrews has even been called 'a Philonian converted to Christianity'; but other scholars have called in question the alleged 'Alexandrianism' of the epistle. Similarly the discovery of the Dead Sea Scrolls led some scholars to think of the author as a former Essene. No doubt it would be perfectly possible to imagine a man growing up in the Qumran community, or one like it, moving at some stage to Alexandria and there coming under the influence of Philo, and then being converted to Christianity and coming under the influence of Paul; but this is speculation. We have no solid grounds for such a construction. All we can say is that all these factors call for consideration when we examine the author's background.

The question is obviously much too large and too wide-ranging to be adequately dealt with in a brief introduction. Fortunately it has been explored in detail in a doctoral thesis by Lincoln D. Hurst, which we may expect to see in the not too distant future in the *SNTS* Monograph Series. All that is attempted here is a brief outline, which may incidentally serve to reinforce one of the points made above. I have read Dr Hurst's work in typescript, but do not have a copy at hand for reference and can no longer remember the detail. Any parallels are therefore due not to borrowing or to influence but to independent work on the same material. Something of the sort may be true of parallels between Hebrews and the others mentioned above.

2. The Old Testament

One element in the author's background which is beyond any doubt or question is the influence of the Old Testament. In his opening chapter he demonstrates the superiority of Jesus to the angels by a catena of Old Testament quotations; in his second chapter he has quotations from the Psalms and Isaiah; a considerable part of the third is devoted to exegesis of Psalm 95:7–11; the discussion of priesthood 'after the order of Melchizedek' is again based on the Old Testament, and in chapter 8 there is an extended quotation of Jeremiah's prophecy about the new covenant. The long roll of the 'heroes of faith' in the eleventh chapter is again largely based on the Old Testament, with some elements which may derive from Jewish legend. It is this prominence of Old Testament quotation and exegesis in the letter which has led scholars in the past to think of a Jewish-Christian author, and indeed of a Jewish-Christian readership. The latter conclusion is however by no means certain: the background of an author is not necessarily that of the people to whom he is writing. Moreover, if he was a Jewish Christian, his use of LXX suggests the Diaspora rather than Palestine. Furthermore, LXX was the Bible of the early Church. Most of the New Testament documents were in circulation by the end of the first century, but they did not enjoy the same status as the Old Testament. A New Testament canon only begins to emerge in the course of the second century, and the development was not complete until the fourth. It was the Old Testament which provided the basis and substructure for early Christian theology. In fact it has been noted that Christianity retained a predominantly Jewish stamp down to the middle of the second century, even when the majority of Christians were of Gentile origin (Jean Daniélou, *Théologie du Judéo-Christianisme*, Tournai [1958], p. 19, following L. Goppelt, *Christentum und Judentum*, Gütersloh [1954]). This however raises questions which cannot be entered into here (cf. for example J. Munck in *NTS* 6 [1959–60], pp. 103ff., who quotes (p. 110) Macaulay's description of the Earl of Crawford: 'It is a circumstance strikingly characteristic of the man, and the school in which he had been trained, that in all the mass of the writing which has come down to us, there is not a single word indicating that he had ever in his life heard of the New Testament'). The point for our purposes is that use of the Old Testament does not provide any firm basis for identifying either the author or his readers as Jewish-Christian, even for those who like the present writer are inclined to take that view. All we can say for certain is that the author was steeped in the Old Testament. That is clear from page after page.

3. Paul

Discussing the reasons for the attribution of Hebrews to Paul, Jülicher notes (p. 147) that not only was Paul the letter-writer *par excellence*, but also the antinomian tendency of Hebrews and its consistent preference for the new revelation, the new covenant, over against the old appeared entirely Pauline, as did many particular words and phrases, e.g. 2:2 (cf. Gal. 3:19), 2:10 (cf. Rom. 11:36). Who but Paul would have written Heb. 7:18f., about the setting aside of the Law because of its weakness and uselessness? 13:19 led people to think of Paul's imprisonment, as already did 13:3; but above all it was the reference to Timothy which suggested Paul as the author (cf. 2 C. 1:1; 1 Th. 3:2; Phm. 1). Later (p. 150) he observes that Hebrews frequently recalls Paul so strongly that claims have been made for its dependence at least on passages from Romans and 1 Corinthians; 'Heb. 5:12ff. for example cannot be independent of 1 C. 3, even if the dependence need not be a literary one'. But the author's point of view is not that of Paul, nor even to be explained as a simple development of the Pauline position. In similar fashion Montefiore (p. 5) writes 'There is inevitably a large overlap with the theology of Paul . . . For both, God is the final and efficient cause of everything (Rom. 2:36; Heb. 2:10). For both the Law is impotent and has been abrogated by Christ (Rom. 3:20: Heb. 10:1ff.). Both set Sinai and the Heavenly Jerusalem in contrast (Gal. 4:24ff.; Heb. 12:18ff.). Both stress the obedience of Christ (Rom. 5:19; Heb. 5:8). Both regard the death of Jesus as a sacrifice, although Paul does not regard Jesus as a high priest. Both have a similar doctrine of the person of Christ'. In the next line, however, Montefiore continues, 'Yet there are striking differences' – for example the absence in Hebrews of Paul's 'in Christ' formula, or his characteristic doctrine of justification by faith. Moreover on the previous page Montefiore draws attention to similarities between Hebrews and the Johannine literature.

The question is quite simply: what do these resemblances mean? To imagine the author sitting in his study with Paul's letters and the Fourth Gospel at hand for reference, drawing now on one and now on another, is frankly an illegitimate modernisation. There is nothing to suggest that he did anything of the sort. It should be noted at the outset that there is a difference between these Pauline and Johannine 'echoes', if such they are, and the clear and unmistakeable use of the Old Testament. One is *reminded* of Pauline or Johannine *ideas* (more will be noted in the commentary as they occur), but there is little or nothing to suggest actual quotation of either. The use of the imagery of milk and solid food at 5:12ff., for example, does indeed recall 1 Cor. 3 if we limit our attention solely to Paul and Hebrews; but when we discover a figurative use of 'milk' at 1 Pet. 2:2 and parallels in Philo and Epictetus (cf. *BAG* p. 149; Schlier in *TDNT* I, 646) the whole matter takes on a

different complexion. It is in fact a metaphor fairly common in
Greek literature, used by different authors in different ways and to
different ends. Vielhauer writes (*Geschichte der urchr. Literatur*
p. 249) that almost all the common elements are not specifically
Pauline, do not prove any literary dependence of Hebrews on Paul,
and also do not allow us to define the theology of Hebrews as a
continuation of the Pauline. There are indeed common elements,
but they are due to a common background in early Christianity, not
to the influence of one author upon another. Paul, John and the
author of Hebrews are all Christians drawing upon the Old Testament in their efforts to further the Gospel, and some similarities are
only to be expected; but they are also separate individuals, each
with a mind of his own, and hence there are differences which must
also be taken into account.

4. Philo

'For many students of the *NT* the problem of the relationship
between Philo and the Epistle to the Hebrews is one that has
long been satisfactorily settled.' So Ronald Williamson begins the
Introduction to his massive study of the subject (*Philo and the Epistle
to the Hebrews*, Leiden [1970]). In the following pages he presents
a long list of those who have argued for the theory of Philonic
influence, as well as of others who have qualified that view, or
argued against it. His own work was undertaken 'in the belief that
there is much to be said for the view that "Philo's influence on early
Christian thought has doubtless been exaggerated" ' (p. 8, quoting
Copleston, *A History of Philosophy* i. p. 462). At the outset, yet
another warning is in order: we have so much of Philo, so little of
many another author, that it is easy to gain a distorted impression
of his significance and influence, simply because it is his writings
that are quoted as supplying parallels. We must beware of the
danger of 'making Philo too much the mirror of his times'. If we
had more from other sources we might well find that what appears
to be Philonic influence was in fact an opinion much more widely
held, and not necessarily derived from him. In this respect a
comparison with Clement of Alexandria, who undoubtedly did know
and draw upon Philo (cf. for example S. R. C. Lilla, *Clement of
Alexandria*, Oxford 1971) could be instructive. In Clement the debt
is clear and beyond dispute; in Hebrews it is very much less certain.
Montefiore (pp. 6ff.) notes 'a whole series of contrasts between Philo
and our author', and sums up: 'These differences of attitude and
outlook between our author and Philo are fundamental. And yet,

at the same time, the non-theological similarities between the two writers are equally striking'. Spicq (1977, p. 13) says that it is not a matter of some chance encounter, but 'the influence of a master on a disciple', revealed in vocabulary, style etc. In his earlier two-volume commentary (i. p. 89) he had gone so far as to suggest that our author might even have known Philo personally. Both Spicq and Montefiore however emphasise that the author of Hebrews is no mere plagiarist. 'His philonism has been adapted to interpret the Incarnation in the spirit of a genuine biblicism' (Montefiore, p. 8).

S. G. Sowers (*Hermeneutics* p. 66) observes that 'many would find dubious some evidence adduced by Spicq', and therefore devotes part of his own study to the establishing of what he regards as a basic point, 'that the writer of Hebrews has come from the same school of Alexandrian Judaism as Philo, and that Philo's writings still offer us the best single body of *religionsgeschichtlich* material we have for this *NT* document'. In dealing with 'reflections of the Philonic doctrine of the Logos', however, he begins with the words *apaugasma* ('reflection') and *character* in the prologue to Hebrews. Both are terms used by Philo (Williamson cites three occurrences of the former from Leisegang's index, and no fewer than 51 for the latter), but on *apaugasma* Sowers adds 'only here in the Bible', which would appear to strengthen the Philonic connection. This overlooks the occurrence of the word at Wis. 7:26, from which both Hebrews and Philo could have derived it. The oversight is the more surprising in that Sowers later (p. 73) writes that 'the writer of Hebrews has come from the Alexandrian school which historically runs from the LXX through the *Wisdom of Solomon*, Aristobulus, and the *Letter of Aristeas* to Philo'.

The most exhaustive and detailed study of the subject is that of Williamson, who examines first the linguistic evidence, the words used by both writers, then various themes and ideas, and finally the use of Scripture. The striking feature is that over and over again we can find the same words, the same ideas, in both, but that they are used in very different ways. 'In the use of the *OT* made by the two writers striking and fundamental differences appear . . . On such fundamental subjects as time, history, eschatology, the nature of the physical world, etc., the thoughts of Philo and the Writer of Hebrews are poles apart' (pp. 576f.). Williamson admits (p. 579) that the author could have been 'a Philonian converted to Christianity', but finds it hard to believe that his conversion 'could have resulted in so thorough-going a rejection of Philo's attitudes, outlook, methods of Scriptural interpretation, and so on'. In particular we may note the point already made by Sowers and others, that there is in Hebrews none of the characteristically

Philonic allegory. Philo was concerned to make Judaism 'intellectually respectable' for Jews attracted to Greek philosophy, and sought
to do so by reading Greek philosophy between the lines of the Old
Testament: all the wisdom of the best Greek minds was already
there in the inspired teaching of Moses. As Williamson says (p. 538
n. 3), 'There is nothing like this in Hebrews. Where Philo discovers
Plato in the *OT*, the writer of Hebrews finds Christ and Christ
alone'. Williamson finally concludes that the author of Hebrews
'had never been a Philonist, had never read Philo's works, had never
come under the influence of Philo directly or indirectly' (p. 579).

This would seem to leave still open the view already quoted from
Sowers, that the author belonged to the Alexandrian tradition which
extends from the LXX to Philo, and beyond to Clement of Alexandria
and Origen. It is this, of course, which lends colour to the theory
that Apollos was the author, a view which has been widely favoured
but which, as already noted, remains conjectural. We simply do
not know enough about Apollos, his background, his teaching, his
movements. All our information comes from two chapters of Acts,
a number of references in 1 Corinthians, and one brief passing
mention in the epistle to Titus (3:13). It has recently been argued
that his role in Corinth was less constructive and more damaging
than is usually thought, and that he was responsible for the introduction into Corinth of a tendency towards gnosticism (S. Pétrement,
Le Dieu séparé, Paris [1984], pp. 343–378). Mlle Pétrement (p. 382)
rejects the view that he was the author of Hebrews, preferring Luke,
but goes on to argue for the hypothesis that he had much to do
with the Fourth Gospel and the Johannine epistles; but this raises
questions beyond our present purpose. It is mentioned here only to
underline the inadequacy of our evidence, and the way in which
hypothesis and conjecture may develop. We have to piece together
scraps of information, interpret them as best we may, and the result,
however careful the exegesis, however plausible the argument, must
often frankly be regarded as no more than speculative and
conjectural.

5. The Dead Sea Scrolls

The discovery of the Dead Sea Scrolls brought a new factor into
the study of Christian origins, revealing an aspect of Judaism in the
New Testament period of which little or nothing had been known
before. For a time it was fashionable to seek parallels between the
Scrolls and the books of the New Testament, Hebrews among them,
to try to establish links with the new documents which might offer

fresh solutions to long-standing problems. As Montefiore (p. 17) puts it, 'Opinion has differed whether the epistle was written to Essene converts to Christianity, to Essenes not yet converted to Christianity, or to Christians in danger of lapsing into Essenism'. In short, every possible avenue has been explored. With the passing of time, it is now possible to see things more in perspective. Parallels can of course be identified, but in some respects Hebrews seems to be closer to Philo than to Qumran (cf. e.g. Montefiore p. 18; Bruce, *NTS* 9 (1962/63) p. 218, who says in closing (p. 232) that it would be outstripping the evidence to call the readers Essenes or spiritual brethren to the men of Qumran). The parallels identified by various scholars have been listed and critically assessed by Herbert Braun (*Qumran und das Neue Testament*, Tübingen 1966, i. (pp. 241–274), who begins his general discussion by listing a catena of judgments as to the relationship, made by different writers and showing a wide range of opinion, from those who find in Hebrews the closest contact with Qumran to those who find it the furthest removed. There are no real verbal parallels with the Qumran texts themselves, although we do find use of the same Old Testament passages; there is however an affinity in biblical exegesis (cf. ii. pp. 183f.), and there are some common ideas. Some of these ideas, however, are simply Jewish, and not peculiar to Qumran and Hebrews. In the end Braun casts his vote for the view that Hebrews is remote from Qumran. The idea that the recipients were in some sense Essenes is therefore without foundation.

6. The Gnostics

One further area calls for attention, perhaps the most difficult of all to assess: the possible influence of Gnosis or Gnosticism. In *Das wandernde Gottesvolk* (Göttingen 1938, 4th edn. [1961]; ET Minneapolis [1984]) Ernst Käsemann sought to interpret Hebrews in terms of the 'gnostic myth'. The book 'made an impression, but met with little general agreement' (Schmithals, *Neues Testament und Gnosis*, Darmstadt [1984], p. 142); according to Schenke-Fischer (*Einleitung* II p. 267) it is open to fundamental objections: all the 'constitutive marks' of gnostic thought are lacking in Hebrews (so too Schmithals). The world is God's own creation, not the work of a demiurge. Nowhere is it seen as dominated by hostile powers, nor is it a prison for the soul; rather it is the place where one awaits the promise. Contact with gnostic thought is limited to the idea that the heavenly world is the true home of the faithful, and to the description of the relation of Christ and the believers as one of brothers. If anything, we should regard Hebrews as anti-gnostic, in view of its emphasis on the fleshly existence of Jesus. Despite this rejection of gnostic influence by Schenke and Fischer, Helmut Köster (*Einführung in das NT*, Berlin [1980], p. 712; English ed. [1982], ii. 274) claims that 'gnostic elements' frequently occur in Hebrews and are decisive for the understanding of what it says. He mentions in particular the pre-existence of the redeemer (1:3; so too Schmithals p. 143), the descent of the redeemer through the heavenly worlds (9:11ff., 24f.; but is this not an ascent, cf. 4:14?), the common origin of redeemer and redeemed (2:11), and the idea that the faithful are on their way to their heavenly home. At the same time he finds the author taking a critical attitude towards 'gnosis', and contesting the 'gnostic' understanding of the redeemer and of redemption. Now such elements may indeed be called 'gnostic' by virtue of their appearance in later developed gnostic systems; what is not clear is that they were already gnostic when the author used them, that he *derived* them from gnostic thought. Here some distinction has to be made between Gnosis in the broader sense, as the term is used by German scholars, and Gnosticism in the narrower sense, referring to the developed systems of the second century. The one flows into the other, but they are not identical. Developments in the direction of the later Gnosticism had already begun at least as early as Paul's letters to Corinth, but we have no clear knowledge of the stages in the process, or how strong the influence of this kind of speculation might have been at any given stage. Reference should also be made to a remark by Schmithals, that some of the motifs adduced by Käsemann might be derived from Jewish or Jewish-hellenistic roots, without necessarily passing through the medium of Gnosis.

Gnostic influence on Hebrews must therefore be regarded as at most very slight, and limited to a few terms and concepts which may already have begun to take on a gnostic colour. There is however another aspect: the influence of Hebrews itself on the development of gnostic ideas. One common motif in Gnosticism is that of 'rest', which of course recalls the interpretation of Ps. 95 in chapters 3 and 4 of Hebrews. However, the motif also occurs in Philo and elsewhere, and moreover Hebrews consistently uses one form of the Greek word, the gnostics (and Philo) another. Too much should not be built on this. W. C. van Unnik (in *The Jung Codex*, ed. F. L. Cross, London [1955], pp. 110, 119) detected a number of echoes in the Nag Hammadi *Gospel of Truth*, there is at least one in the Excerpta ex Theodoto (38.2), and there may be a few more in the *Gospel of Philip* (cf. Wilson, *The Gospel of Philip*, London [1962], p. 190). Perhaps the most striking case is however the Nag Hammadi treatise *Melchizedek* (*Codex IX 1*), which B. A. Pearson suggests 'is a Jewish-Christian product containing an originally pre-Christian Melchizedek speculation overlaid with Christian Christological re-interpretation'. To which he adds, 'It can hardly be doubted that the source of this Christological re-interpretation is the epistle to the Hebrews' (*Nag Hammadi Codices IX & X*, ed. B. A. Pearson, [Leiden] 1981, p. 34). There is however a great deal more in the way of Melchizedek speculation which would require to be taken into account in any full treatment (cf. F. L. Horton, *The Melchizedek Tradition*, Cambridge [1976], who did not have access to the Nag Hammadi text but was able to use among other sources the Qumran 11Q Melchizedek; cf. also Claudio Gianotto, *Melchizedek e la sua tipologia*, Brescia [1984], who traces the development of Melchizedek tradition in Jewish and Christian sources, both orthodox and heretical, down to the Melchizedekian heresies. The Nag Hammadi text is discussed on pp. 193–216).

7. Conclusion

Apart from the Old Testament, none of the areas passed under review can really be said to have exercised any direct or formative influence upon our author. Affinities there certainly are, especially with Philo, but there are also differences in every case. The point of this survey is not so much to find a 'source' for the ideas of our author, documents he might have read or other writers who might have influenced his thinking; rather it illustrates the manifold variety and complexity of his background, the ways in which the same concepts, the same terminology, could be taken up and utilised by different writers for very different purposes. In such a case the short and simple answer may be very far from the truth. When we consider only Philo and Hebrews, for example, we may be struck by the similarities, and even misled into thinking the relationship closer than it actually was. When we take note also of the differences, and bring other factors into the reckoning, other documents which use the same ideas but in different ways, the picture becomes very different; more complicated perhaps, but probably nearer to the truth.

THE LETTER

to the

Hebrews

PROLOGUE

1:1–4

1. The book begins with a polished and elaborate period, marked in the Greek by alliteration and assonance (on the absence of the usual epistolary superscription, see above p. 16). Each of the main phrases in the first verse (**of old, to our fathers, by the prophets**) is matched by a corresponding, and to some extent contrasting, phrase in the second (**in these last days, to us, by a Son**). The 'our' before 'fathers' in *RSV* is slightly misleading, since there is no possessive in the Greek (although some MSS do have it); the fathers are not the actual ancestors of the author or his readers, but the men of ancient Israel, as the following reference to the prophets shows. These could however be described in a general way as 'our fathers', if the readers were Jewish Christians. The two verses cover the whole range of God's word to man, in a former age 'at sundry times and in divers manners' (*AV*), **in many and various ways** (*RSV*), but now fully and completely in the Son. The prophets include not only the writing prophets and their predecessors like Elijah, but also such earlier figures as Abraham (Gen. 20:7), Moses (Dt. 18:15) and Aaron (Exod. 7:1).

2. The phrase **in these last days** (lit. 'at the end of these days') reflects the early Christian conviction that they were living in the climax of the ages, at the close of the existing order and the beginning of a new. As time passed, the delay of the Parousia was to present a problem (cf. 2 Pet. 3:3f.) which was variously answered by New Testament writers, but the author's eschatology affords no real help in the dating of Hebrews. He did believe that the Parousia was near (10:25), but lays no stress upon this conviction. Rather he uses liturgical and philosophical terminology 'to impress upon (his readers) the nearness of the invisible world without insisting upon the nearness of the Parousia' (see C. K. Barrett, 'The Eschatology of Hebrews', in *The Background of the NT and its Eschatology* ed. Davies and Daube (*Dodd Festschrift*, pp. 363ff., esp. p. 391). This may be another way of dealing with the problem, comparable to those of Luke and John, but that does not necessarily mean that Hebrews must be dated late. It should be noted that the reference to the Son has no article in the Greek; it is not 'the Son' or 'His Son' but **a Son**, fixing attention, as Westcott says, 'upon the nature und not upon the personality of the Mediator of the new revelation'.

The name of Jesus is not actually mentioned until 2:9, but Christian readers would of course have no doubt as to who is meant. The reference to the Son is immediately followed by a brief statement of a credal type (cf. Phil. 2:5–11, 1 Tim. 3:16, both introduced, as here, by a relative pronoun) which underlines his exalted status. R. H. Fuller (*Foundations of NT Christology*, pp. 220f.) reconstructs a hymn of two three-line stanzas behind verses 3 and 4, but observes that the two phrases of verse 2b cannot be fitted into this hymn: in these God is the subject, in the rest the Redeemer. However, there is reason at all events to think that the author is drawing on an older liturgical tradition. The words **whom he appointed the heir of all things, through whom also he created the world** reflect some of the developments in Christological thinking in the early Church. 'Son' and 'heir' are naturally related concepts (cf. Rom. 8:17, Gal. 4:7; *BAG* p. 435a), although this should not be pressed too far. There is no suggestion that the Son has entered upon an inheritance with the death of the Father! The point is to establish his exalted status, as second only to God himself. This is reinforced by ascribing to him a part in the work of creation (cf. 1 C. 8:6, Col. 1:16, Jn 1:3). The fact that Paul and John share some of these ideas shows that they are not the author's own invention, but belong in the main stream of early Christian thinking.

The reference to creation points back beyond Christianity to speculations in Judaism, particularly in the Wisdom literature. According to Prov. 8:22 God created Wisdom at the beginning of his works, even before the Creation had begun: 'when he established the heavens, I was there . . . when he marked out the foundations of the earth, then I was beside him, like a master workman' (see the whole passage, 8:22–31). According to Prov. 3:19 'the Lord by wisdom founded the earth', which looks like an interpretation of Gen. 1:1 (cf. Col. 1:15–17 and Burney's analysis, quoted in W. D. Davies, *Paul and Rabbinic Judaism*, London [1948], pp. 150ff.). The theme is further developed in the Wisdom of Solomon, where Wisdom sits beside the throne of God (9:4), and 'spans the world in power from end to end, and orders all things benignly' (8:1 *NEB*). At 9:1 Wisdom is practically identified with the Logos, which prepares the way for yet further development in Philo of Alexandria and in the New Testament. Thus for Philo the Logos is 'the image of God, through whom the whole universe was created' (*Spec. Leg.* 1.81), the first-born son and also the eldest of the angels (*Conf.* p. 146f.). This is enough to locate the author firmly in the Alexandrian Jewish Wisdom tradition, although it is probably going too far to think of him as a disciple of Philo, 'un philonien converti au christianisme' (Ménégoz, *Théologie de l'épître aux Hébreux*, Paris

[1894], p. 198; see Introd. p. 22 and Williamson, *Philo and the Epistle to the Hebrews*, Leiden [1970]).

3. This association with the Wisdom tradition is confirmed by verse 3, which speaks of the Son as the reflection of the glory of God and bearing **the very stamp of his nature**. In Wisdom 7:26 the same Greek word *apaugasma* is used in describing Wisdom as 'a reflection of eternal light, an unspotted mirror of the working of God and an image of his goodness'. There is some difference of opinion as to whether it should be taken as active ('radiance, effulgence'; so *NEB* and many early fathers) or as passive ('reflection'; so *RSV*). As J. H. Moulton puts it (*Grammar of NT Greek* II, p. 298), the choice is between sunlight and moonlight; he himself sees the active – 'effulgence, φῶς ἐκ φωτός' —as fairly certain. Westcott (p. 11) notes that the Greek fathers 'with unanimity' adopted the sense of *effulgence* 'according to the idea expressed in the Nicene Creed, *Light of Light*, and adds that effulgence 'is not any isolated ray, but the whole bright image which brings before us the source of light'. *BAG* 82a consider the active sense preferable for Wisdom and Philo, but Williamson (p. 38) argues that Philo uses the word with both shades of meaning, and notes certain differences in usage which in his view preclude Philonic influence (see pp. 36–41).

A second key-word in this verse (*RSV* **stamp**) has come down to English in transliterated form as 'character'. It means literally 'the stamp or clear-cut impression made by a seal, the very facsimile of the original' (Moffatt, p. 6). The word is used in *1 Clement* (33.4) of man, formed 'as a reproduction of his own image' (cf. Gen. 1:26; in 2 C. 4:4; Col. 1:15 Christ is identified in similar terms as the image of God) while Philo (*Det. Pot.* 83) calls the soul 'a type and stamp of divine power' (see *BAG* 876a). Williamson (p. 74ff.) notes that Philo uses the word 'with a rich variety of connected shades of meaning', but observes (p. 78) that in the case of our author 'the problem is to know whether or not he took over the term from Philo'. Use of the same terminology does not mean that the terms are used with the same significance, and as Williamson (p. 80) remarks, Philo nowhere calls the Logos the 'very stamp' of the divine nature. As Moffatt puts it, 'the unique relation of Christ to God is one of the unborrowed truths of Christianity, but it is stated here in borrowed terms'.

Verse 2 affirms the agency of the Son in creation. The next clause in verse 3 speaks of his providential government of the universe, **upholding the universe by his word of power**. The verb is used by Philo of bringing things into existence, but that would only repeat the thought of v. 2. The idea here is that of sustaining and

governance, expressed by Philo and early Fathers in the metaphor
of a helmsman. Then, having established the status of the Son in
relation to God and to the universe, the author in one brief clause
introduces a theme which will occupy him for much of the letter—
the Son's priestly activity: **when he had made purification for sins**,
i.e. effected their removal. It is one of the author's characteristics
that he quite often introduces a theme casually, almost in passing,
only to return to it later and give it a fuller development. Here there
is only the briefest reference before the prologue is brought to its
climax with an echo of the opening words of Ps. 110, a verse so
often quoted that it was clearly of great significance for early Christians (cf. C. H. Dodd, *According to the Scriptures*, p. 34f.). The
thought thus moves from the pre-existent exalted status of the Son,
his sharing in the creation and governance of the world, to his
earthly activity and self-sacrifice, and finally to his present status as
seated **at the right hand of the Majesty on high**. One is reminded
of the movement of the Christological hymn in Phil. 2:5–11,
although there are details in that passage which find no mention
here.

4. Verse 4 forms a transition to the first main section, which deals
with the superiority of the Son to the angels. It is natural and
convenient to make a break at this point, since in the Greek the
whole of the prologue is practically a single sentence, although in
English translation it is divided into three. This has sometimes,
however, had the unfortunate effect of separating the prologue from
the following section, with which verse 4 in particular is closely
connected. On the other hand it simply is not possible to introduce
a break at the end of verse 3. The Son's superiority to the angels
belongs with his exaltation to the right hand of God.

The sudden introduction of the angels here is at first sight
surprising, and has given rise to various explanations, including the
conjecture (made by Samuel Crell (1660–1747) and independently
in 1913 by Spitta) that 'angels' should be read for 'prophets' in
verse 1. This would certainly fit quite well in the context as stating
the theme of the first two chapters, and prepare the way for the
reference to angels here, but there is no textual evidence to support
it. The number of *NT* manuscripts now available, some of comparatively early date, makes recourse to conjectural emendation only a
last resort, since it is probable that the true reading is to be found
among the variants in these manuscripts. A conjecture without any
manuscript support whatever may be regarded as very doubtful.
Other suggestions (see Montefiore pp. 39ff.) are that the author is
attacking an undue deference to angels (cf. Col. 2:18) or that the
Son has been equated with one of the 'principalities and powers'

which were held to govern and control the universe (cf. I C. 15:24; Eph. 3:10; etc.). There is however nothing to suggest that the readers were addicted to angel-worship (F. F. Bruce, *NTS* 9 (1963), p. 218). It may therefore be that such speculation is quite unnecessary, and that the real explanation is much more simple: the author is claiming for the Son 'the highest place that heaven affords', under God himself. In contemporary thinking the angels were held to rank as intermediaries between God and man, and it naturally follows that one who holds so exalted a place as that ascribed to the Son must rank above the angels. Montefiore's own explanation in terms of an Ebionite view of Christ, revering Jesus as more than human yet denying his divinity and therefore regarding him as neither God nor man but an angel, is perhaps open to the criticism of reading back later developments in Jewish Christianity into the first century (cf. R. N. Longenecker, *The Christology of Early Jewish Christianity*, p. 26ff.; he writes (p. 32) that one of the distinctives for Jewish Christians 'was *apparently* that of angelomorphic Christology' (italics mine). It is possible, but we do not know enough to be absolutely certain, that the Ebionite view was already current in *NT* times). Since Montefiore wrote, the publication of the Qumran Melchizedek fragments (11Q *Melch*) has shed new light on some passages of Hebrews, and serves to illustrate 'the type of thinking about angels and other heavenly beings which the author of Hebrews is up against' (de Jonge and van der Woude, *NTS* 12 (1966), p. 317; for Heb. 1–2 see pp. 314–318).

The **more excellent** name of course recalls 'the name which is above every name' (Phil. 2:9), but opinions differ as to what that name was. Montefiore, for example, while admitting that for Paul the name is 'Lord' (Phil. 2:11), nevertheless argues that 'the name which Jesus has by right must be the name of the Son, as the succeeding verses establish'; the name 'has not been given in virtue of exaltation into heaven, but is his from eternity'. Longenecker on the other hand (p. 128) is equally emphatic on the other side: 'Undoubtedly, it is the name by which God himself has been known; that is, in Greek, κύριος'. Héring prefers to think of 'son'—unless the reference is to an unknown name like that of Rev. 19:12. The fact is that nothing is said to indicate precisely what the name is, and all attempts to identify it are speculative. Westcott (p. 17) is probably near to the truth when he writes that it is 'probably not the name of "Son" simply . . . but the Name which gathered up all that Christ was found to be by believers, Son, Sovereign and Creator, the Lord of the Old Covenant, as is shown in the remainder of the chapter'. Jarl E. Fossum (*The Name of God and the Angel of the Lord*, Tübingen [1985]) has assembled a wealth of material

relating to Jewish (and Samaritan) speculation on the Name of God,
which may be held to support Longenecker's view.

In brief, the prologue is intended to proclaim in the most vivid
terms the exalted status of the Son, the mediator of God's complete
and final word to men. Heir of all things by right, he is also God's
agent in creation, and indeed may be described as the very image
of the divine nature. It is this exalted figure, responsible for the
providential government of the universe, who has intervened in
history for the purification of sins, and now sits at the right hand
of the Majesty on high. At the beginning of the next chapter the
author will draw his conclusion: if the message declared by angels
was valid, and disobedience met with due retribution, how shall we
escape if we neglect the salvation offered by a yet higher authority?
First, however, he must demonstrate the superiority of the Son,
and this he does by a series of Old Testament quotations.

One question which immediately arises from this passage is that
of the author's view of the old dispensation. 'That which is
communicated in parts, sections, fragments, must of necessity be
imperfect; and so also a representation which is made in many
modes cannot be other than provisional' (Westcott p. 4). Such
comments, like the *NEB* translation 'in fragmentary and varied
fashion' or Montefiore's 'only "partial and piecemeal" ', suggest a
rather negative and disparaging assessment, as if the old dispensation was *only* partial and incomplete. It was, however, the same
God who spoke both to 'the fathers' in the prophets and 'in these
last days' in the Son, and much of the letter consists of exposition
of passages drawn from the Old Testament. Further on, Westcott
himself writes 'But while the revelations of the Old and New Covenants are thus sharply distinguished, God is the One Author of both',
while Montefiore after the words quoted above adds immediately,
'Nevertheless it (i.e. the old revelation) was real'. As Moffatt notes,
the author does not mean to exclude variety from the Christian
revelation, nor does he suggest that the revelation given through
the prophets was inferior; 'there is a deeper suggestion of the unity
and continuity of revelation then and now'.

Part at least of the problem lies in the false assumption that
demonstration of the superiority of the new entails the *rejection* of
the old. The author does indeed argue that the old dispensation was
inadequate, ineffective: sacrifices cannot cleanse the conscience, and
the very fact that they have to be repeated proves their inadequacy
(cf. 9:9; 10:1-4). He uses Jeremiah's prophecy of a new covenant
to show that the old is obsolete (8:13). But, as a recent study
observes, 'in spite of the sweeping condemnations made of certain

aspects of the old order, it is by no means a blanket condemnation' (G. Hughes, *Hebrews and Hermeneutics*, pp. 25f.). The message declared by angels was valid, and every transgression entailed due retribution (2:2). It is in the light of this that our author draws the conclusion that the danger in neglect of the new and final revelation is all the greater. He is not seeking to depreciate the old for the sake of exalting the new. Both lay claim to obedience, both convey God's word to men, but the new is superior to the old. It is the climax and culmination of a continuing process, so that the fate of the wilderness generation serves as example and warning to those who are tempted now to fall away. 'The earlier revelation is treated as the preparation for, the foundation of, the latter' (Westcott). It may be added that if his readers were Jewish Christians it would have been tactless and inappropriate to begin at the very outset with a repudiation and rejection of the things which they held dear and to which they were tempted to return. The author's concern is not merely to prevent relapse, but to encourage his readers to press forward to the full realisation of the hope that is set before them. We must beware of the facile assumption that the situation addressed is that faced by Paul, e.g. in Galatians, and that the author is seeking to meet it in the same way. Those who favour a Gentile readership often point out that Hebrews knows nothing of the contrast between Jew and Gentile; for that matter, circumcision is not even mentioned. It is the priesthood and sacrifices of the old dispensation, not the revelation, that the author sees to be superseded.

A second question concerns the relation of the prologue to the letter as a whole. As already noted, it is natural and convenient to make a break at verse 4, but while the next section takes up the allusion to angels in that verse, the transition, and indeed the sudden introduction of the reference to angels, appears somewhat abrupt, and it is not easy to follow the author's train of thought. Hughes (p. 145 n. 4) remarks that most interpreters see a connection between the prologue and the comparison with angels, and some take it as far as the comparison with Moses in chapter 3, but none have taken the prologue as the definitive key to the letter as a whole and few see any connection between it and the high-priestly Christology. He himself argues (p. 24) for a development through 'three elaborate, descending convolute circles of comparison' progressing from the angelic mediators of the law, to the human agent in that revelation, to the priestly organisation based on that Law.

Actually Hughes is not quite accurate in his criticisms. For one thing, he was unable (p. 144 n. 10) to use the work of A. Vanhoye (*Structure littéraire de l'épître aux Hébreux*), who argues in detail for

a much more closely integrated and structured composition than
was often envisaged by commentators. For another Spicq (*L'épître
aux Hébreux*, [1977], p. 34) writes that the prologue 'already
contains the entire subject of the epistle, according to the rule of
the best ancient rhetoric. It presents the person and work of the
Son of God, king and priest, revealer and redeemer, object of faith
for Christians'. As we have seen, verses 2 and 3 declare in the
clearest possible terms the exalted status of the Son, as heir of all
things, agent in creation and sustainer of the universe, sitting on
the right hand of the Majesty on high, while the brief reference to
purification of sins in verse 3b already hints at the priestly function
which will be more fully developed later.

THE SUPERIORITY OF THE SON TO THE ANGELS

1:5–14

The argument of this section consists of a series of seven quotations
from the Old Testament, five from the Psalms and one each from
2 Samuel and Deuteronomy (this last possibly influenced from the
Psalms, see below). By modern standards of exegesis the author's
use of the Old Testament leaves something to be desired, since he
simply quotes what appears to suit his purposes, without regard to
context or to the original meaning of the words he quotes. However,
modern critical methods are a comparatively recent development,
and it is unfair and inappropriate to judge him by modern standards.
We may not be able to follow his example, and certainly we should
often understand the passages he quotes in a very different way,
but if we are to understand his work, and do him justice, we must
assess that work in terms of the standards of his own day, not of
ours. The exegesis of the early Fathers, the writings of Philo of
Alexandria and the *pesher* interpretation employed by the Qumran
sect provide a better standard of comparison than modern critical
and historical methods.

The occurrence here of such a catena of quotations naturally
suggests the use of a testimony-book (that such books did exist in
the *NT* period is now shown by the Qumran 4Q Testimonia; cf.
Vermes, *The Dead Sea Scrolls in English*, pp. 247–249). However,
only one of the seven quotations (Ps. 2:7) is a known *testimonium*
(cf. C. H. Dodd, *According to the Scriptures*, pp. 31f.), although a
second (2 Sam. 7:14) appears in Dodd's list (p. 108, cf. p. 106) of
'subordinate and supplementary sources'; the others do not appear
in Dodd's index. Montefiore (p. 43) argues for an existing catena,

possibly in the form of a testimony book, on the ground that 'if our author had done his own research into the Old Testament, some explanation of his selection would have been likely'. Following F. C. Synge (*Hebrews and the Scriptures*), he claims that the quotations were originally selected 'for a purpose different from that which they serve in this Epistle'. That may be, but the reconstruction of the character and purpose of an author's source when it is no longer extant is at best conjectural, and often highly precarious. It may be that the writer considered the opening words of verse 5, with the comments inserted into verses 6, 7, 8 and 13, to provide sufficient explanation. Granted his presupposition that the texts are applicable to his theme, the first two provide the proof that the mediator of the new revelation is rightly called Son, while the third introduces the motif of his superiority to the angels: *they* are to worship *him*. The fourth and fifth provide a contrast between the status of the angels and that of the Son, and the fifth quotation is then reinforced by the sixth. Finally the last quotation clinches the argument: such words were never addressed to any angel—they are only subordinate **ministering spirits**.

5. The first quotation is drawn from Ps. 2:7, also quoted in Ac. 13:33 with the rubric 'as it is written in the second psalm', but there specifically understood of the Resurrection. The words are also quoted below at 5:5 and in the Western text of Luke 3:22, and in a modified form probably underlie the words of the voice at the Baptism and Transfiguration of Jesus in the Gospels (Mk 1:11 par.; 9:7 par.; cf. 2 Pet. 1:17). The idea that the king was either himself divine or at least the son of the god was widespread in the ancient world, and the psalm probably had associations with the enthronement ritual for a Davidic king. The words here quoted 'are cited in the psalm by the Lord's Anointed as the ground of his confidence in the face of the plottings of his enemies' (F. F. Bruce). Angels are frequently called 'sons of God' in the Old Testament, but LXX practically always translates by 'angels' and no single angel is ever described as son of God. Since author and readers knew only the Greek Bible, 'the proof holds good' (Moffatt p. 10).

The word **today** has occasioned some discussion, since opinions differ as to the 'day' intended. In Acts the reference is to the Resurrection, in the Gospels to the Baptism or the Transfiguration of Jesus, while later theology maintained the eternal generation of the Son. The association of this text with Ps. 110:4 at 5:5 below may suggest that it would be Christ's exaltation and enthronement, but probably, as Moffatt puts it, we are asking a question that was not present to the author's mind. The point of the quotation is for him quite clearly **Thou art my Son**.

The second quotation is drawn from Nathan's prophecy in 2 Sam.
7, a key passage for the idea of the Davidic Messiah. The prophecy
was fulfilled by Solomon, to the extent that he built a temple, but
not exhausted in him. 'The later prophets look forward to a greater
son of David in coming days in whom "the sure mercies of David"
would be adequately realised' (F. F. Bruce). Dodd (p. 106) remarks
that the idea of the Messiah as son of David 'is not conspicuous in
the primary body of *testimonia*'; but it was certainly widespread in
Jewish circles and the fulfilment of the prophecy is in the New
Testament seen in Jesus (e.g. Lk. 1:32f.; 68f.). What is remarkable
is that while the idea of the Messiah as son of God may have been
common enough in Judaism, this particular verse (2 Sam. 7:14) is
not so used except here and in 4QFlor 1.10–13 (Braun, *Qumran und
das NT* I, p. 242; II, p. 312); however, the other texts adduced in
4QFlor are different from those in Hebrews. The verse is also
quoted, with a shift of application, at 2 C. 6:18 and Rev. 21:7.

6. The third quotation has a brief introductory clause which
presents something of a problem, although it is obscured in English
versions. The position of the word **again** admits of its being associated closely with the verb in the temporal clause, to give the meaning
'when he brings the first-born into the world again', i.e. with reference to the Second Coming. For this Westcott argues strongly: 'the
first introduction of the Son into the world . . . had not issued in
an open triumph' (Héring takes the same line, referring to 2:7, or
more accurately 2:8b–9). The Greek word order is however not
decisive, nor is Westcott's grammatical argument. The word picks
up the **again** of verse 5b, marking this as another in a series of
quotations (cf. *BAG* 607a). Moreover there may have been stylistic
reasons; it is difficult to see any other word order which would have
been so euphonious. Accordingly it is better, with *AV*, *RSV* and
NEB, to read **again, when he brings the first-born into the world**.
The point of time in view is probably neither the Second Coming
nor the Incarnation (so Montefiore): 'it is not so much a question
of his being brought into the world as of his being introduced to it
as the Son of God' (F. F. Bruce). Jesus is elsewhere described as
the **first-born** of a new creation (cf. Rom. 8:29; Col. 1:15, 18; Rev.
1:5), but this is the only case in the New Testament where the word
is used absolutely. Philo speaks of the Logos as the first-born or
eldest son, but uses different terms than the word employed here.
In the Old Testament the Hebrew equivalents are frequently used
literally, but also applied to Israel (Exod. 4:22, cf. Jer. 31:9) and
in Ps. 89:27 to David. The word for **world** is different from those
used in verses 2 and 3, and means 'the inhabited universe', including

as Bruce says the realm of angels 'who accordingly are summoned to acknowledge their Lord'.

The quotation is from Deut. 32:43, not in the Masoretic text but in the longer form found in LXX. Moreover verse 43a in LXX, except for one MS, reads 'sons of God', not 'angels'. The word **angels** has been substituted either from verse 43b or under the influence of Ps. 97:7 (96:7 LXX). What is remarkable is that the Qumran fragment 4Q Deut. shows a striking agreement with this reading; the LXX text quoted 'accordingly had a Hebrew *Vorlage*, which was also known at Qumran' (Braun I 243). In the original context it is God who is to be worshipped, but we shall meet with other cases in Hebrews where texts referring to God have been given a new application and transferred to Jesus. Here however there is another factor to be considered: according to rabbinic tradition the angels were summoned to worship Adam (the 'first-born') when he was created ('brought into the world'), but Satan refused (cf. *Life of Adam and Eve*, pp. 13f.). Dodd (*The Bible and the Greeks*, p. 156f.) even goes so far as to say that this re-application of an Old Testament text in Hebrews 'can only have taken place under the influence of a tradition similar to that of the *Life of Adam and Eve*'. That may be too much to say, but it is at least possible that the author was familiar with such a tradition, and transferred it from the first Adam to the last (for Paul's Christological use of the figure of Adam cf. C. K. Barrett, *From First Adam to Last*, London [1962], esp. pp. 68ff.).

7. Thus far, attention has been concentrated on the Son, the first quotation proving his status and the second supporting it, while the third affirms his superiority to the angels, since they are called upon to worship him. The next three quotations present a further contrast, beginning this time with the angels, but once again there is one quotation relating to the angels and two to the Son. There is thus a certain symmetry to the arrangement (2:1/1:2), although not in the length of the quotations, and it is difficult to avoid the conclusion that this careful structuring is deliberate.

The fourth quotation is from Psalm 104:4, which in *RSV* reads:
'who makest the winds thy messengers,
fire and flame thy ministers.'
NEB understands the psalm in the same way, but *AV* interestingly enough comes close to the interpretation in Hebrews: 'who maketh his angels spirits; his ministers a flaming fire' (*RSV* **who makes his angels winds, and his servants flames of fire**). The variation is due to difference of opinion as to which of the Hebrew nouns is the object and which the predicate (the Greek word *pneuma* can mean both 'wind' and 'spirit'; cf. John 3:8). The Hebrew word order

(followed by LXX) suggests the *AV* translation, but the tenor of
thought in the context of the psalm suggests the version in *RSV*
and *NEB*. At all events the author here is following LXX, except
that for the last two words LXX has 'a flaming fire' instead of **flames
of fire**. The verse is quoted in the same form in *1 Clem*. 36:3.

8–9. Verse 8, introducing the fifth quotation, stands in emphatic
contrast. The angels are like wind and fire, transitory and evan-
escent, but 'the throne of God's Son endures for ever; his is the
kingdom that is to know no end' (F. F. Bruce). Here again,
however, there is a problem of translation. At Psalm 45:6 *RSV*
reads 'Your divine throne', with in the margin the alternatives 'your
throne is a throne of God' or 'your throne, O God'. Similarly *NEB*
has 'your throne is like God's throne', but both render the quotation
here **Thy throne, O God**, with 'God is thy throne' in the margin.
Westcott notes that the word 'God' could be taken either as a
vocative or as the subject (or predicate), but decides for the latter
on the ground that 'it is scarcely possible that *elohim* in the original
can be addressed to the king'. That however was prior to modern
investigation into ancient ideas of kingship. R. E. Brown (*Jesus God
and Man*, p. 24) argues from the parallelism that 'throne' and not
'God' is the subject, and adduces this verse as the first of three
passages which explicitly use *theos* (God) of Jesus.

The original psalm is a wedding hymn for some Israelite king,
and commentators are divided as to how it should be rendered. Our
concern now, however, is with the way in which it was understood
by the author of Hebrews, and most modern commentators agree,
against Westcott, in taking the *theos* as a vocative. Some indeed
(Héring, Montefiore) take the first *theos* in verse 9 also as a vocative,
reading 'therefore, O God, thy God has anointed thee' (cf. *NEB*);
but in this verse it is perhaps simpler to take it as a case of repetition
for emphasis. The author's point is already made by the opening
line of the quotation. 'The point of the citation lies in its opening
and closing words: (i) the Son has a royal and lasting authority (as
ὁ θεός), in contrast to the angels, and (ii) he is anointed more highly
than his companions' (Moffatt). The *RSV* variant 'his kingdom' in
the second line of the quotation is probably the result of taking *theos*
as the subject; in an address to the Son the second person singular
is more appropriate. The MS support for the third person is certainly
both old and good (Sinaiticus, Vaticanus and the Chester Beatty
papyrus), while the second person could be suspect as the result of
assimilation to LXX, but the *RSV* text can be justified on the ground
of (a) the weight and variety of the external evidence (a majority of
the MSS and all the versions) and (b) by the difficulty of continuing
the third person (see Metzger, *Textual Commentary on the Greek NT*,

pp. 662f.; but Spicq, Bruce (p. 10) and Montefiore, for example, prefer the third person).

The righteous sceptre is literally 'the sceptre of uprightness' (a genitive of quality). The sceptre is the symbol of authority, but this is no arbitrary authority. Bruce aptly adduces Ps. 89:14 and Isa. 11:5 and comments 'The righteousness and justice which are the foundation of God's throne are equally the foundation of Messiah's throne'. This note is continued in the next verse, with its reference to loving righteousness and hating lawlessness. Such attributes are ideally to be expected of any king, but earthly rulers have all too often disappointed such hopes and expectations. The author sees them completely fulfilled in the Son. In verse 9, **anointed** is a verb cognate with the Greek word which has given us the name of Christ. In the Old Testament, prophets (e.g. 1 Kg. 19:16), priests (e.g. Lev. 8:12) and kings (e.g. 1 Sam. 10:1) were all anointed on installation in their office, but in Ps. 45, as the mention of **oil of gladness** shows, the reference is 'not to the solemn anointing to royal dignity but to the festive anointing on occasions of rejoicing' (Westcott). Since however our author ignores the context, he probably had no thought of the festive associations of the original hymn. It may be a mistake to try to identify any specific moment for the anointing (e.g. the Baptism of Jesus, cf. Ac. 10:38), but it is likely that this verb carried overtones for early Christians; nor is it necessary to identify the **comrades** more precisely. The quotation quite simply celebrates the exalted status of the Son, in contrast to the ministering spirits of verse 7. As Héring notes, it underlines the fact that the Son is no usurper, but anointed by God; and that his reign is one of justice.

10–12. The next three verses are drawn from Ps. 102:25–27, following LXX with some minor changes. In the original psalm they are part of the afflicted sufferer's address to God, but here they are taken out of context as addressed to the Son, an interpretation facilitated by the insertion in LXX of the vocative **Lord**. Verse 2 has already introduced the Son as God's agent in creation, and this is now confirmed, with the added note of permanence and stability in contrast with the transitory nature of even the most stable and lasting elements in the universe. As Bruce notes, the author is not the only New Testament writer to apply to Jesus Old Testament scriptures which in their original context apply to God. One of the earlier Christian confessions, if not the earliest, was 'Jesus is Lord'; given that, it was natural to transfer to him Old Testament passages referring to God as Lord, although as Fuller notes (*Foundations*, p. 68) 'this does not mean that the distinction between Jesus and God is blurred' (cf. his discussion of the Kyrios title, pp. 184–6, 230f. and see also C. F. D. Moule, *The Birth of the New Testament*,

London [1967], pp. 77f.). According to Job 38:7, aptly cited by Bruce and Montefiore, the angels were delighted spectators at the creation; according to Hebrews the Son is God's agent in creation, which again establishes his superiority. More than that, though earth and heaven may pass away he still remains. The comparison with garments expresses this with telling effect: one man in his lifetime wears out many suits of clothes (cf. also Isa. 51:6). The words 'like a garment' in *RSV* margin to verse 12 are probably original to our author. The manuscript support is strong, and their omission in the majority of witnesses can be accounted for by assimilation to LXX. The Greek word order however suggests that they should come at the beginning, not at the end of the line: like a garment, and they will be changed.

13. Finally the author clinches his argument with an explicit quotation of Ps. 110:1, a verse already echoed in the prologue at verse 3. As Dodd notes (*According to the Scriptures*, pp. 34f.), this verse is expressly cited in Mk 12:36 and Ac. 2:34–5 as well as here, while allusions to it are numerous throughout the New Testament (cf. Mk 14:62; Ac. 7:55; Rom. 8:34; Eph. 1:20; Col. 3:1; 1 Pet. 3:22 and perhaps Rev. 3:21; not to mention a few other cases in Hebrews itself: 8:1; 10:12; 12:2). 'It seems clear, therefore, that this particular verse was one of the fundamental texts of the kerygma' (Dodd, p. 35). Sowers (*The Hermeneutics of Philo and Hebrews*, p. 85) notes the 'surprising fact' that this text, which occurs here immediately before a citation of Psalm 8:5–7 at 2:6–8, is also alluded to in 1 C. 15:25 and Eph. 1:20 just before an echo of Psalm 8:7, and that the same phenomenon appears at 1 Pet. 3:22. 'This citing of or alluding to Ps. 8 immediately after Ps. 110 in Heb., Paul, and 1 Pet. cannot be mere coincidence. It strongly suggests the two texts were lying side by side in some document which all three writers consulted.' The original psalm has reference to the enthronement of a king, and promises victory over his enemies. In the New Testament it is interpreted messianically, and applied to the triumph and exaltation of Jesus.

14. Vanhoye (pp. 73f.) notes a similarity between verses 13–14 on the one hand and verses 5–6 on the other, and regards them as forming an *inclusio*. This may be correct, but it must be observed that verse 14 is not a quotation. It is the author's summary comment on what has gone before. It may therefore be better to think of the structure as consisting of two symmetrical groups of quotations, each group containing two quotations relating to the Son and one to the angels, arranged in a chiastic form, with the seventh quotation as the climax. Vanhoye is, however, undoubtedly correct in seeing verse 14 not only as the conclusion to the first section, but also as a preparation for what is to come. The angels are but **ministering spirits** (cf. verse 7) **sent forth to serve, for the sake of those who are to inherit salvation**. What this salvation is, is not explained; it is taken for granted that the readers already know. The salvation is, however, clearly in the future: they are to inherit it, but do not already possess it. What they require, in the author's view, is as the next section shows to realise the danger of treating it lightly, the more especially since the day is drawing near (cf. 10:25).

This section may be regarded as a development and expression of the last verse of the prologue (v. 4), and at the same time as a justification of the claims made in the prologue for the exalted status of the Son. It provides an interesting example of the author's use of the Old Testament, following a 'proof-text' method which selects texts that appear to suit his purpose, regardless of their context or original meaning. Whether or not there was some specific reason for this comparison of the Son with the angels, the final effect is to demonstrate with the utmost clarity his pre-eminence, and this leads naturally to the warning which now follows. The argument is based on the LXX text, but some of the quotations show certain links with Qumran (cf. Braun I, pp. 244f. for an assessment) and some are known from their use in other New Testament writings to have been employed as *testimonia* by the early Church.

THE DANGER OF NEGLECT

2:1–4

As the **therefore** shows, this passage follows closely on what has gone before. The message declared through the mediation of angels is valid, and any disobedience entails due retribution—how much more will this be so in the case of a gospel proclaimed by an even higher authority! It is not actually stated in the Old Testament that the Law was given 'through angels', but the idea is developed in the inter-testamental literature and passed from there into early Christian thought (cf. Gal. 3:19; Ac. 7:38, 53; also Jos. *Ant.* 15:136; cf. Fossum, p. 194). It should, however, be observed that, unlike Paul, the author does not set Law against Gospel. Indeed, he does not speak of 'law' here, but of a message. The old dispensation was valid, but the new is better, because it accomplishes what the old could not achieve. Moreover the author's concern, as will later appear, is with the sacrificial cultus rather than with legal obedience, or as Bruce puts it 'with the ritual law as a means of access to God rather than with the moral law as a way of life'.

1. The verb translated **drift away** means literally to 'flow by, slip away', and is used here in the figurative sense of being washed away or drifting away (cf. *BAG* 622a). The precise metaphor which the author has in mind has been debated: the *AV* 'let them slip' suggests losing hold of something already in one's hand, while *RSV* 'drift away' implies rather 'being swept along past the secure anchorage which is within reach' (Westcott'; the *NEB* 'for fear of drifting from our course' suggests a different image again. In the light of the parallels adduced by Westcott (p. 37), and especially Prov. 3:21 LXX, the *RSV* rendering may claim some preference, but in any case the point is clear: neglect, indifference, disobedience, spell danger.

2. As Bruce observes, 'the sanctions which attended the law given at Sinai were severe and inescapable. Every commandment had the appropriate penalty for its infringement, and for those who deliberately and of set policy defied or disregarded the law of God, there was no reprieve'. The word rendered **just** is not the common word (= righteous) but a cognate term, used also at Rom. 3:8, meaning 'based on what is right' and hence due, deserved or appropriate.

3. Verse 3 is 'the first of several places in the epistle where an inference is drawn *a fortiori* from law to gospel', the type of argument which the rabbis described as *qal wā-ḥōmer* (lit. light and heavy) (Bruce). It also states the grounds on which this salvation is greater: it was proclaimed by the Lord, handed on and confirmed by his hearers, and authenticated by God himself. Montefiore notes 'among the many points of contact between this Epistle and the Lucan writings' that only in Luke among the Synoptics does Jesus himself pronounce salvation (Lk. 19:9), and 'by Luke alone Jesus is called the Saviour (Lk. 2:11) and described as bringing salvation (Lk. 1:69, 71, 77).' This is certainly true so far as the noun 'salvation' is concerned, but the picture is rather different if we look also at the verb 'to save' (e.g. Mt. 1:21); the word is frequently used of physical healing, but sometimes (e.g. Mk 5:34) one may suspect a *double entendre* (cf. Cranfield ad loc.). At all events, the gospel begins with Jesus, and receives its first utterance through him. **It was declared at first by the Lord.** Another passage in Luke (4:17ff.) tells how in the synagogue at Nazareth he read from the prophecies of Isaiah, and went on to claim their fulfilment. The reference to confirmation **by those who heard him** indicates that the author and his readers had no first-hand knowledge of the ministry and teaching of Jesus. He makes no claim to independence, such as Paul does in

Galatians, and indeed there is no trace in Hebrews of the Judaising controversy which elicited Paul's letters. Author and readers alike have received the gospel from those who were 'eye-witnesses and ministers of the word' (Lk. 1:2), but, as noted in the Introduction (p. 5), this is of no assistance in the dating of Hebrews.

4. The witnesses to the gospel are not merely human; God himself has authenticated it by **miracles and by gifts of the Spirit**. As Héring notes, if we are to distinguish the **signs, wonders and various miracles** we might think first of the works of healing, then of phenomena such as Ac. 12:7, and finally of the various gifts of which Paul speaks, such as prophecy and the gift of tongues. These last, however, might be more appropriately included under the **gifts of the Spirit**, and it is open to question whether the first three should be distinguished. The same three nouns appear in Ac. 2:22 and 2 C. 12:12, although in Acts in a different order. **Signs and wonders** frequently occur together (Mt. 24:24; Mk 13:22 (both of false Christs); Jn 4:48; Rom. 15:19; 2 Th. 2:9 (of *pretended* signs and wonders) and often in Acts), but 'wonders' does not appear by itself (cf. *BAG* 748 s.v. σημεῖον 2). **Gifts of the Spirit** is literally 'divisions' (cf. 4:12 below, where the same word is used) or 'distributions' of the Spirit. The first sense might recall the Pentecost narrative in Ac. 2:3, where a cognate verb is employed, but the second sense is more natural here. If the genitive is subjective, there is a parallel at 1 C. 12:11 (but Paul uses a different verb); it is, however, probably more natural to take it as objective: 'it is God who apportions the Holy Spirit according to his (the Father's) will' (Montefiore, comparing Gal. 3:5).

Miracles present a problem for the modern reader; far from providing authenticating evidence, they now themselves require authentication. On the other hand, if first-century people were over-credulous, it may be that we today are unduly sceptical. We have lost the sense of wonder, and take too much for granted. What would a man of the first century say of electricity, the radio, television, or advances in modern medicine? It may be added that the miraculous element in the New Testament is restrained in comparison with the New Testament Apocrypha (e.g. the clay birds in the Infancy Gospel of Thomas 2, the obedient bugs in the Acts of John 60–61, or the dried fish in the Acts of Peter 13). At all events, our author raises no question of the truth of the miracles of which he has heard. For him they set the seal of God's confirmation on the gospel.

At this point another difference may be noted between Paul and Hebrews. In general, Paul tends to deal with theological questions

first, and then turn to the ethical implications (most clearly at Rom.
12:1ff.; the interweaving of ethical and theological discussion in the
Corinthian letters is due to questions raised by the Corinthians).
Our author on the other hand introduces his admonitions in the
course of his theological exposition. It might be thought that the
book is a collection of short sermons on the 'Pauline' pattern, each
containing a theological discourse followed by an ethical admonition;
but, for one thing, the admonitions are unevenly spaced out, and
for another the whole book is too closely integrated to allow such a
theory. We must beware of the danger of modernising: did the early
Christians go in for series of sermons? Would the sermons have
been so short? And are these sections in fact complete and self-
contained? Actually the very next verse (2:5) takes up again the
theme of the first main section: **it was not to angels that God
subjected the world to come.**

THE SUPREMACY OF JESUS

2:5–9

According to Dt. 32:8, 'when the Most High gave to the nations
their inheritance . . . he fixed the bounds of the peoples according
to the number of the sons of God' (both *RSV* and *NEB* here follow
LXX, while *AV* follows the Masoretic text 'sons of Israel'. Many
scholars favour the LXX reading, for which a Hebrew witness has
now been found at Qumran [cf. Bruce, p. 33 n. 16], but G. F.
Moore [*Judaism* I, p. 227, cf. III, p. 62] long ago pointed out the
correspondence between the seventy 'sons of Israel' who went down
into Egypt [Exod. 1:5; cf. Dt. 10:22] and the seventy nations of
the world ['a standing feature of Jewish ethnology']. The Qumran
evidence may thus not be decisive). This theme in Dt. 32 later
developed into the idea that each of the nations had its own patron
among the 'angels of the nations' (cf. Ecclus. 17:17; Dan. 10:20.;
Pal. Targum on Dt. 32:8 in Moore III, p. 62). The Jews also
distinguished between 'this world' and 'the world to come'
(according to Moore II, p. 378 n. 6 the earliest known occurrence
of the phrase is in Enoch 71:15. This is a section not represented
in the fragments from Qumran, and therefore suspect [cf. M. Black,
The Book of Enoch, Leiden [1985] pp. 181ff.], but the idea is
certainly older and goes back to the prophetic tradition. At 6:5
Hebrews uses another formula 'the age to come', which is well
documented in the New Testament [cf. *BAG* 27b s.v. αἰών 2b]).
This **world to come** is 'the new order of things in which the salvation

of 1:14, 2:2, 3 is to be realised, and from which already influences
are pouring down into the life of Christians' (Moffatt). For the Jews,
this new order lay still in the future; for the early Christians it
had already been inaugurated in and through the exaltation and
enthronement of Christ, even though its full consummation was yet
to come. This Jewish distinction of the two ages, incidentally, is
not the same as the Platonic distinction of the visible and intelligible
worlds, although the two could be, and sometimes were, fused
together. It was not difficult to identify the ideal future age of bliss
with the Platonic ideal world, in contrast to this present transitory
world of being.

The author roundly claims that the authority of angels extends
only to this present world, not to the world to come. In certain
circles some at least of the angels were regarded as hostile to man,
and in the later developed Gnosticism they have become the demiurge and his archons, the rulers of this world from whose bondage
the soul longs to escape, but there is nothing of that here. At most
we can see in Jewish apocalyptic and in early Christianity the first
beginnings of what was subsequently to develop into Gnosticism,
and it is a mistake to begin by reading back the developed ideas of
the second-century systems into first-century documents which do
not require these ideas for their interpretation.

6. The trend of the argument so far would lead one to expect an
immediate statement that the world to come is subjected not to the
angels but to the Son, but the author does not take this course and
the connection of thought is not entirely clear. He begins once again
with an Old Testament quotation, this time from Ps. 8:5–7, again
following the Septuagint version. Here the quotation is introduced
by a rather vague formula, literally 'somebody has testified somewhere'. This vagueness is easily explained, in that before the introduction of chapter and verse divisions it simply was not possible to
give precise and specific references. In general one might find the
name of an author and the title of a book, at most a reference to a
well-known passage (e.g. the one about the bush, Mk 12:26). Thus
Philo uses various formulae of introduction (for comparison with
Hebrews see Williamson pp. 504ff.), and indeed on one occasion a
very similar form of words (*De Ebr.* 61). There is, however, another
factor to be taken into account, the author's view of inspiration. In
the Old Testament it is God who speaks; the human author is simply
not important. All his quotations are anonymous, and the one case
which appears to be an exception (4:7) may not in fact be so; 'in
David' may be no more than a general reference to the Psalter (in
any case, 3:7 explicitly identifies the speaker in the psalm quoted
as the Holy Spirit). In the present case there is a slight incongruity,

in that the words of the psalm are addressed *to* God, so that they could not be introduced in the usual way as a divine oracle. In verse 8, however, (verse 6 of the psalm in English versions), there is a clear allusion to Gen. 1:26–30, where God gives to man dominion over all creatures of the earth. Here too, therefore, the words are ultimately God's words and the human author is not important.

Verse 6 shows the parallelism of Hebrew poetry, the second line matching the first with a slight change in the form of expression. **Son of man** is thus simply equivalent to **man** in the preceding line. Psalm 8 is part of the Old Testament background for this sometimes rather enigmatic phrase, which in the Gospels appears only on the lips of Jesus and apparently as a self-designation, but seems to have dropped out of use in early Christianity. When it appears again in early patristic literature, it is with a rather different nuance, as applying to the humanity of Jesus, whereas 'son of God' gives expression to his divinity (cf. the Nag Hammadi *Letter to Rheginus* 44:21–34 for a succinct example). It is not possible here, nor is it necessary, to enter into detailed discussion of the much-debated question of the origin and meaning of the phrase as used by Jesus. What does concern us is the question whether the phrase should be understood as a title here, and the psalm given a messianic interpretation. Thus Westcott writes that the psalm, 'is not, and has never been accounted by the Jews to be, directly messianic; but as expressing the true destiny of man it finds its accomplishment in the Son of Man and only through Him in man'. F. F. Bruce roundly declares, 'The fact remains that, ever since Jesus spoke of Himself as the Son of Man, this expression has had for Christians a connotation beyond its etymological force, and it had this connotation for the writer to the Hebrews', and indeed entitles the whole section 'The Humiliation and Glory of the Son of Man'. These statements may be true enough, and Bruce's heading an apposite title for the section, but the question is whether they should be linked to the phrase 'son of man' in the quotation, and not to the passage as a whole. It may indeed be that the writer knew of Jesus' use of the phrase, but to introduce this connotation here at the beginning of the quotation is to ignore the parallelism and divorce the second line from the first. As Moffatt notes, neither here nor elsewhere does the author use the term 'Son of Man', and while the ideas associated with it are certainly present in the context it is at least open to question whether they should be brought in quite so early. It would therefore seem better to take the quotation as referring, as it does in the original psalm, to mankind and not (on the strength of the Son of Man title) to Jesus. That comes later, in the author's exposition of the text, (cf. however F. J. Moloney, *NTS* 27 [1981] pp. 656ff., who argues

on the basis of the Targums for a non-Christian messianic interpretation of Ps. 8 which could have influenced the *NT* writers).

7. There is a problem for the translator in verse 7, in two small
Greek words which mean 'just a little' and could be used of space
or time or quantity (cf. *BAG* 147a, who cite Isa. 57:17 for use with
reference to time). In the psalm the reference is clearly to rank:
'thou hast made him little less than God' (LXX renders 'than angels',
an interpretation followed here in Hebrews but found also in the
Targum and in Jewish commentators). The psalm is a hymn of
praise expressing the writer's wonder at God's goodness to our
human race. Looking back to the first chapter of Genesis, it recalls
that God gave to man dominion over all creatures, the birds of the
air and the fish of the sea—in fact gave to him a status only slightly
lower than that of God himself. In verse 9 below, however, the
same phrase is almost certainly interpreted of time (cf. also Ac.
5:34) **for a little while lower than the angels**. There is an ambiguity
in the Greek which it is difficult to reproduce in English, and a
choice therefore must be made: do we retain the original meaning
in the quotation in verse 7, and introduce the second meaning in
the author's interpretation in verse 9? Or, since the latter is the
meaning which the author evidently saw in the text, do we (with
RSV and *NEB*) translate **for a little while** in both places? The *AV*
rendering 'a little lower' at both points preserves the ambiguity, but
at the expense of clarity, unless with Bruce (pp. 35f.), we understand the author to be taking the text in its original sense but
applying it not to the first Adam but to the second, the 'true
representative of humanity', who though introduced in the prologue
as 'so much better than the angels' yet had to be made 'a little
lower', in accordance with the psalm (cf. also Héring). There is
certainly food for thought in this interpretation, and it may be that
such ideas were latent in the background, but they are not explicitly
stated and we may wonder whether they would readily occur to the
earliest readers. Here again it seems better to take the quotation in
its straightforward natural sense, as applying to mankind. It is only
in verse 8 that the author begins to expound the text, and give it a
new significance.

At the end of this verse a quite impressive group of witnesses,
including Sinaiticus, Alexandrinus and Claromontanus with several
minuscules and versions, inserts another line from the psalm. The
words are missing however from the Chester Beatty Papyrus P[46]
and from Vaticanus, and marked for deletion by a corrector in
Claromontanus. Since their inclusion may be due to assimilation to
LXX, it is probable that the shorter text should be preferred.

8. The psalm, as already noted, expresses its author's wonder at the goodness of God to the human race. Our author begins his comment by emphasising the last line of the quotation: **in putting everything in subjection to man, he left nothing outside his control.** This line of the psalm is quoted by Paul at 1 C. 15:27, with an exceptive clause to make it clear that God who did the subjecting is, of course, not included. Paul's use of this line does not, however, justify interpreting the quotation as a whole in terms of the Pauline doctrine of the first and second Adam. It is always dangerous to interpret one New Testament author in terms of more detailed teaching given by another, since unless it is explicitly stated we cannot be sure that both shared the same ideas. Later theology, in the attempt to reconcile differences, may have done so, but that is another matter. Here we are concerned with the interpretation and understanding of the text before us. Hebrews makes no such exception, but it is taken for granted. It has, however, been suggested that the difficult reading 'apart from God' (instead of 'by the grace of God') in verse 9 originated in a marginal note by some reader who recalled 1 C. 15:27.

In the second part of the verse, the author prepares the way for his interpretation by bluntly stating that in terms of our ordinary experience the quotation simply is not true. **We do not yet see everything in subjection to him**: Even today, for all man's techno-logical achievement, he cannot control the birds of the air and the fish of the sea—as Montefiore remarks, 'he is far from being monarch of all he surveys'—and first-century readers were a long way short of modern advances. The psalm, however, was to our author Holy Scripture, and therefore must be meaningful. If a straightforward literal understanding is not possible, there must be some other meaning. The text thus presents just the kind of *aporia* which to Philo would have been a pointer to allegorical interpret-ation (cf. J. Pépin, 'Remarques sur la théorie de l'exégèse allégorique chez Philon', in *Philon d'Alexandrie*, (ed.) Arnaldez et al., Paris [1967], pp. 131ff. and especially pp. 161ff.). The **not yet**, if we follow the literal interpretation of the quotation, would mean that the fulfilment of the promise to man in Genesis still lies in the future: 'universal dominion is his future destiny, not his present possession' (Montefiore). On a 'messianic' interpretation, the meaning would be that though the Son has been crowned and enthroned, his foes have still to be subdued. The new order, though inaugurated, has not yet fully come. It should be noted that the word rendered **to man** both in *RSV* and in *NEB* (but in different places) is literally 'to him', so that both interpretations are entirely possible. 'While man is primarily indicated' by this word, 'the Son of Man cannot be totally excluded from its scope' (cf. Bruce, p. 37

n. 35). On the view here followed, the reference is to mankind, and
the *RSV* and *NEB* translators are correct in their interpretation.

9. We do not yet see everything in subjection to mankind, but
we do see the one **who for a little while was made lower than the
angels—Jesus.** The name occurs here for the first time in the letter,
and in an emphatic position which is rather obscured by the *AV*
and *RSV* rendering **But we see Jesus.** It is flanked on the one side
by the reference to his being made lower than the angels, stressing
his humanity, and on the other by **crowned with glory and honour
because of the suffering of death,** which emphasises his work of
salvation (so Montefiore). Mankind is not, or not yet, master of the
universe, and even the Son of Man, though enthroned, has still to
wait for his enemies to be finally subjected, but to the eyes of faith
he is already sovereign, crowned with glory and honour, and that
because of the suffering of death. 'It is precisely because of His
humiliation, suffering and death that He has been invested with
heavenly glory' (Bruce).

At this point some commentators have encountered difficulty,
because the purpose clause **that by the grace of God he might taste
death for every one** appears to follow the crowning with glory and
honour. In the previous clause, however, **because of the suffering
of death** states the ground for the crowning and not its purpose (cf.
Westcott), and the final clause is better explained as epexegetic of
these words: it 'explains and expounds the idea of διὰ τὸ πάθημα
(which consists in) τοῦ θανάτου, gathering up the full object and
purpose of the experience which has just been predicated of Jesus'
(Moffatt). 'That he might taste death for every one' expresses the purpose not merely of the crowning but of 'the whole sequence of preceding events, the humiliation, passion and glory combined' (Bruce).

Another problem here is a textual one. The reading **by the grace
of God** fits so appropriately in the context that it would not be
questioned but for the existence of a variant 'apart from God' (cf.
NEB margin). The latter is undoubtedly the *lectio difficilior*, since
it is easy enough to see how it could have been changed to the
other reading, but difficult to account for a change in the opposite
direction. On this basis, and on grounds of intrinsic probability
(which he does not specify), Montefiore accepts this reading, translating 'separated from God' and interpreting it with reference to the
Cry of Dereliction (Mk 15:34). The criterion of the more difficult
reading is not however to be rigidly applied in every case, and there
is the further fact that 'by the grace of God' is supported by the
great majority of MSS, including the Chester Beatty papyrus and all
the major uncials, whereas the support for the variant is largely
patristic, with only one uncial and a couple of minuscules. The

weight of evidence is therefore heavily on one side, although both readings were already known to Origen. In Montefiore's view, 'the addition of χωρὶς θεοῦ as a scribal gloss, with the subsequent omission of χάριτι θεοῦ, seems an over-complicated explanation'; but that depends on what exactly is envisaged. If the gloss is held to have been inserted where nothing stood before, and subsequently changed, then Montefiore is probably correct (the whole process would have to have been completed before P[46], c. AD 200). On the other hand, if the text already had **by the grace of God** here, and the words 'apart from God' were inserted in the margin *as a gloss on verse 8* suggested by 1 C. 15:27 (see above), then it is entirely possible that later scribes or readers misunderstood them as a correction of verse 9 (cf. Metzger, *Textual Commentary*, p. 664). On the whole, therefore, the reading **by the grace of God** should be given the preference, although there may be still some lingering doubt.

In these verses the author begins by recalling his earlier theme of the superiority of the Son to the angels. Though their message was valid, and any transgression entailed due retribution, they are still subordinate, no more than ministering spirits; nor has the world to come been placed under their control. On the contrary, Psalm 8, looking back to Genesis 1, accords dominion to man. Our author first observes that as it stands, the quotation simply is not true, and then by a bold re-interpretation applies the psalm to Jesus, now introduced for the first time but clearly to be identified as the Son of the opening chapter. He is **crowned with glory and honour because of the suffering of death,** his exaltation the result of his humiliation and suffering. As Bruce notes, 'this interpretation of our author's argument at this point brings it into line with Paul's "therefore also God highly exalted him" in Phil. 2:9'. But there is yet another point, which is still to be developed in the following section: it was by the grace of God that Jesus died for every one, and indeed this was 'consonant with God's character' (Moffatt). As the next verse continues, it was fitting that **in bringing many sons to glory he should make the pioneer of their salvation perfect through suffering.**

THE HUMANITY AND SUFFERING OF JESUS THE HIGH PRIEST
2:10–18

The first part of this passage affirms the full humanity of Jesus, his solidarity with those he came to deliver. As verse 17 puts it, **he had**

to be made like his brethren in every respect, so that he might become a merciful and faithful high priest in the service of God. It has already been noted as one of the characteristics of the author that he frequently introduces a theme, almost in passing, only to leave it aside and return to it later for further treatment. So it is here: the priesthood of Jesus is barely mentioned in 2:17 and 3:1, but then taken up again for detailed discussion at 4:14. Similarly, priesthood 'after the order of Melchizedek' is mentioned in the quotation at 5:6, echoed at 5:10, but detailed treatment of the Melchizedek theme does not come until chapter 7.

10. A further purpose of this section is to explain why Jesus had to suffer and to die, and indeed to show that this was no inconsequential accident, but part of the divine purpose (Montefiore aptly compares Mk 8:31). Some commentators have felt it necessary to defend the author's use of the word rendered **it was fitting**, as if there were something arrogant or presumptuous about affirming what is fitting for, or worthy of, God; but, for one thing, although the word is not so used in LXX it is used by non-Christian writers and in particular by Philo (cf. Williamson, pp. 88ff., who notes that what Hebrews here says was fitting 'is something that to Philo was utterly abhorrent', and quotes Moffatt's remark that 'Philo has the phrase, not the idea'), and for another the choice of a different shade of meaning may make a considerable difference to the sense: it was appropriate, becoming, or in Moffatt's phrase 'consonant with God's character'. The author is *describing* what God appropriately did, not *prescribing* what was fitting for him to do.

The one **for whom and by whom all things exist** must in this context be God, since it is he who makes the 'pioneer of salvation' perfect (for similar usage cf. Rom. 11:36). The same Greek preposition is used with two different cases to describe God, in Westcott's words, as 'the final Cause and the efficient Cause of all things' (a similar thought is expressed in different words at 1 C. 8:6a). Such phrases are employed elsewhere to describe the work of the Son (cf. 1:2 above, also 1 C. 8:6b; Col. 1:16; Jn 1:3,10), but this would not be appropriate in the present context.

The participle rendered **in bringing many sons to glory** is in the Greek in the accusative case, and the only accusative in the sentence with which it could be linked is the word translated 'pioneer' immediately following. The Greek could thus be taken to mean that it was Christ who brought many sons to glory, but the order of words and the run of the sentence are both against this; had the participle been intended to qualify 'pioneer' the order would have been different (cf. Moffatt, p. 31). The reference therefore must be to God, despite the fact that the pronoun in the Greek is in the

dative (Moffatt speaks of 'a common Greek assimilation', comparing
Ac. 11:12; 15:22; 22:17 [which is not quite the same]; 25:27). The
initiative in the work of salvation, as in creation, belongs to God.
The reference to **many sons** does not stand in contrast to the
statement of verse 9 that Christ died 'for every one'; the contrast is
rather with the one and only **pioneer** (Moffatt compares Rom. 8:29;
Mk 14:24. At Mk 1:32, 34 we have a similar change of word, which
does not mean that the people brought *all* their sick, and Jesus only
healed *some* of them! The emphasis is inclusive rather than exclusive,
cf. Cranfield ad loc.). As Montefiore notes, 'the elect are described
as sons, since they have been adopted by God to sonship (Rom.
8:15; Gal. 4:5; Eph. 1:5)'. Westcott aptly quotes the comment of
Chrysostom: 'He is a son, and we are sons; but he saves, while we
are saved'.

The word translated **pioneer** presents another problem for the
translator, since none of the English equivalents conveys its full
range of meaning, and some of them have associations which are
not appropriate. It was used of the hero who founded a city, and
was regarded as its protector, and hence means 'author', 'founder',
'originator', or in a bad sense 'instigator'. It can also be used in a
military or political sense, as often in LXX, as 'captain', 'leader' or
'prince' (see *TDNT* I. 487f.; *BAG* 112b. G. Johnston, *NTS* 27
[1981], pp. 381ff., claims that the biblical meaning 'almost always
denotes *leadership*', and argues for 'Prince'). The word is used three
other times in the New Testament, at Ac. 3:15 (the Author of Life)
and 5:31 (Leader and Saviour) and at 12:2 below (the pioneer and
perfecter of our faith), in addition to the present passage. *NEB*
agrees at Ac. 5:31, but paraphrases at the other three points ('him
who has led the way to life', Ac. 3:15; 'the leader who delivers
them', Heb. 2:10; 'Jesus, on whom faith depends from start to
finish', Heb. 12:2). Commentators speak in terms of 'blazing the
trail' or 'pioneering the way', although one must bear in mind
Johnston's remark about 'paraphrases that must speak vividly to a
Canadian woodsman!' Spicq drily remarks that *Führer* and *Duce* are
no longer possible ([1977], p. 72); he sees an emphasis on Christ's
role as the guide who marches ahead, clearing the way, the first to
cover the route which all must follow, and adds that one who is to
play this part must be fitted for it—hence the *archegos* had to be
'made perfect through suffering'. The word is thus rich in meaning,
and not easily to be rendered by any one English equivalent; sometimes we must resort to paraphrase, particularly when its combination with other words would yield a not very lucid or meaningful
English phrase. The basic idea is that of 'inaugurator' or 'initiator',
but it also has the connotation of leadership, both in the sense of

one leading the way (Michel, p. 144 compares 'fore-runner' at 6:20) and also in that of command.

Perfect through suffering: reference has already been made in v. 9 to Jesus' suffering of death, which must be at least a major part of the suffering mentioned here, although it is not necessarily the whole. We may think of the whole sequence of the Passion story, the mockery, the scourging, as well as the crucifixion itself. On the other hand it is going much too far to treat the whole of Jesus' life and ministry as one of suffering, and speak, like the writer of a hymn, of his 'life and death of woe'. Isaiah's words (55:3) about 'a man of sorrows and acquainted with grief' should not be generalised as if there was nothing else in the life of Jesus (the parable of the children in the market-place (Mt. 11:16–19; Lk. 7:31–35) suggests a different picture). Nor should the inference be drawn that Christians to be like him must be sombre and doleful— that would show small thanks or gratitude for the deliverance bestowed. There *must* be solemnity when we consider the cost, but this whole letter is intended to encourage and inspire, to revive a flagging enthusiasm, to lift up the drooping hands and strengthen the feeble knees (cf. 12:12). There should also be joy and exhilaration—the text, after all, speaks of many sons being **brought to glory**.

A further point to be noted in this verse is the reference to **making the pioneer perfect through suffering**. As Westcott notes (p. 65), the adjective 'came naturally to be used of themselves by those who claimed to possess the highest knowledge of the truth, as initiated into its mysteries', i.e. the gnostics (he quotes Valentinian claims cited by Irenaeus), and the idea of perfection in Hebrews has sometimes been claimed as evidence for a gnostic influence (cf. Introd., p. 25). A moment's reflection is enough to show that this is not necessarily the case. At Mt. 5:48 we read, 'You, therefore, must be perfect, as your heavenly Father is perfect', which surely echoes Lev. 19:2: 'You shall be holy; for I the Lord your God am holy'. The word *is* used by the gnostics later, but this does not mean that it must always be given a gnostic sense. The basic idea (see *BAG* 809) is that of completeness. As applied to persons, **perfect** means full-grown, mature, adult, as distinct from babes (cf. the contrast at 5:13–14). For the use of the word in the New Testament, see P. J. du Plessis, *TELEIOS. The Idea of Perfection in the New Testament* (Kampen, n.d.), and for Hebrews in particular D. Peterson, *Hebrews and Perfection* (Cambridge [1982]), who discusses this passage at length (pp. 55–63).

More relevant is the question how the phrase could be applied to Jesus. Most commentators mention only to reject the suggestion

that he was in any way imperfect: 4:15 is enough to refute any
such idea, which is quite out of keeping with the author's whole
Christology. The real explanation is to be found in the context as a
whole, together with such passages as 4:15, 5:8–9 and 7:28. To
pioneer the way to salvation he must be fully human, sharing in
the temptations which are part of our human lot, and learn obedience through what he has to suffer. It is a major defect of any docetic
Christology that it affords neither inspiration nor encouragement to
the ordinary believer: godhead merely 'veiled in flesh', a divine
being merely masquerading as a man, may be thought to possess
innate advantages that are denied to others. For one thing, the
overcoming of temptation presents no problem. The frailties
common to the rest of us are not really his. But as 4:15 shows, this
is not the author's view. Significantly, the second of Peterson's three
chapters on the perfecting of Christ, devoted to 4:14–5:10, carries
the sub-title 'His earthly struggle' (pp. 74–103), and at the end
quotes Michel's summary: the perfecting of Christ involves 'his
proving in temptation, his fulfilment of the priestly requirements
and his exaltation as Redeemer of the heavenly world'. The phrase
thus refers not to the making good of any defect, but to adequate
qualification for his task. As F. F. Bruce puts it (p. 43): 'The
pathway of perfection which his people must tread must first be
trodden by the Pathfinder; only so could he be their adequate
representative and high priest in the presence of God'. As is so often
the case, the author here merely touches on a point which will be
more fully developed later. A proper understanding of what he
means by 'perfection', both for Christ and for believers, entails
consideration of several other passages (cf. Peterson).

   11. For the moment the argument is concerned with the real
humanity of Jesus: **he who sanctifies and those who are sanctified
have all one origin**. *AV* more literally translates 'are all of one',
NEB 'are all of one stock', Montefiore (to differentiate from Ac.
17:26, where the same phrase is used) 'have a common parent'.
This variety of translation is not important. What matters is that
both have a common **origin**, and because of that **he is not ashamed
to call them brethren**. There is, of course, a difference, in that he
is the sanctifier, they the sanctified (Westcott quotes Theodoret: He
is Son by nature, we by grace; cf. Chrysostom, quoted above at
v. 10), but there is a close bond between them. 'By his death they
are consecrated to God for his worship and service and set apart for
God as his holy people, destined to enter into his glory' (F. F.
Bruce). There would seem to be some slight inconsistency in that
10:10, to which Bruce refers, seems to suggest as he takes it that
the sanctified *become* sons by virtue of their consecration, whereas

here they appear to be sons by virtue of their origin, but it is probable that the author gave no thought to this question. His concern emerges in verse 14, which explains the necessity of the Incarnation. But before that he drives home his point by three Old Testament quotations.

It has been suggested that the 'one' from whom both derive their origin is Abraham (cf. v. 16) or Adam (cf. Ac. 17:26), but Westcott writes 'the reference to Adam or to Abraham is partly inadequate and partly inappropriate'. Most commentators agree that both sanctifier and sanctified are members of the one family of God. Neither common humanity nor membership in the chosen race of Israel is in view in the context, and v. 13 refers to 'the children God has given me'. The reference to Abraham in v. 16 is more remote.

12. The first quotation is from Psalm 22, which Dodd (*According to the Scriptures*, p. 108) lists among the primary sources for *testimonia*. 'The psalm as a whole was clearly regarded as a source of testimonies to the passion of Christ and his ultimate triumph, and probably from an early date, since it is woven into the texture of the Passion-narrative, and used in writings almost certainly independent of one another' (ib. pp. 97f.). The first verse of the psalm is of course the Cry of Dereliction (Mt. 27:46; Mk 15:34), while verse 18 is echoed in all four Gospels (Mt. 27:35; Mk 15:24; Lk. 23:34; Jn 19:24). The words here quoted are from verse 22, and are clearly chosen because of the phrase **my brethren**. This verse stands at the beginning of the second part of the psalm, with its note of vindication and assurance. But there is more. In the parallelism of Hebrew poetry, **the congregation** in the second line corresponds to **my brethren** in the first, which in the author's view justifies his use of the quotation. In the preceding section he identified the Son of Man of Psalm 8 as Jesus, 'crowned with glory and honour because of the suffering of death', who by the grace of God tasted death for everyone. Now by identifying Jesus as the speaker of Psalm 22, he can claim the name of 'brethren' for the Christian community. The word translated **congregation** is the word from which modern English words like 'ecclesiastical' are derived, and is elsewhere commonly rendered 'church', but according to Moffatt our author only uses it (12:23) 'of the heavenly host, never in its ordinary sense of the "church" '. This is only partly correct, and indeed is somewhat at variance with Moffatt's own interpretation (p. 217) of 12:23. Certainly in the New Testament the word is used with various shades of meaning (cf. *BAG* 240f.), and does not always have the associations of the English 'church', but here it is the LXX rendering of the Hebrew *qahal*, the congregation of the people of Israel. The Christian community here steps into the place of Israel as the people of God (on the whole question cf. Richardson, *Israel in the Apostolic Church*, and for Hebrews esp. pp. 175–180).

13. Moffatt deals very concisely with the second quotation, from Isa. 8:17 (**I will put my trust in him**): 'The fact that Jesus required to put faith in God proves that he was a human being like ourselves (cf. 12:2, where Jesus is called the *archegos* of faith, the 'perfect exemplar' and 'supreme pioneer' [so Moffatt, p. 196; for *archegos* see on v. 10 above]). This is certainly true, and fits in with the emphasis of the passage on the humanity of Jesus, his solidarity with his people, which comes to its climax in v. 14: **since the children share in flesh and blood, he himself likewise partook of the same nature**. The author however does not spell out this interpretation, and we may wonder whether the first readers would have taken his point without some explanation. Further, there is more to be said on this verse. Bruce calls it 'a good example of C. H. Dodd's thesis that the principal Old Testament quotations in the New Testament are not isolated proof-texts, but carry their contexts with them by implication' (cf. Dodd, *According to the Scriptures*, esp. pp. 78ff.). Dodd argues (p. 81) that 'there is some ground for believing that Isa. 6:1–9:7 may have formed, for early Christian students of the Old Testament, a single complex unit of prophecy'. Beginning with a vision of the glory of God, the passage proceeds to a prophecy of doom and then, at 7:3, introduces for the first time the idea of the Remnant. At 8:18—the third Old Testament quotation in this passage of Hebrews—the prophet identifies this faithful remnant as 'the children whom God has given me'. In the original context the reference is to Isaiah and his family, but as Dodd notes a first-century reader would understand them as 'the nucleus of the true *ecclesia*' (p. 82). Moffatt remarks that to omit the second **and again** as a scribal gloss 'would certainly improve the sense and avoid the necessity of splitting up an Isaianic quotation into two, the first of which is not strictly apposite', but in the light of the passage as a whole the last clause at least of this comment is open to question. Moreover, as Montefiore says (p. 64), the author 'does not intend to introduce a fresh quotation, but to make a new point'. As Westcott had seen even earlier, the two quotations represent different aspects: 'In the first the prophet declares his personal faith in God in the midst of judgments. In the second he stands forth with his children as representing "the remnant", the seed of the Church, in Israel'.

The application of these three quotations to Jesus supplies three proofs of his kinship with his followers, the other members of God's family, neatly summed up by Montefiore: 'firstly, he calls them brothers, secondly, he shares with them the human attitude of faith in God, and thirdly, he speaks of them as children of God'.

14–15. Verse 14 then goes on to draw out the implications of this solidarity: the kinship implies a full humanity. 'To complete his fellowship with them therefore it was necessary that he should assume their nature under its present conditions' (Westcott). The Christological controversies which eventually led to the formulation of the Nicene and Chalcedonian creeds lie still in the future, and our author offers no explanation as to what he thought of the relation of the divine and human natures in Christ. He stands at a still quite early stage in the development of Christological thinking. In his prologue he has accorded to the Son 'the highest place that heaven affords', under God himself; the following section, culminating in the quotation of Psalm 110 at 1:13, has declared the Son's superiority to the angels, and his exaltation to the right hand of God; at 2:9 the Son is identified as Jesus; now he argues that the solidarity of Jesus with his people involves a real humanity, even to the suffering of death, but exactly how these different aspects are to be reconciled or held together is not discussed. Such questions were to be the concern of theologians and councils in a later age, but at this stage the problems have not yet arisen.

The phrase **flesh and blood** is a common expression for human nature, and not only in Jewish circles (Moffatt quotes 'an apt classical parallel' in the military writer Polyaenus, where a leader urges his troops to think of their enemies as 'men having flesh and blood and sharing the same nature as we do'). The rabbis use it 'chiefly where the corruptible nature of man is compared with the eternity and omnipotence of God', but the usage is older than the rabbinic literature and the idea of mortality and creatureliness seems to be bound up with it from the outset (*TDNT* VII, 116; cf. Sir. 14:18). Here *AV*, *RSV* and *NEB* all have the common order (cf. Mt. 16:17; 1 C. 15:50; Gal. 1:16), although in the Greek (as in Eph. 6:12) the order is inverted, probably as Montefiore suggests because of the importance of blood for the writer's argument later in the epistle (9:12ff.; 10:19).

The purpose of the Incarnation as here stated is at first sight strange, since there is no reference to deliverance from sin: it is not that he might sanctify them (cf. v. 11), cleanse them from sin, deliver them from its bondage, but **that through death he might destroy him who has the power of death.** Death and not sin appears to be the enemy, and it is not entirely clear why he who has the power of death should be identified as **the devil.** However, when we recall

'the fruit
Of that forbidden tree whose mortal taste
Brought death into the world and all our woe',
then all begins to fall into place. According to the Wisdom of
Solomon (1:13f.; 2.23f.), God did not create death: he created man
for incorruption, but through the devil's envy death entered into
the world. Behind this of course lies an interpretation of the story
of the Fall in Genesis 3. So Paul in Romans (5:12) speaks of sin
coming into the world, and death through sin, and later argues (6:9)
that 'Christ being raised from the dead will never die again; death
no longer has dominion over him'. Sin and death are thus linked
together, for 'the wages of sin is death' (Rom. 6:23), and death is
the last enemy to be destroyed (1 C. 15:26). The formulation and
the emphasis may be different, but the association of ideas is the
same. As to **the devil** having **the power of death**, we may perhaps
recall 1 C. 5:5: 'You are to deliver this man to Satan for the
destruction of the flesh', although interpretations of this verse are
very varied. In rabbinic thought the angel of death has the power
of inflicting death (Mechilta 72a on Exod. 20:20), and Héring quotes
the Babylonian Talmud (*Baba bathra* 16a): 'Satan, the evil incli-
nation and the angel of death are identical'.

The Pauline references above do not necessarily mean that
Hebrews is indebted to or influenced by Paul. Rather both stand in
the same tradition of Jewish thought. Nor is the fear of death a
merely Jewish phenomenon. Moffatt (p. 35) notes that 'the Greek
protest against the fear of death, as unworthy of the wise and good,
is echoed by Philo'; but the fear persisted. The classic example is
perhaps the *De Rerum Natura* of Lucretius, 'from end to end a
passionate argument against the fear of death and the superstition
of which it was the basis' (Wickham), but Lucretius was not alone,
as Moffatt's references show. In part this fear is a fear of the
unknown: we know not what lies beyond. At a later point our
author writes of 'a certain fearful looking for of judgment' (10:27
AV), and one of Lucretius' concerns is to demonstrate that there *is*
no hereafter, hence no judgment, and therefore no cause for fear.
That however also entails the conclusion that there is no cause for
hope, that death is absolutely and finally the end, and this was a
conclusion that was perennially resisted, despite all the arguments
of philosophers. Platonism of course always had its doctrine of the
immortality of the soul, Pythagoreanism its doctrine of trans-
migration, but even some of the Stoics admitted some idea of the
survival of the individual. The teaching of the New Testament is
distinctive, in that the future hope is not based on any theoretical
argument but irrevocably tied to the death and resurrection of Jesus.

As F. F. Bruce notes (p. 49), 'it calls for an exceptional effort of
mind on our part to appreciate how paradoxical was the attitude of
those early Christians to the death of Christ. If ever death had
appeared to be triumphant, it was when Jesus of Nazareth . . .
breathed his last on the cross. . . . And yet—within a generation
his followers were exultingly proclaiming the crucified Jesus to be
the conqueror of death and asserting, like our author here, that by
dying he had reduced the erstwhile lord of death to impotence'.

Just how Jesus by dying broke the devil's power is not explained,
any more than Paul explains precisely how by dying to sin Jesus
conquered sin (Rom. 6:10). Moffatt notes the paradox in 'through
death', and quotes Chrysostom's explanation, that the very means
by which the devil held sway is the means by which he was worsted.
Both Paul and Hebrews however express the conviction that the
problem has been effectively dealt with. Hence in verse 15 the
author can go on to speak of the deliverance of those **who through
fear of death were subject to lifelong bondage**. Death no more
has its sting (cf. 1 C. 15:54–55). The translation **destroy him who
has the power of death** (*AV, RSV*) is perhaps too strong: the verb
means to reduce to impotence, to make ineffective, and it is a fact
of common experience that death has not been abolished or done
away with. The point is that **the devil** has been deposed, dethroned,
no longer holds sway, and those who were formerly subject to
bondage are now released. As another writer puts it, 'we have been
born anew to a living hope through the resurrection of Jesus Christ
from the dead' (1 Pet. 1:3 *RSV*).

16. For surely it is not with angels that he is concerned: The
Authorised Version translates 'for verily he took not on *him the
nature* of angels; but he took on *him* the seed of Abraham', indicating
by the italics that for these words there is no equivalent in the
Greek. The verb means to take hold of or grasp (e.g. by the hand,
Mk 8:23), but also to be concerned with, take an interest in or
help (Sir. 4:11; see *BAG* 295a). The *AV* follows the Fathers in
understanding the phrase 'of the fact and not the purpose of the
Incarnation' (Westcott), but Moffatt regards it as 'a warning against
the habit of regarding the Greek fathers as absolute authorities for
the Greek' that they never suspected the real meaning of the word
here. Indeed, when the interpretation now almost universally
accepted was first advanced in the sixteenth century it was roundly
condemned by Theodore Beza as 'false and inept'. The patristic
interpretation however involves the reading in of words which are
not in the text, and would make this verse a repetition of verse 14a,
or an anticipation of 17a. Moreover, the conjunction 'for' indicates
that this verse is explanatory of what has just been said, and finally

there seems to be a reminiscence here of Isa. 41:8. Hence the meaning is 'it is not to angels that he gives help, but to the seed of Abraham'. The latter phrase refers in the first instance to the actual descendants of Abraham, the Jewish people, but Paul had already claimed it for all Christians, irrespective of birth (Rom. 9:8; Gal. 3:29).

17. This verse rounds off the argument of this section, and introduces for the first time one of the fundamental themes of the letter, that of priesthood (for the High Priest in Hebrews, cf. *TDNT* III, pp. 274ff.). As already noted, it is barely mentioned here and in 3:1, before the author turns to deal with another topic; the detailed treatment of it begins at 4:14. The argument is more closely knit than might at first appear. The qualifications required in a high priest are set out in 5:1–4, and when at 5:5 the author sets himself to show how they apply to Jesus he begins with the last. Similarly, here, he deals first with Jesus' faithfulness, in the comparison with Moses (3:2–6), and then with his sympathy and compassion (4:15–16), before taking up the theme of priesthood in chapter 5. The reference to God's house at 3.2ff. leads naturally to warning and admonition against falling into error like the people who formed that house in the days of Moses.

A high priest is chosen from among men to act in relation to God (5:1; 'in relation to God' is the same Greek phrase here rendered **in the service of God**). This adds a further point to the argument for the real humanity of Jesus: he had to become **like his brethren in every respect**, not merely in some, in order to **become a merciful and faithful high priest**. He is to represent men in relation to God, to act on their behalf, and to do that he must himself be fully human. His task is **to make expiation for the sins of the people** (cf. 5:1, 'to offer gifts and sacrifices for sins'). The Greek verb here is one of a group of words deriving from the same root, which in LXX and the New Testament have a different meaning from that of classical and non-biblical *Koine* usage (see Dodd, *The Bible and the Greeks*, 82–95; D. Hill, *Greek Words and Hebrew Meanings*, pp. 23ff.; *TDNT* III, pp. 300ff.). In classical usage the verb and its compounds regularly have the sense 'placate, propitiate', with a personal object; one of them also has the secondary sense of 'expiate', with an impersonal object. In LXX and the New Testament, however, the primary idea is not that of placating or propitiating an angry deity but of the removal or wiping out of the sins which stand between man and God. 'The most striking thing about the development of the terms is that words which were originally used to denote man's action in relation to God cease to be used in this way in the NT and are used instead of God's action in relation to man' (*TDNT* III, p. 317). Here, with 'sins' as the object, the sense is clear, but in other cases the *AV* wrongly introduces the sense of propitiation. 'Propitiation is not a biblical concept, but expiation is the motive underlying atonement sacrifice. Expiation is what the high priest was believed to achieve on the Day of Atonement' (Montefiore). We shall see this worked out in detail as the letter proceeds.

The suddenness with which the idea of Jesus as **a merciful and faithful high priest** is introduced suggests that it is no invention of the author, but a belief already familiar to Christians (A. J. B. Higgins, *NTS* 13 [1967], pp. 235f., who finds the ultimate source of this Christology in the teaching of Jesus himself. It is not that Jesus himself viewed his ministry in priestly terms. 'The early church did that when it interpreted the heavenly intercession of the Son of man in the teaching of Jesus as a priestly function performed by the exalted Jesus himself' (p. 236). On pp. 234f. Higgins adduces Rom. 8:34 (cf. Heb. 7:25), 1 Jn 2:1f. and Jn 17:9 as evidence for the belief outside of Hebrews and in forms 'totally uninfluenced by Ps. 110:4'). As it happens, Philo quite often refers to the Logos as a high priest, and this has formed part of the evidence for the view that our author is indebted to Philo (see Williamson, esp. pp. 409ff.). Certainly there are similarities, but some at least of these are to be explained by a common background in the Jewish Wisdom tradition, shared by both authors. 'It is difficult to believe that the writings of Philo and the doctrines they contain are a primary source of inspiration behind the thought of the Epistle to the Hebrews. It is not just that there is so much in Philo about the Logos and so little in Hebrews, but also that so little, if anything, of the distinctively Philonic conception of the Logos-High Priest appears in Hebrews' (Williamson, p. 430). 'The whole approach of the two writers to their *OT* texts is entirely dissimilar. Philo approaches the *OT* with philosophical conclusions in mind which he has convinced himself can be extracted from it by allegorical exegesis . . . The Writer of Hebrews approaches the *OT* in the light of his Christian beliefs about Jesus and . . . applies to Christ what the *OT* says, e.g., about high priests and clearly implies that the *OT* scriptures in this respect, as in others, found their fulfilment in him' (*ib*. p. 433). It is important to pay due attention not only to the similarities, but also to the differences.

18. Reference has already been made to suffering in v. 10 above. Now it is linked with temptation, a point which will be further developed at 4:15. In the light of 5:7ff., we may naturally think of the temptation to avoid the suffering which led to the cross, but this is not stated, and the temptations of Jesus are not confined to

that. Nor is that a temptation likely to be common to his people,
so that he could help them. We may recall the temptation stories
in the Gospels (Mt. 4:1–11; Lk. 4:1–13), or those occasions when
his friends sought to divert him from his purpose (e.g. Mk 8:32f.).
The point is quite simply that having himself suffered, and endured,
he knows and understands (cf. 4:15) and is able to help—more so
indeed than anyone completely unaffected. 'A man who has not
given way to temptation has thereby borne its whole brunt, and he
knows its full and continuing force better than one who has
succumbed' (Montefiore). When the going is hard, and one is
tempted to give up, it is both stimulus and encouragement to know
that someone has won through and completed the course.

'Many Christian believers do not sufficiently appreciate the
humanity of Jesus. They transfer the picture of the glorified Jesus
back into his public ministry, imagining him to have walked through
Galilee with an aura and a halo about him. They cannot image him
as being like other men; and they are embarrassed by the Gospel
vignettes of Jesus as sometimes tired and dirty, annoyed and
tempted, indistinguishable in a crowd, treated as a fanatic and a
rabble-rouser' (R. E. Brown, *Jesus God and Man* IX). It is not too
much to say that the idea of Jesus held by many people is frankly
docetic: he was not really a man, but deity in the semblance of a
man; but Docetism has long been rejected as inadequate. A brief
note is no place to venture upon the problems of Christology,
but at least some outline may be attempted, to set this passage in
perspective. There are in fact grounds for thinking that the earliest
form of Christology was of what later came to be known as an
'adoptionist' type: 'The distinctively divine, the theologically significant, action began with the resurrection, and the humanity of
Jesus could be for the Church's *thought* as "natural" and uncompli-
cated as there is every reason to believe it was in its memory' (J.
Knox, *The Humanity and Divinity of Christ*, p. 7). This, however,
'did not accord with the growing sense of the importance and the
divine significance of the earthly career' (ib. p. 9). Moreover, 'it
would have followed ineluctably upon the primitive Church's
acknowledgement of Jesus as the Christ that God should have known
him as such before the foundation of the world. But there is obviously only a short step from the idea of this kind of pre-existence
in the mind of God to the conception of a pre-existing hypostasis,
a pre-existent being more personal and objective' (ib. p. 10). Here
we have the beginnings of the long development which was to
culminate in the Nicene and Chalcedonian creeds. It is open to

question whether the Fathers were on the right track in attempting to find a solution in terms of two natures, and even more open to question whether a solution reached in the fourth and fifth centuries can be considered adequate for the twentieth, as numerous modern discussions of Christology serve to show. (cf. for example J. P. Mackay, *The Christian Experience of God as Trinity*, pp. 51ff. 'The New Testament . . . even when it does use pre-existence language, does not convey any information about any divine being distinct from the God that Jesus called Father and distinct at first from Jesus the Messiah' [p. 64]). What is fundamental is the conviction expressed in Paul's affirmation that 'God was in Christ reconciling the world to himself' (2 C. 5:19), 'that God, the Father Almighty, Maker of the heavens and the earth, was back of, present in, and acting through the whole event of which the human life of Jesus was the centre' (Knox, p. 107). It may be a serious error to attempt to classify and label, as if we were dealing with entomological specimens in a glass case.

Hebrews quite clearly stands at an early stage of this development. 'The impression one gets from Hebrews . . .', writes C. F. D. Moule (*The Origins of Christology*, p. 101), 'is that the Jesus of the ministry—and, for Hebrews, especially the Jesus of the Temptation and Agony—has now been lifted to a transcendent state; but that, from there, he will appear at the end, still an individual, however divine and glorious . . . he is the historical, individual person who has gone ahead of us so that he may enable us too to be there, like him . . . Also, of course, Hebrews starts with a fully 'cosmic' Christology, in which the Son of God is associated with creation and so is pre-existent . . . But we are still left asking how the individual of the ministry and the post-resurrection glory is related to that pre-existent Being'.

Perhaps too much effort has been expended in defence of the traditional 'orthodox' doctrine, and we should go back to a point nearer to Christian origins and start afresh in the attempt to understand in modern terms the significance of Jesus. In that case Hebrews presents some basic early Christian convictions with which to begin. The exaltation of Jesus is clear from the echoes of Ps. 110 (1:3, 13) and the references to the great high priest who has passed through the heavens (4:14), who is seated at the right hand of the throne of Majesty in heaven (8:1), the mediator of a new and better covenant (9:15); but also important is the reference to Jesus as 'the same yesterday and today and for ever' (13:8). It is the fully human Jesus of whom the present passage speaks, 'crowned with glory and honour because of the suffering of death' (2:9), the Son who had himself to learn obedience (5:8), who is also the glorious figure of

the exaltation. We do not have a merely human Jesus who walked
the roads of Galilee, and a distinct and separate glorious high priest
in the heavens; they are one and the same. The importance of
this emerges when the author begins his detailed discussion of the
priesthood of Jesus (4:15f.).

JESUS AND MOSES
3.1–6

It is sometimes suggested that, having demonstrated earlier the
superiority of Jesus to the angels, the author now goes on to demonstrate his superiority to Moses (on Moses in Philo and Hebrews,
see Williamson, pp. 449ff.). Fossum (*op. cit.*, see index) affords
ample evidence for the high place accorded to Moses in Jewish and
Samaritan literature. 'He has already shewn that Christ (the Son) is
superior to the angels, the spiritual agents in the giving of the Law;
he now goes on to shew that he is superior to the human law-giver'
(Westcott). In a sense, of course, this is true: Moses was faithful *in*
God's house as a servant, Jesus *over* God's house as a son (verses
5–6); but it must still be asked if this is the author's primary
purpose, if it really brings out the connection of his thought. By
demonstrating the superiority of Jesus to the angels, he claimed for
him the highest status, under God. Was it really necessary to prove
his superiority to Moses also? Why is it done so briefly, almost in
passing, and by affirmation rather than by proof? After all, proof
of superiority to the angels occupies the greater part of the first
chapter. Again, if this were in fact the case, we should expect the
proof of superiority to Moses to follow much more closely. Why
does our author interpose a whole chapter before turning to this
theme? It may be noted that Westcott speaks of angels and the
giving of the Law, of Moses as the lawgiver, which of course is a
traditional association; reference to Moses almost inevitably recalls
the giving of the Law on Mt Sinai. There is, however, nothing in
the context about the Law, and indeed, unlike Paul, our author is
not greatly concerned about the Law, except in so far as it relates
to priesthood and cultus. To introduce Pauline associations here may
be misleading. Héring is more accurate in speaking of 'superiority in
relation to Moses and Aaron, the organisers of the sacrificial cultus
of the old covenant', although Aaron is not actually mentioned until
5:4, and then only in passing, in a single verse. It is in fact the
levitical priesthood of the old dispensation, Aaron's descendants,
that our author has in view. Had he wished, he could no doubt
have found a way of arguing Jesus' superiority to Aaron, and hence

to the levitical priesthood, as he does with Levi at 7:4–9, but this
he does not do.

It is therefore open to question whether proof of superiority to
Moses is our author's primary concern in this passage. It is beyond
doubt that Jesus *is* superior: exalted above the angels, crowned with
glory and honour, he occupies 'the highest place that heaven
affords'; but this is now taken for granted. In this section the author
invites his readers to contemplate this Jesus, consider him more
closely, observe him carefully, and the particular point to which
attention is directed is his faithfulness (cf. 2:17 above).

1. Here for the first time the author directly addresses his readers,
as **holy brethren, who share in a heavenly call**. The first of these
phrases combines two common *NT* designations for Christians,
although elsewhere they are not used together except possibly at 1
Th. 5:27 (a textual variant); at Col. 1:2 we find 'holy and faithful
brethren'. The adjective **holy** is the word used by Paul in the
addresses of his letters, and commonly there rendered 'saints'; as
Montefiore notes, it picks up the use of the cognate verb 'to sanctify'
at 2:11 above. The sense is that of 'dedicated to God' rather than
'saintly' in the common sense of the term: 'it implies a corporate
destiny of holiness rather than the present realisation of sanctity'
(Montefiore). It is indeed one of the concerns of the letter that some
of the readers may fail to achieve that destiny; they have not already
attained, nor are they perfect (cf. Phil. 3:12), and it is our author's
aim to provide stimulus and encouragement. **Brethren** is one of the
commonest of all descriptions of Christians, expressing the kinship
which exists by reason of their common faith, their common relation
to Christ, and their sharing in the heavenly call. There may be a
passing allusion to 2:11ff. above, but there is no direct reference.

They are called upon to **consider Jesus**, observe, take note of
him, or in the words of *BAG* 425a 'to fix the eyes of the spirit'
upon him. It is not just a matter of simple looking, but of reflective
contemplation of what is seen: 'now he instructs them to meditate
on him, considering attentively his role and function' (Montefiore).
The two titles here applied to Jesus are worthy of note: **the apostle
and high priest of our confession**. The second we have already
met, and it will play a large part in the development of the author's
thought, but the first, **apostle**, is not applied to Jesus anywhere else
in the New Testament (the next author so to use it appears to be
Justin Martyr, 1 Apol. 12 and 63). The word is of course predominantly used of the apostles, 'a group of highly honoured believers,
who had a special function' (*BAG* 99b, n. 3), but it is not at first
strictly limited to Paul and the twelve. Thus it is applied to Barnabas
(with Paul, Ac. 14:14), Andronicus and Junias (Rom. 16:7), and on

one interpretation of Gal. 1:19 to James. Elsewhere in the New
Testament it is used more generally in the sense of 'messenger': Jn
13:16 (in contrast with the sender), Phil. 2:25 (of Epaphroditus, the
Philippians' messenger to Paul). It is of course cognate with one of
the Greek verbs meaning 'to send' (cf. e.g. Jn 3:17). The point is
that we should not think of apostleship in the later restricted sense,
but of Jesus as the messenger commissioned and sent by God. The
two titles together sum up his role and function: as the messenger
sent by God, he is God's representative among men; as high priest
(cf. 2:17, 5:1) he is men's representative before God. It may be
added that once again the name Jesus occurs in an emphatic position
in the Greek: '**consider the apostle and high priest of our
confession**—Jesus'. The word **confession** could refer to the act of
confessing (cf. *NEB* margin), but is better understood as referring
to the content of what is confessed, 'the faith which we hold and
openly acknowledge' (Westcott). In Moffatt's words, it is 'almost
an equivalent for "our religion", as in 4:14 (cf. 10:23)' (cf. *NEB*).

2. Verse 2 in the Greek is a participial clause qualifying 'Jesus':
who was faithful (cf. *AV*); conversion into a separate sentence makes
no difference to the sense. The Greek word rendered **faithful** has a
range of nuances: trustworthy, dependable, inspiring trust or faith,
or actively trusting, full of faith, believing (cf. *BAG* 664f.). Vanhoye
(*NTS* 23 [1977], pp. 45of.) remarks that exegetes commonly choose
a nuance for the word at 2:17 (usually 'faithful', 'true' in the sense
of fidelity) and then carry it over to 3:2. There is, however, nothing
to determine the sense at 2:17, and it is only at 3:1–6 that the author
begins to expand upon it; nor does that sense really fit at 3:2. The
primary meaning of the word is 'worthy of trust'. The present verse
echoes Num. 12:7, where the point is not the fidelity of Moses but
his credibility (cf. *NEB* margin: he alone is to be trusted). Perhaps
we may recall also the promise of 1 Sam. 2:35: 'I will raise up for
myself a faithful priest, who shall do according to what is in my
heart and in my mind'; here the contrast is with the 'worthless' sons
of Eli (1 Sam. 2:12). On this line of interpretation, Jesus is worthy
of trust in the sight of God, just as Moses was, although as we shall
see there is a difference. The connotations of loyalty, faithfulness,
fidelity are of course present, but at this point they are secondary.

The word rendered **appointed** is literally 'made', and was understood by some early Fathers as referring to the creation of Jesus'
human nature. But this reflects the Christological speculations of a
later age. It is therefore better to adopt the other interpretation,
already advanced by Chrysostom and Theodoret, and understand it
as referring to Jesus' *appointment* as apostle and high priest (cf. 1
Sam. 12:6; Mk 3:14). The objection that this sense usually requires

a double accusative is easily met: the necessary predicate can readily be supplied from the previous verse.

3–6. Moses according to Num. 12:7 was 'faithful' in God's house but, as verse 5 below points out, **as a servant.** Jesus also is 'faithful', but according to verse 6 **over God's house as a son.** This at once establishes his superiority to Moses. It was a commonplace of ancient thought that a builder is greater than what he builds (cf. Philo, *Plant.* 68; Bruce notes that Justin Martyr (1 Apol. 20) refers to Menander and other writers for this sentiment); how much more then is the builder and master superior to a servant? There is a certain play on the two senses of the word 'house' here, as referring to a building or as in Num. 12:7 to a household or family. **God's house** is primarily his household, his family, his people, the household of faith. The introduction of the reference to the builder and his building has however complicated the argument. In verses 2, 5 and 6 the phrase **in God's house** is literally 'in his house', but a reference to God's house is natural from the context in Numbers. The complication arises when we ask: who is the builder? A natural interpretation of verse 3 would identify Jesus as filling this role; as Montefiore remarks, 'After all, Jesus did found the church'. This would entail taking verse 4 (bracketed in *RSV*) as a parenthetical remark intended to safeguard the sovereign authorship of God, a view which to Westcott 'appears to be unsatisfactory' (but cf. e.g. Héring). But if we recall the prologue things begin to fall into place. God is the author and creator of all things, or as verse 4 puts it, **the builder,** and the house is God's house. According to the prologue (1:2) the Son is God's agent in creation, 'through whom he created the world', and the two are so closely associated that no distinction can really be made between them. To our way of thinking, the founding of the church marks a new departure, a new beginning, but the author does not consider problems which might arise for a later age. As Moffatt remarks, there are not two households. Nor does God's 'house' begin with the founding of the church; it is there already under the old dispensation, in the Old Testament people of God. The emphasis is on continuity rather than disruption. The earliest Christians were Jews, and still saw themselves as Israel (on the whole question see Richardson, *Israel in the Apostolic Church*). Christians are now the people of God, his house, as verse 6 expressly states—if they **hold fast** to their confidence and hope.

A further point emerges in verse 5, although it is not fully spelt out: Moses was faithful as a servant **to testify to the things which were to be spoken later.** His function is thus preliminary, provisional, pointing forward to something that is yet to come. As Montefiore notes, the words to be spoken later 'are not those which

Moses himself was later to speak, nor yet the words of the prophets,
but rather "the message which was announced by the Lord" (2:3)'.
Jesus, although the author does not here expressly say so, brings
the fulfilment. This allows us to get the whole passage into proper
perspective. The contrast is not so much between two persons as
between two dispensations, two stages in divine revelation. Moses
like the prophets in the prologue, or the angels at the giving of the
law, belongs to the old order, worthy of all due respect indeed, but
still inferior to the new. As Hughes puts it (*Hebrews and Hermeneutics*, p. 9), it is not 'an absolute confrontation in which the honour
and integrity of Moses have been eclipsed by the dignity of Jesus',
but neither are they simply equals. 'Their status in the "house",
and the relative weight of δόξα (glory) borne by each, makes this
clear'.

On this line of interpretation, the whole of the argument to this
point is all of a piece. The old dispensation had its value, and is
given due recognition. God spoke to the fathers through the
prophets, gave the law at the hand of angels, acknowledged Moses
to be faithful as a servant; but now there is a new dispensation, of
an even higher order. At the beginning of chapter 2 the author drew
a warning by recalling the retribution entailed by any transgression
of 'the message declared by angels', and in the next section he will
add another warning based on the story of the wilderness. Christians, as noted earlier, are now the people of God, his house; but
there is a condition to be fulfilled: we are his house *if* we hold fast
our confidence and pride in our hope.

The word rendered **confidence** is one of those for which English
has no single exact equivalent. Its first use was to describe 'the right
of the free citizen to express his opinion in the assembly of the
city' (van Unnik, *BJRL* 44 [1962], pp. 471; for Hebrews see esp.
pp. 484–5). Following Schlier (*TDNT* V.), van Unnik notes that it
had three aspects: 'the right to say everything; the plain truth; the
courage to declare one's conviction', while in the private sphere 'it
denoted the free intercourse between friends who speak the truth
and do not flatter one another'. The associations are thus on the
one hand with outspokenness, frankness, plainness of speech, with
speaking frankly and openly, not in whispers or in innuendo; and
on the other with 'courage, confidence, boldness, fearlessness,
especially in the presence of persons of high rank' (*BAG* 630b). In
Hebrews it occurs four times (3:6; 4:16; 10:19, 35), and in Moffatt's
words 'denotes the believing man's attitude to a God whom he
knows to be trustworthy'. As van Unnik observes, this confidence
is 'something more than a human virtue': it has two sides: 'the free
right to approach God, given in the sacrifice of Christ, which is the

essence of the Christian faith, and the open confession of this faith, which is an unshakeable hope'. It is this confidence, with all it carries with it, that the readers are in danger of throwing away.

Pride in our hope is literally 'the boast of our hope'. Moffatt compares Rom. 5:2 (*RSV* 'we rejoice in our hope'). As Montefiore notes, 'this does not mean pride in our own strength, but an expression of trust in God's purpose and a reliance on his promises'. More than that, there is an element of triumph and exultation (cf. *NEB* at Rom. 5:2). In Westcott's words, 'the Christian hope is one of courageous exultation', not a patient resignation but a confident exhilaration.

Several manuscripts and versions insert the words 'firm to the end', but (a) they are not included in Codex Vaticanus or the two early papyri P^{13} and P^{46}; (b) they are grammatically awkward, since the adjective does not agree with the nearest noun; (c) the phrase occurs again at 3:14, with correct agreement. Some scribe familiar with the whole phrase 'hold fast, firm to the end' evidently thought it belonged here, and was followed by a succession of others.

This passage affords a hint, a tantalising glimpse, of the situation confronting the first readers. If they are urged to hold fast their confidence and pride in their hope, we may assume that they are in danger of losing that confidence. Unfortunately there is no indication of the reasons which might cause that loss. The traditional view that the danger was a lapse into Judaism would certainly fit: like the Israelites in the wilderness, mentioned in the following section, they would be hankering for a return to the flesh-pots of Egypt, disillusioned by the hardships of the way and remembering only the more comfortable aspects of their former life, not the bondage and the forced labour. But that is not the only possibility: Gentile Christians who had lost their first enthusiasm, their 'first fine careless rapture', might equally be tempted to fall away. It is by no means uncommon for people to embrace some new movement with enthusiasm, only to become a prey to doubt when the difficulties begin to appear, when progress is not so rapid as was hoped, when success is not so easily come by. We need only recall the interpretation given to the Parable of the Sower in Mark (4:13–20), on which Vincent Taylor writes, 'In the Europe of today every peril mentioned in the section is fully illustrated'. It should be added that Jewish Christians who might be tempted to relapse into Judaism were not confined to Palestine, or to the Jerusalem church. The whole character of the letter in fact suggests rather the Hellenistic wing of Jewish Christianity, which in turn only increases the range of possibilities: Manson's suggestion of a Jewish-Christian wing in

the church at Rome, for example, or that of Schmithals, referring
to the effects of the re-organisation at Jamnia after AD 70 upon
Christians who now found themselves under threat of expulsion
from the synagogue to which they had remained attached. Whatever
the precise details of the situation, which we can no longer determine
with any degree of certainty, the author's response is a vigorous
reminder of all that they are in danger of throwing away, a summons
to go forward in faith and hope and confidence. This essential
message remains relevant today, as it has done in changing situations
through the ages.

The passage does affirm Jesus' superiority to Moses, but as
suggested above this is not its primary purpose. The emphasis lies
rather on his faithfulness, trustworthiness, picking up one of the
two adjectives of 2:17. There he is called a merciful and faithful
high priest; now he is compared with Moses, who according to
Num. 12:7 was 'faithful in all his house'. The point of this
comparison emerges in the next section, which recalls the fate of
the wilderness generation, who were unable to enter the Promised
Land 'because of unbelief' (3:19). This is the danger which our
author sees ahead of his readers, and against which he seeks to warn
them. It is convenient to break up a lengthy document into shorter
sections for study, but sometimes the process may have its dangers,
especially in a book so closely integrated as this one. We need to
take note not only of individual sections by and for themselves, but
also of the run of the argument as a whole. Here the comparison
with Moses serves to introduce a further warning.

LOST IN THE WILDERNESS

3:7-19

The section begins with an extended quotation from Ps. 95 (vv. 7-
11), followed by warning and admonition (vv. 12-15) and then a
string of questions which set out the author's understanding and
interpretation of the psalm. Verse 19 draws the conclusion, and the
first verse of the next chapter begins the application of the lesson
drawn. Once again modern divisions into chapters and sections
break up the continuity of the argument. The *UBS* Greek New
Testament prints the whole passage from 3:7 to 4:13 as a single
section under the heading 'A rest for the People of God'.

7-11. As noted above (on 2:6), it is God who speaks in the Old
Testament; the human author is simply not important. Here the
psalm quotation is introduced as spoken by the Holy Spirit, while

at 4:7 below it is God who speaks 'through David' (lit. 'in David').
It should be observed that the author here uses the present tense:
as the Holy Spirit says. The message of the Old Testament is not
a thing of the past, an old, forgotten, far-off tale; it is addressed
directly to his readers now. The quotation follows LXX, with a
number of variations: LXX has two verbs (cf. *NEB* here 'tried me
and tested me'), where Hebrews substitutes a noun for one of them
('tried me by proving me' F. F. Bruce; *RSV* has simply **put me to
the test**). The reference to **forty years** in v. 9 is attached to the
preceding sentence, instead of to what follows, an easy thing to do
when manuscripts had no punctuation or division of sentences; but
it has the effect of heightening the guilt of the wilderness generation:
although they saw God's works for forty years, they were still
rebellious and disobedient. At 3:17 below we have the other division
of words (**with whom was he provoked forty years?**), which
suggests a deliberate alteration in the quotation. This may be
confirmed by the fact that the author inserts a **therefore** into verse
10 against both the Hebrew and LXX.

Psalm 95 falls into two parts, of which the first (vv. 1–7a) is a
call to worship. The second part begins (v.7b) 'O that today you
would hearken to his voice', here modified into **Today, when you
hear his voice**. This gives an emphasis to 'Today', of which the
author will make use later (3:13, cf. 4:7) to underline the urgency
of his appeal. The prophetic warning contained in this second part
recalls the episode of Exod. 17, where the people of Israel 'found
fault' with Moses because there was no water, and 'put the Lord to
the proof' (Exod. 17:2). Later we are told (Exod. 17:7) 'he called
the name of the place Massah ("proof") and Meribah ("contention")
because of the fault-finding of the children of Israel and because
they put the Lord to the proof'. LXX translates these names instead
of transliterating, and Hebrews follows suit; hence **as in the rebellion** and **on the day of testing**. Apart from this context the word
'to harden' occurs in the *NT* only at Ac. 19:9 and Rom. 9:18, but
the phrase 'to harden the heart' is common in the *OT*, particularly
of course with reference to Pharaoh in Exodus (e.g. Exod. 4:21,
7:13, 9:12; also Dt. 15:7, Prov. 21:29 *AV*, using different Hebrew
verbs). Other passages speak of a hardening of the neck (2 Kings
17:14, Neh. 9:16, 17, 29) or the spirit (Dt. 2:30). The reference is
not so much to callousness or 'hard-heartedness' as to stubbornness
and wilful disobedience. As Montefiore notes, 'the phrase **Do not
harden your hearts** suggests that it was within the power of his
readers to obey'. They have a choice, and are responsible for the
outcome of their decisions.

This stubborn disobedience provokes the wrath of God: **There-**

fore I was provoked with that generation . . . . This is not a theme
on which the author dwells—the reference to anger is provided by
the psalm he quotes, both here and at 4:3, the only place where it
occurs; but there can be no question that it was for him something
very real: 'It is a fearful thing to fall into the hands of the living
God' (10:31; an earlier verse [10:27] speaks of 'a fearful prospect of
judgment'). Some scholars have argued that in the New Testament,
and particularly in Paul's letters, the **wrath** of God is thought of 'in
terms less completely personal' than his love (cf. G. H. C.
Macgregor, *NTS* 7, [1960–61], p. 103, referring to Dodd, *Romans*,
pp. 20–24), as a kind of automatic mechanism of retribution, as it
were, built into the fabric of the universe; but it is doubtful if this
view can stand (Barrett, *Romans*, p. 33). Exodus 34:6f. describes
God as 'merciful and gracious, slow to anger, and abounding in
steadfast love and faithfulness . . . forgiving iniquity and transgression and sin', but adds that he is one 'who will by no means
clear the guilty'. We dare not presume upon his tolerance and
forbearance. It is to be expected that a God who is holy and righteous
will at some time react against what is unholy and unrighteous.
Objections to the attribution of wrath to God are in fact due at least
in part to the idea that it makes him an arbitrary and unpredictable
despot, but that is not the case. A parent who punishes a child for
wrongdoing is not necessarily lacking in love for the child.

Another word in this context which calls for comment is that
translated **rest**, which may refer either to the act of resting or to a
place of rest. In Dt. 12:9 the Greek word is applied to the rest and
inheritance 'which the Lord your God gives you', i.e. the land of
Canaan, and the cognate verb appears in Jos. 22:4. But it is evident
from 4:8 that for our author this is not the real 'rest'. That according
to 4:4 is no less than the rest into which God himself entered after
the Creation (Gen. 2:2). Canaan is thus the imperfect earthly type
of the true heavenly rest. According to Numbers 14 the wilderness
generation, except for Caleb and Joshua, was excluded from the
land of promise; only their children for whom they feared were to
enter. Our author here telescopes into one several narratives from
the story of the exodus: in Numbers the Meribah incident is placed
some six chapters after the repudiation (Num. 20:2–13). But from
the author's point of view his procedure is legitimate. What matters
is that the exclusion of the wilderness generation was due to their
disobedience and unbelief. The details of when and where a
particular incident happened are not important, and after all there
is rebellion and lack of faith in both chapters of Numbers.

Rest is also a common motif in gnostic texts, especially in an
eschatological sense (cf. Foerster, *Gnosis* ii, index p. 339; Siegert,

Nag Hammadi Register, Tübingen [1982], esp. pp. 46, 211). Thus the *Apocryphon of John* speaks of the soul being saved and 'taken up into the rest of the aeons' (*Cod. II* 26, pp. 30–31; *NHLE* p. 113). It is however dangerous to draw conclusions about influence in either direction, since Hebrews consistently uses the form *katapausis*, while the gnostics appear (where the Greek word occurs) to be equally consistent in using the other compound *anapausis* (cf. Vielhauer in *Apophoreta* (FS Haenchen), *BZNW* 30, pp. 281ff.). Probably both are drawing upon a common heritage in the Old Testament and Jewish speculation (for a detailed study of the gnostic concept, see Jan Helderman, *Die Anapausis im Evangelium Veritatis* (NHS 18), Leiden: Brill [1984]). Rabbinic opinion varied in regard to the fate of the wilderness generation, some like Rabbi Akiba (Sanh. 110b) holding that they were excluded from the world to come, while others adopted a more lenient view, maintaining that God later recalled the oath he had uttered in anger. In keeping with his rigorist position (cf. 6:4–6), our author takes the sterner view: the condemnation is final and irrevocable.

12–14. Verse 12 begins the application, with a warning against apostasy (the word rendered **fall away** in *RSV* is the verb from which 'apostasy' derives). In the ancient world the heart was regarded as the focus of personal life, the seat not only of the emotions but of the will. The phrase **an evil unbelieving heart** is literally 'an evil heart of unbelief', a heart characterised by unbelief, unfaithfulness, in contrast as Westcott notes with the faithfulness of Jesus and of Moses. Michel observes that 'unbelief' refers here not to lack of faith but to refusal of faith: 'because the heart does not believe in God, it is evil' (Jer. 16:12; 18:12). **The living God** is a common title for God as sovereign and Creator (cf. e.g. Dt. 5:26; Josh. 3:10; Ps. 42:2; 84:2, Is. 37:4,17), but here as at 10:31 there is an ominous note of the certainty of divine retribution. It may be added that the danger is still potential, and does not necessarily affect the whole community: **take care lest there be *in any of you*** **an evil, unbelieving heart** (cf. v. 13: that *none of you* may be hardened).

The way to meet the danger lies in mutual exhortation and encouragement: **exhort one another every day**—Michel sees here a hint of 'the priesthood of all believers'. As Bruce observes, in isolation the individual is more likely to succumb to subtle temptations, to be impressed by specious arguments; within the fellowship of a community meeting regularly, the resolve of each would be strengthened. 'Any early Christian who attempted to live like a pious particle without the support of the community ran serious risks in an age when there was no public opinion to support him. His isolation,

whatever its motive . . . exposed him to the danger of losing his
faith altogether' (Moffatt, p. 147). A later reference to neglect of
meeting together (10:25) is often taken as relating to public worship,
but the present passage with its **every day** suggests rather personal
encouragement and counsel. The echoing of **today** from the psalm
underlines the urgency: this is the time fixed by God during which
the opportunity still holds. Héring remarks that our author knows
two cases in which it will be too late to make amends: the day of
judgment and the day of complete apostasy (cf. 6:6).

The clause **that none of you be hardened** picks up its verb from
the beginning of the psalm quotation. Once again, as in v. 12, there
is concern lest any individual should go astray. **Sin** is treated almost
as a personal power, as often in Paul's letters (cf. *BAG* 43). As
for **deceitfulness**, *BAG* 82 suggests that the alternative meaning
'pleasure' is also possible, but this must be considered doubtful.
The point is not the pleasure but the seductive, deceptive nature of
sin. The classic example is of course the story of Eve and the serpent
in Gen. 3 (cf. 1 Tim. 2:14).

In verse 14 the clause **we share in Christ** renders a noun which,
apart from Luke 5:7 where it refers to business partners, occurs
only in Hebrews in the New Testament. In the three other cases
where it is used with a following genitive it has the sense of 'sharing
in' (3:1 in the heavenly calling; 6:4 in the Holy Spirit; 12:8 in the
Lord's discipline), and it is therefore natural to give it the same
meaning here (so Westcott: 'The thought is the converse of that in
2:14. Christ partook of our "blood and flesh"; we have become
partakers of Him'. So also Héring). This rendering however suggests
the Pauline 'in Christ' concept, of Christ as the new humanity
incorporating believers, which is alien to our author. It is therefore
better to take the genitive as possessive: we have become Christ's
partners (cf. Bruce, Montefiore). This is then another mark of the
status into which the readers have entered, and which they are in
danger of throwing away. They can retain it only if they hold their
'first confidence' firm to the end. As Montefiore remarks 'It is not
uncommon for converts to begin with an initial flush of enthusiasm
(cf. X. 32), only to flag, falter and fail to persevere'. It was of course
this aspect which gave the letter its relevance for Gentile Christians,
as for succeeding generations in every age; but that does not mean
that it could not have been relevant for Jewish Christians also at an
earlier stage.

Our first confidence is literally 'the beginning of our confidence',
but the last two words present some difficulty. There is no possessive
pronoun in the Greek, although it may be understood, and there is
some difference of opinion over the meaning of the word rendered

confidence, namely *hypostasis*. It was later to play a prominent role in patristic theology, particularly in discussion of the doctrine of the Trinity, but that need not concern us here. The problem is its meaning in the three passages in which it occurs in Hebrews, or at least in two of them. English versions frequently render it differently in each case. The simplest is in the prologue (1:3), where it obviously refers to the reality of the divine nature, 'the stamp of God's very being' (*NEB*). In the other two cases commentators generally follow the versions they are interpreting, rendering 'confidence' here and 'assurance' (*NEB* 'substance') at 11:1, and explaining it etymologically: the word means literally 'under-standing', hence ground or basis, that upon which one stands, the confidence of having a sure footing. Etymology however is not always a safe guide to meaning (cf. J. Barr, *The Semantics of Biblical Language*, Oxford [1961], esp. pp. 107ff.), and moreover this interpretation involves a number of shifts from the basic primary meaning. According to *BAG* 847a this sense 'must be eliminated, since examples of it cannot be found (acc. to Dörrie & Köster)'. Following Dörrie, they suggest here 'frame of mind', i.e. the frame of mind described in 3:6 (where 'confidence' renders another Greek term). Köster (*TDNT* VIII, pp. 585ff.) prefers 'reality' for all three passages, 'contrasting the reality of God with the transitory character of the visible world'. The phrase 'the beginning of our confidence' is 'a description of the *reality* on which the existence of the community rests, as Christ, as the apostle of our confession, is the presence of the reality of God, in which believers share' (Köster, p. 587). To *hold fast the beginning of the reality* is to be 'confident to the very end of the reality of God which has in all actuality commenced in the life of the community' (cf. 2:3, where it is said that salvation took its beginning with the preaching of the Lord). This approach has the advantage of using a single English equivalent at all three points, but presents difficulties for the translator: 'to hold fast the beginning of the reality' without some explanatory supplement is not very meaningful, and moreover one may wonder whether the first readers would have found it altogether clear. This is however not the only case in Hebrews (there is another, for example, at 4:13), where the precise meaning of the words and its formulation in English are obscure, but the general sense is crystal clear: they are to hold fast to the reality which they had in the beginning. Precisely what that reality was may be open to question, but the whole tenor of the letter urges steadfastness and faithful endurance.

15–19. Verse 15 then underlines the warning by repeating the opening lines of the quotation. The following verses relentlessly press home the argument in a series of rhetorical questions. A

3

different punctuation would make the two in v. 16 not questions but a statement (cf. *AV* 'for some . . . did provoke; howbeit not all . . .'), but this as Westcott says is alien to the context. Moreover it destroys the effect: the interrogative **who** corresponds to the pronouns in the first question in each of the succeeding verses (**with whom**, **to whom**), the second part of each verse supplying the answer in question form. A statement as in *AV* would be very weak, whereas the string of questions is like a series of hammer blows relentlessly driving the message home. In verse 17 (contrast v. 10) the forty-year period is linked with God's indignation, as in the original psalm (95:10). The reference to **bodies** falling **in the wilderness** is drawn from Num. 14:29, and uses a word employed only here in the *NT*, literally 'corpses'. Finally verse 19 draws the conclusion: such are the dangers of **unbelief**.

The flow of argument in these two sections now becomes clear, as does its continuity, and the reservations expressed above about any demonstration of the superiority of Jesus to Moses in 3:1–6 are confirmed. Jesus is of course superior to Moses (3:3,6), but the author does not argue the case as he did in the first chapter for Jesus' superiority to the angels. Rather he takes it for granted, and mentions it almost in passing. His point of departure is the reference at 2:17 to Jesus as 'a merciful and faithful high priest'. In developing this, he begins with the word 'faithful' (priesthood will concern him later). This provides a link with Moses, described in Num. 12:7 as 'faithful in God's house' (*RSV* 'entrusted with all my house'), and this in turn leads to thought about the people whom Moses led, who were unfaithful and disobedient. In the process the author passes from the passive sense of 'trustworthy, dependable' (*BAG* 664, 1aα) to the active sense of 'trusting, believing, full of faith' (*ib.* 665, 2), but this was easily done; the English word 'faithful' may also have both shades of meaning. The extended quotation from Ps. 95 provides an example of the dangers of lack of faith, reinforced and recapitulated in the rhetorical questions of verses 16–18 and rounded off by the summary conclusion in verse 19. In 'considering' Jesus (3:1), the readers are to reflect upon what they stand to lose. They are God's house (3:6), partners with Christ (3:14), but only if they remain steadfast, holding to that confidence with which they began their Christian life. The wilderness generation had experienced the grace of God in their deliverance from Egypt, out of the house of bondage, but they had been barred from entry into the promised land because of their unbelief. As Bruce observes, 'the moral must have been plain enough to the recipients of the epistle'.

REST FOR THE PEOPLE OF GOD

4:1-10

Despite modern chapter divisions, there is no break in the argument. As already noted, the *UBS* Greek New Testament prints the
whole passage from 3:7 to 4:13 as a single unit under one heading,
and there are grounds, as can be seen from the notes to the last
section above, for taking in 3:1–6 as well. Continuing his warning
and admonition, the author now turns to the theme of **rest**. The
gist of the argument is that since the wilderness generation did not
enter because of their unbelief, the promise remains open for those
who come after (cf. v. 9), but only on the basis of faith (vv. 2–3).
The argument is complicated by the identification of the **rest** in
verses 3–5 with God's **rest** on the seventh day, and must be
considered rather tortuous and involved. There are also some intricate translation and textual problems.

1. The statement that the promise remains is explained and
justified in v. 6: **those who formerly received the good news** (i.e.
the wilderness generation) **failed to enter**; but some-one must enter
at some time. **So then, there remains a sabbath rest for the people
of God** (v. 9). Given that, there is cause for concern and anxiety
lest any should fall short. At this point in verse 1 modern versions
and commentaries offer a variety of translations, all attempts to
render one Greek word. The most literal is the *AV* 'lest any of you
should seem to come short', defended by Westcott and others: 'it
suggests that the mere appearance or suspicion of failure . . . is a
thing to be earnestly dreaded'. Incidentally Westcott notes that the
perfect tense ('to have come short', translated in *AV* by a present)
'marks not only a present or past defeat but an abiding failure'.
RSV reads **lest any of you** *be judged* **to have failed to reach it**,
while *NEB* has 'the fear that . . . one or another among you should
be found to have missed his chance'. Commentators also differ as to
whether the author is moderating his tone, 'for reasons of pastoral
tact'. According to Westcott, the phrase is 'less stern in expression'
yet 'more comprehensive in warning' (the sentence quoted above
follows immediately). Montefiore however argues that the following
verses 'are not concerned with the disaster of having failed to obtain
the divine promise, but with the danger of thinking that the promise
is no longer operative'. So he offers yet another rendering 'for fear
that any of you . . . *thinks* that he has missed the opportunity of
reaching it' (cf. also Héring).

The first thing to be said is that it is not any semblance or
appearance of failure that is to be feared; it is the reality which is

all too present to the mind of our author. There is a real possibility
that some may fall away. The only way of justifying the *AV*
rendering is on the lines argued by Westcott (who considers the
other renderings 'less natural and less forcible'); but 'seem to have
come short' appears rather difficult in English. The *RSV* **be judged**
takes the word in a forensic sense, which as Héring notes is rare in
the Bible, but is not to be rejected for that reason alone (cf. Moffatt:
'the searching scrutiny which passes this verdict upon lack of faith
is the work of the divine Logos [in v. 12]). On the other hand
Montefiore's interpretation seems to read in more than the readers
at this point already know. At 3:19 the author says **they were unable**
to enter because of unbelief, and it is natural to think that it is
the same shortcoming that is still in view. The fear is that some
through unbelief may come short of what is required. It is only later
that he explains his statement that the promise remains open. To
take the words **while the promise . . . remains** as a warning against
thinking the promise no longer operative is to say the least difficult.
The words 'come short', 'fail to reach' etc. are all attempts to render
a term which means 'to come later, miss, fail to reach, or lack'
(*BAG* 849), but this presents no real difficulty. The crux of the
matter lies in determining whether the author is thinking in terms
of some external outside judgment, or (with Montefiore) of the
thoughts of some individual reader's heart. The run of the argument
would seem to suggest the former.

   2. This would appear to be confirmed in the following verse: **the**
message . . . did not benefit them, because it did not meet with
faith in the hearers. It is still lack of faith that is in view, as with
the wilderness generation, and not some misguided assumption that
the promise of God's rest is no longer open.

   At this point there is a whole cluster of variant readings in the
MSS, some of them merely orthographical (cf. Westcott's Additional
Note). The two most important appear in the text and in the margin
of *RSV*, and differ by no more than a single letter in the Greek.
The text renders a participle in the nominative singular, agreeing
with '**message**', the margin the same participle in the accusative
plural, agreeing with '**them**'. The latter is preferred by Metzger
(*Textual Commentary*, pp. 665) as 'supported by early and diverse
testimony representing both the Alexandrian and the Western types
of text', and as the more difficult reading. On the other hand,
'**them**', also an accusative plural with the same ending, is only two
words in front, '**message**' in the singular another three words away,
and there would be a strong temptation for a scribe to think the
participle referred to the nearer word, and hence write the accusative
plural (it is by no means uncommon in English for an author to

make a verb agree with the nearest noun, and not with the grammatical subject!). Most commentators, with *AV*, *RSV* and *NEB*,
read the singular. The difficulty of reading the plural lies in identifying 'those who heard' (see *RSV* margin), with whom 'they' were
not united. If this reading is adopted, the reference must be to
Moses, Caleb and Joshua, who are not mentioned as a group elsewhere. Readers familiar with the Exodus story would of course
understand, but it is hard to see why the three should be referred
to in this elliptic fashion. It may be added that one rather poorly
attested variant accepts the plural, but changes the final participle
'those who heard' from active to passive ('the things which were
heard'). This of course, as Westcott notes, simply gives the thought
of the other reading in a different form. More important, it probably
shows some scribe trying to make better sense of something he
found difficult.

Whatever the textual complexities, this is another case (cf. on
3:14 above) in which the precise formulation of the author's words
may be obscure, but the general sense is clear: the fault of the
wilderness generation, as the author has repeatedly emphasised, was
lack of faith. Because of that, **the message . . . they heard did not
benefit them**. It is not the hearing of the good news that brings
salvation, but its appropriation by **faith**.

3. In contrast, **we who have believed enter that rest**, although
actually the text reads an explanatory 'for' rather than an adversative
'but'. The explanation of the 'for' is that both verses 2 and 3 clarify
verse 1: there is room for concern lest any be found to have come
short, for (a) good news came to us as to the Israelites of old (but
it did not profit them), and (b) we who have believed are now
entering that rest. Some scholars take the present **'enter'** as a future
(Moffatt, Michel) with the meaning 'we shall (are sure to) enter', and
Michel also regards the participle rendered 'we who have believed' as
conditional ('if we have believed'), but while possible this is not
necessary. The point is that Christians on the basis of faith are
entering; the danger is that through lack of faith they may find
themselves barred, like the Israelites. Initial enthusiasm and
commitment are not in themselves enough; there must be permanent
and persistent faith. The whole aim of the letter is encouragement
to persevere.

The author now adds rather awkwardly an echo of the last verse
of his quotation from Ps. 95, with the comment **although his works
were finished from the foundation of the world.**

4–5. The thought is then made clear in verses 4 and 5: according
to Genesis 2:2, God rested on the seventh day after the work of
creation, while the psalm speaks of **my rest**. The **rest** referred to

in the psalm is thus not just the promised land of Canaan, it is God's own rest into which he entered on the Sabbath day. From our point of view this line of argument must be questionable, but once again we must consider it in the light of the standards of the author's time and not of our own. From his point of view it meets a possible objection that a later generation did after all enter into the promised land (see also v. 8 below). Canaan was not the true rest, it was at most but an earthly type of the true, which is the eternal rest of God which has existed from the foundation of the world. The awkward echo of the quotation in verse 3, with the following comment, thus provides a transition to this next stage in the argument. (For the use of Gen. 2:2 in Philo and Hebrews, see Williamson, pp. 539ff., and for the theme of 'rest' *ib*. pp. 544ff. It is of interest to note that the form Philo uses is *anapausis*, the form later used by the gnostics (see above on 3:11) but never found in Hebrews.)

6–7. The conclusion is drawn in verses 6 and 7: God's rest is prepared, indeed has been since the foundation of the world, when he himself entered into it. It is his will that people should enter into that rest, share its blessings, but **those who formerly received the good news** were excluded **because of their disobedience**. The promise therefore remains open, and God has set a time for its acceptance. The opening words of the quotation from the psalm, spoken **through David so long afterwards** (at 3:7 they are the words of the Holy Spirit), are now taken to mark the critical moment. This is the decisive hour! **Today, when you hear his voice, do not harden your hearts**.

8. Verse 8 adds a further argument, which to the unsuspecting reader of the Greek (or *AV*) is at first perplexing: **If** Jesus **had given them rest** . . . 'Jesus' is the Greek form of **Joshua**, and modern English versions remove any possibility of confusion, but at the cost of obscuring the parallelism. Joshua had led the people eventually into the promised land, but that was not the true rest of God, only an earthly type of it. Otherwise God would not speak through David of **another day**. As Bruce notes, 'the parallel between the Old Testament "Jesus", who led his followers into the earthly Canaan, and Jesus the Son of God, who leads the heirs of the new covenant into their heavenly inheritance, is a prominent theme of early Christian typology, and could scarcely have been absent from our author's mind. Yet he does not dwell on it here; he is more concerned to point the contrast between the temporal "rest" which Israel entered under Joshua and the true rest which is still reserved for the people of God'.

9–10. Finally at verse 9 we reach the culmination of what

Montefiore calls 'this complex biblical exegesis'. In the light of the arguments set forth, and his somewhat involved exegesis of the psalm, the author draws his conclusion: **there remains a sabbath rest for the people of God**. Here he uses a different word, *sabbatismos*, and Westcott finds the change significant: 'not an isolated sabbath but a sabbath-life'. However that may be, the word does not appear to be used by any earlier writer, and Williamson (p. 544), following Spicq, holds that it is the author's own creation. Of the nature of this 'sabbath rest' we are not told in detail, but verse 10 affords a hint. God rested from his labours after completing the work of creation, and so too will those who enter his rest **cease from their labours**. As Spicq [1977] puts it, it is 'a participation in the very beatitude of God (Mt. 25:21)'. (For a comparison of the treatment of the theme of rest in Philo, Hebrews and the Epistle of Barnabas, see Barrett's section, 'The Saints' Everlasting Rest', *Dodd Festschrift*, pp. 366–373. As already noted (see on 3:11 above), the gnostics also took up the theme, and developed it into a description of salvation, but as with Philo and Barnabas there are differences which require to be noted. For one thing, the gnostic texts consistently use *anapausis*, the form employed by Philo, where the Greek word occurs, while Hebrews uses the other compound *katapausis*. It can be dangerous to draw conclusions about possible relationships from similarities in English translations! As Montefiore notes, the Exodus typology 'was formative for Judaism, and also exercised great influence on early Christian thinking'. The similarities go back to a common root in the Old Testament, the differences result from development of the theme by people of differing background, working in different lines of tradition.)

11. There is some difference of opinion as to whether verse 11 should be taken as the last sentence of one paragraph (so e.g. *NEB*, Montefiore) or the first of another (so e.g. *RSV*, Westcott, Bruce). Certainly it fits very well with what precedes, as a final exhortation following the author's deduction from his exegetical argument in verse 9: **There remains a sabbath rest for the people of God . . . let us therefore strive to enter** into it. On the other hand it is also closely connected with what follows, as the connective particle 'for' in v. 12 makes clear. Chapter and verse divisions are a comparatively 'modern' innovation, for convenience of reference and analysis, and when the argument is so closely integrated as in Hebrews, it is not always easy to determine where divisions should be marked. For present purposes it is convenient to make a break at this point, because verses 11–13 contain so much that call for comment and are better treated separately; but due attention should be paid to

the continuity of the argument, which as already noted, extends to
4:13.

One of the major differences between the first century and our
modern 'western' world stems from the industrial revolution, and
the gap is growing wider as the years go by. In the nineteenth-
century there were people who smashed the machines that seemed
to threaten their livelihood; in the twentieth-century, machines have
taken much of the physical effort out of work, and enabled us to
do many things more cheaply and more effectively than before, in
some cases to do things which simply could not be done at all
before. If work is still tedious and wearisome for some people, it is
because of drudgery and monotony, not so much the physical effort
required. In addition, working conditions have improved
immensely, with statutory hours of labour, regular holidays, and so
on. All this makes it difficult for us fully to appreciate the significance of rest for the ancient world, and how it could be elevated into
a symbol of heaven's blessings. Indeed it has been said that the
problem for the future is not one of training for work, but of
education for leisure, of preparing people for life in a world in which
mechanisation and automation have almost completely removed the
need for physical labour. We need to look for a true standard of
comparison to the Third World, where people may still be found
scraping a living from the ground in the sweat of their brows, with
the most primitive of implements, a prey to natural disasters of
every kind, flood, famine, disease.

For people in such conditions, it is not difficult to imagine how
rest could be a blessing to anticipate, their ideal a land of plenty
where food might be had in abundance, without effort; nor is it
difficult to see how such ideas could be transplanted into people's
conceptions of a future life. For many in the modern world, on the
contrary, the experience of having to fill in time on an extended
holiday, in retirement, or in conditions of unemployment, is such
as to make thoughts of everlasting rest rather less attractive, if not
actually repugnant. The life of the world to come is thus one of the
areas in which the ideas of a bygone age are no longer adequate;
but if we are to re-interpret the imagery in modern terms, we must
understand it in the first place (one distinguished scholar in a radio
broadcast included in his own idea of heaven 'a celestial golf course,
and a heavenly day to play on it'! That is only one possibility, and
there are many others. Incidentally one wonders: would such a golf
course include bunkers and other hazards? Would it be worth the
playing without them? But that raises all sorts of other questions).

'The Sabbath was made for man' (Mk 2:7). Whatever its origins and its original function and associations, it provided a regular day of respite from the rigours of daily life and work, and not only for the Israelite but for his entire household, family servants, slaves, even the animals (Exod. 20:10; 23:12). In later ages the emphasis shifted to the hallowing of the day, the preservation of its sanctity, but despite the restrictions imposed the humanitarian aspect remained. In the Decalogue (Exod. 20:11), the institution is already linked with the Creation story, so that it was easy to think of a future life of bliss in terms of a sabbath, anticipated in this life by the weekly day of rest.

Another element in the thought of this passage is the idea of life as a journey, with rest and refreshment awaiting at the end of each day's march and a more lasting rest at the end of the journey. This was natural enough for the Jews, for whom the Exodus story was a fundamental part of their national history. Our author brings all these ideas together in his own way in the working out of his warning and admonition.

THE WORD OF GOD

4.12–13

12. As the connective 'for' indicates, these verses are closely linked with what precedes. The admonition **Let us . . . strive to enter** (v. 11) is the more urgent just because there is no escape from the searching scrutiny that awaits.

The reference to **the word of God** immediately recalls the prologue to the Fourth Gospel, but Hebrews does not have a developed Logos Christology: the Word is nowhere explicitly identified with the Son (perhaps a point against dating this letter unduly late). Nor should we assume too readily a connection with Philo's doctrine of the Logos (see Williamson, pp. 386ff. on this passage). As Williamson writes (p. 430), 'It is difficult to believe that the writings of Philo and the doctrines they contain are a primary source of inspiration behind the thought of the Epistle to the Hebrews. It is not just that there is so much in Philo about the Logos and so little in Hebrews, but also that so little, if anything, of the distinctively Philonic conception of the Logos-High Priest appears in Hebrews. The Messianism of Hebrews, and the idea of a High Priest-Messiah, is something that was clearly not derived from Philo'. Similarities there are, but we have to ask just what these similarities mean. It is sometimes all too easy to fall into the trap of converting 'parallels into influences, and influences into sources'

(I owe this formula to E. E. Ellis, *Paul's Use of the Old Testament*, Edinburgh [1957], p. 82). Here the similarities are probably due to a common background in the Old Testament and Jewish speculation. Williamson (*loc. cit.*) speaks of 'the plain fact that Philo and the Writer of Hebrews represent quite different (perhaps even entirely unconnected) strands in the intricate pattern of Jewish Christian Logos speculation.' The Alexandrian Logos concept *may* be implied here (*BAG* 479), but this way of thinking was very widespread, and it is dangerous to draw hasty conclusions.

Reference to a concordance is enough to show the frequency in the Old Testament of phrases like **the word of God** or more particularly 'the word of the Lord', often in the sense of a message delivered but also with other associations. At the beginning of Genesis we read 'God said: Let there be light', and it was not a long step from that to the phrasing of Ps. 33:6,9: 'By the word of the Lord the heavens were made . . . For he spoke and it came to be; he commanded, and it stood forth'. In such passages there is sometimes an element of personification, as here in Hebrews, but it is slight, much less than the personification of Wisdom in the Wisdom literature or of the Logos in Philo. The difference can be clearly seen from comparison of a few passages. Thus in the Wisdom of Solomon (18:14ff.) we find: 'All things were lying in peace and silence, and night in her swift course was half spent, when thy almighty Word leapt from thy royal throne in heaven into the midst of that doomed land like a relentless warrior, bearing the sharp sword of thy inflexible decree, and stood and filled it all with death' (*NEB*; the allusion is to the slaying of the first-born in Exod. 12:28ff., there described as the direct act of the Lord himself). In Rev. 19:11ff. the rider on the white horse is called 'Faithful and True' (cf. the description of Jesus as. 'faithful' in Heb. 2:17; 3:1–6 above), and the passage continues (v. 13): 'He is clad in a robe dipped in blood, and the name by which he is called is The Word of God' (*RSV*). Two verses later (19:15) we read 'From his mouth issues a sharp sword with which to smite the nations' (cf. also Rev. 1:16).

A notable feature of these passages is the association of **the word** with a **sword**, probably due, as Montefiore says, to 'the similarity of shape (and on some occasions of function) between a tongue and a dagger'. Similarly for Philo the flaming sword of Gen. 3:24 is a symbol of the Logos (*de Cher.* 28); in *Quod det. pot.* 110 the Logos (here the human reason) is a pruning knife for the cutting out of vices; in *Quis rerum* 130–132 the human reason distributes into endless parts what it receives by the intelligence, while the divine Logos has separated and apportioned all things in nature. Finally, the Nag Hammadi *Gospel of Truth* (26:1–5) describes the judgment

which has come from above as 'a drawn sword, with two edges,
cutting on either side', and in the next sentence continues 'when
the Word came into the midst' (*NHLE* 41f.). It is clear enough that
we are dealing with the same imagery, but there are also differences
which should warn against hasty assumptions of dependence: in
some cases the **word** *is* the **sword**, in others he bears it, as again in
others it proceeds from his mouth. In particular, Hebrews speaks
of the **word** as **sharper than any two-edged sword,** and not simply
likened to a sword. We are dealing with a common imagery, which
each writer uses in his own way. It cannot be invoked as a proof
for the dependence of one upon another. It may be added that there
is of course a Greek Logos tradition running from Heraclitus to the
Stoics, but whatever its relevance for Philo or for later patristic
theology this does not appear to come into question here. The Old
Testament and Jewish background is completely sufficient.

This word is **living and active.** In Moffatt's terms, 'no dead letter,
this *logos*!' It is no mere empty form of speech, but 'effective, active,
powerful' (*BAG* 265); commentators frequently recall the words of
Isaiah (55:11 *AV*): 'it shall not return unto me void, but it shall
accomplish that which I please, and it shall prosper in the thing
whereto I sent it'. The particular activity singled out here is its
penetrating discernment of the inmost thoughts and intentions of
the heart. The reference to **the division of soul and spirit** has
sometimes been taken in terms of a distinction between two parts
of human nature, on the lines of Paul's distinction between 'psychic'
and 'spiritual' in 1 Corinthians or the later gnostic threefold division
into spiritual, psychic and fleshly, but the addition of **joints and
marrow** makes this difficult, to say the least. The point is rather
that there is no part of man's being to which the Logos cannot
penetrate. **All are open and laid bare.**

13. This last phrase is another of those cases in which the general
sense is clear but the precise formulation, the imagery intended, is
obscure (cf. on 3:14, 4:2 above). **Open** is literally 'naked' (so *AV* &
NEB), but that is merely a different choice of words. The problem
lies with the word rendered **laid bare,** which occurs only here in
the New Testament, although it is used by Philo and Josephus in
the sense of prostrating or overthrowing. Héring claims that it is a
technical term in wrestling, and waxes caustic at the 'acrobatic
tricks' of those who wish at all costs to see in it a synonym for
'open' or 'naked'. Even those who think in terms of wrestling are
sometimes wide of the mark, speaking of a wrestler 'downing' his
opponent by seizing his throat or suggesting that wrestlers 'were
said to down their opponents by pushing back their necks, thus
exposing their faces'. It is surely not a question of 'downing' an

opponent, but of some grip that left him helpless. Thus Josephus
uses it (*BJ* IV. 375) of the paralyzing effect of civil war and dissension within the Jewish ranks.

The Greek Fathers were already perplexed by the word, Chrysostom for example understanding it of animals hung up by the neck
to be flayed. Another suggestion is in terms of animal sacrifice: if
an animal was to be killed by having its throat cut, the slayer would
first have to pull back its head to expose the neck. One might also
think of a defeated warrior lying prostrate and helpless, with an
enemy sword at his throat. The term is derived from a Greek word
for 'neck', but etymology is not always a safe guide to meaning.
Indeed the problem arises from efforts to find a meaning relating
to the neck. The evidence in Philo (*de Cher.* 78. *vit. Mos.* 1, 297)
and Josephus should probably be considered decisive. As Montefiore
puts it, 'the only attested meanings of the verb are "to grip by the
neck" or (metaphorically) "to prostrate" '. However, whatever the
difficulty of determining the precise analogy in view, the general
sense is clear.

Finally the last words of v. 13 can be taken in various ways.
Moffatt roundly calls the rendering 'of whom we are speaking' (a
similar phrase occurs in the Greek of 5:11) impossibly flat, while
Montefiore regards the *RV* and *RSV* rendering **with whom we have
to do** as giving "a particularly jejune meaning". The latter rendering
is perfectly good Greek usage; all that is required is the recognition
that it must be taken in the sense of reckoning or giving account
(cf. *NEB*: with whom we have to reckon). Most commentators
prefer some such form as 'to whom we must render account', which
is in keeping with the whole sense of the passage, and with the
author's earlier warnings. What he has to say is not a matter to be
shrugged off lightly.

In dealing with an extended discourse such as this, it is often
useful to pause at some point and review the way by which we have
come, to pick out the main lines of the author's argument and see
how it all hangs together, otherwise we may fail to see the wood for
paying undue attention to particular trees! In Hebrews, this is an
appropriate place for such a pause. It is not that there is any real
break in the argument; rather the author returns to the theme which
he left at 2:18, and proceeds to take up the other element in his
description of Jesus as 'a merciful and faithful high priest' (see verse
15 and 5:2). At the same time one is conscious of a certain transition,
as for the next few chapters the author concentrates his attention
on his main theme, the High Priesthood of Jesus.

We began with a prologue (1:1–4) proclaiming the status of the

mediator of the new and final revelation and establishing his credentials, including his superiority to the angels. This superiority was
then justified by a catena of quotations from the Old Testament
(1:5–14), after which the author introduces the first of several
admonitions (2:1–4): if the message declared by angels entailed
retribution for any transgression, what of those who neglect a
salvation proclaimed by an even higher authority? In point of fact,
it was not to angels that God subjected the world to come: a
quotation from Ps. 8 speaks in the highest terms of man, but is
contradicted by the facts of experience, and the author claims that
the true reference is to Jesus, now mentioned for the first time (2:5–
9). The next section then establishes his solidarity with those he
came to save, his full humanity: since the children of God share in
flesh and blood, he too partook of the same nature (2:10–16). At
the end of this section we have the first reference to the main
concern of the letter, the theme of priesthood. He had to be like
his brethren in every respect, in order to be a merciful and faithful
high priest for them; having himself suffered and been tempted, he
can help those who are tempted (2:17–18).

Chapter 3 forms something of a digression: the reference to faithfulness recalls the faithfulness of Moses (though Jesus ranks even
higher), and this in turn leads to thought of the lack of faith and
disobedience of Israel in the wilderness (3:1–11). Another Old
Testament quotation includes the vow, 'They shall never enter my
rest', and the author uses this as the basis for an argument that God's
rest is still open now for his readers. At 4:8 a possible objection is
countered: the land of Canaan into which Joshua led the people was
not the true rest, which still remains open. Further admonitions
and warnings are introduced at 3:12f., 4:1 and 4:11ff., that the
readers may be left in no doubt as to the seriousness of the issue.

THE COMPASSIONATE HIGH PRIEST

4:14–16

The author now picks up the thread which he dropped at 2:18. In
the previous verse (2:17) he had spoken of Jesus becoming 'a
merciful and faithful high priest', and in 3:1–6 he began by
comparing the faithfulness of Jesus with that of Moses. Now at 4:15
he takes up the other element of the description, explaining here
and in 5:2 how Jesus can be called merciful or compassionate. The
point was already touched on at 2:18: because he himself has
suffered and been tempted, he is able to help those who are tempted.

14. Verse 14 in a way recapitulates what has gone before with its confident assertion that **we have a great high priest who has passed through the heavens**. The Hebrew title means literally 'great priest', but Greek has two words, a simple form meaning 'priest' and a compound meaning 'high priest' (cf. English bishop and arch-bishop); when the latter was used in rendering the Hebrew, it was very natural to add the adjective, even if the result was slightly pleonastic. That this is not our author's own invention is shown by its use in Philo (*de Somn.* 1:219). That this high priest **has passed through the heavens** is a new element, but is prepared for by the earlier reference to Jesus being 'crowned with glory and honour' (2:9) and in particular by the quotation of Ps. 110:1 at 1:13. One of the Jewish cosmologies of the time envisaged the earth as surrounded by seven heavens, with God's own realm beyond them. Thus if Jesus has taken his seat at God's right hand, this presupposes his passage through the heavens. As Héring notes, the idea of a heavenly journey was known to Jewish literature (he cites Slavonic Enoch 1–20; Asc. Is. 7–9 and the Greek Apocalypse of Baruch). We may add that in 2 C. 12:2–4 Paul speaks of being 'caught up to the third heaven', which provided at least part of the inspiration for the Nag Hammadi *Apocalypse of Paul* (*NHLE*, pp. 239ff.). It is not however necessary to think of influence from such sources here: the early Christian conviction that Jesus has ascended to the right hand of God (cf. Eph. 4:10 and the use of Ps. 110:1 as a testimonium, see Dodd, *According to the Scriptures*, pp. 34f.) provides sufficient explanation. Commentators often note the 'implied contrast' (F. F. Bruce) which is brought out more fully later, between Jesus and the Jewish high priests: they entered into the presence of God, in the Holy of Holies, just once in the year, whereas he is for ever permanently at God's right hand. The readers therefore have reason to **hold fast** their **confession** (cf. 3:6, 14 above). The Greek verb here is however different, with a suggestion of laying hold on or grasping rather than 'holding firmly that which is already completely in our possession'. As Westcott says, 'the words imply danger and incite to effort'.

15. Verse 15 deals with a possible objection, that one so exalted could not truly sympathise with our human frailties. This would be fatal to any merely docetic Christology, or to one which over-emphasised the divinity of Jesus, but the author has already pointed another way: Jesus was 'crowned with glory and honour because of the suffering of death' (2:9) and 'because he himself has suffered and been tempted, he is able to help those who are tempted' (2:18). So here **we have not a high priest who is unable to sympathise . . . but one who in every respect has been tempted as we are, yet**

without sinning. The Greek word (from which our 'sympathise'
derives) does not here refer merely to emotions of sympathy or
compassion felt by an outsider; rather 'he sympathises because he
has, through common experience, a real kinship with those who
suffer' (Montefiore). The picture is of one who was truly human in
every respect, not a divine being masquerading in human disguise,
and the sufferings he had to endure were real. The phrase **as we
are** is literally 'according to likeness', and could be rendered in two
ways: the natural amplification is 'according to our likeness' or 'the
likeness of our temptations', i.e. 'as we are'; but at 2:17 'he had to
be *made like* his brethren in every respect' (a cognate Greek verb).
The *NEB* rendering 'because of his likeness to us' affords food for
thought (cf. Héring, Bruce).

The last words of this verse present something of a problem.
Montefiore sees here 'an ambiguity which is for once best left in the
English translation'. Literally the meaning is 'without sin' or 'apart
from sin', but in what sense can Jesus be said to be without sin?
One interpretation is that his temptations were exactly the same as
ours, except that he never yielded (i.e. **without sinning**, as *RSV*),
a second that they were the same apart from temptations resulting
from previous sins. As Moffatt wrote long ago, 'a number of our
worst temptations arise out of sin previously committed', but he
adds immediately 'but this is not in the writer's mind at all'. A third
suggestion, that the reference is to original sin and that Jesus was
consequently invulnerable to sin, should be ruled out at once: it
would flatly contradict the rest of the verse, and make him something less than fully human; but the whole point of 2:14–17 is to
emphasise his real humanity. A divinity in human guise who was
invulnerable to sin could not be **tempted as we are**. Accordingly
the first interpretation must have the preference. Jesus was fully
human, therefore he was tempted, just as we are; but he did not
give way. The Gospels describe a time of temptation in the wilderness (Mt. 4:1–11; Lk. 4:1–13; only briefly mentioned in Mk 1:12–
13), and there are other passages in which we can see an element
of temptation (e.g. the rebuke to Peter at Caesarea Philippi, Mk
8:31–33, or the mockery of the bystanders at the Cross, Mk 15:29–
32); but nowhere does Jesus yield. It may be added that the conviction of Jesus' sinlessness is well attested in the New Testament (2
C. 5:21; 1 Pet. 2:22; 1 Jn 3:5; cf. Jn 8:46), but nowhere is the
thought employed quite as here. Our great high priest is one who
knows and understands, from experience, the temptations to which
we are exposed. Having successfully met and faced them, he can
help us to face ours (cf. 2:18); and more than that, he can sympathise

with our weakness. This is no austere and relentless judge, deciding
according to the letter without feeling or understanding.

16. Therefore we may approach with boldness, confident in the
assurance that the barriers between God and man have been broken
down. We may look for pardon, and for **grace to help** should need
arise. The phrase **the throne of grace** is formed by analogy with
the phrase 'throne of glory' (1 Sam. 2:8; Jer. 14:21; 17:12; Ecclus.
47:11; cf. Mt. 19:28; 25:31), which refers in the first place to God's
throne, but in Matthew to that of the Son of man. Here it is 'that
revelation of God's Presence in which His grace is shewn in royal
majesty' (Westcott.). Montefiore notes that it is 'where God sits (not
where Jesus sits)', but at 1:13 our author has already applied Ps.
110:1 to Jesus, with its reference to sitting at God's right hand. As
1 Jn 2:1 puts it, 'we have an advocate with the Father', at the very
highest level.

These three verses serve as a transition to the main theme of the
letter, recapitulating what has already been said about Jesus in
preparation for the extended discussion of his priesthood. In verse
14 Jesus is for the first time given the full title 'the Son of God',
but this is only a spelling out of what has gone before: the prologue
began by speaking of 'one who is a son'(1:2), while from 2:9 on it
becomes clear that this figure is to be identified with Jesus. The
thought of priesthood was first introduced at 2:17, the reference to
temptation at 2:18, while the idea of his sympathy for our weakness
was prepared for in the demonstration of his full humanity at 2:10
ff. There is thus a gradual but steady build-up of the argument,
and as we move forward we can see each piece falling into place.
One thing however still remains to be done: the author has spoken
of Jesus as our great high priest, but he has not yet shown how
Jesus can be, how he is qualified for this function. To this he now
turns.

QUALIFICATIONS FOR HIGH PRIESTHOOD

5:1–10

The first four verses of this section set out three criteria which
require to be fulfilled by any true high priest, then verse 5 begins
the demonstration that they are met by Jesus, characteristically
starting with the last. It is equally characteristic that the author
shows no interest in the contemporary situation or in the facts about
some holders of the high priesthood. In the post-exilic era the high

priest was the political as well as the religious leader of the nation
(see Schürer, *History of the Jewish People*, rev. ed., ii. p. 227), and
'both Herod and the Romans deposed and appointed high priests
at will' (p. 228). Earlier, in the reign of Antiochus Epiphanes, there
was the case of Jason, who 'obtained the high priesthood by corrupt
means' (2 Mac. 4:7 *NEB*), only to lose it to a higher bidder (*ib*. 24;
see Schürer i. pp. 148–149). Again, 'it could only be with
suppressed rage that they (the Pharisees) saw that a fierce warrior
like Alexander Jannaeus discharged the office of High Priest in the
sanctuary, certainly not with a scrupulous observance of ordinances
regarded by the Pharisees as of divine origin' (Schürer i. p. 222).

1. All this the author simply ignores. His high priest is an ideal
figure, a purely religious leader, whose sole function is to represent
men before God, **to offer gifts and sacrifices for sins**. To do that,
he must be a man himself, a point in fact already made in the
demonstration of Jesus' full humanity at 2:10 ff. above. The phrase
gifts and sacrifices could be understood as referring to two different
kinds of offerings, the meal-offerings and the blood sacrifices, but
the two terms are closely co-ordinated in the Greek and probably
form a general expression to cover all offerings for sins. Later on it
becomes clear that it is the offerings on the Day of Atonement that
the author particularly has in mind (cf. 8:3 and 9:9, where the same
phrase is used).

2. Being a man himself, the high priest is **beset with weakness**,
simply because he is human. Montefiore calls the phrase 'a remarkable understatement about the high priesthood during the Roman
era', but rightly adds 'our author is concerned only with general
biblical principles, not with the known weaknesses of actual high
priests'. The legislation in Leviticus (4:3–12; 9:7; 16:6, 11) provides
for the priest to make offerings on his own account before acting
on behalf of the people, and of course Aaron, the first high priest
of all, provides a classic example of human weakness in the episode
of the golden calf (Exod. 32); here Moses himself has to seek to
make atonement.

Conscious of his own frailty, the high priest should be able to
deal gently with the ignorant and wayward. This phrase **deal gently**
renders a word which literally means 'to moderate one's feelings',
and denotes 'the golden mean between indifference and mawkish
sentimentality' (Bruce, quoting E. K. Simpson, *EQ* 18 [1946] 36f.).
It indicates tolerance, sympathy, understanding over against the
indifference advocated by the Stoics on the one hand and the indul-
gence shown by Aaron or by Eli (1 Sam. 2:12–17, 22–25) on the
other. This is another word used by Philo, but in a more philosophical sense of 'moderating one's passions' (cf. Williamson,

pp. 25ff.), e.g. of Abraham resolving not to grieve over-bitterly after
the death of Sarah (*de Abr.* 257). It is worthy of note that this
tolerance and understanding is extended to **the ignorant and
wayward** or 'the ignorant and erring' (*NEB*), i.e. those who sin
through ignorance. Numbers 15:27–31 makes a clear distinction
between those who sin unwittingly and the person who sins 'with
a high hand', who is to be 'utterly cut off'.

3. In these four verses the author is dealing with general principles, with criteria which apply to **every high priest** (v. 1). As
already noted, the Leviticus legislation required the priest to make
atonement **for his own sins** before acting for **the people**, which
appears slightly incongruous when Jesus has just been said (4:15)
to have been tempted even as we are, yet without sinning. Later on
however (7:27) the author will make the point that this is precisely
what distinguishes Jesus from the priests of the Aaronic succession:
he had no need to offer a preliminary sacrifice on his own account,
and his priesthood is of an altogether higher order. But that is to
anticipate.

4. Finally, the honour of high priesthood is not one that a man
arrogates to himself; the true priest must be **called by God**, like
Aaron (Exod. 28:1ff.; Lev. 8:1ff.). Numbers 16 relates the disaster
which befell Korah and his company, who sought to claim the
priesthood for themselves. The call of Aaron's heirs and successors
is meticulously documented (Num. 20:23ff.; 25:10ff.), and others
not of Aaronic descent who like Samuel exercised a priestly ministry
did so at the express call of God (1 Sam. 3:20 calls Samuel a prophet,
but in earlier chapters he 'was ministering to the Lord' (3:1), and
it would be easy to take 2:35 as referring to him). Num. 16:40
points a fearful warning lest anyone not of the descendants of Aaron
should presume to exercise priestly functions.

These four verses make no reference to any regulations regarding
the high priesthood, apart from what is contained in the Old Testament. They are the author's own formulation of what he regards as
the necessary qualities in any true high priest. Few high priests in
Israel during the last two centuries before the fall of Jerusalem
would have met his criteria, but as Montefiore remarks he shows 'a
splendid indifference to the actual circumstances of his day'.

5–6. As already noted, the first requirement has in fact been dealt
with above at 2:10ff. Our author begins with the third: **Christ did
not exalt himself** (lit. glorify himself); it was he who spoke to him
in the words of Ps. 2:7 who did so. There is no verb in the Greek
to correspond to **was appointed** (cf. *AV*): it has to be understood
from the previous clause, and English versions use various expedi-
ents to bring out the meaning. The psalm has already been quoted

at 1:5, clearly because of the title 'son'. Here the emphasis may be rather more on **today**, suggesting in conjunction with the following quotation the day of Christ's enthronement or installation (cf. Bruce). If so, this quotation appears to be used by different writers as referring to three or four different occasions, the baptism of Jesus, his transfiguration, his resurrection and his enthronement, which provides a warning against the facile assumption that the same words, or the same quotation, must always mean the same thing. Authors could use the same quotation for different ends. At all events this verse is one of C. H. Dodd's 'primary *testimonia*', employed by at least three *NT* authors and probably without literary dependence on one another (*Acc. to the Scriptures*, p. 31f.). The first verse of Ps. 110, from which the next quotation comes, was quoted at 1:13 above, and Dodd speaks (p. 104) of 'the immense importance' of this verse as a *testimonium*. Here in v. 6 we have a quotation of the fourth verse of the psalm, which provides our author with a theme for elaboration later: priesthood **after the order of Melchizedek**. Dodd writes, 'It is clear from the elaborate argument of which the citation is the basis and centre that the author to the Hebrews is conscious here of being an innovator. Yet his argument rests upon secure grounds if he could count upon the general acceptance of the hundred-and-tenth psalm as being, in its entirety, a testimony to Christ'. The two quotations together provide a scriptural basis for the statement of 4:14, that we have **a great high priest . . . Jesus, the Son of God**. All the author requires to do is to assume that these verses apply to Jesus, as was done with earlier quotations.

Bruce notes that some branches of Jewish expectation (e.g. at Qumran) distinguished two Messiahs, a lay and a priestly, and that it has been argued that the addressees belonged to some such group. This would certainly fit if we had other grounds for thinking that they were former Essenes. However, the affinities appear to be due rather to a common background in the *OT* and Judaism, not to any specific connection with Qumran (cf. Introd., p. 24), and this point certainly cannot be used as an argument for that position. As Bruce observes (p. 29), the most that can be said is that the addresses 'were probably Jewish believers in Jesus whose background was not so much the normative Judaism represented by the rabbinical tradition as the non-conformist Judaism of which the Essenes and the Qumran community are outstanding representatives, but not the only representatives'. In fact it has already been suggested (above, p. 20) that the background should be sought rather in Hellenistic Jewish Christianity, or more specifically, with Sowers (cf. Introd., p. 23) in Alexandrian Judaism. With so many other possibilities to take into account, it is a mistake to place undue emphasis on affinities with Qumran. Other scholars have thought the author is trying to meet the objection that Jesus could not be a high priest because he was not of Aaronic descent (see Braun I, pp. 252f.), a point he does deal with later (7:14), but which the development of his argument has not yet reached. In any case, as Braun notes, this too cannot be used in proof of a Qumran connection: the requirement that a priest should be of Aaronic descent was never quite forgotten, and was not peculiar to Qumran. What we have here is rather the climax and culmination of a carefully developed argument which provides the basis and the text for a discussion which is yet to come: the priesthood of Jesus **after the order of Melchizedek**, and its superiority to the priesthood of the old dispensation. We began with an exalted figure, ranked high above the angels, who for a short time was made lower than them, becoming fully human and sharing completely in the trials and temptations of our human life, yet without surrendering to temptation, without sinning. He is 'crowned with glory and honour because of the suffering of death', made perfect through suffering, and therefore by virtue of his human experience qualified at once to deal understandingly with 'the ignorant and wayward' and to help those who are tempted. How the exalted figure and the human Jesus can be one and the same is a question the author does not ask; that was to be the cause of much debate in later controversy. All we know is that for him they are certainly one (cf. 13:8), and it is in this Jesus that he sees the fulfilment of the two psalm verses he has quoted.

Commentaries on the Gospels frequently refer to this passage by way of comment on the agony in the garden of Gethsemane, as commentaries on Hebrews refer to the Gospels (Mt. 26:36-46; Mk 14:32-42; Lk. 22:40-46). There might conceivably have been other such occasions, but as Bruce says 'restricted as we are to the Gospel narratives, "Gethsemane seems to offer the most telling illustration" of these words' (quoting A. E. Garvie, *Exp.T.* 26 [1914-15], p. 549). The similarities, however, are not such as to suggest quotation from the Gospels; for example, the Gospels do not specifically mention **loud cries and tears**. This may be the author's own expansion and interpretation of the gospel reference to sorrow (Mt. 26:37-38; Mk. 14:33-34; not in Luke, although some MSS include something similar at Lk. 22:43-44); or it may be due to the influence of Ps. 22, which 'was clearly regarded as a source of testimonies to the passion of Christ and His ultimate triumph, and probably from an early date' (Dodd, *Acc. to the Scriptures*, p. 97). Verse 22 of the psalm has already been quoted above (2:12), and verse 24 appears to be echoed in the statement that **he was heard**.

7. Verse 7 begins in the Greek with a relative pronoun, which is sometimes a pointer to a quotation of a credal type (cf. 1:2 above; Phil. 2:5–11; 1 Tim. 3:16); but the fact that it may introduce such a quotation does not make every relative clause a credal formula. Probably it is simply an echo of early Christian tradition, recorded in slightly different form in the Gospels. **In the days of his flesh** refers to Jesus' earthly life with its human weakness, and should not be taken to contrast his incarnate life with some other form of existence. As Bruce remarks, if the expression meant the termination of an incarnate state with Jesus' exaltation to the right hand of God, 'it would seriously weaken our author's argument that Christians have right now a high priest who feels for them and with them in all their temptations and sorrows'. For our author, Jesus is 'the same yesterday and today and forever' (13:8). Questions of the relation of the divine and human natures lie still far in the future, and are not his concern. An interesting piece of speculation appears in an unfortunately fragmentary passage of the Nag Hammadi *Gospel of Philip* (66.32–37; *NHLE*, p. 141), which seems to contrast the flesh of Jesus with ours: his is true flesh, ours but an image of the true. At an earlier point (56.32–57.7 [*NHLE*, p. 134], quoting 1 C. 15:50 and Jn 6:53) it is the flesh and blood of Jesus that will inherit the kingdom of God, and his flesh is identified with the Logos, his blood with the Holy Spirit. Such passages illustrate the kind of speculation current in certain circles at a later date, but are remote from our author's concerns. He is merely singling out from the earthly life of Jesus an incident which proves his claims for the humanity and sympathy of the great high priest.

The prayer **to him who was able to save him from death** naturally recalls the Gethsemane prayer 'remove this cup from me' (Mk 14:36), but the closing words of the verse present a problem: **he was heard for his godly fear**. If **he was heard** is understood of the taking away of the cup, i.e. of deliverance from death, then in Montefiore's words, 'it is denied by the facts. For Jesus' prayer to be delivered from death was not granted; and he died'. Harnack sought to resolve the difficulty by inserting a negative, and has been followed by others, but while on the surface this might remove the problem, it is only superficial; moreover there is no manuscript evidence to support it, and the number of textual witnesses at our disposal makes any recourse to conjectural emendation very dubious. Another expedient is to take the word rendered **godly fear** as meaning 'fear, anxiety'. Thus Montefiore renders 'and being heard (was set free) from fear'. He admits that the phrase is cryptic,

and that 'Jesus' liberation from fear is only indirectly relevant to
the main point of the sentence, which is that Jesus learnt obedience
from his sufferings'. Yet he argues for this position: 'If Jesus was to
release those who through fear of death had been in life-long ser-
vitude (2:15), he himself had to be triumphant over his own fear of
death'. Peterson (*Hebrews and Perfection*, p. 90) remarks 'We may
indeed ask whether, in the light of his later use of Psalm 22:1 (Mk
15:34 = Mt. 27:46), Jesus was in fact delivered from fear of death'
(cf. his discussion of the whole section 4:14–5:10, pp. 74–103).

The only other occurrence in the *NT* of the Greek word in view
here is at 12:28, where it means awe or reverence in the presence
of God. The cognate verb appears once, at Heb. 11:7, in connection
with Noah's building of the ark (*RSV* and *NEB* 'took heed'; possibly we might paraphrase by the adverb 'prudently'). The adjective
occurs four times in the *NT* (Lk. 2:25; Ac. 2:5; 8:2; 22:12), all
with the meaning 'devout' or 'God-fearing' (and all incidentally in
Lucan writings). In the light of this, the primary meaning of the
word in Hebrews would indeed seem to be **godly fear**, and Montefiore's 'cryptic' phrase a rather desperate attempt to overcome an
alleged difficulty.

We must therefore turn our attention to the other element in this
phrase, the statement that Jesus **was heard**. On the surface, this is
not true, but only if we limit the content of the prayer to deliverance
from death. In the first place, we need to ask if the 'answering' of
prayer must always and necessarily involve the granting of the
request that is made, as if we had to do with some kind of automatic
slot-machine. Every parent knows of occasions when for one reason
or another a child's earnest entreaties have to be refused, but not
out of any lack of love for the child: it may not be in the child's
best interest, or the parent may have something better in mind. In
the second place, the Gethsemane story in the Gospels contains not
one prayer but two, the second being 'not what I will, but what
thou wilt' (Mk 14:36; Mt. 26:39). Moreover the Fourth Gospel as
well as the Synoptics underlines Jesus' deliberate acceptance of 'the
cup', the destiny which awaits him (cf. Jn 12:27–28; 18:11). In the
light of this, there is justification for Peterson's claim (p. 92) that
'in verse 7, our writer recalls the struggle of Jesus to do the will of
God when the ordinary human fear of death and suffering, and
the particular fear of death as the place of expulsion and God-
forsakenness, tempted him to turn aside. When, in reverent awe,
he submitted himself to the Father's will, his prayer was heard and
answered in the death, resurrection and ascension-enthronement
that followed'. Earlier (p. 89) he sees in both John and the Synoptics
a 'two-stage presentation' of which Hebrews also shows awareness:

Jesus prays for deliverance from the approaching crisis, but then submits to the Father's will. 'The offering of "prayers and petitions, with loud cries and tears . . ." corresponds to the first stage and the statement that "because of his humble submission his prayer was heard" (*NEB*) corresponds to the second'. The problem thus arises only if we restrict the 'hearing' to the prayer for removal of 'the cup', which patently was not granted. When we take into account the second petition, and the whole complex of the Passion story, things become very different. In particular we are given food for thought in regard to the vexed question of 'unanswered prayer'.

8. Verse 8 then 'draws out the significance of the previous verse: the process of learning to obey God in the face of suffering was necessary even for the Son' (Peterson, p. 92). The statement **he learned obedience** has occasioned some perplexity, since learning normally implies the acquisition of some skill or knowledge not previously possessed. There is however 'no suggestion of an original imperfection in Christ that must be gradually overcome' (Peterson, p. 93); in fact, 4:15 above has spoken of him as 'tempted . . . yet without sinning'. That he learned obedience therefore cannot mean that he was previously disobedient. Indeed, any such idea would be quite incongruous where the exalted figure of the prologue is concerned. Some have felt that there may be some inconsistency, even contradiction, in the author's Christology, but it is more probable that the questions which were to exercise later generations had not yet been raised. The context, and particularly verse 9, shows that this learning has to do with the struggle towards perfection. Now the exalted being of the prologue was presumably already perfect, but this 'perfection' would not be of the kind required in 'a great high priest': for one thing, his obedience would never have been tested, and for another such an exalted being who had never had to face trial would be but poorly qualified as a saviour for people constantly under the pressures of life. He would be quite unable to 'sympathise with our weaknesses'. Tennyson in his *Lucretius* has some lines about

> . . . the Gods who haunt
> The lucid interspace of world and world,
> Where never creeps a cloud or moves a wind,
> Nor even falls the least white star of snow,
> Nor ever lowest roll of thunder moans,
> Nor sound of human sorrow mounts to mar
> Their sacred everlasting calm.

These lines are modelled on Lucretius; *de rerum natura* III. 18–24,

a passage itself a translation of Homer, *Od*. VI. 42ff. Commenting
on the Lucretius passage, J. D. Duff wrote, 'This peace of the gods,
which nothing impairs at any time, is only possible on condition
that they have nothing to do with the affairs of men'. With this,
'one of the most important doctrines of Epicurus', our author's view
is completely at variance. The exalted figure of the prologue is not
remote and aloof, untouched by human frailties; he was 'made like
his brethren in every respect', and in the words of Phil. 2:8 'became
obedient unto death, even death on a cross'. The path to perfection,
and to his becoming **the source of eternal salvation to all who
obey him**, lies through obedience and suffering.

Son here, as applied to Jesus, 'means something special'
(Moffatt). As Bruce says, 'it is the most natural thing in the world
for a son to learn obedience by suffering; indeed, our author makes
this very point in 12:4ff. But it is not any ordinary son that he is
speaking about here, but the Son of God: "Son though He was" . . .
even He was granted no exemption from the common law that
learning comes by suffering' (a play on two Greek words which is
common in Greek literature as far back as Aeschylus). Earlier on
(v. 7) Bruce had written 'the fact that the cup was not removed
qualifies Him all the more to sympathize with His people; when
they are faced with the mystery and trial of unanswered prayer they
know that their high priest was tempted in the same way and did
not seek a way of escape by supernatural means of a kind that they
do not have at their disposal. At no point can the objection be
voiced that because he was the Son of God it was different, or easier,
for Him'. Any Christology which does not do justice to the real
humanity of Jesus is quite inadequate, whatever problems that may
involve.

9. On verse 9, Peterson (p. 102) insists that the writer's presentation of the perfecting of Christ 'is specifically related to the preparation of Christ for his high-priestly ministry'. 'In the final analysis,
it is his redemptive death that qualifies Christ to act as heavenly
high priest, since the primary function of priesthood is "to expiate
the sins of the people" (2:17; cf. 5:1; 7:27; 8:3; 9:28)'. Moral
progress is not to be excluded, but in one who is sinless it must
play a somewhat subordinate part. It is through obedience that he
is made perfect and becomes **the source of eternal salvation** to all
who in their turn obey him. At 2:10 above, Jesus was called 'the
author or pioneer of salvation'. Here **source** renders a different
Greek word, which might equally be translated 'author' or more
precisely 'cause of salvation', a phrase found in classical Greek and
in Philo. Spicq noted four 'exact parallels' in Philo, but Williamson
(pp. 84–88) while admitting the 'verbal closeness' of the parallels

points out (a) that there is nothing in Philo to match 'eternal'
salvation in Hebrews, and (b) that Philo is not the only source from
which our author could have derived the words which are parallel.
A coincidence of two Greek words cannot be considered significant
when the phrase is used by other authors also. If Philo, and no
other writer, had spoken of 'eternal salvation', it might have been
another matter. The phrase 'everlasting salvation' occurs at Isa.
45:17 LXX, and may be derived from there. It should be added that
the adjective does not merely mean 'everlasting' in the sense of
unending duration. It appears frequently in the *NT*, especially in
the phrase 'eternal life', and there are grounds for interpreting it in
the sense of 'the life of the age to come'. It thus has not only a
temporal but a qualitative reference (see D. Hill, *Greek Words and
Hebrew Meanings*, Cambridge [1967], pp. 186ff.). This salvation is
not merely of infinite duration; it belongs to the world to come.

The theme of priesthood was first formally introduced at 2:17,
although there is a hint of it already in the prologue in the reference
to purification for sins (1:3). After his usual manner, the author at
first mentions it almost in passing, picking it up for further development later. The transitional passage 4:14–16 for the first time speaks
of a great high priest, and gives the full title 'Jesus the Son of God',
drawing together the main threads of what has gone before. The
present section spells out in detail Jesus' qualifications for office,
supplementing and expanding what has already been said, and
adding a telling illustration of his real humanity, and the sympathy
and understanding deriving from it. The way is now clear for the
development of the Melchizedek theme, first introduced in the
quotation in verse 6 and echoed in verse 10; but before that the
author embarks on a lengthy exhortation, containing some of his
severest strictures, his sternest warnings and admonitions to his
readers.

A FURTHER ADMONITION

5:11–6:12

11. There is another problem for the translator at the beginning of
verse 11: the Greek has a relative pronoun which might be either
masculine (*AV* 'of whom') or neuter (*RSV* **about this**). The latter
would refer generally to the whole topic under discussion, but it is
probably more natural to take the relative as referring to the last
named subject (*NEB* 'about Melchizedek'). Once again it is a matter

of finding a precise English equivalent; in terms of sense either
would be quite appropriate. Our author has much to say, but it is
difficult because his readers have become **dull of hearing**. This does
not refer to physical deafness, but to a spiritual torpor. The word
rendered **dull** is used below at 6:12 (*RSV* 'sluggish'), and occurs in
1 Clem. 34:1 with reference to a careless workman (cf. Lightfoot,
The Apostolic Fathers, London [1891], p. 71: 'the slothful and careless dareth not look his employer in the face').

12. Verse 12 shows that they have been Christians for some time
past, but there is nothing to indicate how long, and the verse is
thus of no assistance in dating the letter. The reference to being
teachers does not imply special qualifications, or that they are 'a
small, specially cultured community'. Similar phrases used by Greek
philosophers show that this is 'a general expression for stirring
people up to acquaint themselves with what should be familiar'
(Moffatt). Schoolmasters have been known to tell pupils in senior
classes that they ought to be back in the preparatory school! They
need 'someone to teach you the ABC of God's oracles over again'
(*NEB*). The word rendered **first principles** (*RSV*) or 'the ABC'
(*NEB*) occurs seven times in the *NT*, with a variety of meanings
(see *BAG* 768b). At 2 Pet. 3:10, 12 it refers to the basic elements
of which the natural world is composed, and which on the day of
the Lord 'will be dissolved with fire'. Outside the *NT* it is sometimes
used of the heavenly bodies (e.g. in Diog. Laert. of the signs of the
Zodiac). At Gal. 4:3, 9 and Col. 2:8, 20 the meaning is debated.
Some scholars think the reference is to 'the *elemental spirits* which
the syncretistic religious tendencies of later antiquity associated with
the physical elements' (*BAG* 769a), whereas others prefer to take it
as referring to elementary forms of religion. Here no such problems
arise: the reference is quite clearly to the basic fundamental elements
of learning, the very letters of the alphabet. 'Oracles' (*NEB*) is a
word meaning literally 'a saying', used by Polycarp (7:1) of sayings
of Jesus and also in the title of Papias' book *Exposition of the Oracles
of the Lord* (ap. Euseb. HE 3.39.1). Elsewhere it refers to revelations
received by Moses (Ac. 7:38), or to God's promises to the Jews
(Rom. 3:2). Here the reference is to the words of Scripture in
general (cf. *BAG* 476b), at this stage, it should be remembered,
still primarily the *OT*, although the sayings of Jesus may have been
included. The contrast of **milk** and **solid food** 'is one of the most
common in Greek ethical philosophy' (Moffatt), and had already
been used by Paul (1 C. 3:1-2). Along with the contrast in the next
two verses of the **child** and the **mature** (lit. 'perfect'), also at least
hinted at in Paul (1 C. 2:6), it has sometimes been taken to indicate
Pauline influence on Hebrews, or hellenistic or even gnostic

influence on both. However, the use is so widely spread (cf. also 1
Pet. 2:2), and is found in writers who cannot by any stretch of the
imagination be called 'gnostic', that theories of alleged 'gnostic'
influence must be considered doubtful. As Montefiore puts it,
'although the vocabulary is pagan, it has been baptised into Christ',
and in particular the meaning of the word used to describe 'mature'
Christians 'is not controlled by Greek philosophy or Hellenistic
mystery religions' (where it was used to describe initiates). The
gnostics also used the same terminology, but whether they derived
it direct from pagan sources or through the medium of the *NT*
remains obscure (on the use of this word see P. J. du Plessis,
ΤΕΛΕΙΟΣ: the idea of Perfection in the NT; D. Peterson, *Hebrews
and Perfection*).

13–14. The author now develops and explains the contrast drawn
in v. 12: **milk** is for children, indeed for infants, who in the nature
of the case have no experience and are unaccustomed to more
advanced instruction. The phrase **unskilled in the word of
righteousness** is literally 'unacquainted with the word'; the child
has not yet completed his apprenticeship, is unfamiliar with the
drill, is not practised in the techniques—there are numerous metaphors to express the same idea. **The word of righteousness** has
given rise to some discussion: it has been understood to mean
'incapable of speaking correctly', which as Moffatt observes may be
the mark of an infant, but is irrelevant in this connexion; a variant
of this, 'incapable of understanding normal adult language', would
be more to the point, but does not explain why our author should
speak in terms of righteousness. A third proposal, 'unacquainted
with the righteousness of God revealed in Christ', introduces 'a
Pauline conception, uncharacteristic of our author' (Montefiore) and
moreover requires an explanatory supplement to make it clear.
'Unacquainted with the teaching of righteousness found in scripture
as a whole' is according to Montefiore 'a phrase parallel to the
previous remark about the oracles of God, but not a particularly
appropriate comment about infants'. It is however, without the
explicit reference to scripture, perhaps the best literal translation
available, the point being brought out in v. 14 where the mature
are said to have their faculties trained **to distinguish good from
evil**. The child, the infant, does not have the experience to make
such judgments, and is unfamiliar with these questions. This is the
condition of his readers as our author sees it, but they ought to be
mature, trained and efficient. *NEB* takes a short cut in v. 13:
'Anyone who lives on milk, being an infant, does not know what is
right' (*or* is incompetent to speak of . . .). As often noted, the
language is that of Greek ethical philosophers, but it is no less

important to observe that our author uses this language for purposes
of his own. Thus Williamson argues (p. 290; see the whole
discussion of Philonic parallels, pp. 277ff.) that 'though there is a
practical, moral aspect to the maturity towards which he urges his
readers to advance, it is also and primarily a matter of progress
towards a correct Christological interpretation of the *OT* . . . He is
not interested in the ethical condition of human life as analysed by
the ethical teacher in terms of a need to produce by training a
capacity for moral discrimination, but only in so far as the language
of the ethical teacher supplied him with a vocabulary by means of
which to draw attention effectively to the theological backwardness
of his readers' (cf. his paraphrase of the whole passage, p. 291).
Peterson also (p. 181) questions whether it is a matter of *moral*
stagnation only; 'it is rather a question of general spiritual lethargy,
with a definite disinclination to explore more deeply the implications
of their Christian position, that our writer reveals'. Montefiore's
own rendering 'without experience of discourse between right and
wrong' is thus unduly narrow. It is not just their ethical judgment
that is defective and immature, it is their whole grasp and comprehension of the Christian faith.

6:1. The opening **therefore** of this verse has occasioned some
surprise, since the author now seems to ignore the rebuke he has
just uttered. Bruce aptly recalls 1 C. 3:2, where Paul uses the same
metaphor of milk and solid food, and adds 'Even yet you are not
ready'. We should thus expect 'however' or 'nevertheless'. Peterson
however notes (p. 182) 'If the readers continue on their diet of
"milk", they will remain "unacquainted with" or "unaccustomed
to" the teaching which alone can motivate them to righteousness
and give them that discernment which is the mark of spiritual
maturity'. They are immature Christians, but the only way to
maturity is to go forward. Héring sees here a resort to a well-known
pedagogical device, to stimulate their effort. A constant stream of
criticism and censure might only make things worse, so our author
blends in an element of encouragement, as he does again below at
6:9 after a paragraph in which, in Moffatt's words, he 'practically
tells his readers that they must either advance or lose their present
position of faith, in which case there is no second chance for them'.
The foundations have already been laid, and there is no point in
doing it all over again. What matters now is to get on with the
building. The **elementary doctrines of Christ** are literally 'the word
of the beginning of Christ' (cf. the similar phrase at 5:12 above, lit.
'the elements of the beginning of God's oracles'). The following list
gives some insight into what the author regards as these rudiments.
Six items are mentioned, which as Bruce remarks fall naturally into

three pairs: repentance and faith, baptism and laying on of hands, resurrection and judgment. In at least one case, however, this summary (based on *AV*) could be misleading: the reference to 'baptism and the laying on of hands' immediately suggests Christian initiation, but that is not the only possibility (see below; *RSV* uses 'ablutions'). There is also a textual question: one reading has **foundation** in the accusative, followed by a string of genitives, which makes all six items part of the foundation (cf. *RSV* and *NEB* margins); this reading has by far the strongest numerical support. The other reading has **instruction** also in the accusative, in apposition to 'foundation', with the following genitives depending on it (*RSV*: **instruction about ablutions**; cf. *NEB* instruction *about* cleansing rites . . . *about* the resurrection). This reading, found only in the Chester Beatty papyrus *P⁴⁶*, the Codex Vaticanus, the Old Latin of Codex Claromontanus (the Greek has the genitive) and the Peshitta Syriac, is undoubtedly early, and the choice is difficult. The difference is no more than a single letter in the Greek, and the genitive might be due to assimilation to the other genitives in the list; hence many commentators prefer the accusative. Metzger however (*Textual Commentary*, p. 666) notes that a majority of the *UBS* committee regarded it as 'a stylistic improvement introduced in order to avoid so many genitives'. On the other hand Westcott (who thought it 'simpler to take the genitive') long ago noted that baptisms, laying on of hands, resurrection and judgment 'form characteristic subjects of teaching'. Moreover there is an inversion of order in the Greek, which makes the genitive appear decidedly clumsy. All things considered, therefore, it would seem that the minority reading should have the preference. We have then the foundation defined as repentance and faith, and in apposition to it instruction about ablutions, the laying on of hands, resurrection and judgement. Michel notes that the first two could refer to public Christian preaching, the other four to the instruction of catechumens and, more important, that all six would be familiar to Jewish Christians from their synagogue days.

Repentance is commonly thought of in terms of remorse, of 'sorrow after sin', but the basic meaning of the Greek word is 'a change of mind'. According to *BAG* 512b it is used 'mostly of the positive side of repentance, as the beginning of a new religious and moral life'. Here it refers to a turning away from **dead works**, a renunciation of old habits, a conversion to a new way of life. The reference to 'works' should not be understood in a Pauline sense as 'works of the law'; Paul himself can speak of casting away 'the works of darkness' (Rom. 13:12; cf. Col. 3: 5–8). Ephesians (2:1), using a slightly different formulation, speaks of people being 'dead'

through trespasses and sins, before their conversion. Such works
are 'dead' because they are evil, and do not lead to life. The
Bruce compares the 'Two Ways' doctrine in the Didache and Barnabas,
but older than either, with its contrast of the way of life and the
way of death. At 9:12 below we find 'purify your conscience from
dead works to serve the living God', which suggests that such ideas
are in the author's mind.

Repentance and **faith** are frequently associated, as two aspects of
the conversion experience. According to Mark (1:15), Jesus began
his ministry with the call 'Repent and believe in the gospel'.
According to Acts (20:21), Paul reminded the elders of Ephesus of
his life among them, 'testifying both to Jews and to Greeks of
repentance to God and of faith in our Lord Jesus Christ' (in Paul's
letters however 'repentance' occurs only at Rom. 2:4 and 2 C. 7:9,
10). The Greek word rendered 'faith' has a wide range of meaning
(cf. *BAG* 663ff.), but in this kind of context it denotes not intellectual assent to a body of doctrine but a personal trust and confidence
in God or in Christ. **Repentance** thus signifies the turning away,
the renunciation of the old life, **faith toward God** the new direction
and attitude that is involved.

2. The *AV* reference to baptism and the laying on of hands, as
already noted, naturally suggests Christian initiation, and is so taken
by many scholars. Montefiore is quite emphatic: 'There is no reference in this passage to Old Testament ablutions . . . Our author is
not describing dead works to be renounced, but the positive content
of elementary Christian instruction'. The first part of this last
sentence is correct: instruction about baptism and the other matters
does not belong to the 'dead works'. The second part however
misses the point. Reference has already been made to Michel's note
that all six items in the list would be familiar to Jewish Christians
from their synagogue days. As Bruce puts it, each takes on a new
significance in a Christian context, 'but the impression we get is
that existing Jewish beliefs and practices were used as a foundation
on which to build Christian truth'. We need to remember the point
made by Goppelt and Daniélou (see Introd., p. 20) that Christianity
retained a predominantly Jewish stamp down to the middle of the
second century. Now as Montefiore himself notes, the word used
here is not the usual word for Christian baptism (according to *BAG*
132 used only in Christian writers), but a related word, used in Mk
7:4 of the washing of dishes and in Josephus (a non-Christian
writer!) of the baptism of John (*Ant.* 18.5.2). The only other *NT*
occurrence of this form is at 9:10 below, where it refers to 'various
ablutions' included among temporary 'regulations for the body'.
Moreover in all three *NT* cases it is used in the plural. There is

thus reason for doubting whether Christian baptism is directly in view. It may be included, but along with other similar rites. The *RSV* **ablutions** (*NEB* 'cleansing rites') is therefore a better translation. The question then arises of the nature of these ablutions. Montefiore, in keeping with his theory about Apollos, points to Ac. 18:25: 'If he had known only the baptism of John, he would have been rebaptised into the name of Jesus, and in these exceptional circumstances he would also have had hands laid on him (cf. Ac. 19:5f.)'. This is of course possible, and would explain the plural, but it is not the only possibility. If we were to follow the Rabbinic principle adopted by the author at 7:3, that what is not mentioned in scripture does not exist (cf. Philo, *De ebr.* 61), it could be noted that in Acts Apollos, unlike the disciples at Ephesus, is not said to have been baptised again; presumably he was, but that is an inference, and not expressly stated. In any case ablutions of various kinds were practised by other groups in the ancient world. Mention has already been made of Old Testament ablutions, and such rites were important to the Qumran sect. There was a considerable baptist movement in Palestine at the beginning of the Christian era (see J. Thomas, *Le movement baptiste en Palestine et Syrie*, Gembloux [1935]. K. Rudolph, *Antike Baptisten*, SB Leipzig, Phil.-hist. Klasse, 121, 4 Berlin [1981]), and finally there is the Jewish baptism of proselytes, not to speak of ablutions or lustrations that may have been practised in other religions. If Christian baptism is included in the reference here, the elementary instruction might have involved explanation of what made it different from other rites.

The laying on of hands was an early Christian practice, associated especially with bestowal of the Holy Spirit (Ac. 8:17; 19:6), but also with ordination to office (Ac. 6:6; cf. 2 Tim. 1:6) and with healing (Ac. 9:12, 17; Mk 6:5 etc.). Later it was to become particularly associated with the rite of Confirmation (on the whole question see G. W. H. Lampe, *The Seal of the Spirit*, London [1951]), but that lies still in the future here. This too was, in Bruce's words, 'inherited from the Old Testament, where it is used especially in commissioning someone for public office (Num. 27:18, 23; Dt. 34:9), or as part of the sacrificial ritual (cf. Lev. 1:4; 3:2; 4:8 etc)'. He adds that in rabbinical Judaism the term appears regularly in the sense of ordination (of elders; cf. Mishnah, *Sanhedrin* IV. 4). D. Daube (*The NT and Rabbinic Judaism*, London [1956], pp. 224–245) discusses the usage in the Old Testament, Rabbinic literature and the New Tesstament, and notes that the English phrase, or its equivalent, is often employed indiscriminately for different uses of the rite, for which Hebrew has three different verbs.

Resurrection of course immediately recalls the resurrection of
Jesus, which was fundamental for early Christians, but here the
reference is more general: **the resurrection of the dead**. This
conception finds little or no place in the Old Testament, apart from
the book of Daniel (12:2), but it was developing in inter-testamental
Judaism, and indeed was one of the points at issue between Pharisees, who accepted it, and Sadducees, who did not (cf. Ac. 23:6ff).
According to Schürer (*History of the Jewish People*, rev. ed. [1979],
II. 539) 'On this point there are so many opinions in Jewish religious
thought that it is not feasible to enter into them all at the present
time' (on Jewish ideas of the hereafter cf. G. F. Moore, *Judaism*
II., pp. 279ff. and index s.v. Resurrection; G. W. E. Nickelsburg,
Resurrection, Immortality & Eternal Life in Intertestamental Judaism.
[1972]; M. Hengel, *Judaism & Hellenism*, ET London [1974],
pp. 196–202). Ideas of **judgment** also differed, e.g. as to whether
the judgment would fall at the beginning or at the end of the
Messianic Age (Schürer II., p. 544), but resurrection and judgment
are commonly associated: once the idea of resurrection developed,
it was a short step to thoughts of a judgment when life and conduct
would be assessed, and reward or retribution meted out.

3. The *Larger Catechism* approved by the Westminster Assembly
of divines speaks of 'the needful but much neglected duty of
improving our baptism', to be performed by us all our life long. It
is to this kind of attitude that our author here gives expression.
These six items form a basic programme of Christian instruction,
not necessarily exhaustive or universally current, but indicating the
sort of teaching which could serve as a foundation. They are clearly
based on Jewish antecedents in the teaching of the synagogue. But
they are only the foundation, and matters cannot be left at that. It
is important to pass on: **and this we will do**, says our author,
if God permits. The simple future is preferable to the hortative
subjunctive of the reading in the margin, both because of the weight
of evidence supporting it and because it is more congruent with the
following clause (cf. Metzger, *Textual Commentary*, pp. 666f.). The
difference is due to a confusion of letters which occurs quite
frequently in the manuscripts.

4–6. Before fulfilling his promise to press on, the author adds
another warning, indeed the strongest and sternest yet. It is
contained in one long and rather involved sentence, which may be
summarised thus: if people have enjoyed the privileges mentioned
and then fall away, they cannot be restored again to repentance.
There is no second chance. From this it would seem to be clear that
the danger chiefly in view is that of apostasy (cf. 3:12 above, with
its reference to 'falling away' from the living God); also that our

author adopts a 'rigorist' position (cf. also 10:26ff.; 12:17). But, as verse 9 shows, all is not yet lost: it is a danger the author seeks to avert, not one to which his readers have already fallen victim. The question of post-baptismal sin was the subject of much debate in later centuries (cf. K. E. Kirk, *The Vision of God*, London [1941]), particularly in times of persecution: what was to be done about those who lapsed in the face of the threat of martyrdom, and subsequently, when the danger was over, sought re-admission to the Church? However, the problem was already present in *NT* times. In theory, a Christian could not sin (cf. 1 Jn. 3:9: 'No one born of God commits sin'): to use Pauline terms, he or she has put off 'the old man' and put on the new. In practice, Christians did sin, and the same Johannine letter affirms that to deny this is self-deception (1 Jn. 1:8ff.). One solution was to adopt the Old Testament distinction between unwitting and wilful sins (cf. on 5:2 above; also 1 Jn 5:16), but then the problem was to determine which was which. The Synoptics speak of sin against the Holy Spirit as unforgiveable (Mk 3:29 and parallels), and Kirk observes (p. 171) that while Hermas proposed one post-baptismal reconciliation for *all* grave sins without exception, which aroused the wrath of Tertullian, 'the Church excluded even from this strictly limited amnesty the three mortal sins of apostasy, adultery and homicide'. Later ages were to adopt a more tolerant and more lenient attitude, but the problem remains; indeed it may happen that the very people in need of the Church's help are excluded from its membership. Kirk (p. 9) makes a distinction which could be developed further, between the attitudes of the evangelist and the pastor: the evangelist, concerned for decision, conversion, commitment, must see things as either black or white, with no shades of grey. In an age of itinerant evangelists and prophets, he had no concern for a continuing congregation (cf. Did. 11: if he abide three days, he is a false prophet). The pastor on the other hand has to deal with a continuing congregation, some of whom at some time are bound to lapse in one way or another. He has to uphold the standards, but at the same time, like the Great High Priest, 'deal gently with the ignorant and wayward' (5:2). This is one area in which the twentieth century is little different from the first.

Bruce suggests that the wilderness narrative may still be in the author's mind (cf. 3:7ff. above). In that case it is not without interest to compare Paul's use of the same theme, also in a context of warning (1 C. 10:1–13): ' . . . all were baptised into Moses in the cloud and in the sea, ate the same supernatural food, drank the same supernatural drink . . . Nevertheless with most of them God was not pleased . . . Now these things are warnings for us . . .'

What emerges from such passages is the deep concern and seriousness of both writers. This is not a matter to be taken lightly.

Paul speaks of 'the light of the knowledge of the glory of God'
(2 C. 4:6, cf. also v. 4), John of 'the true light that enlightens every
man' (1:9). The imagery is common not only in the *NT* but in
ancient religion generally (cf. Conzelmann, *TDNT* IX, 310ff.). At
least from the time of Justin (1 Apol. 61,65) 'enlightenment' became
a technical term for baptism (Conzelmann 357f.), and it is natural
to see the beginnings of this development here. It may not yet
be a technical term, but Christian initiation and reception of the
knowledge of the truth (10:26) go together. Those who are converted
have, in the proverbial phrase, 'seen the light', and should walk in
the light (1 Jn 1:7). The **once** does not mean 'once upon a time',
but 'once and for all'. The tenses here are all Greek aorists, indicating complete and decisive action. There can be no second baptism
into Christ.

The reference to 'tasting' might suggest the eucharist, but is not
to be restricted to that; **the heavenly gift** 'is the richness of the
whole Christian life, and this gift belongs properly to the world of
heaven' (Montefiore). Moffatt notes the partiality of Philo for this
metaphor, but adds 'indeed it is common throughout contemporary
Hellenistic Greek as a metaphor for experiencing'. He also draws
attention to the fact that, as here, the food metaphor follows on the
light metaphor in Philo's remarks about the manna of Exod. 16:15,
16 (*De Fug*, 135); but Williamson (p. 306) calls it 'surely a pure
coincidence'. Another parallel occurs in 1 Pet. 2:3, echoing Ps. 34:8,
although it is perhaps closer to v. 5 below.

The gift of **the Holy Spirit** is commonly associated with baptism
(cf. Ac. 1:5; 2:38; 19:6; 1 C. 12:13. At Ac. 9:17–18 and 10:44ff.
baptism *follows* the gift of the Spirit, while at 8:14ff. reception of
the Spirit comes in a later rite, at the hands of Peter and John. This
was the pattern subsequently followed, in the separation of baptism
and confirmation). Despite the form used in English translations,
there is no article in the Greek (lit. 'partakers in holy spirit', rather
than 'in the Holy Spirit'), which makes it difficult to be certain
whether the gifts of the Spirit are here distinguished from the
person. The gifts however are probably included in the 'powers of
the age to come' in the next verse, the 'present manifestations of
the Spirit' (Montefiore, comparing 1 C. 12:1ff. We may also recall
the 'signs, wonders and miracles and gifts of the Spirit' mentioned
at 2:4 above, where 'miracles' translates the same Greek word).
There is therefore good reason for the rendering **partakers of the
Holy Spirit** here, although the gift of the Spirit and his gifts are
not always clearly distinct. As already noted, the first part of verse

5 has a partial parallel in 1 Pet. 2:3, where the reference is to the kindness of the Lord (cf. Ps. 34:8; 119:103).

These clauses provide a summary of the privileges the readers have enjoyed, as part of their Christian experience, and which they are now in danger of throwing away through apostasy. One is reminded of Paul's similar appeal to the Galatians (e.g. Gal. 3:1–5; 5:2–4), although that does not of course mean that the situations in view are exactly the same. It is simply that in both cases there is a danger of falling away, which admits of no repentance. To bring out the enormity of apostasy, the author affirms that those guilty are in fact crucifying the Son of God **on their own account** (*NEB*: with their own hands). The verb here is a compound which in non-biblical Greek means simply 'to crucify', but was understood by the Greek Fathers and some versions to mean 'crucify afresh'. According to BAG 61a the context seems to require this meaning, but as Marcus Dods observed long ago 'any crucifixion by the Hebrews must have been a *fresh crucifixion*, and needs no express indication of that feature of it' (*Expositor's Greek Testament* IV, London [1910], p. 298). In Origen's account of the Quo Vadis story, quoted by Moffatt (p. 80), the simple verb is used, with a separate adverb to express 'again'. Since in the *NT* the simple verb is normally employed, and the compound occurs only here, it is easy to see how the Fathers reached their interpretation. The word rendered **hold him up to contempt** (NEB 'making mock of his death') is a reminder that crucifixion was in the ancient world the most abhorred of all deaths, too degrading for a Roman citizen and reserved for slaves, and in Jewish eyes involving a curse upon the victim. It was not merely a matter of the pain inflicted, but also of the shame involved (cf. 12:2; 13:13 below). Dods and Bruce both note that this word is used in LXX at Num. 25:4 of the leaders of the Baal-peor apostasy, who were 'hung up in the sun before the Lord'. The reference is to exposure to open shame and contempt.

7–8. Verses 7 and 8 underline the point by what has been called 'an agricultural parable'. Land which drinks in **the rain that falls upon it** (cf. Dt. 11:11; the image is quite common) and produces fruit is blessed; it is fulfilling God's purpose at the creation (Gen. 1:11f.). If on the other hand it produces **thorns and thistles**, it is worthless. Here there are echoes of Gen. 3:17f., God's curse on the ground following the fall of Adam and Eve. Bruce recalls Isaiah's song of the vineyard (5:1ff.), of which verse 6 is particularly apposite: 'I will make it a waste . . . and briers and thorns shall grow up; I will also command the clouds that they rain no rain upon it'. Such land is indeed **near to being cursed**. In point of fact, the burning of the land is normally not to destroy it, but to clear the ground and allow new shoots to grow, or leave it clear for crops. The author may therefore be a man of the city, unfamiliar with country ways, or more probably simply ignores the point. Fire as the fate of the wicked is common in the *NT* (cf. for example Mt. 3:10–12; 13:30, 42; 25:41); or he may have in mind the fate of Sodom and Gomorrah (cf. Dt. 29.23). Apostasy leads to doom and desolation.

9–12. Despite this frightful warning, the author is confident that his readers are 'in better case' (*NEB*). In these verses there is a marked change of tone, and for the only time in the letter he addresses them by the affectionate term **beloved**. This is a common enough device: constant harping on deficiencies and shortcomings may fail of the desired effect, for very repetition. There is a place also for positive encouragement. Moreover the author has grounds for his confidence: he refers to their past works, the love for God shown in their service to the saints (cf. also 10:32–34). Similar language is used at Rom. 15:25ff.; 1 C. 16:1 and 2 C. 9:1 with reference to Paul's collection for 'the saints' at Jerusalem, but there is no need to limit the present reference to that. For one thing, the phrase is used, with the cognate noun instead of the verb employed here, at 1 C. 16:15, on which C. K. Barrett writes (commentary, p. 394): 'The saints here are not those of 16:1, since Stephanas has already begun his ministry to them, whereas the collection for the Jerusalem saints is only at this point being set in motion'. For another, such mutual service was one of the salient characteristics of early Christianity. Bruce notes that if the intended recipients were in Rome 'the behaviour for which our author commends them was a precedent for the reputation for Christian charity which the Roman church enjoyed in later times' (cf. Ignatius *ad Rom.* preface; Dionysius of Corinth ap. Euseb. HE IV, 3.10).

In the words of the prayer, 'it is not the beginning of any good work, but the continuing therein even unto the end that yieldeth the true glory'. So our author here expresses his earnest desire that each and every one of his readers may show the same zeal for the full and complete realisation of their hope. They must continue 'even to the end'. They are not to be **sluggish** (cf. 5:11), but rather **imitators of those who through faith and patience inherit the promise**. The word rendered **patience** here carries the meaning not only of patient waiting, in a temporal sense, but of steadfastness and endurance (cf. *BAG* 488a). The Greek present tense can have a durative force, 'are inheriting', which would lend colour to Monte-fiore's suggestion that our author has the example of contemporaries in mind; at 4:3 above he had written, 'we who have believed enter (*or* are entering) that rest'. Paul twice urges his readers 'Be imitators

of me' (I C. 4:16; 11:1), and on two other occasions speaks of a
different group becoming 'imitators of us and of the Lord' (I
Th. 1:16) or 'imitators of the churches of God . . . in Judaea' (I
Th. 2:14), so that thought of the example of contemporaries is
not impossible. Other scholars however (e.g. Bruce) see here an
anticipation of the long roll of the heroes of faith in chapter 11.
Admittedly 11:39 says they did not receive what was promised, but
the remainder of the verse suggests that in due time they will. For
the moment, reference is made only to Abraham (v. 13) as a signal
example of one to whom a promise was made, and mention of
Abraham eventually leads back to the theme of Melchizedek (7:1).

THE PROMISE BACKED BY AN OATH

6:13–20

13–15. The reference to promises in v. 12 recalls the **promise** made
to Abraham when he proved himself faithful and obedient, even to
the extent of being ready to sacrifice his only son at God's command
(Gen. 22:1–14); in the words of 'the angel of the Lord': 'By myself
I have sworn, says the LORD, because you have done this, and have
not withheld your son, your only son, I will indeed bless you, and
I will multiply your descendants as the stars of heaven and as the
sand which is on the seashore' (Gen. 22:15–17). Hebrews quotes
only the actual promise, but it is clear from the reference to an oath
that the context is also in mind. Moreover we may remember the
earlier promises made to Abraham, even before the birth of Isaac
(Gen. 12:1–4; 17:1–8, 15.21). The command to sacrifice Isaac must
have seemed to put an end to these promises, so far as Isaac was
concerned, to destroy all Abraham's hopes; yet he **patiently
endured**, in striking contrast to the disobedient wilderness generation, and received confirmation of the promise, in yet more
emphatic terms. Actually the *RSV* translation '**having patiently
endured**' is slightly misleading here (*NEB* 'after patient waiting').
The Greek word refers not so much to endurance as to forbearance
(cf. I C. 13:4: love is patient), or more generally to patient waiting
(*BAG* 488a). As Montefiore notes, the birth of Isaac came twenty-
five years after the call of Abraham (Gen. 12:4; 21:5), while Paul
sees the fulfilment of the promise of numerous descendants in the
Christian church (Rom. 4:13, 16: the promise is 'not only to the
adherents of the law, but also to those who share the faith of
Abraham'). One might indeed feel a certain contradiction between
the present verse and 11:39, where it is said that 'all these (Abraham

included, cf. 11:17), though well attested by their faith, did not
receive what was promised'. The solution is of course that Abraham
received the promise (6:15; 11:17), but not its final realisation and
fulfilment (11:39). **Abraham** thus, in Montefiore's words, provided
'a signal example of faith and patience'. This echo of v. 12, where
the cognate noun is used, suggests that the idea of endurance and
steadfastness should not entirely be ruled out here; the point is that
when reference is made to endurance of suffering or hostility at
10:32, 36 and 12:1–3, the terms employed belong to a quite different
group of words. The associations may be close, but they are not
perhaps quite so close as is suggested by the use of the same English
words in each case.

16. On the human level, an oath is 'a decisive appeal to the
highest power to close all controversy' (Westcott); it calls upon God
as witness to the truth of what is said, invokes his wrath upon the
taker if the promise is not fulfilled. Here there is another point of
contact with Philo, who writes that 'God does not swear by another,
for there is nothing better than he, but by himself, who is best of
all' (*L.A.* III. 203). It is however evident that Philo is rather embarrassed by the idea. At *Spec. Leg.* II.10 he speaks of an oath as
'nothing but God's witness in a debated matter', and adds that to
call upon God if it is not the truth is the most impious thing of all.
In his comment on the Genesis passage however he seems to quote
the same formula as the opinion of others (*L.A.* III.203), indeed
'thousands' of them (*de Sac. Ab.* 91, where the formula appears
again), for whom the idea that God should swear an oath is odd
and inappropriate. He therefore finds it necessary to provide some
justification (see *L.A.* III. 203–207; also Williamson, pp. 201–212):
'God is the strongest guarantor, first for himself and then for his
works, so that it was reasonable for him to swear by himself in
giving assurance regarding himself, which was impossible for anyone
else'. Our author has no such scruples.

17. Rather he sees in the **oath** evidence of God's desire **to show
more convincingly** the unchangeable character of his purpose. The
promise in itself was sure and certain; the addition of an **oath** makes
it doubly sure. The verb rendered **interposed** means to mediate,
act as surety, hence to guarantee (cf. *NEB*). The **heirs of the
promise** are not just Abraham's lineal descendants but 'all who
under different circumstances and different degrees succeed to the
promise' (Westcott). As noted above (on 2:16; 6:15), Paul had
already claimed the title 'seed of Abraham' for all Christians, irrespective of birth. Hence the promise made to Abraham has direct
relevance for the author and his readers.

18. God's purpose is **unchangeable**, and it is impossible for God to lie (cf. Tit. 1:12); therefore the promise and the oath are also unchangeable, and therefore we **have strong encouragement to seize the hope that is set before us**. This is the first occurrrence in Hebrews of a word with a fairly wide range of meaning: encouragement, exhortation; appeal, request; comfort, consolation (cf. *BAG* 618a). At 13:22 (cf. Ac. 13:15) it is used in a phrase describing the letter as a whole as 'a word of exhortation', or perhaps better 'of encouragement'. The author's whole purpose in writing is to encourage and re-assure, to give his readers confidence and stimulate them to further effort. The hope lies before them; it is for them to grasp and hold it fast. At the end of the verse *NEB* offers a different construction 'who have claimed his protection *by grasping* the hope', but this seems to require an unusual use of a Greek infinitive; the reading of the *NEB* margin 'to give to us, who have claimed his protection, a powerful incentive to grasp . . .' is much more natural. The words **we who have fled for refuge** have suggested to some commentators that the readers are refugees and exiles; as Spicq notes ([1977], p. 114), the refugee has no treasure left but hope, and the instability of his situation would contrast very effectively with the following metaphor of the anchor (v. 19). There is nothing in the letter to suggest that they are refugees, although they may be exiles (e.g. Jews in Rome). It is therefore better to take the description metaphorically: as 13:14 puts it, 'here we have no lasting city'. 1 Pet. 2:11 speaks of Christians as 'aliens and exiles' ('aliens in a foreign land', *NEB*). This world is not their permanent home (13:14 *NEB*). As William Manson puts it, 'Christians are "refugees of God", persons who have sought asylum, ultimate deliverance as offered in Him' (p. 65). Westcott notes that the word (here rendered by an English relative clause) is used in connection with the cities of refuge in Dt. 4:41f. and other *OT* passages, and that 'the thought of these cities appears to be in the mind of the writer'. For Philo these cities symbolise the divine powers, the Logos being the one to which 'it is most profitable to fly first' (see Drummond, *Philo Judaeus* II. 83, 161); he can speak of flight to 'the God of the things that are' (*L.A.* III. 12) or describe eternal life as 'a flight to pure being' (*de Fug.* 78). 1 Clement (20) speaks of those 'who have taken refuge in His compassionate mercies through our Lord Jesus Christ' (Lightfoot, *The Apostolic Fathers*, p. 66). As we can see from Num. 35:9ff., these cities were established as places of sanctuary where the unintentional slayer might live secure, without fear of vengeance. It is not difficult to see how the idea could be extended to that of an ultimate sanctuary at the throne of God and under his protection. The idea of 'aliens and exiles', incidentally, that in this world mankind has no permanent home, was later to be prominent in

Gnosticism, and has sometimes beem claimed as a 'gnostic motif'
in the New Testament; but with the *OT* background and the Exodus
tradition it is not necessary to seek for any extra-Biblical sources
for this idea.

   **19. We have this as a sure and steadfast anchor of the soul, a
hope that enters into the inner shrine behind the curtain**: This
translation is one way of resolving the problems presented by the
Greek text. Verse 19 is literally 'which we have as an anchor of the
soul, sure and steadfast and penetrating into the inner part of the
curtain' (i.e. into the inner sanctuary behind the curtain). The
relative clearly refers back to **hope** in the previous verse. The
problem lies in the phrase beginning **sure and steadfast**, two adjectives and a participle, all feminine, which could grammatically agree
either with 'anchor' or with 'hope'. *AV*, translating word by word,
takes them with 'anchor', but in Montefiore's words 'it is, of course,
hope and not the anchor which is said to enter the sanctuary!' *NEB*
and *RSV* both attach **sure and steadfast** to **anchor**, but 'entering
within the veil' (*AV*) to 'hope', which as Westcott says 'gives
distinctness to two aspects of hope, its immovable stability and its
penetrative vigour'. However, he regards this division as artificial,
and thinks it best 'to connect the whole description with the principal subject (hope)'. The combination **sure and steadfast** is
common enough in Greek ethical literature (cf. e.g. Philo, *Quis
Rerum*, 314), and is appropriate enough to **an anchor**; moreover
these two adjectives are more closely linked together than they are
to the following participle, which lends support to the rendering in
NEB and *RSV*; but a sudden change, linking the participle with
'hope' instead, is distinctly awkward. The best solution is to recast
as in Montefiore's version: 'This hope we have like an anchor for
our life. It is safe and sure; and it enters into the inner sanctuary
of the veil'. The metaphor of the **anchor** is not used elsewhere in
the Bible, but was airly common in the Greek world. Montefiore's
choice of 'life' instead of **soul** is a reminder that this Greek word is
not to be confined to some spiritual or immaterial part of human
nature, distinct from the body and thought to survive death; as
BAG put it (893a), 'it is often impossible to draw hard and fast lines
between the meanings of this many-sided word', but to translate
uniformly by 'soul' may be to introduce ideas and associations which
belong to the philosophy of Plato rather than to the Bible (cf. 10:39
below). The 'veil' or **curtain** separated the inmost sanctuary, the
Holy of Holies, from the outer sanctuary, the Holy Place (Exod.
26:33 etc.; at Lev. 16:2 Moses is bidden to tell Aaron 'not to come
at all times into the holy place within the veil', a point to which our
author will come later (cf. 9:7).

20. Into this inmost sanctuary **Jesus has gone as a forerunner on our behalf**. One cannot but recall the *archegos* of 2:10, although a different Greek word is used here. As Montefiore puts it, 'Jesus constitutes the advance guard who is already in heaven and who by his entry has assured the consequent entry of all who are his. It is in this representative capacity that he "entered on our behalf" '. With this our author picks up again the theme which he left at 5:10: by virtue of Ps. 110:4, quoted at 5:6, Jesus has become a high **priest for ever, after the order of Melchizedek**. The significance of this he now proceeds to expound.

Before we go on to the discussion of this theme, it may be well to look back again at the main lines of this lengthy admonition. From some points of view it may seem a digression, but our author is not one to waste words. His difficulty is, as Manson (p. 60) puts it, 'that his hearers are backward hearers who have remained virtually at the ABC stage of religious understanding. The sally that they need elementary instruction at a time when they ought to be teaching others excludes the possibility of the community in question being regarded as an intellectual *elite* of some kind to whom the writer desires to communicate some higher Christian *gnosis* . . . Something is retarding the advance from first principles which might have been expected of them'. Peterson (p. 176; cf. his whole discussion, pp. 176–187) notes that there has been division over the author's emphasis in this passage. As can be seen, 5:11–14 and 6:4–8 administer rebuke, the latter passage in the strongest terms, whereas 6:9–12 is much more cordial. 5:11 speaks of the readers as 'dull of hearing', while 6:12 expresses the fear that they may *become* 'sluggish'. The solution here is probably just that the author is blending encouragement and rebuke in the effort to stimulate his readers; we might in fact see an alteration of sternness and conciliation in this whole section: rebuke in 5:11–14, a more conciliatory tone in 6:1–3, followed by even sterner warnings in 6:4–8, and finally the closing note of encouragement in 6:9–12. The reference to training and practice in 5:14 provides food for thought: the musician must keep in practice if he is to maintain his standard of performance, and participants in any form of sport are well aware that at the beginning of a new season it may take some time to reach their peak. This offers a useful analogy, although of course analogies must not be pressed too far. In our author's eyes, his readers have failed to realise their full potential, and are in danger of losing what they already have. They cannot simply rest on their laurels, still less abandon their past achievement. We do not know the exact situation of the readers, or the problems with which they were

faced, but they seem to have become discouraged, to have lost their
first enthusiasm, to be wondering whether it is worth going on. As
Bruce says (pp. 117f.), it was possible for the recipients, 'yielding
gradually to pressures from various quarters, to give up more and
more those features of faith and practice which were distinctive of
Christianity, and yet to feel that they had not abandoned the basic
principles of repentance and faith, the realities denoted by religious
ablutions and the laying on of hands, the expectation of resurrection
and the judgment of the age to come'. This would certainly fit
with Schmithals' theory that they were former synagogue adherents
under pressure at the time of the re-organisation at Jamnia (see
Introd., p. 14), but this is not the only possibility. Peterson (p. 181)
speaks of 'general spiritual lethargy, with a definite disinclination
to explore more deeply the implications of their Christian position',
a lethargy 'involving loss of zeal, lack of confidence and faltering
hope' (p. 186); he thinks it 'most likely that the original recipients
were Jewish Christians, tempted to slip back into a form of Judaism
in order to escape the hostility and suffering associated with being
Christian'. Certainly 6:11 would seem to show that in our author's
view a renewal of zeal is what is required.

This is perhaps the point at which the letter is most directly
relevant to the modern world. Too many people have made little or
no advance in their knowledge and understanding of Christianity
since their childhood. They are content with an elementary and
superficial knowledge, and gradually slip away. The pressures of
modern life may not include actual persecution, although in some
circumstances that too is possible, but these pressures are none the
less present. It is all too easy just to conform and go along with the
crowd. Or again, there is the perennial problem of relevance. It is
not enough to go on repeating the outworn shibboleths of a bygone
age. What was meaningful and significant for one generation may
no longer be meaningful for another. Our understanding of the faith
must continually grow and deepen, otherwise it may simply wither
away. The problem is that attempts to present it in terms more
relevant to the modern situation are often viewed with suspicion by
those who cling to the past. What is not always realised is that this
is not simply a modern problem, though it may be more intensely
felt today. It is a problem that has faced the Church all through the
centuries. And the way to a solution is to press forward to maturity,
**to show the same earnestness in realising the full assurance of
hope**.

The final section (6:13–20) serves two purposes. First of all,
reference was made at 4:1 to 'the promise of entering his rest'. At
6:12 the reference seems to be more general, 'the promises'. At 6:13

the author recalls the promise made to Abraham, which was backed by God's oath. This allows him to claim the strongest encouragement to perseverance, for here we have not one but two **unchangeable things, in which it is impossible that God should prove false.** The promise is certain and irrevocable, and we have every ground for hope. Secondly, the passage introduces Abraham, who has indeed been mentioned earlier at 2:16, but only in passing; in the next chapter he will play a more prominent role in relation to Melchizedek. With the stage now set, the author can go on to speak of Jesus entering in as our **forerunner** into **the inner shrine behind the curtain,** as 'a **high priest for ever after the order of Melchizedek'.**

AFTER THE ORDER OF MELCHIZEDEK

7:1–28

The case of Melchizedek offers a salutary warning against the danger of the argument *e silentio*. In 1964 Montefiore wrote that in the *Genesis Apocryphon* from Qumran he receives only a bare mention, adding 'among people such as the Qumran covenanters the name Melchizedek may have become suspect owing to their distrust of those who claimed a priesthood like that of Melchizedek'. Similarly Braun in 1966 says that for the Qumran community Melchizedek was 'evidently quite uninteresting'. In terms of the evidence available when they wrote, they are certainly correct; but the whole situation changed with the publication in the summer of 1966 of the fragments of a scroll from Cave 11 at Qumran, *11Q Melchizedek* (the *editio princeps* was actually in *Oudtestamentische Studien* XIV (Leiden [1965]), pp. 354–373, but it was an article by M. de Jonge and A. S. van der Woude in *NTS* 12 [1965–66], pp. 301–326 which brought it to the notice of New Testament scholars; for Heb. 7 see pp. 318–323). Authors must of necessity form their conclusions on the basis of the evidence available to them, but one can never be completely certain about a negative conclusion, since it may at any time be falsified by some new discovery. More recently a further item has been added to the dossier on Melchizedek, with the publication of the tractate *Melchizedek* from *Codex IX* of the Nag Hammadi library (*NHLE*, pp. 399–403; introduction, text and translation by B. A. Pearson in *Nag Hammadi Codices IX and X* (*NHS* 15), Leiden [1981], pp. 19–85).

Thus far our author has quoted only the reference to Melchizedek in Ps. 110:4, the background and origins of which are uncertain:

some scholars have thought the psalm composed in honour of some
Hasmonean king while others date it back to the pre-exilic period.
There is nothing in the psalm itself to explain the allusion, although
it may be noted that the preceding lines contain another divine oath:
'The Lord has sworn and will not change his mind . . .', a point
on which our author will lay stress later (7:20–21). Here he goes
back to the only other passage in the Old Testament in which
Melchizedek is mentioned, his meeting with Abraham after the
defeat of the four kings (Gen. 14:17–20). On this slender basis a
considerable amount of speculation was to develop (see F. L.
Horton, *The Melchizedek Tradition*), some of it in the Christian
period clearly drawing upon Hebrews, as with the Nag Hammadi
treatise (Pearson, p. 34). The Hebrews passage itself has attracted
enough attention for a monograph to be written on the history of
its exegesis (B. Demarest, *A History of the Interpretation of Hebrews
7,1–10 from the Reformation to the Present*, Tübingen [1976]). With
so much material available, it is impossible in brief compass to do
more than sketch the main outlines. A more recent monograph by
C. Gianotto (*Melchisedek e la sua tipologia*, Brescia [1984]) traces the
development of Melchizedek speculation in Jewish and Christian
sources, orthodox and heretical, down to the later Melchizedekian
heresies; this includes discussion of the Nag Hammadi text, not yet
available to Horton.

Philo (*Leg. All.* III. 79) offers the same explanation of Melchizedek's name and title as does Hebrews (righteous king, king of
peace), but this similarity is not significant; such etymologies are
fairly common. What is more important is that Philo never mentions
Ps. 110:4, which is the foundation text for our author (see Williamson, pp. 434–449, and for this point, pp. 446f.). At *Leg. All.*
III. 82 Philo allegorises Melchizedek's gift of bread and wine, at *De
cong. quaer.* 99, Abraham's gift of tithes, but neither of these passages is relevant for Hebrews. In 11Q Melchizedek this first priest
to be mentioned in Scripture (Jos. *BJ* VI. 438) has become a
heavenly deliverer who protects the faithful people of God; indeed
'he is so much "God's warrior" that his priestly activities remain
completely in the shadow' (de Jonge and van der Woude, p. 306).
There is a basis for this development in the following lines of the
psalm. From this it is clear that, in Montefiore's words, 'our author's
exposition of Melchizedek is highly original'.

1–3. He begins with a summary of the Genesis passage, and then
in verse 2 goes on to his explanation of the name and title (actually
the name means 'My king (is) righteous', or possibly 'My king is
Zedek', perhaps the name of a Canaanite deity; Josh. 10:1 mentions
Adonizedek, king of Jerusalem, 'My Lord is Zedek'). **Salem** was

identified by most of the Fathers with Jerusalem (cf. Ps. 76:2), but Jerome knew a tradition identifying it with a town near Scythopolis, the Salim of John 3:23. Josephus (*Ant.* I.180) says that Melchizedek was king of Soluma, and elsewhere (*Ant.* VI.67; *BJ* 6.438) that this was the former name of Jerusalem. Héring notes that, like Philo, our author does not know this equation, or he would certainly have made the point that Melchizedek officiated in the very city where the new High Priest sacrificed himself. The author also makes no reference whatever to Melchizedek's gift of bread and wine, which later writers of course linked with the Eucharist.

It is probable that 'the most high God' was a Canaanite deity, identified with Yahweh after the Hebrew conquest. In Greek literature the superlative is often an epithet for Zeus, as the chief god of the pantheon. Dodd (*The Bible and the Greeks*, pp. 11ff.) notes that in hellenistic inscriptions it is often difficult to know whether the title is Jewish or pagan: for the Jew it meant 'God most high', for the pagan 'the supreme deity' (among other gods). See also Nock, *Essays*, pp. 416ff., who concludes (p. 426) that 'Jewish influence, though sometimes a contributory factor, was not all-important' in the widespread use of the title. Here of course there is no problem: for our author **the most high God** is the God of the Old Testament, who spoke in time past in the prophets and has now spoken to us in a Son (cf. 1:1–2).

Verse 3 follows the principle that what is not recorded in Scripture may be presumed not to exist. In the Genesis story Melchizedek suddenly appears, with no preparation, no indication of who he was (except that he was king of Salem), no mention of his birth or lineage, and equally suddenly disappears; there is no record of his death. Therefore, our author claims, **he is without father or mother**, and in Moffatt's phrase 'void of any genealogy'; with no record of his birth or death, he is eternal. The three Greek terms rendered 'without father', 'without mother', 'without genealogy' occur only here in the Bible, and it has been suggested that the third is our author's own coining. The other two are used by Greek writers to describe orphans or illegitimate children, but also for the supernatural birth of gods or goddesses (e.g. Hephaestus or Athena). There is thus a suggestion of a supernatural origin for Melchizedek. Philo uses only the second of these three words (Williamson, pp. 20–23). The phrase **resembling the Son of God** is at first sight incongruous, since Jesus has earlier been described as a priest 'after the order of Melchizedek' (cf. also v. 15 below). In terms of earthly chronology Jesus is of course later, but from our author's point of view Jesus is the archetype of whom Melchizedek is the earthly

type. As Bengel puts it, it is not that the Son of God is assimilated
to Melchizedek, but the reverse. He is like the Son of God.

4–10. The author now proceeds to develop his argument,
deducing from the Genesis story he has just quoted a) the superiority
of Melchizedek to Abraham, and b) the superiority of his priesthood
to the levitical priesthood. In the first place, Abraham **gave him a
tithe of the spoils,** and thereby acknowledged his superiority. In
the second place Abraham received his blessing, and it is beyond
question that it is **the inferior** who **is blessed by the superior** (v. 7).
Verses 5–6 underline the curious fact that while the levitical priests
take tithes from their fellow-Israelites according to the law, here
we have a man who does not have **their genealogy** (i.e. the Aaronic
descent necessary to the priesthood) actually tithing Abraham, to
whom the promises were made. Verse 8 then points a contrast: the
levitical priests are **mortal men** (cf. v. 23 below), whereas Melchizedek is 'a priest for ever', and therefore is alive, eternal. This is
not stated in the text of Genesis, and is an inference from Ps. 110.
We should remember that behind Melchizedek the author sees the
figure of Jesus. Finally verses 9–10 introduce an idea which on the
usual translation (**one might even say,** 'so to speak') the author
himself seems to find a little extravagant. Héring however objects
that while this may match *our* way of thinking, the author has no
reason to weaken his affirmation; the phrase may also mean 'to use
just the right word' (cf. *BAG* 305b). At all events ancient ideas of
corporate personality provide a sufficient explanation: Levi, the
ancestor of the priestly tribe, had not yet been born at the time of
the Genesis incident (he was the third son of Jacob and Leah, and
is first mentioned at Gen. 29:34). Since an ancestor was held to
contain within himself the seed of his future descendants, Levi
could be said to have paid tithes when Abraham did so (Levi was
still in the loins of his ancestor), and thus to have acknowledged
the superiority of Melchizedek.

11–14. The effect of the preceding argument is to demonstrate
the superiority of Melchizedek over the levitical priesthood, and
consequently the superiority of a priesthood 'after the order of
Melchizedek'. The fact that by modern standards such an argument
would not hold is not relevant; our author clearly considered it to
be valid, and we must not allow our standards to prevent us seeing
the power of his argument for his own day. Verse 11 then introduces
a further argument, the insufficiency of the old priesthood (cf.
Peterson, pp. 108ff.). Here we return again to Ps. 110. **If perfection
had been attainable** through the old priesthood, there would have
been no need for another priesthood; but the psalm speaks of
another priesthood, therefore the old priesthood was inadequate. If

it had been effective, why should God speak in the psalm through David, long after the ordination of Aaron and his sons (Exod. 29:4–9; Lev. 8), of **another priest** of a different order? In fact, as our author will establish later, the sacrifices and offerings of the old priesthood were not effective in cleansing the conscience (9:9) or in taking away sins (10:1–4).

The parenthesis in v. 11 is a reminder of the close connection between the institution of the Aaronic priesthood and the giving of the law in Exodus and Leviticus. It was **under it** ('on this basis', *NEB*) that the law was given; the whole system belonged together. A corollary to this follows in v. 12: **a change in the priesthood** entails **a change in the law** as well. 'The new priesthood implies that the old Law . . . the Old Covenant are abrogated' (Manson, p. 114). Commentators frequently note the similarity with Paul's conclusions about the law, but as Manson notes there is a difference: Paul and Hebrews arrive at the same conclusion, 'but they come to it by different roads'. 'In St Paul the abrogation of the Law as a source of rightness with God implicitly carries the fall of the cultus with it. In Hebrews the supersession of the cultus explicitly involves the repeal of the Law' (p. 115).

For Peterson (p. 109) v. 12 'forms a parenthesis to the main argument' (cf. Westcott), as becomes apparent when v. 13 refers back to v. 11 and explains how another priest can arise who is not **after the order of Aaron**: Jesus belonged to a different tribe (Judah), and there is nothing in the Old Testament about priests from that tribe. There is actually a reference to a priest from the tribe of Judah in the Testaments of the Twelve Patriarchs (TLevi 8.14), but this 'is one of the clearest signs of Christian influence in the extant recensions' (Bruce). David and Solomon are both reported to have offered sacrifice on various occasions (2 Sam. 6:13, 17f.; 24:25; 1 Kg. 3:4; 8:62ff.), but these our author ignores; he is concerned with the principles governing the institution of the priesthood in the pentateuchal legislation, not with the exercise of priestly functions by one king or another. It might even be said that he skilfully turns what might have been a serious objection into a support for his case: as **descended from** the tribe of **Judah**, Jesus could not be a priest according to Mosaic principles—but he *is* a priest, of a new and different order. As it happens, attempts were later made to provide Jesus with a levitical lineage, and so justify his priesthood, but as Bruce observes these would have been dismissed by our author, had he known them, 'not only as irrelevant but as perverse, because they blunted the point of his argument—the calculated supersession of the Levitical priesthood by one of a different kind'.

15–17. Verses 15–17 return to Ps. 110 to add a further argument, based on the phrase 'for ever'. This new kind of priesthood is **not according to a legal requirement concerning bodily descent** (*RSV*), 'a system of earth-bound rules' (*NEB*), or more literally 'the law of a carnal commandment' (*AV*). This reference to the flesh does not carry the Pauline associations of flesh and sin; the point is rather its transitory, this-worldly character. The priesthood was to belong to Aaron and his sons 'by a perpetual statute' (Exod. 29:9); at Exod. 40:15 it is called 'a perpetual priesthood'. However its permanence was due entirely to priestly succession (cf. v. 23 below): the priesthood might be everlasting, but only because generation after generation new priests were installed to replace those who died. The phrase thus carries both the sense of bodily descent, i.e. in the line of Aaron, and also, more particularly, that of the transitory, earth-bound character of this priesthood. In contrast the new priest is one 'for ever', by the power of a life that nothing can destroy. According to Westcott, 'The life of Christ was not endless or eternal only. It was essentially "indissoluble". Although the form of its manifestation was changed and in the earthly sense he died, yet his life endured unchanged even through earthly dissolution. He died and yet he offered himself as living in death by the eternal Spirit (cf. 9:14)'. Peterson (p. 111) finds the last clause 'an incomprehensible notion', and also (p. 245, n. 43) criticises the preceding sentence as 'not the *NT* way of thinking about death and resurrection at all: the resurrection is a totally new beginning after the experience of death'. The issue here is whether we are to regard this life as possessed by Jesus from the beginning, in which case his death upon the cross becomes a problem, or whether we should not think rather of his risen and exalted life. The problem ties in with the question when Jesus is to be thought of as becoming 'priest after the order of Melchizedek', at the beginning of his life or at the resurrection. It may be that this is another point which the author has not completely thought through, and certainly he nowhere seems to give an answer; but there is something to be said for the view that 'the writer envisaged no time interval between Christ's self-sacrifice and his entrance into the heavenly sanctuary. Having brought the perfect sin offering once and for all, the victim became almost simultaneously the high priest' (B. A. Demarest, quoted by Peterson p. 245, n. 40). What is certain is that our author's faith centres in the great high priest who ministers in the heavenly sanctuary now as the author writes. Whether he thought of Jesus as possessing **indestructible life** in the days of his flesh we do not know. It is the risen and exalted Jesus who ministers as our great high priest. This may be another case of problems arising from our desire for answers to questions that simply had not occurred to the mind of the author. But one thing is certain: at a later point (13:8) he speaks of Jesus as 'the same yesterday and today and for ever', and the whole point of his argument in earlier chapters about the humanity of Jesus, his qualification to be a merciful and sympathetic high priest, would be lost if there was not a continuity. It is this Jesus, who shared our life, knew our temptations, endured suffering and death, who now lives in **the power of an indestructible life**. The resurrection marks a new beginning.

18–19. Verses 18 and 19 draw the conclusion: the former commandment is set aside as weak and useless—**the law made nothing perfect**; or rather, as will be argued later, the sacrifices ordained by the law proved ineffective (cf. 9:9–10; 10:1). On the positive side, in contrast, there is the introduction of **a better hope . . . through which we draw near to God**. This is not to deny that people under the old dispensation could have any access to God; as Bruce observes, the Psalter provides evidence enough that they could enjoy 'peace of conscience and a sense of nearness to God'. But there is a very real sense in which 'the whole apparatus of worship' associated with the Aaronic priesthood 'was calculated rather to keep men at a distance from God than to bring them near'. Whatever may be said of personal devotion, sacrifice had to be offered by the priests, while in the ritual of the Day of Atonement only the high priest was allowed to enter the Holy of Holies, and that only on one day in the year. This remoteness, this separation, is symbolised by the curtain screening off the inner shrine, into which Jesus 'has gone as a forerunner on our behalf' (6:19–20). At Exod. 19:24 even the priests are debarred from approaching Mt Sinai, at Exod. 24:2 even Aaron: Moses is to go up alone. Under the new dispensation, in contrast, 'we have confidence to enter the sanctuary by the blood of Jesus' (10:19); the way is open for all to draw near 'in full assurance of faith' (10:22).

20–22. The first quotation of Ps. 110–4, at 5:6 above, included only the words immediately relevant to the author's argument: 'Thou art a priest for ever after the order of Melchizedek', and it is to these words that the author has constantly referred in the course of his discussion. There is however more to the verse, and to this he now turns. The full quotation of the first part of the verse is given at v. 21: **The Lord has sworn and will not change his mind, 'Thou art a priest for ever'**. The significance of this is that while, in Montefiore's words, 'a lot of ceremonial was required at the consecration of Aaron and his sons (Exod. 28–99; Lev. 8–9)', there is no reference to **an oath**. Here we need to remember what was said of God's oath to Abraham at 6:13ff. above: 'When God desired to show more convincingly to the heirs of the promise the

unchangeable character of his purpose, he interposed with an oath'
(6:17). As already noted, the Aaronic priesthood was said to be
perpetual (Exod. 29:9; 40:14), but now it is declared to be superseded. What guarantee could there be that the new priesthood which
supplanted it would not also be superseded? After all, the history
of the high priesthood would have afforded examples in plenty, had
our author wished to use them, of men who usurped the office, only
to be supplanted in their turn. But Ps. 110:4 is proof that in the
present case this cannot be: the Lord has sworn and will not change
his mind. The priesthood which Jesus holds is therefore truly
permanent, and this in turn makes him the guarantor of **a better
covenant**. Once again the author mentions in passing a theme to
which he will give fuller attention later (cf. 8:6ff.). In the Greek,
incidentally, these verses form a single complex sentence, with the
name of Jesus in the emphatic position at the end: so much the
better is the covenant of which the guarantor is Jesus!

23–28. The following verses draw the conclusions from what has
gone before. Under the old order priests officiated in their lifetime,
and were replaced by others when they died. They were consequently **many in number**. As Bruce notes, Josephus (*Ant.* 20.227)
counts eighty-three high priests from Aaron to the fall of the Temple
in AD 70. Jesus in contrast continues for ever, and his priesthood is
therefore permanent. The Greek adjective, translated by the adverb
permanently, occurs only here in the New Testament, and it is
tempting to take it, on etymological grounds, as meaning 'which
cannot pass to another' (so Montefiore). This would certainly
contrast with the priestly succession of the old order, but there
appears to be no justification for it in Greek usage. The word means
rather 'inviolable, permanent, unchangeable' (see BAG *80*; *TDNT*
V. 742f.). The corollary to this permanence of his office is that he
is fully and completely able **to save those who draw near to God
through him**. The Greek phrase has evidently caused some
perplexity to the ancient translators (see *BAG* 608): the Armenian
understands it to mean 'completely, fully', the Vulgate, Syriac and
Coptic 'for all time'. The only other occurrence in the *NT* is at
Lk. 13:11, where there is a similar ambiguity: some take it that the
bent woman could not fully straighten up, others that she could not
do so at all. In the present instance both meanings are perfectly
apposite: as priest for ever, Jesus is able to save **for all time**, but
he is also able to save 'absolutely' (*NEB*), 'to the uttermost' (*AV*).
It is simply that the English translator has to choose one rendering
or the other. Since the thought of permanence is expressed in the
next clause (**he always lives**), perhaps that of completeness should
have the preference here. As Bruce notes, the intercessory work of

Christ 'is not a doctrine peculiar to our author'; like others, he aptly quotes Rom. 8:33ff., and of course there is 1 Jn 2:1 with its reference to 'an advocate with the Father'. At Lk. 22:32 Jesus says to Simon Peter 'I have prayed for you that your faith may not fail', while in the Fourth Gospel there is the great high-priestly prayer of John 17. It is therefore very natural to trace here 'the echo of an early Christian confession of faith, which in addition to acknowledging the death, resurrection and enthronement of Christ made mention also of His intercessory ministry' (Bruce). Commentators frequently make the point that this intercession is not the prayer of a suppliant, as the intercessions of earthly priests could only be. This great high priest is risen and exalted, enthroned at the right hand of God, his intercession therefore the more effective.

The *RSV* rendering of v. 26, **For it was fitting that we should have such a high priest,** is rather flat and prosaic, and obscures the fact that 'high priest' is the subject of the sentence: 'such an high priest became us' (*AV*), 'does indeed fit our condition' (*NEB*). This is the kind of high priest we need. It should be noted that Melchizedek is not mentioned further; he has served his purpose. Attention is now concentrated entirely on Jesus. Montefiore sees the following string of attributes as presenting a series of contrasts between Jesus and the levitical priesthood, but as he himself admits these contrasts are 'only implicit'. It is not likely that the author, had he intended them, would have left it to the ingenuity of his readers to spell them out, and in any case he has already demonstrated to the full the superiority of Jesus. The climactic, culminating contrast is still to come, in verses 27–28. It is better and simpler to take these attributes as a characterisation of the kind of priest who is appropriate to our condition, rather than to read into them something the author may never have intended. First come three adjectives, **holy, blameless, unstained**; then two descriptive phrases, **separated from sinners, exalted above the heavens.** The adjectives, as a glance at English versions will show, admit of various renderings: **holy** is not the common word (*hagios*) used with reference to the Holy Spirit at 2:4; 3:7 and 6:4 above and commonly translated 'saints' when it refers to people, but another word (*hosios*) which means 'holy' in the sense of 'devout (*NEB*), pious, pleasing to God' (*BAG* 585b). In LXX it frequently renders the Hebrew *hasid* with reference to the godly man (e.g. Ps. 16:10). Its connotations are thus of piety and devotion, of consecration to the service of God, and this in the most genuine sense, without any of the associations of sanctimonious piety which sometimes attach to such terms. **Blameless** is more accurately 'innocent, guileless' (*BAG* 29a); the word is used at Rom. 16:18 of the unsuspecting (*RSV* 'the simple-minded';

NEB 'innocent people). If etymology were given weight, it would refer to one in whom there is no evil. **Unstained**, finally, is 'undefiled' (*NEB*), 'pure' in a religious or moral sense. It is used of the inheritance 'imperishable, undefiled and unfading' in 1 Pet. 1:4, but this appears to be the only case in which it is used of a person (cf. *BAG* 46a). Bruce observes that Philo 'can speak of the Logos as the ideal high priest, free from all defilement', using this same word (*Spec. Leg.* I.113; *Fug.* 108ff.), but adds in a footnote: 'Philo is concerned to present the undefiled character of the Logos as the truth denoted allegorically by the law forbidding the high priest to touch a corpse or mourn for the dead'. Christians on the other hand 'have as their high priest one who does not remain in the realm of ideas but is the incarnate Logos, one who preserved His purity while treading the common ways of this world and sharing our human lot'. This is in fact one more illustration of the danger of assuming that common ideas and common terminology are pointers to a genetic relationship between two authors, or two groups. We have to examine the ways in which the ideas and the terminology are used on either side, for there may be not only similarities but also distinctive differences (on the Logos and the High Priest in Philo and Hebrews, see generally Williamson, pp. 409ff.). In the present instance we have on the one hand a Jew endeavouring to interpret the Old Testament in terms of Greek philosophy, using the allegorical method of exegesis in the attempt to demonstrate that all the wisdom of the Greeks is already there in the inspired teaching of Moses; and on the other hand a Christian seeking to use the same Old Testament to encourage his fellow-Christians to perseverance and to greater zeal. The similarities are due to a common background, the more especially if the author of Hebrews was like Philo a man of Alexandria, but they are not such as to require direct dependence on the writings of Philo.

The levitical priests were required to be 'holy to their God' (Lev. 21:6) by the observance of strict rules of ritual purity (see the whole chapter in Leviticus, and for the high priest verses 10–15; the priest in the parable of the Good Samaritan, who 'passed by on the other side' (Luke 10:31), would have been defiled had he come into contact with a dead body). These three adjectives in v. 26 affirm that Jesus possesses in himself the purity and holiness which the priests were required to maintain by ritual observance. The two descriptive phrases following go together, the second explaining the first. **Separated from sinners** might at first sight seem to suggest an aloofness at variance with the solidarity with his 'brethren' for which the author has argued earlier (according to rabbinic sources the high priest was required to go into seclusion for seven days before the ceremony of the Day of Atonement), but in fact it is clarified by the addition of **exalted above the heavens**. It is the risen and exalted Jesus who is in view here, who in the words of the prologue 'when he had made purification for sins, sat down at the right hand of the Majesty on high'. He was known in his earthly life as the friend of sinners, but in his sinlessness (cf. 4:15) remained in some sense apart from them. Now in his exaltation he is definitely separated from them, but as 4:15 reminds us is still able to 'sympathise' with their weaknesses. This separation involves no ostracism.

27. Verse 27 presents a problem, in that the high priest did not offer sacrifices **daily**, first for his own sins and then for those of the people. That was the ritual of the Day of Atonement, which was celebrated only once in the year. Daily sacrifices were offered by the priests, but the high priest did not necessarily himself take part. There were also offerings *for* the high priest, but again he did not always himself officiate. Attempts have been made to meet the difficulty, e.g. by suggesting that the meaning is 'on each Day of Atonement', but that does violence to the meaning of the Greek (Williamson, pp. 178ff. lists no fewer than five explanations which have been advanced). Since Philo also speaks of the high priest offering up prayers and sacrifices 'every day' (*Spec. Leg.* III. 131), it might be thought that both writers are guilty of a confusion due to their remoteness from Jerusalem; but a later verse (9: 7: **and he but once a year**) shows that our author is perfectly aware of the real situation. It must be concluded that he is combining the two rituals for his own purposes. The one offering of Christ is contrasted with the repeated sacrifices of the levitical priests; that the daily sacrifices were offered by other priests does not greatly matter, since the high priest was at their head and might be presumed to be acting through them. What is more important is the second part of the verse: **he did this once for all when he offered up himself**. Later our author will argue that the very repetition of the sacrifices of the old dispensation is proof of their inadequacy. Jesus by offering up himself has accomplished **once** and **for all** what the repeated sacrifices of the old order could not achieve. Verse 28 then sums up the argument and underlines the contrast: **the law appoints men in their weakness as high priests, but the word of the oath, which came later than the law, appoints a Son who has been made perfect for ever**. Some commentators, like Montefiore, attach the words **for ever** to the verb **appoints**, but the Greek word order rules this out. The point is, as the perfect tense shows, that the struggle towards perfection is now over. We have thus the contrast between the priests of the old order, beset by human frailty and

operating on the purely human level, many in number because of
the essentially transitory character of their office (v. 23), and on the
other hand the one great high priest of the new order, who is
supremely qualified to fulfil his function, the Son made perfect for
ever. In the following chapters the author will develop and enlarge
upon this theme.

   This chapter is clearly central to the letter, and not just in the
superficial sense that there are six chapters before it and six more
to follow. The chapter and verse divisions were introduced at a
much later date, and in any case the symmetry is not quite complete.
The six following chapters are somewhat longer than the first six,
and while the earlier chapters can be said to prepare the ground it
is not altogether the case that the following chapters spell out the
implications of this seventh chapter. That is certainly true for the
next three chapters, but it is not so clear for the long roll of the
'heroes of faith' in chapter eleven or for the two final chapters. It
is in terms of content that this chapter is central: the ground was
prepared in the demonstration of the humanity of Jesus in earlier
chapters, his 'sympathy' with his 'brethren', and in the anticipatory
allusions at various points to his priesthood 'after the order of
Melchizedek'. Having now dealt with this theme, and demonstrated
the superiority of this other priesthood, the author will go on in
what follows to show what it means in terms of covenant and
sacrifice, and in effective dealing with sin.
   The evidence of *Melchizedek* speculation provided by Philo and
in such texts as the Qumran *11Q Melchizedek* or the Nag Hammadi
tractate *Melchizedek* shows that there was a considerable amount of
interest in this figure, but not all of this speculation is directly
relevant for Hebrews, and indeed some of the later speculation is
based on Hebrews itself. For our author, Melchizedek is only a
starting-point, the basis for an argument to prove the superiority of
the new order. It is significant that he disappears once he has served
his purpose; there is no further mention of him after verse 17.
The Genesis narrative with its reference to Melchizedek's blessing
Abraham, and receiving from him 'a tenth part of everything',
provides the basis for the argument that he is therefore superior to
Abraham, for 'the inferior is blessed by the superior'. Not only that,
since Levi was yet unborn he could be claimed to have paid tithes
through Abraham. This holds also for Levi's descendants the levitical priests, so that a priesthood 'after the order of Melchizedek' is
superior to the levitical priesthood. The possible objection that Jesus
belonged to a different tribe altogether is brushed aside: the old
priesthood was ineffective, or there would have been no need for

change. Since priesthood and law were closely linked, the 'old
commandment' itself is set aside, and in its place a 'better hope' is
introduced, guaranteed by the divine oath with which Ps. 110:4
begins. A further argument is drawn from the fact that 'the former
priests were many in number, because they were prevented by death
from continuing in office'. Their priesthood was at best temporary
and transient, whereas Jesus 'holds his priesthood permanently,
because he continues for ever'. Finally the closing verses of the
chapter draw the threads together in their description of the perfection of this great high priest, who is completely appropriate to our
need. Where the sacrifices of the levitical priesthood require to be
constantly repeated, his sacrifice was offered once and for all. Where
the law 'appoints men in their weakness', the oath which came after
the law appoints a Son 'made perfect for ever'.

PRIEST IN THE HEAVENLY SANCTUARY

8:1–7

1. The author now begins a new section which extends to 10:18,
comparing and contrasting the ordinances of the old covenant and
the new, the ritual and sacrifices of the old order which are but a
shadow and the reality that is now available. The *RSV* translation
now the point in what we are saying might seem to suggest that
he is beginning with a summary and recapitulation of what he has
already said, and this has in fact been a common interpretation
(Moffatt: 'the point of all this'; *NEB* 'now this is my main point';
cf. Coverdale's rendering 'the pith'); but it is open to question
whether it is correct. Montefiore for example writes: 'The reasoning
was complex, and our author, instead of giving a summary of it all,
underlines its salient point so that he can build upon it the next
stage of his argument', but even this is not entirely correct. Verses
1–2 barely mention that **we have such a high priest**, only to go on
to an echo of the prologue **who is seated at the right hand of the
throne of the Majesty in heaven** (cf. 1:3), and then introduce a
new theme, **a minister in the sanctuary and the true tent**. Manson
(p. 123) writes that the accepted rendering does not do justice to
the writer's train of thought, or to 'the heightened elevation of the
stage to which the argument ascends'. The Greek word can refer to
a sum of money (Ac. 22:28, the only other occurrence in the *NT*),
or it can mean 'gist' or 'point' (cf. *BAG* 429b–430a), but such a
rendering here 'throws us too much back on the past course of the
argument, and fails to bring out the transcendent character of the

vista which here opens to our eyes'. Accordingly he suggests the translation 'And now to crown the argument' (cf. Williamson pp. 123–129: the word occurs in Philo, but in the sense of 'pith' or 'main point' it is so common in other writers also that there is nothing distinctively Philonic about it; in the sense of 'crown of the argument' there are no parallels in Philo). These verses, then, do not merely summarise what has gone before; they introduce the crown and culmination of the author's argument. This is no mere earthly priest, but a great high priest eternal in the heavens, ministering in the heavenly sanctuary. What this means he now goes on to show.

2. The word rendered **minister** was used of the angels at 1:7 above ('servants') and the cognate adjective ('ministering') at 1:14; at Rom. 13:6 it is used of civil authorities as 'ministers of God', at Rom. 15:16 of Paul himself as 'minister of Christ to the Gentiles', at Phil. 2:25 of Epaphroditus as the Philippians' 'minister' to Paul's need. It is the context here that marks the difference: this is no ordinary service, but a ministry in the true and eternal sanctuary. In classical Greek this group of words, from which our English 'liturgy' is derived, was used of public service rendered by an individual to the state (e.g. the fitting out of a warship), but in the *NT* and early Christian literature they have almost exclusively religious connotations (cf. *BAG* 470b–471). The **sanctuary** is literally 'the holies' or 'the holy things', a sense in which the word is used in Philo (*Leg. all.* III. 135 'minister of sacred things', actually the same three Greek words as here, but in a different order; cf. *de Fug.* 93); but for one thing the word is used regularly for the **sanctuary** or Holy Place in the following chapter (9:2, 8, 12, 24, 25; cf. 10:19; 13:11), and for another it is more precisely defined by the following reference to **the true tent which is set up not by man but by the Lord.** Here the Greek contains an echo of Num. 24:6 LXX (cf. Exod. 33:7). The word translated **true** is not the usual word, which does not occur in Hebrews, but a cognate term with associations of genuineness or reality. What is meant is made clear in verse 5: when Moses was about to pitch the tabernacle in the wilderness, he was instructed: **See that you make everything according to the pattern which was shown you on the mountain** (Exod. 25.40). The 'tent' which Moses pitched was therefore only a copy and shadow of the heavenly sanctuary, the true tent set up not by man but by God himself.

3. Verse 3 recalls what was already said before (5:1), that **every high priest is appointed to offer gifts and sacrifices.** That is the normal function of priesthood. Therefore **it is necessary for this priest also to have something to offer**: Jesus is no exception. The

nature of his offering has already been indicated at 7:27, and is
further developed at 9:14, 24ff., but there is one small nuance of
Greek grammar which calls for attention here: the first **to offer** in
the present verse renders a present infinitive, which implies continuity and repetition, whereas the second translates an aorist
subjunctive ('something which he might offer'), which refers simply
to the action without specifying its time or suggesting repetition.
The latter is therefore 'consistent with our author's repeated
emphasis on the singularity of the sacrifice which Christ offered'
(Bruce, comparing 7:27, 10:12). Jesus has no need to offer sacrifices
daily, like earthly priests; he did that once for all when he offered
up himself (cf. 7:27). There is no implication that he continues to
offer himself in expiation for sins: expiation is mentioned as part of
his priestly function at 2:17, but already in the prologue it is said,
'when he had made purification for sins, he sat down at the right
hand of the Majesty on high' (1:3). We may therefore conclude that
for our author the sacrifice offered by the great high priest is already
in the past. 'Jesus' present ministry in heaven is intercession, not
offering' (Montefiore, who removes all ambiguity by translating 'it
was necessary for him too *to have had* something to offer'; cf. *NEB*
margin 'must have had'). As Moffatt noted long ago, the analogy
of the high priest 'had its obvious limitations'; it is important not
to press analogies too far. The point is made explicitly by our author
himself at 9:25 below: 'Nor was it to offer himself repeatedly, as
the high priest enters the Holy Place yearly . . .'. As to the nature
of Christ's offering, the author will speak in the next chapter of his
entering the heavenly sanctuary 'taking not the blood of goats and
calves but his own blood' (9:12). This must refer to his sacrificial
death, but that was for cleansing and purification (9:14); the closing
verses of the chapter make it abundantly clear that it is something
not to be repeated (9:25–28).

4–5. The following verse seems at first sight to hark back to the
argument of 7:11, where the author was concerned to demonstrate
the inadequacy and insufficiency of the levitical priesthood. Here
however the emphasis is different: in fact, he gives a positive recognition to that priesthood. It was divinely appointed and the priests
offered their gifts **according to the law**. Because of this Jesus, **if
he were on earth, would not be a priest at all**. There can be no
thought of anyone usurping the status, the privileges and the duties
of the levitical priesthood. Yet their ministry and service are still
inadequate, because they are offered on a merely earthly level. As
verse 5 puts it, **they serve a copy and shadow of the heavenly
sanctuary**, whereas Jesus is priest in the heavenly sanctuary. The
argument here, as already noted, is based on the instructions given

to Moses at Exod. 25:40, that everything should be made **according to the pattern which was shown you on the mountain**. The earthly sanctuary is thus only a reproduction, a copy, of the true heavenly sanctuary (cf. v. 2). This contrast of the earthly and the heavenly sanctuaries readily lends itself to interpretation in terms of Plato's theory of ideas, the contrast of the real and ideal worlds, and has been a major factor in the views of those who have stressed the 'Alexandrianism' of the epistle. As Williamson remarks, 'At first sight 8:5 seems to consist of pure Platonism' (p. 557; see the whole section, pp. 557–570). This is however another case where a superficial similarity may be misleading. At 2:5 above it was noted that the Jewish idea of the two worlds, this present world and the world to come, could be, and sometimes was, fused together with the Platonic conception of the visible and intelligible worlds, although they are in fact distinct, and the same is true here. The idea of heavenly worship in a heavenly sanctuary had long been familiar in Judaism, quite apart from any Platonic influence (Manson, p. 124 notes that R. H. Charles cites as evidence *Test. Levi* III.5, where the angels and archangels of the presence 'minister and make propitation to the Lord for all the ignorance-sins of the righteous'). To see what a Platonising interpreter could make of the Exodus passage we have to turn to the Philonic evidence examined by Williamson (*Qu. in Ex.* II. 52; *Leg. all.* III. 102; *de Plant.* 27; *vit. Mos.* II. 74–75). One of Philo's aims is apologetic, to show that all the wisdom of the Greeks is already contained in the inspired teaching of Moses, but there is nothing of that in Hebrews. If our author's background was in Alexandrian Judaism, as would seem quite likely, he could have known the language of Alexandrian Jewish philosophy as represented by Philo, even perhaps have read some of Philo's writings; but that does not mean that he must have been profoundly influenced by them. What we have in fact is two ways of thinking developed independently, which in some respects show clear similarities and could therefore be combined; but we must beware of converting 'parallels into influences and influences into sources' (Ellis, *Paul's Use of the OT*, Edinburgh [1957], p. 82). As Williamson says (p. 569), 'the "Platonism" of Hebrews has to be sought for; it is at most vestigial'. Similarly Manson writes (p. 125) that 'the element of Alexandrianism does not enter into the Epistle until this point is reached, and it is not continued after this point is passed'. One small but telling point is that the word here rendered **pattern** is used by Philo, in a technical sense, 'to designate the more insignificant copy, not to designate the more important prototype' as in Hebrews (Goppelt, *Typos*, ET Grand Rapids [1982], p. 177; for typology in Hebrews, see pp. 161–178).

6–7. Verse 6 sums up the argument, and introduces a new element, already hinted at, after the writer's usual custom, at 7:22 above ('This makes Jesus the surety of a better covenant'): **he has obtained a ministry which is as much more excellent than the old as the covenant he mediates is better.** This is developed and expounded in the following section, on the basis of an extended quotation from Jeremiah. Verse 7 puts the argument in a nutshell: as with the priesthood at 7:11 above, the very fact that there is reference to a new covenant is proof that the old was inadequate. If the old covenant had been perfect, there would have been no need for it to be superseded. The idea of the **covenant** goes back to the Old Testament, where there are numerous references: a covenant with Noah (Gen. 6:18 and especially ch. 9), with Abraham (Gen. 15:18 and esp. ch. 17), but above all the covenant made with the people under Moses on Mt Sinai (Exod. 24:7–8; cf. Dt. 5:2f.). The word employed in LXX and in the New Testament is not the usual Greek word for a contract or agreement, evidently because it was felt to suggest a compact between equals, but a related word which in hellenistic Greek means a will or testament (it is so translated at 9:16f. below; cf. Gal. 3:15, where however some commentators prefer the translation 'covenant' (e.g. Lightfoot or Duncan *ad loc.*), the more particularly in view of the clear reference to the covenant with Abraham in v. 17). It is from this usage, via the Latin *testamentum*, that our modern division of the Bible into the Old Testament (or Covenant) and the New is derived. The point here is that the usual Greek word refers to an agreement between two parties on a more or less equal footing, but in God's covenant with Israel that is not the case: the covenant is a mark of God's gracious goodness towards his people. It is God who initiates the covenant; the duty of Israel is acceptance, and the responsibility of obedience. There are repeated references to Israel's breaking of transgression of the covenant, but throughout the Old Testament there is a firm confidence in God's faithfulness to his promises. Since it is God alone who sets the conditions, the word used here sometimes takes on the meaning of 'decree' or 'ordinance', a declaration of God's will (cf. *BAG* 183a). Incidentally, it is sometimes used in LXX even for an agreement between two persons (e.g. Gen. 21:27, of the 'covenant' between Abraham and Abimelech). The one place in the Old Testament which speaks of a new covenant superseding the one made through Moses is the passage in Jeremiah quoted below (Jer. 31:31–34), but this idea was to be of great importance in later Judaism and particularly for the Christian Church. It was for example fundamental to the Qumran community, who saw themselves as fulfilling Jeremiah's prophecy in their separ-

ation from the 'wicked of Israel': 'Consistent with their approach
to legal matters, their attitude in regard to the Covenant was that
only the initiates of their own "new Covenant" were to be reckoned
among God's elect' (Vermes, *The Dead Sea Scrolls: Qumran in
Perspective*, Cleveland [1978], p. 170; see the whole chapter,
pp. 163ff.)

At 7:22 above Jesus is called the surety (*NEB* 'guarantor') of a
new covenant; here he is its mediator. The translation **the covenant
he mediates** (cf. *NEB*) paraphrases slightly (lit. he is mediator of
a better covenant), but brings out the sense more clearly. A mediator
is one who intervenes between two parties, with a view to effecting
reconciliation, an arbiter in a dispute; so Jesus in 1 Tim. 2:5 is
called mediator between God and men. The covenant however, as
already noted, is not an agreement between two parties of equal
standing, so that this sense is not altogether appropriate here. At
Gal. 3:19-20 the word is applied to Moses: the law was 'ordained
by angels through an intermediary'. These two verses in Galatians
present problems of interpretation, but it is clear that they are meant
to show the inferior character of the law (cf. 2:1-4 above). Whether
the author is consciously thinking of Moses here may be open to
question, but the Galatians passage points to the right interpretation:
Jesus is the intermediary through whom the new and better covenant
is given. It may be added that the cognate verb is used above (the
only occurrence in the New Testament) at 6:17, where it is said
that God 'interposed' with an oath. The sense is that of intervention
as the agent in transmission from one party to the other. The new
covenant is **enacted**, legally secured, **on** the basis of **better promises**. What these promises are will be shown in the following verses.

These verses form the transition to a new section in a carefully
constructed argument, preparing the way for the quotation from
Jeremiah which follows in verses 8-12 and the discussion of the
heavenly service rendered by Jesus at 9:11ff. In earlier chapters the
author has demonstrated the humanity of Jesus, his sympathy and
understanding, and claimed for him a new priesthood 'after the
order of Melchizedek', a priesthood of a new and different quality,
far surpassing that of the old dispensation. The theme of priesthood
was first introduced, almost in passing, at 2:17, then developed with
a reference to the great high priest who has passed through the
heavens at 4:14ff. This new priesthood is contrasted with the old
in chapter 7: the very fact that a new priesthood should be spoken
of is proof that the old was inadequate and ineffective. This theme
will be further developed later. Now we move to the 'transcendent
vista' of which Manson wrote, the heavenly service rendered by the

great high priest in the heavenly sanctuary. One point should be emphasised, that it is the same Jesus who 'in the days of his flesh . . . offered up prayers and supplications' (5:7), who 'in every respect has been tempted as we are' (4:15), who now ministers in the heavenly sanctuary. As the author himself puts it later (13:8), 'Jesus Christ is the same yesterday and today and forever'. There can be no question of a merely human Jesus who walked on earth and a distinct and separate great high priest transcendent in the heavens; they are one and the same. This has important implications, some of which our author himself spells out, but he never explains in detail the relation between the Son of his prologue, the earthly Jesus and the great high priest. That for him they are one is clear enough, and the transition from the earthly Jesus to the exalted great high priest can easily be accounted for on the basis of the resurrection and exaltation of Jesus; but whether he considered the earthly Jesus as in some sense divine, and if so how he thought of the relation between the divine and the human, is by no means clear. That was to be a problem for a later age. There are obvious affinities with the *Carmen Christi* in Philippians 2, but that passage too presents its problems, as the literature devoted to it shows.

THE OLD COVENANT AND THE NEW

8:8–13

8. As already noted, verse 7 puts the argument in a nutshell: **if that first covenant had been faultless, there would have been no occasion for a second.** This is now developed and expanded by a scriptural proof from the prophecies of Jeremiah, the one passage in the Old Testament, as it happens, to speak of a new covenant. Here the difference between our author's approach and that of a modern scholar is particularly marked. The modern scholar would have to consider the authenticity of the passage, since it has been questioned, and then try to set it in its proper context. An agreement between two parties is only valid so long as both abide by it. Now there are numerous references in the Old Testament to Israel's transgression or breach of the covenant; even the reforms of Josiah (2 Kings 22–23) proved ineffective. It is in this context that Jeremiah (31:31–34) proclaims his vision of a new covenant, no longer a matter of outward regulation but one of inner renewal, a law written not on tablets of stone like that of Moses, or in a book like Josiah's 'book of the law', but in the hearts of men. For our author some of these questions are of no concern; it is the idea of a new covenant

that draws his attention. As with his other quotations, he regards
these words as spoken by God himself, a procedure here facilitated
by the fact that Jeremiah already proclaimed them as a word of the
Lord (cf. verses 8, 10). Hence God **finds fault** with his people **when
he says: 'The days will come . . . when I will establish a new
covenant'**.

9–12. Comparison with the Old Testament shows only a few
changes, although occasionally the same thing is said in slightly
different wording by the use of synonyms. In verse 9 **and so I paid
no heed to them** probably goes back to the use of a different
Hebrew text by the LXX translators; a difference of one letter would
be enough. The Hebrew 'though I was their husband' recalls the
frequent use in the prophets of the imagery of Israel as the errant
bride of Yahweh (there is an interesting *catena* of such passages in
the Nag Hammadi *Exegesis on the Soul*, *NHC* II 129.5ff.). In verse
10 the Hebrew reads **I will put** my law within them, but **into their
minds** is a natural expansion, forming a parallelism with **on their
hearts** in the next line. The point about this new covenant is that
it will not be a series of external regulations to be observed; obedience will come from the heart. Bruce compares Ezek. 11:19f.: 'I
will take the stony heart out of their flesh and give them a heart of
flesh, that they may walk in my statutes and keep my ordinances
and obey them'. The flaw in the old covenant was that it was
external; at Sinai and later under Josiah the people promised to
keep it, but they were unable to fulfil their promise. In similar
fashion Paul can write that 'the law is holy, and the commandment
is holy and just and good' (Rom. 7:12), but continue later 'I do not
do the good I want, but the evil I do not want is what I do' (verse
19). The new covenant involves a new relationship, based on direct
and first-hand knowledge of God: **they shall not teach every man
his fellow . . . for all shall know me** (v. 11). The promise in verse
10, **I will be their God and they shall be my people**, is not in itself
new, but in substance a promise oft repeated from the time of the
Exodus on (cf. e.g. Exod. 6:7; 29:45; Lev. 26:12; Ezek. 37:27. In
the latter context (v. 26) Ezekiel speaks of a covenant of peace. At
2 C. 6:16 the promise is claimed for the people of the new covenant).
What is new is the character of the relationship which Jeremiah
prophesied and our author claims to be now inaugurated. Finally
the last verse of the quotation brings the promise of forgiveness: **I
will be merciful toward their iniquities, and I will remember their
sins no more**. This too is a note often struck in the Old Testament,
as numerous references to God's mercy, long-suffering and forgiveness show. The God of the Old Testament is not an arbitrary and
vindictive tyrant—the distinction between the merely righteous God

of the Old Testament and the loving God and Father of our Lord
Jesus Christ was the heresy of Marcion in the second Christian
century, the degrading of the Old Testament Creator into a hostile
Demiurge who seeks to hold the human race captive was the work
of Christian gnostics about the same period. Of this there is nothing
in Hebrews. It has to be remembered that the Old Testament is the
product of development over many centuries, during which ideas
about God changed quite considerably. There is undoubtedly an
aspect of sternness and severity, particularly where the sins of the
people are in view, and this continues into the New Testament (cf.
for example 10:26–27 and 31 below); but the covenant was a mark
of God's love and grace in the first place.

13. Verse 13 finally rounds off the section: **in speaking of a new
covenant he treats the first as obsolete** (lit. has made it old or
antiquated). **And what is becoming obsolete** (the same verb in the
present tense) **and growing old is ready to vanish away** (lit. is near
to disappearance or destruction; cf. *NEB*: anything that is growing
old and ageing will shortly disappear). The old covenant belongs to
the past; it is the new that now matters. The old is indeed still in
existence, but it is antiquated and outmoded, superseded by the
new, and will soon pass away.

At this point there is one telling argument which the author might
have used at any time after the fall of Jerusalem and the destruction
of the Temple in AD 70: that destruction proves that the old order
is a thing of the past. The fact that he does not use this argument,
but speaks of the old covenant as soon to pass, **ready to vanish
away,** has been taken by some to show that he wrote before that
date. This is however not so conclusive as might at first appear.
The author nowhere mentions the Temple, nor is he greatly
concerned with events in contemporary history. It is of the tent that
he speaks, the tabernacle in the wilderness, and his whole argument
is based on interpretation of Scripture, not upon contemporary
history. This point is therefore not so conclusive for the dating of
the letter as some have thought. Whatever the date at which he
wrote, our author shares the conviction of early Christians that they
were living in the last days (cf. 1:2): the Day is approaching (10:25),
the time of reformation (9:10) drawing near; he and his readers have
already tasted the heavenly gift, the powers of the age to come
(6:4–5); all the more reason for holding their first confidence firm
to the end (3:14). The old age is passing away, and the new age has
already dawned, but there is a danger that all may yet be lost. It is
this that gives urgency to his message (on the eschatology of
Hebrews cf. C. K. Barrett in *The Background of the NT and its*

Eschatology, (ed.) Davies and Daube, Cambridge [1964], pp. 363–393).

The name of Jeremiah has become proverbial for a prophet of doom. Like other prophets, he castigated the sins and shortcomings of the people, in particular their reliance on the external formalities of religion at the expense of the realities. But the 'dismal jeremiad' is not the whole story: he bought a field at Anathoth when the area was in enemy hands, which is not the act of a thorough-going pessimist; as Jer. 32:15 indicates, it was intended to be symbolic of confidence that God had a future for Israel. There are other such passages, but the most influential was undoubtedly the one quoted here. As already noted, it was fundamental for the Qumran community, who saw themselves as 'men of the covenant' (the Damascus Rule actually speaks of 'the members of the New Covenant in the land of Damascus'; see Vermes, *The Dead Sea Scrolls in English*, p. 103, also pp. 35ff.). There is however a difference, in that for them, in Vermes' words, 'the obligations imposed by the New Covenant were materially the same as those implicit in the Old'. In other words, it was a renewal of the old covenant and a stricter observance, whereas what is in view in Hebrews is rather a new covenant altogether. Paul in similar terms contrasts the splendour of the old dispensation with that of the new (2 C. 3:7), and speaks of himself as minister of 'a new covenant, not in a written code but in the Spirit; for the written code kills, but the Spirit gives life'. In his account of the Last Supper, the earliest report we have, Paul records the words of Jesus over the cup as 'This cup is the new covenant in my blood' (1 C. 11:25). This suggests the possibility that Jesus himself may have thought in terms of the inauguration of a new covenant, but the question is complicated by textual problems in the Synoptic narratives: the word 'new' in some manuscripts at Mt. 26:28 and Mk 14:24 is not in the major manuscripts, and while it has strong support is open to suspicion of being a later assimilation. The longer text at Lk. 22:20 (see *RSV* margin) does speak of a new covenant, but here there are no fewer than six forms of the text, and it has been claimed that the long version including verse 20 is due to assimilation to Paul. However, as Barrett points out (*The First Epistle to the Corinthians*, p. 268), both forms of the saying, with or without the word 'new', presuppose 'that the shedding of the blood of Christ inaugurated a new covenant between God and man'. For background, Barrett refers to Exod. 24:8 and Jer. 31:31–34. It is therefore not without reason that Dodd can write, 'Although there is only one place where the prophecy of the New Covenant is expressly cited as from scripture, it seems clear

that it was widely influential in the Church from an early date'
(*According to the Scriptures*, p. 46; see his discussion, pp. 44ff.). As
to the 'better promises' mentioned in verse 6 above, they are neatly
summed up by Dodd (p. 45) as follows: (a) the law written on the
heart; (b) the intimate relation of God and his people; (c) knowledge
of God; and (d) forgiveness of sins. As Dodd says, 'These features
crop up in various combinations in New Testament writers'.

THE INSTITUTIONS OF THE FIRST COVENANT

9:1–10

1. In the preceding chapter the author compared and contrasted the
old or first covenant and the new in general terms. Now he goes on
to a more detailed comparison. Verses 1–10 set out the ordinances
and arrangements of the first covenant, while the remainder of the
chapter is devoted to a series of contrasts demonstrating the superiority of the new. **Even the first covenant had regulations for
worship and an earthly sanctuary**. It was not deficient in that
respect, indeed the description that follows is explicitly related to
the account of the making of the tabernacle in Exodus, where Moses
acts according to God's express command (Exod. 25: 1; detailed
instructions follow in succeeding chapters. See also the account of
the execution of the work in chapters 35–40, the last two of which
have the recurrent refrain 'as the Lord had commanded Moses').
Having mentioned first the regulations and then the sanctuary, the
author characteristically begins with the latter. The word translated
earthly occurs in the New Testament only here and at Tit. 2:12,
where it refers to 'wordly' passions, but it could be understood in
a variety of ways. Philo and Josephus use it of the Temple as a
place of *public* worship as opposed to local synagogues or houses of
prayer. They also toy with the idea that the Temple is symbolic of
the universe (it is the word from which the English 'cosmic' is
derived), but there is nothing of that here. Our author refers to this
sanctuary simply as **an earthly sanctuary**, in contrast to the heavenly
one which will be described later. Here again it is easy to see possible
links with Plato's theory of ideas, but as Barrett roundly declares
'the heavenly tabernacle in Hebrews is not the product of Platonic
idealism, but the eschatological temple of apocalyptic Judaism'
(*Dodd Festschrift*, p. 389).

2. The description of the **tent** is at first confusing, since our
author seems to speak of two tents, one behind the other. Actually
the description in Exodus 26 is of a single tent (the tabernacle,

verses 1–6) with an outer covering (the tent over the tabernacle, verses 7–14). The inner tent was divided into two parts by a veil or curtain (verses 31–33), which separated the holy place from the most holy. This our author calls **the second curtain**, naturally enough since there was also a screen at the outer door of the tent (Exod. 26:36–37). The whole was intended to be a portable shrine which could be set up where the people camped on their journeyings. The outer 'tent' contained **the lampstand** with its seven branches, described in Exod. 25:31–39, **the table** described in Exod. 25:23–29, and **the bread of the Presence** (Exod. 25:30). This bread, better known as the shewbread, consisted of twelve 'cakes' or loaves of fine flour set out in two rows upon the table (Lev. 24:5–9). This bread was renewed every sabbath, and the loaves removed consumed by the priests. Jesus in the Gospels (Mk 2:27 par.) recalls the episode of 1 Sam. 21:1–6, in which David is given the shewbread, 'which it is not lawful for any but the priests to eat', because there was no other bread available. This outer tent the author, like Exodus, calls the Holy Place. Montefiore objects to this translation, on the ground that the usage would be unparalleled in the epistle. The Greek word could be either a feminine singular, agreeing with 'tent', or a neuter plural referring to the (inner) sanctuary (as at 13:11; at 9:25 *RSV* wrongly translates as 'the Holy Place'). Accordingly he translates 'this Tent is called Holy'. In terms of Greek grammar and consistency of usage this may be right, but it is in any case the Holy Place of Exodus 26:33 that is in view.

3–5. **Behind the second curtain** was an inner tent called **the Holy of Holies**, to which the author later refers as the second tent (verse 7) or simply the sanctuary (see above). His usage is perfectly natural and presents no problems once it is related to the description in Exodus: there was a first or outer tent, and a second or inner tent, or more precisely an area partitioned off within the whole. In a modern frame tent there is a living area entered immediately from outside, and an inner tent, which may have several compartments, to serve as sleeping quarters. All becomes clear when we realise that the tabernacle was originally a dwelling-place for God when he chose to visit his people (cf. A. R. S. Kennedy in Hastings' *Dictionary of the Bible*, IV. pp. 655f.): the inner tent was thus his private quarters. The pattern was preserved in the construction of the Temple later, although of course the buildings were larger and more elaborate. The tabernacle itself was comparatively small. Incidentally, the use of the past tense in this description cannot be employed to suggest that the Temple was no more. As already noted, it is with the tabernacle in the wilderness that our author is concerned: this is how it was in his authority, the book of Exodus.

Verses 4–5 proceed to describe the furnishings of this inner sanctuary. The reference to **the golden altar of incense** presents some
problems: first of all, the word here used means 'properly a place
or vessel for the burning of incense, usually a censer' (*BAG* 365a),
and it is in this last sense that it is used in LXX. There is however
no mention of a censer in the Exodus description, and both Philo
(*Quis rerum* 226f.; *vit. Mos.* II. 94, 101 etc.) and Josephus (*Ant.*
III. 147, 198) employ the word for the altar of incense described in
Exod. 30:1–10, as do the translations of Theodotion and Symma-
chus. Since the word can refer either to a place or to a vessel for
burning incense, there is no real difficulty about understanding it
to mean the incense altar here (so *BAG*); the contemporary evidence
of Philo and Josephus is fairly decisive. It is almost certainly not
the censer of Lev. 16:12, which was brought within the veil from
outside. There is no indication that it was kept inside the inner
sanctuary, and in any case it was scarcely a significant enough item
to be mentioned separately. The real problem here is that in Exod.
30:6 Moses is told to place the incense altar 'before the veil that is
by the ark of the testimony 'cf. Exod. 40:26), which seems to mean
in front of or outside the curtain. Moreover Aaron is to burn incense
on it 'every morning when he dresses the lamps' (Exod. 30:7), which
would conflict with the ruling that the high priest should enter the
Holy of Holies only once a year: he could not burn incense daily
on an altar within the inmost sanctuary. It seems that there has
been some confusion here, but if there was a mistake, it was an
easy one to make: the Exodus description is in some respects vague,
the account of the incense altar comes not in the instructions for
the making of the tabernacle in Exod. 25–27 but later in Exod. 30,
and at 1 Kg. 6:22 we are told that Solomon overlaid with gold 'the
whole altar that belonged to the inner sanctuary'. Moreover at Exod.
30:10 Aaron is to 'make atonement upon its horns once a year' (cf.
atonement for the altar of sacrifice at Exod. 29:36–37). The altar of
incense played an important part in the ritual of the Day of Atonement (cf. Lev. 16): the Holy of Holies was never entered without
incense from this altar, and the blood of the sin-offering was sprinkled on the altar of incense as well as on the mercy seat (Exod.
30:10; Lev. 16:15, 18).

The ark of the covenant, made of acacia wood and **covered on
all sides with gold**, was the chief item of furniture in the tabernacle,
and indeed is the first to be mentioned in the instructions given to
Moses (Exod. 25:10ff.). At Exod. 25:16 Moses is commanded to
put into it 'the testimony which I shall give you' (hence it is sometimes called 'the ark of testimony'); in Dt. 10:1–5 it is said to have
contained the two tables of the ten commandments (the **tables of**

the covenant), and according to 1 Kg. 8:9 there was nothing in the
ark except these two tables. The jar of **manna** (Exod. 16:33–34,
called in Hebrews a **golden urn**) was placed 'before the Testimony,
to be kept', as was **Aaron's rod** (Num. 17:1–10), but the biblical
evidence does not say that they were kept in the ark. That they
were is a natural inference on the part of the author, or the tradition
before him, but still an inference. It should be remembered that
the last reference to the ark in the Old Testament is Jer. 3:16, and
that verse suggests that it was already lost: 'it shall not come to
mind, or be remembered, or missed; it shall not be made again'.
Our author knew only what was recorded in his Bible. In earlier
ages the ark was regarded with an awe and reverence verging on
superstition, as can be seen from 1 Sam. 4:3ff., where the people
took it into battle in the hope that it would bring them victory,
with disastrous results (cf. its effect upon the victorious Philistines
in the sequel, and the story of the unfortunate Uzzah in 2 Sam. 6).

The mercy seat was placed on top of the ark, with the two
cherubim, one at each end, overshadowing it with their wings
(Exod. 25:17–21). Both mercy seat and cherubim were of gold.
From the following verses in Exodus, the mercy seat appears to be
envisaged as a kind of throne from which God speaks; it is therefore
the earthly counterpart of the throne of grace mentioned above at
4:16. This also explains the phrase **the cherubim of glory**: the glory
is that of God himself, and they are the guardians of the divine
presence. The Greek word used here for the mercy seat is also
employed at Rom. 3:25, where Christ is put forward 'as an expiation
by his blood', the means of dealing with sin and reconciling man to
God; but there are problems in that passage which do not arise
here. The mercy seat was the place of expiation, and was sprinkled
with blood by the high priest every year on the Day of Atonement
(cf. Lev. 16:11–15).

All these items are simply listed one after the other, to set out
the furnishing and arrangements of the first sanctuary, but without
any detailed discussion: **of these things we cannot now speak in
detail**. Philo in particular enlarges upon them at various places, but
our author is not concerned with allegorical interpretation of the
Old Testament. He has more important interests, and is anxious to
press on.

6–7. Having dealt with the sanctuary, he now goes on to the
regulations for worship. **The priests go continually into the outer
tent, performing their ritual duties**. These included the trimming
of the lamps and the offering of incense, morning and evening
(Exod. 30:7–8), and the weekly changing of the shewbread (Lev.
24:5–9). These were the normal priestly duties in which every priest

took his part. In contrast, **only the high priest** entered into the 'second' tent, **and he but once a year.** His access to the inmost sanctuary, to the very presence of God, was therefore strictly limited. At 7:27 above it was noted that our author is guilty of an apparent error when he writes of the high priest offering sacrifices daily, but this verse shows that he is fully aware of the actual procedure. He was not a modern scholar writing with meticulous attention to every slightest detail! For his purposes his statement at 7:27, as with regard to the position of the altar of incense at v. 4 above, was accurate enough. It is not uncommon for preachers to make similar errors if they have not checked their references.

The one occasion was on the Day of Atonement. Lev. 16:1 speaks of the two sons of Aaron, who 'drew near before the Lord and died', because they had done so without due authority and observance of the correct formalities; so holy was the place. The rest of the chapter prescribes in detail the procedure to be followed by Aaron and his successors in the high priestly office: bathing to remove any bodily uncleanness, the wearing of special clothing, the 'holy garments'. The high priest was first to offer atonement for himself and his family with the blood of a bull, and then make the sin-offering for the people with the blood of a goat. He thus entered the inmost sanctuary at least twice on this day. Our author seems to telescope the whole procedure into one entrance when he writes **and not without taking blood which he offers for himself and for the errors of the people.** This is however due once more to the compression of his statement: the main point is that the high priest entered only once a year, and not without blood. Jesus on the other hand is permanently in the heavenly sanctuary, and has no need of atonement sacrifice: he accomplished the necessary sacrifice once for all when he offered up himself (7:27). It may be added that no reference is made to the second goat 'for Azazel' mentioned in Leviticus; it has no relevance to our author's purpose. **The errors of the people** are literally their sins of ignorance (cf. Num. 15:27–31: sins 'with a high hand' could not be atoned).

8. Verse 8 presents the author's interpretation: **By this the Holy Spirit indicates that the way into the sanctuary is not yet opened as long as the outer tent is still standing.** The following parenthesis **which is symbolic for the present age** comes close to the idea found in Philo and Josephus, that the Temple is symbolic of the universe, but the distinction here is the Jewish one between this present age and the age to come, not the Platonic distinction between the visible and intelligible worlds. Direct access to God is not possible under ordinary human conditions. At most one person, and he but once a year, after due preparation and under stringent precautions, might venture to enter into the holy place. The modern reader cannot but think of precautions against radio-activity at a nuclear plant. Such is the old order, which as 8:13 says is 'ready to vanish away'. The new has not yet fully come, but it has been inaugurated, for Jesus has already entered into the inner shrine behind the curtain as a forerunner on our behalf (6:19–20).

9. In the Greek, verses 6–10 form a single complex sentence, which in English versions is broken up into three or more shorter sentences for ease of comprehension. The parenthesis at the beginning of verse 9 is in some editions not so marked; in the Greek it is a relative clause which may be taken in several ways. The word behind **symbolic** is literally 'parable', and the obvious antecedent to the relative is 'tent' in verse 8 (both feminine singular). *NEB* however makes the reference more general: 'All this is symbolic, pointing to the present time'. The following clause is another relative clause, again with a feminine relative the natural antecedent to which is 'parable'. On a literal translation, then, the tent is a parable according to which gifts and sacrifices are offered. This is not entirely perspicuous and it is not surprising that modern English versions paraphrase in various ways, but the general sense is clear enough: in the old order, symbolised by the tent and all that pertains to it, **gifts and sacrifices are offered which cannot perfect the conscience of the worshipper.** The whole purpose of the ritual of atonement was to expiate the sins of the people, to remove their guilt, but this was possible only to a limited degree. As Bruce remarks, 'The reality effective barrier to a man's free access to God is an inward and not a material one; it exists in his conscience. It is only when the conscience is purified that a man is set free to approach God without reservation . . . And the sacrificial blood of bulls and goats is useless in this regard'.

10. Verse 10 then explains further: these gifts and sacrifices **deal only with food and drink and various ablutions, regulations for the body imposed until the time of reformation.** In other words they are in the first place purely external, and secondly they are of only temporary validity. It is not said that they are no longer valid; on the contrary, as with the priesthood above, their validity is expressly recognised. But it is for a limited period only. The most obvious explanation of the reference to food and drink is that it relates to the laws about clean and unclean foods (Lev. 16; Dt. 14:3–21), but the only reference to drink there concerns a vessel into which a dead unclean animal had fallen: 'all drink which may be drunk from every such vessel shall be unclean' (Lev. 16:34). It is important to remember that, strange though some of these regulations may appear to us, they were based on practical considerations of hygiene and are not merely arbitrary rules. In the present context however it is more probable that the reference is to food and drink *offerings* (cf. Exod. 29:40–41; 30:9; Lev. 23:13, 18, 37), the more particularly since so much of the preceding section has been based on Exodus.

The word translated **ablutions** was used at 6:2 above, where some commentators have seen a reference to Christian baptism (cf. *AV*), with or without reference to other rites. It was there argued that the reference is more general, and this is confirmed by the present passage, where even *AV* has 'washings'. The most obvious and natural reference here is to the requirement that the high priest should bathe before and after the ritual of the Day of Atonement (see Lev. 16:4, 24), but there were also other washing rites for the removal of defilement from persons or from objects (e.g. Lev. 6:27; 14:8; Num. 8:7; 1199:7f.). In this connection we may recall Josephus' description of John the Baptist (*Ant.* XVIII.117), according to which John taught that baptism would be acceptable to God if it was undertaken 'for purification of the body after the soul had been purified by righteousness'. A similar idea appears in the Qumran Community Rule (*IQS* III.4–9), where the 'stubborn of heart' 'shall neither be purified by atonement, nor cleansed by purifying waters, nor sanctified by seas and rivers, nor washed clean with any ablution'. Later we find, 'He shall be cleansed from all his sins by the spirit of holiness . . . And when his flesh is sprinkled with purifying water and sanctified with cleansing water, it shall be made clean by the humble submission of his soul to all the precepts of God' (Vermes, *The Dead Sea Scrolls in English*, pp. 74–75). Our author was not alone in stressing inward purity of conscience over against any mere outward cleanliness.

As the references supplied above show, this section summarises fairly accurately the instructions for the making of the tabernacle and its furnishings. There is an apparent slip with regard to the placing of the altar of incense, but that may be due to the compression of the account. Another possibility is that the author was misled by Lev. 16:13, where the high priest is to 'put the incense on the fire before the Lord'. This might have suggested that the altar of incense was already inside the inner sanctuary. At any rate such points of detail are not relevant to the author's main purpose. He is concerned only to sketch in broad outline the character and furnishings of the tent of the first covenant, and the ritual associated with it, in order to set over against them the greater splendours of the new covenant. It is however important to note that he does not merely repudiate or disparage the old. Like the

priesthood it has its validity, even if it is but a temporary one. It is
but a copy and shadow of the heavenly sanctuary, and is soon to
be superseded. Now he is ready to set forth the glories of the new
order.

THE ETERNAL REDEMPTION

9:11–14

We now approach the point for which the author has been carefully
preparing. The institutions and ordinances of the first covenant have
their validity, but it is a limited one. The gifts and sacrifices offered
deal only with external matters; they cannot perfect the conscience
of the worshipper. **But when Christ appeared as a high priest of
the good things that have come . . . he entered once for all into
the Holy Place.** This introduces the first of a series of contrasts: the
ritual of the old covenant is recognised as valid for the purification of
the flesh (v. 13), but Jesus secures an eternal redemption (v. 12),
his blood can purify the conscience (v. 14). Whereas the high priest
entered the earthly sanctuary yearly (v. 25). Christ enters once and
for all (this point was already made at 7:27, and will be repeated
and developed below).

    11. As the *RSV* margin notes, other manuscripts read *good things
to come*. This reading actually has a majority of manuscripts in its
favour, and is accepted by Montefiore for example, on the ground
that while Christians have tasted the powers of the age to come
(6:5), their salvation still lies in the future (1:14). The reading in
the text he considers 'intrinsically improbable'. On the other hand
Metzger (*Textual Commentary*, p. 668) writes that the reading **good
things that have come** 'appears to have superior attestation on the
score of age and diversity of text type ([p46] B D 1739 itd syrp, h pal
Origen *al*.)'. His suggestion that copyists writing the variant may
have been influenced by the expression in 10:1, where the text is
firm, is however less happy: why should copyists be influenced by
a passage that still lies ahead? The real arguments in favour of the
reading in our text are a) that of age and diversity of text type, and
b) that of content: salvation does indeed still lie in the future for
the readers, as it does for all of us, but it has already been inaugurated with the appearance of Christ as a great high priest. Commentators rightly remark on the note of triumph with which this section
begins. As Bruce puts it, Christ's entrance into the presence of God
'is not a day of soul-affliction and fasting . . . but a day of gladness
and song' (he refers to Lev. 16:29, 31; 23:26, 32). At 10:1 the whole

situation is different: from the standpoint of the law, the good things were indeed yet to come. In our author's view, it offered not the reality but only a shadowy anticipation.

Following the analogy of the ritual in the earthly sanctuary, as it is explained in verses 6–7 above, one might naturally think that the words **through the greater and more perfect tent** refer to the 'outer' tent. **The Holy Place** in verse 12 is then more properly the Holy of Holies, the inmost sanctuary. In that case Christ has passed through the greater and more perfect tent, the heavenly tabernacle, into the inmost sanctuary. This is of course true to the author's thought, but there are problems here: it is not what he actually says, and the order of the phrases is against it. The preposition 'through' can indeed refer to passage through a place, but it occurs three times in this sentence, and it would be distinctly awkward for it to be used with two different meanings (cf. *RSV* margin *through* for **taking** in verse 12). Since it is used instrumentally in the second and third instances (with reference first to **the blood of goats and calves** and then to **his own blood**), it should probably be given more of an instrumental than a local force here. In any case our author is not concerned with details of the ritual, or with establishing an exact parallel; these details belong to the old order that is 'ready to vanish away' (8:13). What matters to him is that Christ has passed through the heavens (4:14), has **entered once for all into the Holy Place** (9:12), and is now there permanently to appear in the presence of God on our behalf (9:24). The emphasis is not on the details of his progress into the sanctuary, but on the fact that he has entered once and for all.

The form of words used for the outer tent is literally 'the holies' and that for the inner sanctuary 'the holies of holies' (i.e. the most holy place of all). It is the first of these that is used in verse 12, as also at verse 15 below, so that to this extent the *RSV* rendering **the Holy Place** at both points is justified. At verse 25 however, the reference is unmistakably to the inner sanctuary, and as noted above the same may be true here. Since our author thought of the tabernacle as made by Moses 'according to the pattern which was shown you on the mountain' (8:5), he presumably envisaged the heavenly sanctuary as likewise consisting of two chambers, but he lays no stress upon this point. It is enough for him that the earthly tabernacle is but an inferior copy of a heavenly prototype; once he turns to his discussion of that heavenly prototype the details no longer seem important. At 8:2 above the phrase is more precisely defined by the following reference to the true tent, while at several points (9:8, 24; 10:19; 13:11) it is translated in *RSV* simply by 'sanctuary'. Possibly the author used the shorter phrase simply for the sake of brevity; once he had explained the ritual of the earthly sanctuary there was no need for him to make precise distinctions. At verse 24 the true sanctuary is said to be heaven itself. It might be simpler at all these points just to speak of 'the sanctuary'.

This greater and more perfect tent is **not made with hands, that is, not of this creation**. In our modern world, the description 'hand-made' is often a mark of quality and craftsmanship, in contrast to goods mass-produced in a factory, but these are not the associations of the word used here; rather it has frequently a sense of disparagement. We might convey this better by translating 'not made by human hands': it contrasts what is man-made with something of a different order. Thus this word is used with reference to the Temple in Stephen's speech (Ac. 7:48: 'the Most High does not dwell in houses made with hands'), and again in Paul's speech on the Areopagus (Ac. 17:24: 'The God who made the world and everything in it, being Lord of heaven and earth, does not live in shrines made by man'). The idea however goes much further back: the occurrence of the word in Stephen's speech is immediately followed by a quotation of Isa. 66:1–2: 'Heaven is my throne and the earth is my footstool; what is the house which you would build for me?'; and this in turn recalls the words of Solomon's prayer: 'Heaven and the highest heaven cannot contain thee; how much less this house which I have built!' (1 Kg. 8:27). At Mk 14:58 both this word and its negative form are used in the 'false witness' brought against Jesus at his trial (cf. Taylor, *The Gospel according to St Mark*, pp. 566f., who regards it as an original saying, supported by Mk 13:2; 15:29; Jn 2:19; Ac. 6:14. Its original form however is less certain). When we add that LXX and Philo employ the word with reference to idols, its derogatory associations are clear (cf. also Isa. 2:8; 40:19–20 and the classic denunciation of idolatry in 44:9–20). The following words **not of this creation** amplify the point: this perfect tent is not made by human hands, and is not even of this world. It belongs to a new order altogether.

12. As already noted above (on verse 7), the high priest on the Day of Atonement went into the Holy of Holies first with the blood of a bull to offer for himself, and then with the blood of a goat, to offer for the people (cf. Lev. 16). Our author's inversion of the order (**goats and calves**) is another indication that he is not greatly concerned about exactness of detail here. In the next verse he speaks of goats and bulls, at 9:19 of calves and goats, at 10:4 of bulls and goats. At Lev. 16:3 Aaron is to take 'a young bull', and the word used in LXX is the word here translated 'calves' (so also 9:19; in verse 13 and at 10:4 the normal word for 'bulls' is employed). The LXX word for the goats is not however used. The plural can be explained in various ways: as a generalising statement, or as including other sacrifices as well (for the sacrifices in the Temple, see Schürer, *History of the Jewish People*, revised ET [1979], II, pp. 295ff.), or finally as due simply to the annual repetition of the ritual. Over centuries numerous bulls and goats had been sacrificed, and this multiplicity contrasts very effectively with the one offering made by the great high priest of the new dispensation.

The frequent references to **blood** in this context have to be understood in the light of ideas widely spread in the ancient world, and in particular in the Old Testament and in Israelite religion. According to Lev. 17:14, 'the life of every creature is its blood'; hence the regulations about the killing of animals earlier in the chapter, and the prohibition in the immediate context (verses 10–14) of the eating of blood. The blood was considered to be invested with a mysterious potency, which made it an appropriate medium for sacrifices of expiation, for rites of purification or for acts of consecration. As our author puts it later, 'under the law almost everything is purified with blood, and without the shedding of blood there is no forgiveness of sins' (9:22). It must be remembered, however, that the Old Testament is the product of more than a thousand years of history, during which ideas changed and developed even where the rites and ceremonies continued to be performed. Thus the prophets already are critical of the sacrificial system (e.g. Hos. 6:6: 'I desire steadfast love and not sacrifice, the knowledge of God, rather than burnt offerings'; Mic. 6:6–8: 'Will the Lord be pleased with thousands of rams, with ten thousands of rivers of oil?'); there was a growing recognition that what God required was 'to do justice, and to love kindness, and to walk humbly with your God' (Mic. 6:8), a spiritual rather than a material offering. In the present context, our author is building his argument on the description in the Pentateuch, and drawing a parallel: the blood which the high priest offered gave him the right of access into the inner sanctuary; so also Jesus gains access to the heavenly sanctuary, **not** with **the blood of goats and calves, but** with **his own blood**. Since 'the life of every creature is its blood', the reference is clearly to his death. There is no thought here of the metaphors of cleansing and purification developed in other New Testament writings (e.g. 1 Jn 1:7; Rev. 7:14); the argument is strictly based on its Old Testament text.

The effect of all this is now stated in a final clause: **thus securing an eternal redemption**. At 5:9 above, Jesus is said to have become 'the source of eternal salvation to all who obey him', and here the idea is the same although a different word is used. 'Salvation' may have connotations of health and well-being, as well as of deliverance,

and is the more general term. 'Redemption' has associations rather
with the ransoming of captives or the release of slaves (Paul uses a
compound form which appears in 9:15 below; the only other occurrences of the simple form in the New Testament are at Lk. 1:68;
2:38); it is appropriate in the present context as conveying the idea
of a costly deliverance (against a false emphasis on the idea of a
'ransom' see Hill, *Greek Words and Hebrew Meanings*, pp. 66ff., and
for the present passage, pp. 68f.). This redemption is **eternal** in
contrast to the temporary atonement affected by earthly priests:
they had to repeat their offerings every year, whereas Jesus made
his sacrifice once and for all.

13–14. There is still a further point to be adduced by way of
explanation. At verse 9–10 above it was said that the gifts and
sacrifices of the old dispensation cannot perfect the conscience of
the worshipper; they deal only with external matters. Now our
author grants them a certain limited validity, but then goes on to
one of the most impressive examples of his familiar *qal wā-ḥōmer*
argument: **if the sprinkling of defiled persons with the blood of
goats and bulls and with the ashes of a heifer sanctifies for
the purification of the flesh, how much more shall the blood of
Christ . . . purify your conscience.** The reference to **goats and
bulls** here may include not only the sacrifices of the Day of Atonement but other sacrifices also. Just how these sacrifices sanctified
the flesh our author does not say; it was enough for him that this
was the procedure laid down in the Old Testament. The ritual of
the red **heifer** is described in Num. 19: it was slaughtered outside
the camp, and the whole corpse burnt with 'cedar wood and hyssop
and scarlet stuff'; the ashes were kept 'for the water of impurity,
for the removal of sin'. This water was used for the cleansing of
persons polluted by contact with a dead body. Once again we are
not told how the cleansing was thought to be effected; but this is
the ritual prescribed. Here it is interesting to compare and contrast
the Epistle of Barnabas (ch. 8), where the ritual of the red heifer is
completely allegorised. There is nothing of that in Hebrews. Rather
the point is that if, according to the Old Testament, these
ceremonies were effective **for the purification of the flesh**, there is
now a greater and more effective purification through **the blood of
Christ**, one that can even **purify** the **conscience**. As James Denney
puts it (*The Death of Christ*, p. 224): 'The Old Testament sacrifices
had an outward efficacy; they removed such defilements as excluded
a man from the communion of Israel with God in its national
worship. The New Testament sacrifice has an inward efficacy; it
really reaches to the conscience, and it puts the man in a position
to offer religious service to a living God. In some way it neutralises

or annuls sin so that religious approach to God is possible in spite of it.' So this section ends with the triumphant cry: **how much more shall the blood of Christ . . . purify your conscience from dead works to serve the living God**! Repentance from dead works was mentioned at 6:1 above, among the 'elementary doctrines': they are dead because they do not lead to life. In Bruce's words, they are 'those practices and attitudes which belong to the way of death, which pollute the soul and erect a barrier between it and God'. So Paul writes (Rom. 8:6–8): 'To set the mind on the flesh is death . . . for the mind that is set on the flesh is hostile to God . . . and those who are in the flesh cannot please God'. In reading such passages we have to remember the radical newness of life in Christ for the early Christians: conversion to Christianity was for them nothing less than a passage from death to life. According to the Nag Hammadi *Apocalypse of Adam* (*NHC* V 65.10ff.), the 'eternal knowledge of the God of truth' departed from Adam and Eve after the separation of the sexes. On one translation the text continues: 'From that time we learned about dead works, like men' (Böhlig-Labib, *Koptisch-gnostische Apokalypsen*, [1963], p. 97; Morard, *L'apocalypse d'Adam* [1985], p. 23; *NHLE* p. 257 translates 'dead things'). In this gnostic application of the phrase the 'dead works' belong to the service of the Demiurge who seeks to hold the human race in subjection; the way to life is through *gnosis*, the knowledge of God and of one's own true nature.

One clause has not yet been mentioned: **who through the eternal Spirit offered himself without blemish to God**. The word translated **without blemish** is figuratively used to describe the ideal for Christians at Eph. 1:4, Phil. 2:15, Col. 1:22, Jude 24 (cf. also Rev. 14:5 of the redeemed; at Eph. 5:27 it is used of the Church): they are to be blameless, without blemish, spotless. More relevant to the present context however is the use in 1 Pet. 1:19, which speaks of 'the precious blood of Christ, like that of a lamb without blemish or spot'. This reminds us that in the Old Testament the animals offered in sacrifice were required to be perfect, without spot or blemish. In other words, Christ's sacrifice is perfect in every respect, fulfilling every least requirement. 'The perfection of this sacrifice is clearly associated with the perfection of the victim, in this case, the priest himself' (Peterson, p. 116).

The real problem in this clause lies in the words **through the eternal Spirit** (*NEB* paraphrases: he offered himself without blemish to God, a spiritual and eternal sacrifice). The Greek word *pneuma* can refer to the inmost part of the human personality, the soul or spirit, and some scholars accordingly interpret the phrase here as referring to the divine nature of Christ. Moffatt for example

remarks that what was called an indestructible life at 7:16 is here
called eternal spirit, while Montefiore translates 'in his eternal
nature', with the comment: 'he, who in self-sacrifice offered to God
his full and perfect humanity, was himself eternal by nature; and
because of this, the salvation he procured is everlasting'. Bruce
however objects that if the author had wanted to say 'through his
eternal spirit' he could have said so, while H. B. Swete long ago
wrote 'to think here of our Lord's human spirit as "the seat of His
Divine Personality" seems too much like an attempt to read the
formal theology of a later age into a document of the first century'
(*The Holy Spirit in the New Testament*, London [1910], p. 252). The
author does in his prologue introduce the exalted figure of a Son,
and from 5:8 it is clear that Jesus and this Son are one and the same
('Although he was a Son, he learned obedience . . .'); but it is
nowhere stated that Jesus carried the divine nature of his pre-
existent life into his earthly existence. On the contrary, the emphasis
throughout is upon his real humanity, and indeed any emphasis
upon the divinity could have been detrimental to the whole argument: a divine being might be held to possess advantages which are
not shared by ordinary human beings. It is however fundamental
to our author's case that Jesus in every respect has been tempted as
we are (4:15), that because he himself has suffered and been tempted
he is able to help those who are tempted (2:18). Furthermore, the
'indestructible life' of 7:16 is not simply to be identified with 'eternal
spirit' here: in that earlier passage the 'indestructible life' is most
naturally to be understood as the life which the risen Jesus *now*
possesses. He has passed through death and been raised again to a
life which nothing can destroy (here we may recall the 'Gethsemane'
passage at 5:7, where Jesus offers up prayers and supplications to
him who was able to save him from death, and 'was heard for his
godly fear'. There is no suggestion here that he possessed in himself
the power to escape from death). In short, the view that the phrase
'through the eternal Spirit' refers to Jesus' divine nature is very
seriously open to question. 'Eternal spirit' must therefore refer to
something else. Bruce points in the right direction when he notes
that when the Servant of the Lord is introduced for the first time
at Isa. 42:1 it is said, 'I have put my spirit upon him'. That this is
not just an attempt to bring in divinity by another door can be seen
from other references to the Spirit of the Lord in the Old Testament;
thus at Jg. 6:34 'the Spirit of the Lord took possession of Gideon',
but there is no suggestion that Gideon was divine. The point is that
God was working in and through Gideon, as with others upon whom
the Spirit came. On this view, the 'eternal spirit' is the Spirit of the
Lord which appears in numerous Old Testament passages. It has

to be remembered here that our author still stands at a relatively
early point in the development of Christianity: like the Philippians
hymn, he affirms the pre-existence of Christ, but he does not say
how he envisaged the relationship between the exalted Son of his
prologue and the earthly Jesus, except that they are one and the
same. The detailed working out of that relationship was to be a
problem for later ages. What is more important here is that if the
'eternal spirit' is to be understood in terms of the Spirit of the Lord,
it emphasises God's involvement. In Denney's words (*The Death of
Christ*, p. 208), 'in Christ's sacrifice we see the final revelation of
what God is, that behind which there is nothing in God'; 'it was
the final response, a spiritual response, to the divine necessities of
the situation' (*op. cit.*, p. 228). As to the word **eternal**, Denney
collects the references in this letter (5:9; 6:2; 9:12, 14, 15; 13:20;
see *op. cit.* pp. 207ff.) and notes that they all have a certain character
of finality; the word means not merely 'everlasting' or unending,
but ultimate and absolute.

'A Jesus who walked through the world, knowing exactly what
the morrow would bring, knowing with certainty that three days
after his death his Father would raise him up, is a Jesus who can
arouse our admiration, but still a Jesus far from us . . . On the
other hand, a Jesus for whom the future was as much a mystery, a
dread, and a hope as it is for us and yet, at the same time, a Jesus
who would say, "Not my will but yours"—this is a Jesus who could
effectively teach us how to live, for this is a Jesus who would
have gone through life's real trials' (Brown, *Jesus God and Man*,
pp. 104f.). The preceding paragraph affirms with equal emphasis
the relevance of the Nicene doctrine of the divinity of Christ, but
it is this paragraph which is most directly relevant to the thought of
Hebrews. The definitions of Nicaea and Chalcedon were formulated
several centuries later, after long debate and discussion, and were
themselves the subject of controversy, but the formulae of a later
orthodoxy are not simply to be read back into the work of an author
in whose day the problems had not yet arisen. Denney (*The Death
of Christ*, pp. 209ff., 318ff.) criticises the tendency 'to put the Atonement out of its place, and to concentrate attention on the Incarnation' (p. 320) as shifting the centre of gravity in the New Testament. In his view 'the atonement, and the priestly or reconciling
ministry of Christ, are the end, to which the incarnation is relative
as the means' (p. 211). Historically this is undoubtedly correct: it
was the conviction of redemption in Christ that gave him the central
place in the thought of early Christians. They clearly accorded to
Jesus a special relationship with God, but as Brown shows it is only

in the later strata of the New Testament that he is actually called
God; and even here the New Testament writers are concerned only
to state the fact, not to explain the relationship of the divine and
the human. That is a problem to which every age must address
itself anew, in the light of changing circumstances.

The point of this section can be summed up in the words of
Denney (p. 217), that 'in the death of Christ God has dealt effectu-
ally with the world's sin for its removal'. His sacrifice is 'the basis
on which the eternal priesthood of Christ is exercised, and the
sinner's access to God assured' (p. 225). The sinless Jesus, offering
himself without blemish to God, has opened the way into a new
relationship. This is further explained and developed in the next
section.

MEDIATOR OF THE NEW COVENANT

9:15–22

15–17. Verse 15 first picks up two points from the earlier discussion:
Jesus is **the mediator of a new covenant** (cf. 8:6 with the following
quotation from Jeremiah; at 7:22 he is called the surety of a better
covenant), and the purpose of this is **that those who are called
may receive the promised eternal inheritance** (cf. the promise of
entering into God's rest at 4:1 and the references to heirs and
inheriting at 6:12, 17). In the Greek the last clause of this sentence
is actually a subordinate clause preceding the second of these (cf.
NEB; lit. in order that, a death having taken place . . . those who
are called may receive). The passage plays on the two meanings of
the word rendered **covenant**, which may mean either a treaty or
compact *or* (its normal meaning in hellenistic times) a last will or
testament (cf. *NEB*: 'covenant, or testament'). The train of the
argument is rather difficult to follow, since the author seems to
combine two different sets of ideas. In verses 16–17 he speaks in
terms of a will: **where a will is involved, the death of the one who
made it must be established**. It **takes effect only at death** (lit. is
valid in the case of deceased persons), and **is not in force as long
as** the testator **is alive**. The Revised Version incidentally treats this
last clause as a question: 'for doth it ever avail while he that made
it liveth?' This has the advantage of removing an apparent tautology,
and also does justice to the grammatical form, which could be a
question expecting a negative answer. Most editions and modern
versions however take it as a statement. In verse 18, in contrast, we
are back to the idea of a covenant: **even the first covenant was not**

ratified without blood. As the following verses show, the reference is to the Mosaic covenant (cf. Exod. 24:3–8).

The difficulty for the modern reader lies in verses 16–17, the more particularly since two words are employed, **will** and **covenant**, where the Greek uses the same word throughout. It would be easier had the author gone straight from verse 15 to verse 18: the first covenant was inaugurated with blood, and so must the second be. This however would not explain why the death *of Jesus* should be necessary. He is in some sense not only the mediator, the guarantor, of the new covenant, but also the testator; it was necessary for him to die before it could be inaugurated. Such an argument might not be valid in terms of modern logic, but our author evidently thought it cogent. The association of the new covenant with the death of Jesus is not peculiar to Hebrews, for it is already present in the earliest recorded tradition of the Last Supper: This cup is the new covenant in my blood (1 C. 11:25, cf. Mk 14:24. The addition in Matt. 26:28 of 'for the forgiveness of sins' only makes explicit what is implicit in the other versions, but underlines the connection made by early Christians between the death of Christ and the forgiveness of sins). The real problem lies in the idea of Jesus as in some sense the testator: as Moffatt remarks, 'A will does not come into force during the lifetime of the testator, and yet Jesus was living!' However, he adds further on: 'The slight incongruity in this illustration is not more than that involved in making Jesus both priest and victim'. The difficulty is not to be evaded by using the translation 'covenant' throughout, and claiming that the maker of the covenant was identified with the victim slaughtered on the occasion. As Bruce points out, there is no suggestion either in Gen. 15:1–18 (the covenant with Abraham) or in Exod. 24:3–8 that God was represented by the covenant-victims. Despite the incongruity, the main point is clear, the efficacy of the death of Jesus for dealing with sin: **a death has occurred which redeems them from the transgressions under the first covenant**. It is in fact this conviction of the saving power of the death of Jesus that controls the argument, rather than any considerations of logic.

The phrase **which redeems them** in verse 15 is literally 'for redemption of the transgressions', using a compound form (also employed by Paul, Rom. 3:24; 8:23; 1 C. 1:30) of the word used at verse 12 above. Originally it had to do with the buying back of a slave or captive, making him free by payment of a ransom (cf. *BAG* 96a), but in a figurative sense it means 'release' or 'deliverance'. As already noted above, Hill warns against undue emphasis on the idea of a 'ransom' (*Greek Words and Hebrew Meanings*, pp. 66ff.; for the present verse see p. 69). He notes that the word

is rare in non-biblical Greek, but is 'obviously an important term
in the New Testament salvation vocabulary' (p. 71: seven times in
the Pauline corpus, twice in Hebrews and once in Luke). A close
parallel to the thought of our present passage is provided by Eph.
1:7: 'In him we have redemption through his blood, the forgiveness
of our trespasses'.

In verse 17 the phrase **at death**, as noted above, is literally 'in
the case of dead persons', but this rendering actually goes slightly
beyond the Greek, on the assumption that what is referred to is a
will. There is no noun in the Greek, but one has to be supplied in
English, and it might well have been 'animals'. This could be an
argument in favour of using the term 'covenant' throughout, but
for one thing the reference to animals is only a possibility, and not
beyond question; for another, verse 16 would still remain difficult.
Most modern versions and commentators accept a shift of meaning
to 'will' or 'testament' in these two verses. There is a similar ambiguity at Gal. 3:15 ('no one annuls even a man's will, or adds to it,
once it has been ratified'), although here there is a stronger case, in
view of 3:17 following, for keeping the sense of 'covenant' and
translating 'no one annuls even a human covenant'. The Nag
Hammadi *Gospel of Truth* (*NHC* I 20.15-27; cf. *NHLE* 39) makes
use of the same analogy, along with other New Testament echoes,
for its own purposes: 'As in the case of a still unopened testament
the estate of the deceased master of the house is concealed, so is
the case of the All which was concealed, because the Father of the
All was invisible . . . Therefore Jesus appeared. He took that book
to himself. He was nailed to a tree. He published the disposition of
the Father on the cross' (tr. K. H. Kuhn in Foerster, *Gnosis* II, ET
[1974], p. 58; for the New Testament echoes, cf. van Unnik in *The
Jung Codex*, London [1955], pp. 108ff.; Ménard, *L'évangile de
Vérité* (*NHS* 2) [1972], pp. 96ff.; H. W. Attridge (ed.), *Nag
Hammadi Codex I* (*NHS* 23: notes), pp. 57ff.).

18. Difficult as they may be for us, these verses are clearly
intended to explain the necessity of the death of Jesus. Verse 18
then draws the conclusion: **hence even the first covenant was not
ratified without blood.** Actually, it was probably the fact that a
covenant often required a blood sacrifice (although not in the case
of Noah, Gen. 6:18; contrast the covenant with Abraham in Gen.
15) that led the author to think of the death of Jesus in covenant
terms in the first place.

19-20. The following verses then go on to describe the inauguration of the first covenant under Moses (Exod. 24:6-8). According
to Exodus, Moses first sent young men who 'offered burnt offerings
and sacrificed peace offerings to the Lord'. Then he put half the

blood in basins, and threw half against the altar. Finally, after reading the book of the covenant in the hearing of the people, 'he took the blood and threw it upon the people'. The account in Hebrews is plainly a summary of this, with some modifications. The words **when every commandment of the law had been declared by Moses** correspond to Exod. 24:3, if they do not also include the whole of the ordinances in the preceding chapters, beginning with the Ten Commandments in chapter 20. Exodus makes no mention of **goats** in this context, which leads to an intricate textual problem in the present text of Hebrews: some manuscripts, including the early Chester Beatty papyrus and a corrector in the Codex Sinaiticus, have no mention of goats; two other groups, one including the original scribe of Sinaiticus as well as Codex Alexandrinus and Codex Ephraemi Rescriptus, include a mention of goats, in the one case with the article, in the other without; finally the Codex Claromontanus (both Greek and Latin) with one or possibly two Old Latin manuscripts has not 'calves and goats', but 'goats and calves' (cf. on verses 11–12 above for the author's variations of this phrase). The omission of any reference to goats could be the result of an assimilation to the LXX version of Exod. 24:5 or, on the other hand, the addition of the words could be influenced by the formulation in verse 12 just above (which refers to the Day of Atonement, not to the inauguration of the covenant). The choice is difficult, as is shown by the somewhat hesitant discussion in Metzger's *Textual Commentary* (pp. 668f.). However, it may be noted that the variants including the reference differ among themselves, a) by the inclusion or omission of the article, or b) by an inversion of order. Such points are sometimes an indication of later insertion, so there may be some justification for omitting any reference to goats; but since scribes were sometimes prone to correcting the 'errors' of their authors, doubts must remain. A further point is that in Exodus there is no reference to **water and scarlet wool and hyssop**. All three are mentioned in the ritual for the cleansing of a leper in Lev. 14:4–7, hyssop and 'scarlet stuff' in connection with the ritual of the red heifer at Num. 19:6 (where verse 7 adds that the priest shall bathe his body in water). Num. 19:17 specifies: 'For the unclean they shall take some ashes of the burnt sin offering (i.e. the heifer), and running water shall be added in a vessel; then a clean person shall take hyssop, and dip it in the water, and sprinkle it . . .' This suggests how our author came to his formulation here: he has simply assumed that the Exodus reference to Moses throwing the blood upon the people refers to an aspersion such as those of which we read elsewhere (AV as it happens has 'sprinkled' where *RSV* has 'threw' and *NEB* 'flung'; the Hebrew word means 'to throw, toss' or 'to sprinkle'. Too much should not be made of the translator's choice of an English equivalent!).

Thirdly, there is no reference in Exodus to the sprinkling of **the book**, while in verse 20 there is a slight modification in the quotation: **This is the blood of the covenant**: Exod. 24:8 reads: 'Behold the blood of the covenant'.

21–22. Finally in verse 21 our author says: **In the same way he sprinkled with the blood both the tent and all the vessels used in worship**. At Exod. 24 the tabernacle and its furnishings are not yet in existence: the instructions for their making begin in Exod. 25, while the account of their construction begins at Exod. 36. At Exod. 40:9f. instructions are given for the consecration of the tabernacle, the altar and all the utensils by anointing with oil; there is no reference to water or scarlet wool or hyssop, although Aaron and his sons are to be washed with water (Exod. 40:12) and there is reference to blood in connection with the altar at Exod. 29:12. All this suggests that our author is here making a general statement from memory, in line with the principle stated in verse 22: **under the law almost everything is purified with blood**. In the ancient world it was not so easy to make a detailed check of every reference! According to Josephus however (*Ant*. III. 206) the tabernacle and its vessels were consecrated with oil and with the blood of bulls and rams. Our author may be drawing on a similar tradition; at any rate he is not alone.

There is a basis for the principle of verse 22 in the law of the sin offering in Lev. 4–5, where the offerings required are minutely regulated. It may be noted that even here, if a man could not afford the minimum offering of two turtle doves or two young pigeons (cf. Lk. 2:24, fulfilling the law of Lev. 12:2–8), he could offer 'a tenth of an ephah of fine flour for a sin offering'. Almost everything was to be purified with blood, but there were exceptions. Reference has been made above (verses 13–14, 19–20) to the ritual of the water of impurity, made with the ashes of the red heifer, while Lev. 15 prescribes purification by ablution in certain circumstances. Metals according to Num. 31:22 were purified by fire. The burning of a garment infected by a leprous disease (Lev. 13:47ff.) might appear to be simply a public health measure, but it is mentioned in the context of regulations regarding cleansing of various kinds, and judgment as to what should be done was in the hands of the priest, so that here too there is an element of ritual purification. Our author's qualification **almost everything** is therefore justified.

There is however no such qualification to his summary conclusion: **without the shedding of blood there is no forgiveness of sins**. There is nothing in the Greek to match the last two words (cf. *NEB*), but this is a natural explanatory expansion (cf. Mk 1:4; 3:29 etc. The only place in the New Testament where the word rendered 'forgiveness' has no reference to sin in the context is Lk. 4:18, where it is translated 'release'). As already noted (on verses 11–12 above), the prophets were critical of the sacrificial system, calling for justice and righteousness rather than sacrifice (Am. 5:21–24; cf. Hos. 6:6; Mic. 6:6–8 and numerous other passages). In the prophetic tradition John the Baptist preached a baptism of repentance for the forgiveness of sins (Mk 1:4). The Qumran sect repudiated the sacrifices of a Temple they regarded as contaminated, and looked for the day when true sacrifice would be offered in a Temple rededicated and restored to its former glory; pending that, the council of the community was itself to be a 'most holy dwelling for Aaron' where 'without the flesh of holocausts and the fat of sacrifice' a 'sweet fragrance' was to be sent up to God, and prayer serve as 'an acceptable fragrance of righteousness' (see Vermes, *The Dead Sea Scrolls: Qumran in Perspective*, [1978], p. 181; also Gaertner, *The Temple and the Community in Qumran and the New Testament*, [1965]). At a later point (13:15–16) the author will himself speak of 'a sacrifice of praise to God', 'the fruit of lips that acknowledge his name', with the comment that 'such sacrifices are pleasing to God.' Here he is not concerned with prophetic criticism, or with the relative merits of material and spiritual sacrifices. He is simply summing up the legislation of the Pentateuch with regard to rites of purification; had he wished, he might have quoted Lev. 17:11: It is the blood that makes atonement, by reason of the life. It was noted above, with reference to the priesthood, that he shows little interest in contemporary or recent history: so here he ignores any later developments and adheres firmly to exegesis of the Pentateuch and its prescriptions. However, as Hughes points out (*Hebrews and Hermeneutics*, [1979], p. 89), he *has* reflected 'at impressive depth' upon the sacrificial system, and 'is very clear in his assessment of it', as a later passage shows (cf. 10:5–10 below). There is more still to come before he has done with his exposition.

Taken by itself, as an independent statement, the final assertion of this section, that without the shedding of blood there is no forgiveness of sins, simply is not true; even in the Old Testament, as noted above, there is provision for forgiveness to be received in other ways. These words however take on a totally different complexion when they are read in context, and seen not as a general statement but as a statement of the situation under the law which governed priesthood and sacrifice in the old dispensation. The whole of verse 22 belongs together, as a summary of this situation: *under the law* almost everything is purified with blood, and without that there is no forgiveness. A second point to be noted is that since 8:6 our author has shifted the focus of his attention from the ritual of the Day of Atonement to the inauguration of the covenant. If the first covenant had been faultless, there would have been no need for a second (8:7); but God through Jeremiah has spoken of a new covenant, and therefore treats the first as obsolete (8:13). Now that first covenant was inaugurated by sacrifice, and it is therefore appropriate that the second should be also. As 9:23 puts it, it was necessary for the copies of the heavenly things to be purified with these rites, but the heavenly things themselves with better sacrifices. This provides an explanation for the necessity of the death of Jesus: it is the sacrifice which inaugurates the new covenant. The shift of focus was the easier in that the high priest on the Day of Atonement was carrying out a ritual which had been celebrated year by year since the inauguration of the first covenant under Moses. The statement of 9:7 holds good not just for any given high priest, but for every high priest in the long succession from Aaron on; but all that now belongs to the past. A new covenant has now been inaugurated, in and through the death of Jesus, opening up the promised inheritance for those who are called and offering them redemption from their transgressions.

Reference has been made in the notes above to certain discrepancies between verses 19–21 and the description of the inauguration of the first covenant in Exodus, but they are not such as to invalidate the author's argument. It would be a mistake to expect of him that he check every statement in his sources—a much more difficult thing to do before the days of concordances and chapter and verse divisions! What he does in these verses is to combine various elements of the Old Testament sacrifical ritual into one comprehensive general statement in order to bring out the significance of blood in the ritual of atonement. The next two sections recapitulate some of the points that have been made, in order to round off this part of the author's argument.

PURIFICATION BY BETTER SACRIFICES

9:23–28

23. According to 8:5 the levitical priests serve a copy and shadow of the heavenly sanctuary, for Moses constructed the tabernacle according to the pattern which was shown him on the mount. The preceding section (9:18–21) describes the ritual for the inauguration and consecration of this earthly sanctuary. Now our author draws the conclusion: **it was necessary for the copies of the heavenly things to be purified with these rites, but the heavenly things themselves with better sacrifices than these**. This is another point at which an element of 'Alexandrianism' may be detected, but as already noted the basis for the contrast between the earthly and the heavenly is already given in the author's Old Testament text, and does not require Platonic theory to inspire it. Exod. 25:40 could of course be interpreted in a Platonic sense, as it is by Philo, but Sowers (p. 106) observes: 'This brief remark in Exodus was of apologetic value for Philo because it proved that Moses taught a basic Platonic doctrine centuries before Plato lived. But the very text which Philo uses to Judaism's advantage was turned in Hebrews to its disadvantage. Hebrews sees the text as a clear indication that Judaism is based upon an earthly cult all of whose institutions are mere copies of heavenly archetypes'. This provides yet another warning of the danger of placing too much weight upon parallels and similarities that may be no more than superficial. It is reasonable enough to think in general of an Alexandrian background, but there is always a danger of making too much of our author's alleged 'Alexandrianism'. Manson indeed plays it down, holding that this Alexandrianism is limited to a few chapters in the middle of the letter: '*his great elaboration of the Alexandrian contrast between earthly and heavenly reality has been but an interlude in the development of his central theme*' (pp. 141f.; italics original).

The problem in verse 23 lies in the statement that the heavenly things required to be purified with better sacrifices. The plural **sacrifices** in fact presents no great difficulty, since it is fairly obviously due to the antithetic parallelism of the sentence: as we proceed, it is clear that there is but one such 'better sacrifice' (cf. e.g. verses 26 and 28; 10:10, 12). That better sacrifice is Christ's sacrifice of himself. The real crux is the idea that **the heavenly things themselves** require to be purified: 'when the writer pushes the analogy so far as to suggest that the sacrifice of Christ had, among other effects, to purify heaven itself, the idea becomes almost fantastic' (Moffatt). Attempts have been made to solve the problem by suggesting that the cleansing was necessitated by the presence of Satan (the 'great red dragon' of Rev. 12:3–12) or 'the spiritual hosts of wickedness in the heavenly places' (Eph. 6:12); a gnostic might think of the expulsion of the Demiurge and his archons! These suggestions however introduce ideas of which our author shows no sign: it is always dangerous to try to interpret one book in the light of another, one author by the writings of another, unless we have reason for holding that there is some connection. In seeking a solution we may note in the first place that Moffatt himself pushes things too far: the author does not speak of purifying heaven itself, but of the heavenly things, the things that belong to heaven. We are not to think of heaven being cleaned out like a house in preparation for a new occupant! Further, we may recall verse 14 above, which speaks of the blood of Christ purifying the conscience. It is the consciences of men and women that require to be cleansed and purified. It may at first sight appear difficult to see any connection between the human conscience and a heavenly sanctuary, but there are some indications which may help towards an understanding. Paul writes to the Corinthians 'Do you not know that you are God's temple?' (1 C. 3:16–17; cf. 2 C. 6:16. At 1 C. 6:19 the body of the Christian is called a temple of the Holy Spirit). Eph. 2:19–22 uses the same imagery, speaking of the Christian community as members of the household of God, a holy temple in the Lord, a dwelling-place of God in the Spirit, while 1 Pet. 2:5 uses a cluster of images similar to those in Hebrews, a spiritual house, a holy priesthood, to offer spiritual sacrifices acceptable to God. The Qumran texts also 'contain a consistent temple symbolism, in which the community is represented as the new temple, and in which the true sacrifice is seen as being spiritual in character' (Gaertner, *Temple and Community*, p. 47). At 3:6 above our author wrote 'We are his house if we hold fast our confidence and pride in our hope', which would seem to suggest that such ideas were not unfamiliar to him. It is therefore legitimate in this case to adduce the passages mentioned from other authors to help our understanding. Bruce makes the point when he paraphrases 'while ritual purification is adequate for the material order, which is but an earthly copy of the spiritual order, a better kind of sacrifice is necessary to effect purification in the spiritual order'. This also helps to explain why, as already noted, the author shows no particular interest in matching the details of the heavenly sanctuary with those of the earthly: it is enough for him to have established the idea of a great high priest ministering in a heavenly sanctuary, immeasurably superior to anything that exists on earth. The lay-out and the furnishings of such a heavenly sanctuary are not matters of concern. There is however a distinction that requires to be made: it was said above that there is but one 'better sacrifice', the sacrifice offered by Christ himself, but later our author will speak of 'a sacrifice of praise to God' and of sacrifices 'pleasing to God' (13:15–16). The difference is that the sacrifice of Christ is that which inaugurates the new order; the sacrifices of praise and well-doing, the 'spiritual sacrifices' mentioned in other passages, are the continuing offering to be made by God's people. They are to be holy, as God himself is holy, drawing near, as 10:22

puts it, 'with a true heart in full assurance of faith, with our hearts sprinkled clean from an evil conscience'.

24–26. Verses 24–26 recapitulate points already made, to drive home and emphasise the argument. **Christ has entered, not into a sanctuary made with hands** (cf. 9:11), **a copy of the true one** (cf. 8:5), **but into heaven itself, now to appear in the presence of God on our behalf.** At 4:14 above the author spoke of a great high priest who has passed through the heavens, which suggests a heavenly journey through the celestial spheres; similarly at 7:26 the high priest is exalted above the heavens. The analogy of the true tent and its earthly copy on the other hand might seem to suggest that this true sanctuary was somewhere *in* heaven, as the earthly sanctuary was at a given point on earth. These apparent inconsistencies are however merely superficial. What really matters is our author's conviction that this great high priest is seated at the right hand of the throne of the Majesty in heaven (8:1, cf. already 1:3), in the very presence of God, and therefore able to intercede on our behalf. This confirms the view expressed at 8:3 above, that Christ's ministry in heaven is one of intercession (cf. 7:25, also Rom. 8:34; 1 Jn 2:1). In the next verse it is expressly stated that this ministry is not a sacrificial one: **Nor was it to offer himself repeatedly, as the high priest enters the Holy Place yearly with blood not his own.** The **Holy Place** is literally 'the holies', the form normally used for the 'first' or outer tent, not the full phrase employed for the inner sanctuary ('the holy of holies'; cf. above on verse 12. The word is used without the article in verse 24, just above, where it is translated 'sanctuary'). The author is either using the shorter form for brevity, or he is simply no longer interested in the distinction between the inner and outer chambers. To translate 'sanctuary' in both verses (cf. *NEB*) would be perfectly adequate. There is here a double contrast, first with the repeated annual sacrifice offered by the earthly high priest, and secondly in the fact that it was **blood not his own** which the earthly high priest presented. This verse picks up the theme of verse 12, with some modification: there Jesus is said to have entered once for all into the Holy Place, taking not the blood of goats and calves but his own blood. His sacrifice is unique and not repeated, and it involves his own death, not the death of animal victims. Verse 26 then spells out the point: if it had been a question of offering himself repeatedly, **he would have had to suffer repeatedly since the foundation of the world**; but that is not the case—Jesus died only once, and had no predecessors. His death is a once and for all event: **But as it is, he has appeared once for all at the end of the age to put away sin by the sacrifice of himself.**

This marks the decisive effect of the death of Jesus: the putting

away of sin, the breaking down of the barrier between man and
God, the opening of the way to life everlasting, the inauguration of
a new covenant and a new sanctuary—the imagery varies, but there
is no question that this was a fundamental conviction of the early
Christians (cf. for example Rom. 5:8; 1 C. 15:3; Gal. 1:4; 1 Pet.
3:18; 1 Jn 2:2). Equally, it is a sacrifice not to be repeated, for that
would reduce it to the level of the sacrifices of the old dispensation:
it was offered once for all. **At the end of the age** (*NEB* 'at the
climax of history') is literally 'at the consummation of the ages', and
like the reference to 'these last days' in the prologue reflects the
early Christian belief that they were living in the last days. As
Barrett notes (*Dodd Festschrift*, p. 385), the 'once' in this verse
'refers to an eschatological event that has taken place, and is followed
by the plainest assertion of an eschatological event yet to come—
the return of Christ' (see verse 28). This incidentally may point a
warning against dating the letter unduly late: as time went on, and
the expectation of an imminent Parousia was not fulfilled, the delay
presented a problem which different authors sought to meet in
various ways; but there is nothing of this in Hebrews. That may
however be due to the author's consistent concentration upon
interpretation of his Old Testament material, and his equally
consistent ignoring of contemporary events. The phrase **to put away
sin** (*NEB* 'to abolish sin') is literally 'for the removal of sin', using
a word which in the New Testament occurs only here and at 7:18
above (lit. 'on the one hand there is the annulment, or cancellation,
of a preceding commandment'). The word is a legal technical term
(*BAG* 21a), and the cognate verb occurs below at 10:28 ('A man
who has violated the law of Moses', lit. declared it invalid, set it
aside). Whatever the choice of an English equivalent, the author's
conviction is clear: sin has been effectively dealt with. At 2:14 above
it was noted that the purpose of the incarnation as there stated
appears to be strange, since there is no reference to deliverance from
sin. It is now clear that dealing with sin is also part of that purpose.

27–28. Verse 27 is at first sight strange, with its reference to death
and judgment, here introduced without any preparation or warning.
Moffatt indeed calls verses 27–28 a parenthesis, arguing that the
thought of Jesus' first 'appearance' (verse 26) suggests that of the
second, the thought of his dying once suggests that men too have
to die once; 10:1 then carries on the argument from 9:26. What our
author actually says however suggests that his train of thought runs
in precisely the opposite direction: **just as it is appointed for men
to die once . . . so Christ**. It is not expressly stated that it is
appointed for him too to die once, but that is readily understood
from the context. This is, in Montefiore's words, 'a comparison of

similarities', and provides a further link in the chain of the argument for the uniqueness and finality of the sacrifice of Christ. It is appointed for men to die once, **and after that comes judgment**. So far as earthly existence is concerned, that is the end of it (there is more on the theme of judgment at 10:26ff.). In the same way there can be no second earthly existence for Jesus, no repetition of his sacrifice; his ministry is now in heaven. Yet with all the similarity there is a difference: for men, 'after that comes judgment', but **Christ . . . will appear a second time, not to deal with sin but to save those who are eagerly waiting for him**. This expectation of a Second Coming was widespread in early Christianity, and not merely in the earliest strata of the New Testament: 'It is in 1 Peter (e.g. 4:7, 17; 1:5f.) which probably dates from the final quarter of the first century; 1 Jn 2:18, 28 testifies to its appearance in the Johannine literature which is at least as late as this; Rev. in its final form also comes from the same period and in it the belief is widespread' (E. Best, *First and Second Thessalonians*, London [1972], p. 360; cf. his appendix on the Parousia, pp. 349–354). 2 Peter (3:3–13) speaks of mockers who say 'Where is the promise of his coming? For ever since the fathers fell asleep, all things have continued as they were from the beginning of creation', which does indeed indicate that the delay had become a problem; but it should be noted that even here the author is concerned to defend the belief. As noted above, there is no sign that our author felt any problem, which may perhaps warn against any unduly late date; but as so often the point is inconclusive. It is a mistake to think of early Christian thought and belief as moving steadily and uniformly forward, like the production line in a factory. Some authors were more conservative than others, some more innovative, more ready to see the implications of their faith and work out their meaning.

More important in the present context is the clear statement **not to deal with sin**. This is in keeping with our author's consistent emphasis in these chapters on the 'once and for all' character of the sacrifice of Jesus: he is a priest, ministering in a heavenly sanctuary, but he does not offer sacrifice there. That has already been done, as indeed the whole of this chapter is concerned to establish: it is the blood of Christ, already offered, that will purify the conscience (cf. verse 14). Bruce notes that to speak of this sacrifice as 'the eternal sacrifice' can be misleading: 'If it means that His sacrifice is the historical expression of the eternal mercy of God, or that its efficacy is eternal, no exception can be taken to the term; but if it means (as it does for many who use it) that He is eternally offering Himself in heaven (with the corollary that in the Eucharist His sacrifice is repeatedly re-enacted on earth), then it is in plain contra-

diction to the emphatic teaching of this epistle'. Christ's Second
Coming is not to deal with sin (lit. 'without' or 'apart from sin'.
The phrase was used at 4:15 in its simple sense; here it means
'without any relation to sin'), but to save those who await his return.
But this is the very hope and expectation which the readers are in
danger of abandoning!

An earlier phrase, **to bear the sins of many**, is an echo of one of
the Servant songs in Isaiah (53:12; cf. 1 Pet. 2:24). As at 2:10 above,
the **many** is not exclusive: for one thing, it is given in the LXX text,
and for another this is common usage in many New Testament
passages (e.g. Mk 10:45; 14:24). It refers to 'many' in contrast to
one or a few, not in contrast to 'all'. Westcott observes that Chrysostom's note 'is strangely wide of the meaning': he writes that Christ
did indeed die for all, to save all, but he did not bear the sins of all
because all were not willing; not all believed. That may be true
enough, and indeed our author has earlier underlined the dangers
of unbelief (e.g. 3:19; cf. 4:11), but this is not in question here.
Chrysostom was probably misled by the fact that in Greek usage
'many' is exclusive, in contrast to 'all', whereas in Jewish Greek it
has an inclusive sense (cf. Jeremias, *TDNT* VI, 536). For the
meaning here Jeremias points to 2:9 above, 'that by the grace of
God he might taste death for every one'. It may be dangerous to
make a homiletic point without regard to what the author actually
intended!

These verses round off the chapter, recapitulating some of the
points made earlier. The chapter and verse divisions are however,
as already noted, a comparatively modern invention, and in fact the
recapitulation continues into the following chapter. The divisions
are useful, as a matter of practical convenience, breaking up this
lengthy discourse into shorter and more manageable units, but they
are not the author's own. If sometimes, as at 4:11 above, it is
difficult for a modern editor to decide whether a verse belongs with
what precedes or with what follows, it is because for the author the
whole was all of a piece. So here the next section opens with a
connective 'for'. There are further points to be made before the
exposition is complete.

It may be added that on the Day of Atonement the people waited
outside while the high priest entered the inner sanctuary. His emerg-
ence was an occasion for rejoicing, for it signified that the sacrifice
offered had been accepted. Bruce aptly quotes Ben Sira's description
of Simon, son of Onias, coming from behind the temple curtain
'like the morning star appearing through the clouds or the moon at
the full' (Ecclus. 50:5–10; the whole passage to verse 21 conveys a

vivid impression of the ritual). If we may see a parallel here, the implication is that the readers should be waiting with no less eager expectation for the appearance of their own great high priest.

SHADOW AND REALITY

10:1-4

1. At first sight there is another element of Platonism in the opening verse: **the law has but a shadow of the good things to come instead of the true form of these realities**. Williamson however points out (p. 566) that there is no contrast here between an ideal heavenly law and its imperfect earthly shadow or copy. As Manson writes (p. 184), 'shadow may suggest something which in itself is unreal or even deceptive as in the Platonic philosophy. But the writer to the Hebrews is not primarily a Platonic idealist but an eschatologist, and when he says that the Law had in it the shadow of the Christian order, though not the reality, he means that the new order was at hand, at the door'. Earlier (p. 144) he had warned against any undervaluing of 'the real, though negative, function assigned to the cultus in bringing home to the soul the "remembrance" of sin. The sacrificial worship kept alive the sense of the Holiness of God and, like the Law in the Pauline theology, it prepared the way for the higher revelation of grace in the gospel'. In fact, the law represents rather a *fore*shadowing of something yet to come, not an earthly copy of a heavenly pattern. There would be more justification for thinking of Platonism at 8:5 above, but even there, as we have seen, Platonic influence is by no means certain. Williamson (*loc. cit.*) writes that we do have 'language reminiscent of Plato', but adds that 'the similarity is word deep only'. At an earlier point (p. 159) he had made an illuminating remark about our author's conviction that the Jewish sanctuary 'represents an attempt to reproduce on earth conditions of access to God for the sinful believer obtainable only in heaven'. Once this is seen, then all begins to fall into place: the use of the Old Testament as the basis for the author's argument, the analogy drawn from the priesthood and sacrifice of the old dispensation, in particular the use of the ritual of the Day of Atonement—they all point forward to what was yet to be, they are shadows of a reality yet to come, which for our author has indeed come in the perfect sacrifice of Christ. It is thus a mistake to think of him as merely disparaging the old in order to exalt the new: the old had its value, but it was a limited value and it has now been superseded. A similar use of

the shadow imagery occurs at Col. 2:17, where regulations about
food and drink and feast-days are called 'only a shadow of what is
to come; but the substance belongs to Christ' (Lightfoot here quotes
Philonic parallels, but no commentator appears to suggest Philonic
influence, although reference is made to the present passage in
Hebrews).

In the light of what has just been said, it can be seen that there
is a difference between 9:11 above and the present passage, and one
which confirms the reading 'good things that have come' at that
earlier point: there the author was speaking from his own point of
view—Christ has appeared, a new situation has been inaugurated,
the good things have already come, if not yet in all their fullness.
Here in contrast he is thinking of the situation under the law, when
the good things still lay in the future and were yet to come.

Comparatively little has so far been said in Hebrews about the
law, in contrast with Paul's repeated reference to it in Romans and
Galatians, which should give warning against interpreting Hebrews
too much in Pauline terms. The levites have a commandment in the
law to take tithes from the people (7:5), and under the law almost
everything is purified with blood (9:22), but the law made nothing
perfect (7:19). The law appoints men in their weakness as high
priests (7:28), and there are priests who offer gifts according to the
law (8:4), but the word of the oath, which came later than the law,
appoints a Son made perfect for ever (7:28). All this fits in very
well with what has just been said above. The author's assessment
of the law is positive, up to a point. The law is valid (cf. 2:2), every
transgression duly punished; but it could not bring perfection, as
the rites and ceremonies connected with it could not cleanse the
conscience. This is precisely what our author claims for the new
priesthood and the new order; the law offered but a shadowy fore-
taste of what was yet to be. Moreover, law and priesthood in the
old dispensation were so intimately connected that a change in the
one necessitated a change in the other: where there is a change in
the priesthood, there is necessarily a change in the law as well (7:12).
This shows very clearly the close-knit character, and the coherence,
of the author's argument.

According to Bruce the good things to come 'embrace the unrepeatable sacrifice of Christ and His present high-priestly ministry,
which carry with them eternal redemption and uninhibited access
to worship the living God'. Montefiore (who accepts the variant
reading at 9:11) in contrast claims that they 'are not to be identified
with the Christian dispensation which has superseded the abrogated
Law . . . The good things will come at the consummation of the
age, i.e. they are the "promises" '. In the light of the discussion

above it must be clear that Bruce is right. 'The most natural way to take the verse is to interpret τῶν μελλόντων ἀδαθῶν and τῶν πραδμάτων (these realities) as parallel expressions and see them as a reference to the boons and blessings of the new age, from the standpoint of the Law. That which was only *foreshadowed* in the *OT* cult is now a reality available to men through the New Covenant' (Peterson, p. 145).

2–4. Since the law has only the shadow and not the reality, **it can never . . . make perfect those who draw near.** This takes up the point already made at 9:9, with its reference to gifts and sacrifices which cannot cleanse the conscience of the worshipper, but gives it a sharper edge by referring to **the same sacrifices which are continually offered year after year.** The very multiplicity of the sacrifices is proof of their ineffectiveness: **otherwise, would they not have ceased to be offered?** Obviously, if the worshippers had once been cleansed, their sins effectively dealt with, they would no longer have any consciousness of sin; there would no longer be any need for atonement by sacrifice. In point of fact, however, the sacrifices did continue, which proves that the atonement was not complete, the consciousness of sin was not removed. Indeed, **in these sacrifices there is a reminder of sin every year**; year by year they remind the worshippers of their own shortcomings, without effectively dealing with the problem. In contrast, the prophecy of the new covenant, quoted at 8:12 above, contains the promise 'I will remember their sins no more'. Verse 4 then makes the author's point with uncompromising clarity: **it is impossible that the blood of bulls and goats should take away sins.** At 9:13 above it was said that sprinkling with the blood of goats and bulls sanctifies for the purification of the flesh: it is valid and effective so far as it goes, but on a purely external level. For the cleansing of the conscience a better sacrifice is required, and this has now been offered once and for all (cf. 9:12, 14, 26); the very fact of its unique and unrepeatable character is proof of its efficacy and sufficiency.

The statements in these four verses could refer to sacrifices in general, but a reference back to 9:25 together with the point that they are offered **year after year** must suggest that it is still the ritual of the Day of Atonement which is primarily in mind. The high priest entered yearly, the sacrifices here mentioned are offered year by year; while thought of other sacrifices need not be excluded, it is the ritual of the great Day of Atonement, one of the central festivals of the religious year, that is in the background throughout. The passage affords another occasion for comparison and contrast with the writings of Philo (cf. Williamson, p. 160ff.): both speak of sacrifices involving **a reminder of sin** (lit. of sins), but where in Philo it is the sacrifices of the wicked which put God in remembrance of the sins of those who offer (de Plant. 108; cf. Spec. Leg. 1.215, Vit. Mos. 2.107), here the reference is more general and covers all sacrifices; also it is the *worshipper* who is reminded. Moreover Philo 'much prefers to allegorize the *OT* regulations dealing with sacrifice', whereas in Hebrews there is no such allegorizing (Williamson, p. 173f., where the main features of Philo's view are summarised). The real background to our author's thought lies not in Philo but in the prophetic tradition with its criticism of the sacrificial system.

According to Montefiore, the order of the Greek words and the use of the same phrase later in the chapter (verses 12, 14) forbid our taking the phrase rendered **continually** with the subordinate clause. He therefore takes it with what follows: the law can never bring the worshippers to perfection *for all time* (cf. *NEB*; the *NEB* margin 'the worshippers who come continually' seems even more difficult to reconcile with the Greek). There is some justification for this in that of the four occurrences of the phrase in this letter (cf. also 7:3) three have the meaning 'for ever'; moreover this would certainly fit the context: these sacrifices have no permanent and lasting effect, they cannot make perfect for ever; but the argument from the Greek word order must be considered dubious: the words 'can never make perfect those who draw near' form a self-enclosed unit, and the most natural way of understanding a rather involved construction is to take the phrase with which we are concerned with what precedes, as part of the description of the sacrifices. They are offered year by year, for all time, i.e. continually. Several passages in the Old Testament indicate that the sacrifices were to be continued in perpetuity: 'Fire shall be kept burning upon the altar continually; it shall not go out' (Lev. 6:13).

The use of the present tense in this passage (*are* continually offered, *is* a reminder) might suggest that the sacrifices are still being offered, the Temple ritual still in being, and hence that the letter must be dated before the Fall of Jerusalem and the destruction of the Temple in AD 70. As already noted, however, our author never mentions the Temple (cf. Introd., p. 6). His whole argument in this section is based entirely on the Old Testament, on the description of the tabernacle in the wilderness and the rites associated with it, which were continually repeated through the centuries; this is how things are in the old dispensation recorded there. Quite apart from the fact that it is possible to argue a case for the continuance of sacrifice in Jerusalem even after AD 70, there is the telling point that Clement of Rome a quarter of a century later can still write of 'the priests and levites who minister unto the altar of God' (32:2), with no hint that the Temple had long lain in ruins. In the same way our author says at 5:1 that every high priest is appointed to act on behalf of men, at 8:3 that the high priest is appointed to offer gifts and sacrifices, at 8:4 that there are priests who offer gifts according to the law; in the description of the Atonement ritual (e.g. 9:25) the high priest enters. All of these can be adequately explained on the basis that the author is thinking purely in terms of the situation described in the Old Testament. Even the statement that the former priests were many in number (7:23) could have an Old Testament basis: quite a number of high priests are mentioned there by name. Had our author wished to use it, the history of the high priesthood might have afforded ample material for condemnation of the old order, but he shows no interest in contemporary or recent history. His concern is to present the new dispensation as immeasurably superior to the old, and he finds his evidence in the very documents of the old itself. It had its value, but it was at best a limited value and it has now been superseded. This point is thus not so relevant for the dating of the letter as some have thought.

As the connective 'for' in verse 1 indicates, these verses are closely linked with what precedes. Not for the first time, the chapter divisions introduced at a later date break up the flow and continuity of a connected argument. Looking back, we can now trace the development since the beginning of chapter 9. The first ten verses of that chapter set out the ordinances and arrangements of the old covenant, as described in Exodus. Verses 11–14 then present the first of a series of contrasts, arguing that the sacrifices of the old dispensation are effective only for the purification of the flesh, whereas the blood of Christ will purify the conscience. In verses 15–22 there is a comparison of the old and new covenants, leading to the conclusion at verse 23 that just as the earthly copies required to be purified by appointed rites, so it was necessary for the heavenly things themselves to be purified with better sacrifices. Verse 24 contrasts the sanctuary made with hands with the true sanctuary in heaven, verses 25–26 the yearly sacrifices offered by the high priest with the single sacrifice offered 'at the end of the age' by the great high priest. Verses 27–28 underline the finality of this single sacrifice: it is appointed for men to die once, and so it is with Christ. He has been offered once, and when he appears again it will not be to deal with sin but to save those who await his coming. Finally in 10:1–4 the repetition of the old sacrifices, their very multiplicity, is used as proof of their ineffectiveness. At various places the author takes up some point he has already made, recapitulating his argument, sometimes giving it a new turn, relentlessly driving it home. The following section, as the initial 'consequently' shows, continues

the argument, characteristically adducing and expounding an Old
Testament quotation to serve as proof.

THE TRUE OFFERING

10:5–10

5–7. As already noted, the **consequently** links this section to what
precedes: it is because the sacrifices of the old dispensation are
inadequate, the blood of bulls and goats ineffective, that some other
resource must be found. That resource for our author is the blood
of Christ, his offering of himself, as the whole of the preceding
argument makes clear. He now finds confirmation for his position
in Ps. 40:6–8, which he puts in the mouth of Jesus. This is the
same procedure as was adopted at 2:12–13, where the speaker of
Ps. 22:22 and Isa. 8:17–18 was identified as Jesus. Here the very
occasion of the utterance is specified: **when Christ** (lit. he) **came
into the world**. One naturally thinks of 1:6 which speaks of God
bringing the first-born into the world, but it should perhaps be
noted that two different Greek words are employed ('world' at 1:2
translates yet another word): that used at 1:6 (also for the world to
come at 2:5) means literally the inhabited earth, while the word
used here is the much more common *cosmos* (already used at 4:3;
9:26 with reference to the foundation of the world, and later
employed at 11:7, 38 in a sense akin to that common in John, of
the world or human society as organised in opposition to God. For
the range of meanings, see *BAG* 445b–447a; *TDNT* III. 883ff.).
The obvious reference is to the Incarnation, but attention may be
drawn for comparison to the Naassene Psalm preserved by Hippo-
lytus (Ref. X.2; see Foerster, *Gnosis* I. 282), where the pre-existent
Jesus asks the Father to *send* him into the world to convey the
saving *gnosis*. This shows how such ideas could develop at a later
stage, but here it is not necessary to think of the pre-existent Jesus:
it is **when he came into the world** that these words are said to be
spoken.

The quotation follows the LXX version, with some slight modification. It also offers one of the clearest examples of the author's
reliance on LXX over against the Hebrew, which in the second line
reads 'thou hast given me an open ear' (lit. 'ears thou hast dug for
me'). It does not seem possible to explain the LXX rendering as due
to a corruption or variant in the Hebrew text, or as a corruption in
the transmission of LXX itself, and the most likely explanation is
that the translators regarded the Hebrew as an example of *pars pro*

toto and rendered it in terms which express *totum pro parte* (cf. Peterson, p. 266 n. 132, quoting Bruce. He also notes Westcott's comment: 'The "body" is the instrument for fulfilling the divine command, just as the 'ear' is the instrument for receiving it'. It is thus not a corruption but an interpretative paraphrase). What is clear is that the rendering **a body hast thou prepared for me** 'seems to have struck our writer as being particularly relevant to express the idea of the pre-existent Son becoming man, to fulfil the divine purpose for man (cf. 2:14, 17)' (Peterson, p. 147). The reference to a body naturally suggests the incarnation, and Bruce goes so far as to say 'his incarnation itself is viewed as an act of submission to God's will and, as such, an anticipation of his supreme submission to that will in death'; but as Peterson points out (*loc. cit.*), the words **Lo, I have come** in verse 7 'stress the attitude of one who has already come' (the *NEB* 'Here am I' is misleading; but it has 'I have come' in the next line). As Peterson says, 'If obedient submission to God's will characterised Jesus' life as a whole (cf. John 4:34; 6:38), it is pre-eminently the attitude with which he faced the climax of his life and ministry, and thus became "the source of eternal salvation" (5:7–9)'. Comparison with the Naassene Psalm shows the difference when it is the pre-existent Jesus who is in view.

The quotation serves a double purpose for our author: in the first place, it goes further than many other Old Testament passages in affirming God's rejection of sacrifice, and 'the powerlessness of sacrifices in themselves to please God and bring about a proper relationship between God and man' (Peterson); and in the second place it provides him with the basis for a new understanding. At 9:22 above, mention was made of Hughes' remark that 'the author *has* reflected at impressive depth' on the sacrificial system 'and is very clear in his assessment of it'. This was in criticism of the view that our author simply takes up and re-affirms 'the Old Testament conviction that sacrificial blood has a mysterious, expiatory power'. 9:22 is 'a simple observation of what happened inside the old, legal dispensation' (cf. the notes on that verse). The author's own view appears at 10:4: It is impossible that the blood of bulls and goats should take away sins. Hughes continues (*Hebrews and Hermeneutics*, p. 89): 'In his massive reinterpretation of the Old Testament cultus . . . he has actually replaced the sacrificial ritual with the infinitely more profound concept of the sacrifice of the will. In his understanding, the sacrificial worth of Jesus' death therefore consists not so much in his physical death as in the sacrifice of his human will which that death presupposes: 'In burnt offerings and sin offerings you take no pleasure. Then I said, "Behold I have come . . . to do your will, O God" '. There can be no question but that this

psalm statement has been thought through and applied to Jesus in
such a way that the principle of radical obedience has replaced the
outward, ineffective, constantly repeated sacrificial ritual of the old
covenant: "He abolishes the old in order to establish the new"
(10:10)'.

8–10. Sacrifices and offerings in the first line of the quotation
translates two nouns which in the Greek are in the singular (cf.
NEB), probably just for conformity with the plurals **burnt offerings**
and sin offerings in verse 6 and because the author himself uses
plurals in his comment at verse 8. The four terms appear to be
intended to cover the main types of offering prescribed in the
levitical ritual; as our author says in his parenthesis, **these are**
offered according to the law. Sacrifice could refer to any form of
animal sacrifice, but in the Old Testament is frequently associated
with the peace-offering; the **offering** referred to in the psalm is the
minhah or meal offering, while the **sin offering** needs no further
explanation. The **burnt offering** is literally a whole burnt offering,
the peculiarity of which was that it was wholly consumed by fire,
whereas in some other sacrifices a portion might be set apart for
consumption by the worshippers. As Peterson remarks (p. 147), 'In
our writer's exposition of the psalm, these sacrifices are relegated to
the period of the Law in God's dealings with his people'. In his
comment the author brings all four terms together, ignoring the
intervening line, which has served its purpose. The points he wishes
to emphasise are first the rejection of sacrifice, and secondly the
obedience expressed in the words **Lo, I have come to do thy will**.
He then draws his conclusion in words which Hughes by an oversight transposes into the next verse: **He abolishes the first in order**
to establish the second.

Denney (*The Death of Christ*, [1903], p. 231) writes that this
passage 'is often read as if it signified that sacrifice was abolished in
favour of obedience, and the inference is drawn that no use can be
made of the conception of sacrifice in the interpretation of Christ's
death'. At an earlier point (p. 215) he had set out the sacrificial
significance of the death of Jesus; indeed the frequent references to
the blood of Christ in earlier chapters would be meaningless if
obedience were what atones. Now Denney continues 'What is
contrasted in this passage is not sacrifice and obedience, but sacrifice
of dumb creatures . . . with sacrifice into which obedience enters,
the sacrifice of a rational and spiritual being, which is not passive
in death, but in dying makes the will of God its own.' Similarly
Manson (pp. 144f.) writes 'the Christ of the psalm is not rejecting
sacrifice and offering in favour of something else, but rejecting
animal sacrifice in favour of that personal sacrifice which God has

willed for him, and for which he has prepared by appointing for
him the body of his incarnation.' Peterson (p. 148) notes that verse
10, **and by that will we have been sanctified through the offering
of the body of Jesus Christ once for all,** 'indicates that our writer's
focus is on Jesus' willingness to offer himself as a sacrifice in
death . . . God's will is for Jesus to offer himself as a sacrifice for
sins and so achieve the sanctification of his people.' Some scholars
would attach the final **once for all** to **sanctified** rather than to
offering, thus making the effect of the work of Christ, the sanctification, once for all like the offering which effects it. This in itself
may be true enough, but the position of this one Greek word at the
end, which gives it an added emphasis, and the frequent reference
in earlier chapters to the once for all character of the sacrifice suggest
that it should be taken so here also. The completeness and finality
of the sanctification are adequately expressed by the perfect tense
we have been sanctified. 'The definitive consecration of men to
God, promised in the prophecy of Jeremiah, is accomplished by the
offering of the body of Christ, once for all (10:10), because that
offering is a "sin-offering" (verse 18), providing the essential assurance that God "will remember their sins and their misdeeds no
more" ' (Peterson, p. 149). Here we are faced with a familiar
problem, the tension between the already and the not yet. The
Pastoral Epistles refer to Hymenaeus and Philetus, who 'have
swerved from the truth by holding that the resurrection is past
already' (2 Tim. 2:17), the implication being that Christians are
already living in the new order, are already perfect, that there is no
need for further effort, that life and conduct are of no significance.
The whole point of this letter is however to encourage the readers
to a greater effort, to a fuller realisation of the possibilities opened
up for them. To put it briefly, the final consummation is yet to
come, but the decisive victory has already been won. As Peterson
writes elsewhere (p. 186), 'our writer's emphasis on the perfecting
of believers by Christ is designed to encourage *confidence about their
relationship with God* and to encourage them *to persevere in that
confidence*, even in the face of hostility and suffering. Although in a
sense there is a journey of faith to be completed towards that final
goal, the end is already experienced and *enjoyed as a gift from God*
(12:22–4, 28)' (italics original). They have been sanctified, brought
into a new relationship with God, and they are in danger of throwing
it all away. What they should be doing is to go forward in faith and
hope and confidence, in the knowledge that the decisive act has
already been accomplished.

For the modern reader there is something incongruous about the

use of an Old Testament passage which involves its being placed on
the lips of Jesus, who lived long after the passage was actually
written. One solution is to argue that the passage is taken as in
some sense prophetic, 'a factual prediction of the Incarnation by
the pre-existent Son of God speaking overhead of the psalmist'
(Manson, p. 144), or to think of the pre-existent Christ as speaking
through the psalmist (Westcott). This however involves ideas which
are also difficult for many a modern reader, in particular a conception of inspiration that entails the superseding of any human reason
in the prophet or seer by the divine power that has taken possession
of him. Such ideas were prevalent in the ancient world, as can be
seen for example in the works of Philo (e.g. *Spec. Leg.* I.65, IV.49);
but there is no indication that the author of Hebrews shared Philo's
'ecstatic' view of prophecy. He does indeed come close to it, in that
as noted above at 2:6, it is God who speaks in the Old Testament
and the human author is not important; but there is no suggestion
that the human author, or the interpreter, had to be possessed by
a 'corybantic frenzy' for the author to write or the interpreter
expound his words (cf. for example Philo, *Mig. Ab.* 34–35). Here
Hughes makes a point worth considering: in a survey of our author's
use of the Old Testament (pp. 47ff.) he detects a pattern according
to which that use 'is always through the screen provided by the
revelation in Jesus' (p. 62). Indeed, 'the author sees such a close
conformity between the Old Testament and New Testament forms
of the Word of God that the former can now be appropriated to
give expression to the latter' (*ibid.*). According to the prologue, God
who spoke through the prophets has now finally spoken in a Son.
Now there are numerous places in the Old Testament where reference is made to the Word of the Lord which came to one prophet
or another. For our author this Word is now embodied in the person
of Jesus, and this for him justifies the use of these quotations with
reference to Jesus: the Old Testament texts are ' "up-dated" in the
light of the new form of the Word so that they can actually be
identified with the *logoi* (words) of Jesus' (*ibid.*). On the same page
Hughes lists a number of gospel passages which 'show that there
were in the early church strong traditions of words and acts of Jesus
which coincide with the attitudes here described in scripture words
but attributed to him'. Out author was thus not alone, although no
other writer worked out these ideas at such length and in such
detail. By our standards it may be an arbitrary approach, as Hughes
admits (p. 57) but it is not so arbitrary as the mere 'proof-text'
method of which the author is sometimes accused, and it is rather
less difficult than the idea of a pre-incarnate Christ already at work
in Old Testament events or speaking through Old Testament

figures. What emerges, as Hughes had written earlier (p. 47), is a
theology of the Word of God—not a Logos theology like that of
John, or a Logos doctrine like that of Philo, but a theology of the
Word that is our author's own. 'The continuity which binds Christians to the Old Testament scriptures and them to the Christians
is for the writer grounded in his conception of God. Because God
is wholly consistent, his Word is discernible in the Old Testament
to those who also have the New Testament, in spite of the external
differences within the old and new modes of address' (Hughes, *loc.
cit.*).

SEATED AT THE RIGHT HAND OF GOD

10:11–18

11–12. One further contrast remains to be drawn before the author
turns to his next admonition after this lengthy exposition of the
theme of priesthood. Verse 11 actually adds nothing new, but now
the scope is widened to include not the high priest only, but every
priest, and not only the sacrifice of the Day of Atonement but the
regular daily sacrifices: **every priest stands daily at his service,
offering repeatedly the same sacrifices, which can never take
away sins.** In contrast, **when Christ had offered for all time a
single sacrifice for sins, he sat down at the right hand of God.** It
has been noted before as one of the author's characteristics that he
often mentions some theme in passing, only to leave it and then
return to develop it at some later point. So here: it was already
stated in the prologue (1:3) that 'when he had made purification for
sins, he sat down at the right hand of the Majesty on high', while
8:1 speaks of a high priest 'seated at the right hand of the Majesty
in heaven'. Now the point about his sitting down fulfils several
functions: for one thing, it signifies the completion of Christ's sacrificial offering, so often said to have been made once and for all. The
priests stood at the altar in the performance of their duties, and
would only sit down when these duties had been fulfilled. 'A seated
priest is the guarantee of a finished work and an accepted sacrifice'
(Bruce). Moreover, as the author has repeatedly emphasised, their
sacrifices were ultimately ineffective, incapable of dealing with the
real problem, which is sin. As Bruce's comment suggests, Christ's
sitting at the right hand of God implies the acceptance of his
sacrifice, and hence its efficacy. It also underlines his exaltation to
the highest dignity and status, and this in turn provides an additional
basis for confidence and assurance on the part of the readers as they

approach the throne of grace. At 2:18 and 4:15f. above the emphasis
was on his sympathy and understanding, based on the fact that he
had himself suffered and endured; now the confidence that he is
able to help is given a further support, in that in his exalted position
he has direct and immediate access to God and is therefore the more
able to help should advocacy be required. His priestly work is done,
so far as sacrifice is concerned, but he remains 'a priest for ever'
according to Ps. 110:4, so often quoted already. His function now
however is not sacrifice but intercession. Here commentators note
the 'misleading influence' (Moffatt) of the Vulgate Latin version:
Latin has no perfect participle active, unlike Greek, and therefore
the Vulgate uses a present participle here, which suggests that Christ
is offering for all time a single sacrifice for sins. The Greek however
has a perfect: the sacrifice is over and complete.

13. Verse 12 clearly echoes Ps. 110:1, which also lies behind 1:3
and 8:1, although in none of these cases do we have a direct
quotation. The whole verse is quoted at 1:13, and now the substance
of the second part is echoed here in verse 13: **then to wait until his
enemies should be made a stool for his feet.** The enemies are not
identified, but the reference is probably not to the devil (said to
have been 'destroyed' at 2:14) or hostile powers (who are nowhere
mentioned in this letter). Bruce plausibly suggests that 'there may
be an implied warning here to his readers not to let themselves be
numbered among the enemies of the exalted Christ, but rather to
be reckoned as His friends and companions by preserving their
fidelity to the end (cf. 3:14)'. Clement of Rome (36:5–6) quotes 1:13
in a string of quotations from Hebrews (three of them quotations
from the Psalms) and then continues: 'Who then are these enemies?
They that are wicked and resist His will' (tr. Lightfoot). We may
compare and contrast Paul's use of the text along with Ps. 8:6 at 1
C. 15:24–28, where Christ must *reign* until *he* has put all enemies
under his feet—and the last enemy to be destroyed is death. Thereafter he is to deliver the kingdom to God the Father. In this version
(*RSV*) it might appear that it is Christ himself who is to effect the
conquest, but as Barrett notes (*The First Epistle to the Corinthians*,
p. 358) it is not clear what subject should be supplied; a few lines
later he adds that Paul's use of a loose quotation from Ps. 110:1
suggests that the subject here is God, while *NEB* in fact translates
'he is destined to reign until God has put all enemies under his
feet'. However that may be, it is clear that the two authors have a
somewhat different emphasis. If our author knew Paul's letter, he
is using the material in a rather different way. It is not without
interest to note that while the quotation of Ps. 110:1 leads Paul at
this point to think of the similarly worded passage in Ps. 8, Hebrews

uses the latter verse at a different point (see 2:6–8 above) and for another purpose.

14. Verse 14 then sums up the whole argument: **by a single offering he has perfected for all time those who are sanctified**. As Montefiore remarks, 'each particular phrase in this sentence has been the subject of full exposition earlier in the Epistle'. This is no mere vain repetition, however, but a deliberate and concentrated effort to drive the message home. Whatever the situation of the addressees, it gave our author deep concern and he is at pains to deal with it. In this verse there is a small point of Greek grammar which calls for notice: at verse 10 above the author says 'we have been sanctified', using the perfect tense to indicate a completed action the effects of which continue into the present. Here however, as at 2:11 above, **those who are sanctified** translates a present participle, literally 'those who are being sanctified'. It is possible to make too much of this difference, but a difference there is; the English past participle might suggest that the process of sanctification is already complete, whereas the Greek rather indicates that it is still going on. We cannot assume that we *have been* sanctified, and that that is the end of it; there is no more to be done, no need for effort. Once again, there is a certain tension between the 'already' and the 'not yet'. What is clear is that the words **he has perfected** emphasise 'that the sacrifice of Christ has a permanent result for believers' (Peterson, p. 149). This does not however mean that they are already in the full sense perfect: they still have to live in the conditions of this life, with all its problems and its temptations; the final consummation is yet to come. What it does mean is, in Peterson's words (pp. 151f.), that 'the *consummation* of man in a direct and lasting personal relationship with God . . . is proclaimed a present possibility, through the finished work of Christ'. Barrett (*Dodd Festschrift*, p. 365) sums up the matter very neatly when he writes that 'Christians, though living in this world, have already begun to experience the world to come. In their baptism they have tasted the heavenly gift, become partakers of the Holy Spirit, tasted the good word of God and the powers of the age to come (6:4f.); and they have approached Mount Sion, the heavenly Jerusalem (12:22–24). Their life is one of hope and struggle, in which they are sustained by the fact that that for which they strive has already been achieved for them, and that they have already begun to enjoy it'. In this new situation the vital question is one of the proper response: apathy, indifference, still more apostasy, must clearly be unthinkable, nor can one simply presume upon this new relationship and conclude that there is nothing more to be done. The proper response must be to strive for a full realisation of the possibilities

that are now opened up. From this we can see the aim and object
which our author has in view.

15–17. The next three verses find confirmation for the argument
in a summary of the New Covenant passage in Jeremiah which was
quoted at 8:8–12 above. There it was used as proof that the old
covenant was obsolete, here the summary is adduced as the testimony of the Holy Spirit to the new order: **the Holy Spirit also
bears witness to us.** Verse 16 presents the first part of Jer. 31:33,
with some minor changes from the original quotation: **This is the
covenant that I will make with them** (instead of 'with the house
of Israel'); in the third and fourth lines 'hearts' and 'minds' are
interchanged. Then verse 17 adds the last line of Jer. 31:34, which
is clearly the vital one for our author's purpose; **I will remember
their sins and their misdeeds no more.** Again there is a slight
modification, in the insertion of 'and their misdeeds', but these
changes do not affect the meaning. Only what is essential to the
author's purpose is adduced: the promise in Jeremiah involved first
a new relationship between God and his people, and secondly the
blotting out of their sins and transgressions from God's memory.
This for our author has been accomplished by the sacrifice of Christ.

18. Verse 18 then draws the logical conclusion: **Where there is
forgiveness of these, there is no longer any offering for sin.** The
old sacrifices had to be repeated because they could not actually
deal with sin; indeed they provided a reminder of sin, year after
year (cf. verse 3 above). In the new order sin has been dealt with,
once and for all. Sacrifices and sin-offerings are therefore obsolete.
In fact, although the earliest Christians at first continued to attend
the temple in Jerusalem (cf. for example Ac. 2:46; 3:1), the practice
of animal sacrifice was in time to be abandoned; it was the prophetic
tradition as to what God requires in the way of service that was to
become dominant, mercy and not sacrifice, righteousness and truth
and justice rather than burnt offerings. There is indeed a place for
sacrifice, but it is the sacrifice of praise, of well-doing, of mutual
sharing (cf. 13:15–16 below).

As noted above at 4:13, it is sometimes useful in dealing with a
lengthy discourse to pause and review the way by which we have
come. Otherwise close attention to the details may leave us unable
to grasp the full range and sweep of the argument. This is another
such point. The author has now completed his doctrinal exposition,
and at 10:19 he launches into a lengthy exhortation and admonition
in which he seeks to draw out the practical implications for his
readers of all that has been said.

The theme of priesthood was first introduced in a single brief clause in the prologue (1:3), followed immediately by another clause which apart from the quotation of Ps. 110:1 at 1:13 and an echo at 8:1 is left without further mention until 10:13: when he had made purification for sins, he sat down at the right hand of the Majesty on high. A second brief allusion occurs at 2:17: he had to be made like his brethren in every respect, so that he might become a merciful and faithful high priest in the service of God (cf. also 3:1: the apostle and high priest of our confession), and then at 4:15 we have a verse which sums up the point of the earlier part of the letter: we have not a high priest who is unable to sympathise with our weaknesses, but one who in every respect has been tempted as we are, yet without sinning. The aim of these early chapters is to provide encouragement and reassurance by emphasising the humanity, the sympathy, the understanding of this great high priest who has 'passed through the heavens' (4:14). Exalted he may be, crowned with glory and honour (2:9), but this is no remote and austere figure, untouched by feelings of human sympathy. Because he himself has suffered and been tempted, he is able to help those who are tempted (2:18).

The development of the theme of priesthood begins at 5:1–10 with a statement of the qualifications required in any high priest, and the proof that they are fulfilled in Jesus. This section introduces another quotation which will receive fuller attention later, the fourth verse of Ps. 110 with its reference to 'a priest for ever, after the order of Melchizedek'. These words are repeated like a recurring refrain at 5:6; 5:10 and 6:20, where they serve to bring the discussion back to the theme of priesthood after the long admonitory section which begins at 5:11. The detailed discussion of the theme begins in 7:1–10 by harking back to the story in Genesis (14:17–20) of Melchizedek's meeting with Abraham, and includes further echoes of Ps. 110:4 in the remainder of the chapter (verses 11, 15, 17, 21, 28). The Genesis story is used to provide the proof of Melchizedek's superiority to Abraham, and consequently to Levi, who at the time was yet unborn ('still in the loins of his ancestor', 7:10). This in turn entails the superiority of a priest 'after the order of Melchizedek' to the levitical priesthood. The implication of a new and different priesthood is that perfection was not attainable through the old (7:11–19); indeed, the former commandment is set aside because of its weakness and uselessness (7:18). A further argument is introduced at 7:23–28 in the contrast between the many priests of the old order and the one permanent priest of the new.

At 8:1 a further echo of Ps. 110:1 serves to introduce a contrast between the true sanctuary which is in heaven (cf. 9:24) and its earthly 'copy and shadow' (8:5). Not only is there now a new priest

and a true sanctuary, there is also a new covenant, according to the
prophecy of Jeremiah 31:31–34, which is quoted at length. In
speaking (through Jeremiah) of a new covenant, God treats the first
as obsolete (8:13). The old is indeed still in existence, but 'what is
becoming obsolete and growing old is ready to vanish away'. Chapter
9 then compares and contrasts the ordinances of the old order and
the new: first the tabernacle and its furnishings are described (verses
1–5), then the atonement ritual is outlined (verses 6–10). Over
against the annual entrance of the high priest on the Day of Atonement, our author sets Christ's entrance once and for all into the
Holy place, 'taking not the blood of goats and calves but his own
blood, thus securing an eternal redemption' (9:11–12). The sacrifices
of the old dispensation are given a limited efficacy, as sanctifying
'for the purification of the flesh', but it is the blood of Christ which
alone can cleanse the conscience (verses 13–14). He is therefore the
mediator of a new covenant, which brings about a new relationship
between God and his people, 'so that those who are called may
receive the promised eternal inheritance' (9:15). He has entered 'not
into a sanctuary made with hands, a copy of the true one, but into
heaven itself, now to appear in the presence of God on our behalf'
(9:24). This suggests that there are two distinct aspects to Christ's
priestly work, the single sacrifice of himself, offered once and for
all, through which he effected a true purification for his people
and inaugurated a new relationship with God, and the continuing
intercession, help and assistance which he is ever ready to afford to
those in need. He is after all 'a priest for ever', according to Ps.
110:4, and even on a merely human level 'every high priest chosen
from among men is appointed to act on behalf of men in relation
to God' (5:1). His sacrifice is complete, and needs no repetition,
but he remains a priest, with a ministry to fulfil.

Finally the first part of chapter 10 echoes some of the themes
which have already been introduced, employing them in new ways
to drive home the author's message. The law, possessing only the
shadow and not the reality, can never with its multiplicity of sacrifices make perfect those who draw near: it is impossible that the
blood of bulls and goats should take away sins. A quotation of Ps.
40:6–8 adduces one of the strongest Old Testament passages
affirming God's rejection of sacrifice, and at the same time points
the way to a new and deeper understanding: the rejection of sacrifice
in the first part of the quotation is balanced in the second by 'Lo,
I have come to do thy will'. Sacrifice is to be replaced by obedience.
In our author's words, 'he abolishes the first in order to establish
the second'. A final contrast at 10:11 sets on the one hand 'every
priest' standing daily at his service and on the other Christ, his

sacrificial work completed, seated at the right hand of God. The
two themes enunciated at the beginning in the prologue (1:3) are
thus here brought together once again. An echo of Jeremiah's
prophecy leads to the conclusion of this long discussion: where there
is forgiveness of these, there is no longer any offering for sin.

Drawing the main threads together in this way allows us to see
something of the scope and sweep of our author's argument.
Working through it verse by verse, we may at times feel it arbitrary
and repetitive, perhaps even perverse. As Hughes puts it (p. 56),
'we have to say quite simply that some of the devices used no longer
meet the exegetical standards required by the critical method'; but
he adds immediately after that 'in comparison with other exegetical
traditions of his time' our author 'has an appreciably high regard
for the Old Testament text and for historical principles of exegesis'.
His methods are not ours, but he is a man of the first century, and
should be judged accordingly. What is beyond doubt or question is
the deep concern and seriousness with which he approaches his
task. It is of the utmost importance to him that his readers should
fully comprehend the significance of his Old Testament quotations
as he expounds them in a new situation, in the light of Christ. His
work is in fact a reminder of something all too easily forgotten, that
a true theology is not static, a mere repetition of the formulae of a
bygone age, however hallowed they may be; it must grow and
develop, in ever new and deeper understanding. Part at least of the
problem is that his readers, as he told them at 5:12, 'need milk, not
solid food'. Much is said today about relevance, in the changed and
changing situations of modern times; but it is not always realised
that this is not a modern problem. It has been present almost from
the beginnings of Christianity. From some points of view Hebrews,
and particularly these chapters, might seem unlikely to have any
relevance to our modern world, but near the end of his book Hughes
says (p. 135), 'it is difficult to resist the instinct that this message
of buoyant hope to Christians who are confused and dispirited is
also a message for our times as well as those in which it was written'.

From a Christological point of view it is clear that the focus of
these chapters is on the great high priest of the heavenly sanctuary,
i.e. the risen and exalted Jesus. It is however also clear from earlier
chapters that our author places considerable weight on the humanity
of Jesus, while the prologue proclaims his pre-existence. A later
verse (13:8) will affirm that 'Jesus Christ is the same yesterday and
today and for ever'. That is important, because it is the human
Jesus who has suffered and been tempted who is also the great high
priest, and who is therefore able to be sympathetic and understanding; but while it is easy enough to relate the human and the

exalted Jesus, our author nowhere spells out their relation to the
pre-existent, except that they are one and the same. There is no
talk of divine and human natures; that was to concern a later age.

CONFIDENCE TO ENTER THE SANCTUARY

10:19–25

19–22. At Rom. 12:1 Paul turns from his discussion of theological
topics to the practical implications with the words 'I appeal to you
therefore, brethren . . .' So here our author, with a similar **therefore**, turns to the practical implications of his long discussion. It is
in the light of all that he has said above that **we have confidence
to enter the sanctuary by the blood of Jesus**; his single sacrifice
has established a new relationship which makes that confidence
possible. The word rendered **confidence** has already been used
above at 3:6 ('we are his house if we hold fast our confidence',
which suggests that the readers are in danger of throwing that
confidence away, cf. 10:35 below), and also at 4:16 in a similar
invitation to this ('let us then with confidence draw near to the
throne of grace'). There is however a difference of emphasis, slight
though it may be: at 4:16 the readers are urged to draw near with
a confidence based on the assurance that the high priest who has
passed through the heavens is one who can sympathise; here they
now have that confidence, and are summoned to act upon it. As
noted at 3:6 above, the word referred originally to the right of a
free citizen to express his opinion in the assembly of his peers, and
hence has associations of openness, frankness, candour and boldness
(see W. C. van Unnik, *BJRL* 44 [1962], pp. 466–488). Actually the
summons **let us draw near** (verse 22) has a double basis: first the
confidence which the readers now have, and secondly the fact that
we have a great priest over the house of God (verse 21; cf. 4:14–
16). As noted at 4:14 above, the Hebrew title means literally 'great
priest' but Greek has two forms, the simple meaning 'priest' and a
compound meaning 'high priest', to which the adjective 'great' is
often added, as frequently in the preceding chapters. Here we have
the simple Greek form with the adjective, corresponding exactly to
the Hebrew title.

Verse 20 presents some problems, particularly in regard to the
final words **through the curtain, that is, through his flesh**. The
construction of the passage as a whole is literally: we have confidence
for entrance . . . which he inaugurated for us as a new and living

way ('entrance' is a noun, followed by a relative pronoun in agreement, with 'a new and living way' in apposition. *RSV* thus paraphrases slightly, but preserves the meaning). The verb translated **opened** means to inaugurate or dedicate, and is used of the first covenant at 9:18 above (*RSV* 'ratified'). The **new and living way** naturally recalls Jn 14:6, where Jesus says 'I am the way, the truth and the life'. The way is new because it has not been open before; that is clear enough, but it is not so clear why it should be called living. Montefiore's explanation 'because it is the way opened up through the death of him who lives for ever' would seem to be little more than playing with words. It is indeed the way to life, but that does not make the way itself 'living'. The most probable explanation would seem to be to link the thought of John 14:6 with 7:25 above: he is able for all time to save those who draw near to God *through him*, since he always lives to make intercession for them. Jesus is himself the way to God, and can truly be described as living. The **curtain** is most probably the one which screened off the inner shrine (6:19f.), corresponding to the 'second curtain' of 9:3; there was also a screen at the outer door of the tent (Exod. 26:36–37), but such details no longer call for mention. It is enough that Jesus has gone into the inner shrine behind the curtain as a forerunner on our behalf (6:19–20), and in so doing has opened the way for others. The problem lies in the addition of the words **that is, his flesh**: to what do they refer? It is certainly very natural to take these words as standing in apposition to, and explanatory of, the curtain which has just been mentioned. The effect of this is to identify the curtain with the flesh of Jesus, which incidentally is one of the points listed by Ernst Haenchen (*RGG*[3] II, cols. 1652ff.) as evidence for 'gnostic' influence in the New Testament. Now it is beyond question that the gnostics treated the veil or curtain as symbolic of the firmament: according to the *Hypostasis of the Archons* (*NHC* II 94.9–10; *NHLE* 158) 'a veil exists between the world above and the realms that are below' (the Coptic retains the Greek word used here in Hebrews; in *SJC* (*NHLE* 225) the curtain is 'between the immortals and those that came after them'). The *Gospel of Philip* (*NHC* II 84.23–85.10; *NHLE* 150) contains a passage which appears to combine the rending of the veil in the Passion story (Mt. 27:51; Mk 15:38) with echoes of Hebrews: 'The veil at first concealed how God controlled the creation, but when the veil is rent and the things inside are revealed, this house will be left desolate, or rather will be [destroyed] (cf. Mt. 23:38; 24:2) . . . If some belong to the order of the priesthood they will be able to go within the veil with the high priest' (cf. Heb. 6:19–20). It is urged that the veil was not rent at the top only, or at the bottom, but from top to bottom: 'Those

above opened to us who are below, in order that we may go in to
the secret of the truth'. The *Second Treatise of the Great Seth* (*NHC
VII* 58.24–28; *NHLE* 333) has its own version of the Passion story:
'They nailed him to the tree, and they fixed him with four nails of
brass. The veil of his temple he tore with his hands'. All these
texts are considerably later, and some of the references show clear
evidence of the influence of the New Testament itself. These passages show how the imagery of the veil of the Temple, or the tabernacle, could be used to symbolise the division between the higher
and the lower worlds, and the rending of the veil the opening up
of access into the higher realm, and to that extent are relevant here;
but Gnosis is not the only source from which the imagery could
have been derived. We need to go further back to the use of the
motif in late Jewish speculation, from which the gnostics derived it
(cf. A. Adam, *Die Psalmen des Thomas*, *BZNW* 24, p. 35 n. 15 and
the unpublished thesis by G. W. MacRae, Cambridge [1966]). In
any case these passages do not explain the identification. They
illustrate how the curtain could be understood, but do not resolve
the problem of the addition.

An alternative solution which is generally rejected is to regard
these words as a later gloss. In itself this is of course possible, but
excision of anything that proves to be difficult is the easy way out;
surgery should be the very last resort. A third solution links the
clause not with the curtain but with the new and living way (so e.g.
Westcott, Montefiore). Montefiore objects to the first solution that
the function of the curtain is to conceal, not to reveal, whereas Jesus
in this letter does not hide the glory of God, but God speaks through
him. The primary difficulty with this third view is that the clause
and its antecedent are so far apart (although admittedly not so far
in the Greek); moreover it is simply not the natural way to understand the passage. Montefiore's objection to the first solution can
be met *if* the author in fact had the rending of the veil in mind. It
is precisely the rending of the veil that opens the way into the
heavenly sanctuary. Now it has to be admitted that the rending is
not expressly mentioned, but there are other indications of our
author's familiarity with traditions recorded in the gospels, whether
or not he knew the gospels themselves (cf. the 'Gethsemane' passage
at 5:7 and the parallels listed by Hughes, p. 62). It is difficult to
improve upon Moffatt's comment: 'instead of saying that (Jesus')
sacrificial death meant the rending of the veil (like the author of
Mk 15:38), i.e. the supersession of the Old Testament barriers
between God and man, he allegorises the veil here as the flesh of
Christ; this had to be rent before the blood could be shed, which
enabled him to enter and open God's presence for the people. It is

a daring, poetical touch, and the parallelism is not to be prosaically pressed into any suggestion that the human nature in Jesus hid God from men (in the days of his flesh), or that he ceased to be truly human when he sacrificed himself'. **His flesh** in this verse, like **the blood of Jesus** in verse 19, clearly refers to the life offered up in sacrifice; it is the association with the curtain that occasions the perplexity.

In the light of what he has just said, the author continues: **let us draw near with a true heart in full assurance of faith, with our hearts sprinkled clean from an evil conscience and our bodies washed with pure water**. At 3:12 above the readers were warned to beware 'lest there be in any of you an evil, unbelieving heart, leading you to fall away from the living God'. Here in contrast we have a positive expression of the same idea, with an admonition to sincerity and faith. A **true heart** is one in which there is no hypocrisy or deceit, no hesitation or doubt. The theme of **faith** has not so far received much attention, but will be given detailed treatment in the next chapter. It is however interesting to note that the word rendered **full assurance** is used at 6:11, with reference to the full assurance of hope, and is immediately followed by an injunction to be 'imitators of those who through faith and patience inherit the promises'. Here again our author has touched in passing on a theme to be more fully developed later. The other references to faith in earlier chapters are at 6:2, where faith toward God is among the 'elementary doctrines', and 4:2, where it is said that the message which came to the wilderness generation 'did not benefit them, because it did not meet with faith in the hearers'. When we add 3:19 with its statement that 'they were unable to enter because of unbelief', it is clear that faith for our author means belief and trust in God and in his promises. Faith and hope belong together: it is not a matter of mere wishful thinking, of 'hoping against hope', but of a confident assurance and expectation based on trust in God.

The mention of **hearts sprinkled clean from an evil conscience** recalls the ritual of the red heifer (Num. 19), but the author has already made it plain at 9:13f. that it is the blood of Christ which alone can cleanse the conscience (cf. 10:10: it is through the offering of the body of Jesus Christ that he and his readers have been sanctified). Aaron and his sons were to be **washed** with water before their consecration (Exod. 29:4; 40:12); also 'when they went into the tent of meeting, and when they approached the altar, they washed; as the Lord commanded Moses' (Exod. 40:32; cf. Exod. 30:20–21). In the same way the high priest 'shall bathe his body in water' before putting on the sacred vestments for the ritual of the Day of Atonement (Lev. 16:4). There may be an element of superstitious awe here, but there is also a proper sense that the holiness of the place demanded an appropriate reverence in those who entered. What in Exodus is required of the priests is now extended to all believers. In themselves the words could be taken to refer to bodily cleanliness in general; as Moffatt notes, 'ancient religious literature is full of orders for the penitent to approach the gods only after moral contrition and bodily cleansing, with a clean heart and a clean body, in clean clothes even'; but as he adds, such ablutions had to be repeated. There is however a more specific reference, to Christian baptism. Paul uses similar language: 'But you were washed, you were sanctified, you were justified in the name of the Lord Jesus Christ' (1 C. 6:11; cf. Eph. 5:26; Tit. 3:5). Some commentators have felt a certain incongruity in the association of inward and outward cleansing here in Hebrews: baptism is for them 'a spiritual washing to be contrasted with the outward washing of the body' (Montefiore cites 1 Pet. 3:21, which describes baptism 'not as a removal of dirt from the body', and adds 'yet our author seems to mean here an outward rite'). This is however to overlook the significance of the outward rite as the visible sign and symbol of an inward cleansing. The Qumran Community Rule offers an interesting parallel: of the man who persists in walking 'in the stubbornness of his heart' it says 'he shall neither be purified by atonement, nor cleansed by purifying waters, nor sanctified by seas and rivers, nor washed clean with any ablution. Unclean, unclean shall he be'. In contrast, 'it is through the spirit of true counsel concerning the ways of man that all his sins shall be expiated . . . He shall be cleansed from all his sins by the spirit of holiness uniting him to His truth . . . And when his flesh is sprinkled with purifying water and sanctified by cleansing water, it shall be made clean by the humble submission of his soul to all the precepts of God' (*1 QS* III, in Vermes, *The Dead Sea Scrolls in English*, pp. 74–75; cf. F. F. Bruce in *NTS* 9 [1963] pp. 224–227). We may recall also the description of John the Baptist in Josephus (*Ant.* 18.117), where it is said that he thought baptismal ablution would be acceptable 'if it were used not to beg off from sins committed, but for the purification of the body when the soul had previously been cleansed by righteous conduct' (tr. Thackeray, Loeb ed.). The point of all these passages is that the outward rite in and of itself is of no significance; it requires the cleansing of heart and conscience also.

23. Verse 22 is but the first of three admonitions in this section, which as Westcott noted long ago presents 'the three members of the Christian triad of earthly discipline' (i.e. faith, hope and love) 'in the familiar order of St Paul (1 C. 13:13)'. The second follows in verse 23: **let us hold fast the confession of our hope without**

wavering, for he who promised is faithful. This echoes a number of points which have already been made earlier: **let us hold fast** recalls the admonitions of 3:6, 14, where the same Greek word is used with reference to holding fast to their confidence. Almost the same phrase 'let us hold fast our confession' appears at 4:14, but with a different Greek verb which means rather to lay hold of or grasp (cf. 6:18, where it is rendered 'to seize the hope set before us'). It is difficult to say how far this distinction should be pressed, but what is clear is that this hope and confidence is something to be laid hold of and firmly held. The word rendered **confession** occurs not only at 4:14 but earlier in 3:1, where Jesus is described as 'the apostle and high priest of our confession'. Taking all this together, one might perhaps say that the confession of Jesus, in the light of all that has been said in the preceding chapters, affords ground for confidence, and this in turn is the basis for hope. **Without wavering** is actually an adjective agreeing with 'confession': as Bruce says, 'if the confession wavers it is because the confessors waver'. The author's call is for a steadfast, tenacious and unswerving adherence to their confession and to the confidence and hope for which it is the basis. It should perhaps be added that in some Nag Hammadi texts there are references to a self-designation of the gnostics, sometimes translated in the form 'the race that does not waver'. This is another case in which conclusions drawn from a similarity in English could be dangerous. There is admittedly some affinity, but the Greek word which appears to underlie the Coptic is different (in one passage it is retained as a loan-word), and so too are the associations involved: in the *Apocryphon of John*, for example (e.g. *NHC* II 25.23), *NHLE* 112 translates 'the immovable race'. The associations are not so much with unswerving confidence and steadfast faith as here in Hebrews, but rather with an unshakable stability that seems to owe more to the 'sage' of Greek philosophy than to the Bible (cf. M. A. Williams, *The Immovable Race* (*NHS* 29), Leiden [1985], who writes that to belong to this race is to realise full human potential, 'a potential which is in theory open to anyone who "seeks and finds", but which in practice is achieved by only certain persons' (p. 172). Our author too is concerned that his readers should realise their full potential, but he expects it of all of them. As often happens, we need to pay attention to the (sometimes subtle) differences as well as to the similarities). Jesus was described as **faithful** at 2:17 above, and also in the comparison with Moses at 3:2–6, but **he who promised** suggests that the reference here is to God (cf. 11:11 below; also 6:17–18 above. The faithfulness of God is almost axiomatic, cf. 1 C. 1:9; 10:13).

24–25. The third admonition turns to relationships within the community. At 3:1 above the readers were enjoined to 'consider' Jesus; here the same verb is used: lit. 'let us consider one another for provocation of love and good works'. The word here rendered 'provocation' may, like the English word, be used in a bad sense: its one other occurrence in the New Testament is at Ac. 15:39, of the 'sharp contention' between Paul and Barnabas. Here however it refers to mutual stimulation to **love and good works**, and the *RSV* paraphrase **let us consider how to stir up one another** brings out the meaning: it is a question of *mutual* stimulus and encouragement, and this is only possible within the fellowship of a Christian community; hence the **not neglecting to meet together, as is the habit of some.** Who these were is not stated: it has been suggested that some regarded themselves as a kind of spiritual elite, and refused to associate with others, but that may be to import into Hebrews the situation found in some other texts, and for this there is no real evidence. It could also be that some were withdrawing because of pressures of one kind or another, the hostility of family or neighbours, the threat of persecution, in whatever form. We simply do not know. What is vital is that individualism and self-sufficiency, the desire to 'go it alone', may be disastrous. Christians *need* the fellowship of the community for the full development of their faith, each contributing as he may be able and receiving strength and encouragement from others. It is a matter of **encouraging one another**, and all the more urgent **as you see the Day drawing near.** Such mutual encouragement was already advocated at 3:13 above, and there too there is the note of urgency: exhort one another every day, as long as it is called 'today'. The verb rendered 'encourage, exhort' in these verses is cognate with the noun our author uses at 13:22 to describe his own work: a word of exhortation, or of encouragement. **The Day** is the Old Testament Day of the Lord, the day of judgment, the consummation of the ages, which early Christians associated with the return of Jesus (cf. 9:28); it is a day of vindication for the righteous, but of doom and judgment for the wicked (cf. verse 27). The early expectation of an imminent Parousia gave rise to problems with the lapse of time, when that expectation remained unfulfilled (cf. 2 Pet. 3:3ff.), although it is open to question whether modern scholars have not made too much of this. Christians in every age have had to live with what Goppelt called 'the tension between the eschatological existence of being aliens in this world and everyday life as people within secular history' (*Apostolic and Post-Apostolic Times*, p. 137). 'He who confesses Christ stands already on the ground of that new abiding world (12:27f.), and he who denies him will perish at the end' (ib. 138).

A FEARFUL PROSPECT OF JUDGMENT

10:26–31

26–27. The reference to the Day leads directly into the second part of this extended exhortation, which contains a stern warning of the dangers of apostasy and unbelief. In keeping with the rigorist attitude adopted earlier (cf. 6:4ff.), the author uses firm and uncompromising language: **if we sin deliberately after receiving the knowledge of the truth, there no longer remains a sacrifice for sins** . He and his readers have already been sanctified through the offering of the body of Jesus Christ, once and for all (10:10), and the process is not to be repeated; in earlier chapters our author has constantly emphasised the single sacrifice of Jesus over against the many sacrifices of the old priesthood. The logic of his argument entails that there can be no repetition. It should be noted that he says **if we sin deliberately**: Num. 15:22–31 draws a clear distinction between sins done unwittingly and those committed 'with a high hand'. Sins of ignorance could presumably still be atoned for under the rules of the old dispensation, but nothing is said of that; it is with wilful and deliberate sin that our author is here concerned (Paul in Gal. 6:1 speaks of restoring 'in a spirit of gentleness' one who is overtaken in any trespass, and our author himself is realistic enough (cf. 2:17f.; 4:15f.; 5:2) to realise that Christians are not immune to temptation). The phrase **the knowledge of the truth** occurs four times in the Pastorals (1 Tim. 2:4; 2 Tim. 2:25 [*RSV* to know the truth]; 3:7; Tit. 1:1), and of course there are numerous references to **the truth** in the Johannine literature. Those who accept the gospel and then abandon it have nothing to look for but **a fearful prospect of judgment, and a fury of fire which will consume the adversaries**. This is no light matter. As already noted (at 6:7–8 above) the association of fire and judgment is common in the New Testament, but it is not merely a fire of punishment. There are other associations also: at 12:29 below our author speaks of God himself as a consuming fire (cf. Dt. 4:24), and the famous passage in Malachi (3:2) describes the expected Lord as like a refiner's fire. The Coptic Gospel of Thomas (log. 82) contains an agraphon known also to Origen, 'he that is near me is near the fire', which Jeremias interprets in terms of the fire 'of testing, of tribulation, of suffering (1 Pet. 1:7; Rev. 3:18)' (*Unknown Sayings of Jesus*, [1964], p. 72; cf. also Mk 9:49). There is thus a whole cluster of associations to be taken into account, although the primary reference in the present context is clearly to judgment. The verse contains an echo of Isa. 26:11.

28–29. In his first admonition (2:2f.) the author noted that transgression against 'the message declared by angels' entailed due retribution, and used this as a warning against neglect of the salvation now offered. Here he repeats the warning, with a similar *qal wā-ḥōmer* argument in which he adduces the gist of Dt. 17:2–6: **A man who has violated the law of Moses dies without mercy at the testimony of two or three witnesses.** Two things call for mention here: in the first place the requirement of two or three witnesses is in the nature of an addendum, to save the accused from conviction on the evidence of one witness only, and to that extent is a mitigating factor. But there was no mercy for the convicted offender, so our author's use of the reference is justified. Secondly, the specific sin in view in Dt. 17:3 is that of idolatry and apostasy. It is not just a matter of transgression or disobedience, as at 2:2, but of a breach of the covenant, a repudiation of the law. The word translated **violated** means to set aside or reject, to declare invalid. As Bruce remarks, this suggests that our author has in mind something much more serious than what Paul calls being overtaken in any trespass, and the strong language of verse 29 bears this out: **How much worse punishment do you think will be deserved by the man who has spurned the Son of God, and profaned the blood of the covenant by which he was sanctified, and outraged the Spirit of grace?** Apostasy is tantamount to an insult flung in the face of a gracious God.

30–31. The following verses drive home the warning by adducing two further quotations, both from the Song of Moses in Dt. 32. The first, **'Vengeance is mine, I will repay'** (Dt. 32:35), differs both from the Hebrew ('vengeance is mine, and recompense') and from LXX ('in the day of vindication I will repay'), and even more from Philo's quotation at *Leg. All.* III.105. It is however quoted in the same form by Paul (Rom. 12:19); but before any hasty conclusions are drawn regarding Pauline influence it should be added that a very similar version appears in the Targums (as can be seen, the first part agrees with the Hebrew, the second with LXX). The most probable solution is that both Paul and Hebrews are drawing on a Greek form of a textual tradition related to that of the Targums. It should be noted that they make use of the quotation for different ends: Paul is warning his readers against revenge and retaliation, whereas our author is closer to the sense of the original. As the following verse in Deuteronomy shows, the passage is about God's vindication of his people (cf. Ps. 135:14). There are however two aspects to judgment, the vindication of the righteous and innocent and the condemnation of the wicked. The association of judgment and vindication is not uncommon (cf. e.g.

Ps. 43:1: Judge me, O God, and plead my cause (*AV*; cf. *NEB*),
which *RSV* renders: Vindicate me, O God, and defend my cause),
and indeed can still be found in the modern world in certain groups
who insist on the vindication of their cause, regardless of wider
considerations of equity and justice. A minority should be fairly
treated, but it should not expect to have everything tailored to its
requirements. On the other hand there is also a sense, particularly
emphasised by the prophets, that God's people themselves are not
exempt from a righteous and impartial judgment (e.g. Am. 3:2:
You only have I known . . . therefore I will punish you for all your
iniquities). It is in keeping with this that when our author goes on
to quote Dt. 32:36 it is the thought of judgment that is more
prominent: 'The Lord will judge his people'. The actual form of
words is the same, but the emphasis suggested by the context is
different. As at 2:13 above, two consecutive verses of the original
are quoted, with an **and again** to separate them. In that earlier
passage, the effect of the insertion was to make a new point of the
second verse; here it serves to isolate the first verse in a sense
suggested by the context, and the second then naturally follows to
reinforce it.

As Bruce remarks, 'our author has a deep conviction of the
awesome holiness of the divine majesty'. At 3:12 above he has
already warned his readers against falling away from **the living God**,
using a familiar Old Testament title, while at 12:29 below he speaks
of God as 'a consuming fire'. Here he rounds off his warning with
the ominous words **it is a fearful thing to fall into the hands of the
living God**. That God is good, gracious, long-suffering, plenteous in
mercy, is of course beyond doubt; but we may not presume upon
that goodness. In contrast, there is a curious passage in the apocryphal Gospel of Peter in which the elders of the Jews are made to
say 'it is expedient for us to be guilty of a very great sin before God,
and not to fall into the hands of the people of the Jews and be
stoned' (tr. H. B. Swete, London [1893], p. 27). Had he known it,
our author would have rejected it with horror.

YOU HAVE NEED OF ENDURANCE

10:32–39

In an earlier admonition (5:11–6:12; see the discussion following
6:20), our author blends encouragement and rebuke in an alter-
nation of sternness and conciliation, recognising the service rendered
in the past by his readers but urging that they show 'the same

earnestness in realising the full assurance of hope until the end' (as noted above, the word translated 'full assurance' is used in 10:22 as well as in 6:11). Similarly here, the first section of this admonition (verses 19–25) contains three exhortations embracing the three cardinal virtues of faith, hope and love (verses 22, 23, 24–25). The second (verses 26–31) presents a warning, couched in the strongest terms: apostasy means the spurning of the Son of God, profanation of the blood of the covenant, an insult to the Spirit of grace (one is reminded of the saying in the Gospels [Mk 3:28–29 and parallels] about the unforgivable sin of blasphemy against the Holy Spirit).

32–34. Now in this third section he strikes a more conciliatory note, seeking to encourage them by reminding them of their past experience. **Recall the former days,** he writes, **when after you were enlightened, you endured a hard struggle with sufferings.** The word **enlightened** provides another link with the earlier admonition, for it is used at 6:4 in the description of the apostates for whom there is no second chance. The occasion of this **hard struggle** we simply do not know: this is one of those allusions which would be readily understood by the readers, but leave us completely at a loss. All our information is contained in the text before us: it was subsequent to their baptism (**after your enlightenment**), and involved public exposure to **abuse and affliction.** The **struggle with sufferings** is literally a contest of sufferings, while **publicly exposed** suggests that they were made a public spectacle (cf. *NEB*: abused and tormented to make a public show. Paul uses the cognate noun at 1 C. 4:9). The imagery is that of contestants in an arena, but it would be dangerous to forge an immediate link with the persecution under Nero, in which as Tacitus relates (*Annals* 15.44), Christians were indeed made a public spectacle in the arena. Bruce remarks 'it could never have been said to Roman Christians after AD 64 that they had "not yet resisted unto blood, striving against sin" (cf. 12:4), and this is one of the major problems for any theory which seeks to combine a Roman destination and a late date. On the other hand, it could have been said *to the survivors* that they had not resisted unto blood, as others had done, and in any case a reference to martyrdom is not the only possible explanation of 12:4 (see below). More important for the present context is that it does not mention any martyrs: the sufferings listed are **abuse and affliction,** imprisonment, the **plundering of your property.** These suggest something short of an actual persecution like that of Nero, although still a severe trial to those who had to face it. Bruce draws attention to the famous passage in Suetonius (*Claud.* 25.4) reporting the expulsion of the Jews from Rome by Claudius because 'they were constantly indulging in riots at the instigation of Chrestus'.

Accepting the common inference that these riots resulted from the introduction of Christianity into the Jewish community in Rome, he suggests that 'a large-scale eviction of this nature would inevitably have been attended by widespread looting by the city proletariat, together with many other kinds of insults and indignities'. This certainly points in the right direction, but the events of AD 49 are not the only possible reference for this passage: Acts relates several instances of disturbances arising from the proclamation of the gospel in Jewish synagogues, and indeed Paul and Silas were imprisoned at Philippi (Ac. 16:19ff.). The same thing could have happened in many places: Christians were exposed to hostility from the outset. What is more important is our author's statement that his readers had **endured** these **sufferings, sometimes** themselves **exposed** to them, **sometimes being partners with those so treated**. They had thus shown their solidarity with the victims, had compassion on the prisoners, even shared their sufferings (so *NEB*). The mutual support of its members in times of trial and hardship has been one of the strengths of Christianity from the beginning. They had also accepted **the plundering of your property**, not in despair or in stoic indifference but joyfully, because they knew that they **had a better possession and an abiding one**. As Montefiore notes, 'their treasure was in heaven (Mt. 6:20), a city that lasts (13:14), the heavenly Jerusalem (12:22)'.

35–36. They have, then, proved the quality of their faith in the past. What is required of them now is perseverance and endurance. **Therefore do not throw away your confidence, which has a great reward**. It would be tragic if, having endured so much, they were now to fall away. **Confidence** is one of the recurring themes of the letter: the word is used at 4:16 and 10:19 of the assurance with which they may approach the throne of God, and at 3:6 of the confidence and pride in their hope which they are to hold fast. As noted above, it has associations of boldness (cf. Ac. 4:13 with its reference to the boldness of Peter and John in the face of the Sanhedrin): this is no time for faint hearts! **Reward** is the word translated 'retribution' at 2:2, and in the Greek Bible occurs only in Hebrews (cf. also 11:26). Some writers might take exception to the association of reward with well-doing, as if it made the action no longer meritorious but merely mercenary; but that raises questions which cannot be entered into here. Certainly our author has no such scruples: he has spoken repeatedly of hope and of promise, and if there is to be retribution for wrong-doing (cf. 2:2) it is natural to think that there should be reward for doing good, for faith and perseverance. The promise is sure, guaranteed by God himself (cf. 6:17–18), but the readers **have need of endurance, so that you**

may do the will of God (cf. Mk 7:21) **and receive what is promised.**
Whether they attain the goal or fall by the wayside depends on their
attitude now, their willingness to press on with confidence. The
word rendered **endurance** is another of those terms with a range of
meanings: *AV* has 'patience', but in modern usage this suggests
patient waiting for something to happen, whereas the Greek word
means rather more. It connotes steadfastness, fortitude, perseverance, 'especially as they are shown in the endurance of toil and
suffering' (*BAG* 846a). The cognate verb is used just above in verse
32, and again at 12:2, of Jesus enduring the cross. The author never
suggests that the living of the Christian life is an easy thing; there
are trials and tribulations to be expected; but the promise is
supremely worth the effort.

37–38. The following verses underline the urgency of the admonition by a scriptural proof: the delay will not be long. The main
part of the quotation comes from Hab. 2:3–4, with some modification, but it is prefaced by three words which in the Greek bible
occur together only here and at Isa. 26:20: **'yet a little while'.** Our
author appears to be drawing on the LXX version of Isaiah to
reinforce his quotation from Habakkuk. In the Hebrew text of
Habakkuk the reference is to a vision which will surely come and
not delay, but only the last part of the verse is quoted, without
specific reference to the vision. The Hebrew is literally 'coming it
will come', but LXX already makes it a masculine 'he will come'; by
inserting the definite article before 'coming' our author makes the
messianic reference clear: **'the coming one'** (cf. Mt. 11:3 par.) **'shall
come and shall not tarry'.** In verse 38 the order of the phrases in
Habakkuk is inverted: where the prophet has a contrast between
the man whose soul is not upright and the righteous, Hebrews
makes the righteous the subject of both verbs. It is a question
whether he perseveres or shrinks back: **'if he shrinks back, my soul
has no pleasure in him'.** A further point is the insertion of a
possessive in the first phrase here: **'my righteous one shall live by
faith'.** This is actually the reading of some LXX manuscripts, but
others attach the possessive to 'faith'; it is possible that the agreement when it occurs is the result of influence from our present text.
There are in fact several ways of understanding this short phrase.
Basically there are three elements (in the order of the Greek): the
subject 'the righteous', a prepositional phrase 'by faith', and the
verb 'shall live'. Paul quotes it twice, without any possessive
pronoun (Rom. 1:17; Gal. 3:11), in a way that suggests he took it
to mean 'he that is righteous by faith (and not by works) shall live'.
This of course makes it a key text for his doctrine of justification
by faith. The addition of 'my' to 'faith' in some LXX manuscripts

suggests that it is by God's faithfulness that the righteous will live. According to the Qumran sect (*IQ pHab*. VIII, 1–3; Vermes, *The Dead Sea Scrolls in English*, p. 239), the text concerns 'all those who observe the Law in the House of Judah, whom God will deliver from the House of Judgment because of their suffering and because of their faith in the Teacher of Righteousness'. This shows how the sect applied the text in their own situation. The majority of late manuscripts of Hebrews, with one papyrus, omit the possessive, but this is probably an assimilation to Paul. Only a few agree with the majority LXX reading, attaching 'my' to 'faith', but there is strong support for the reading 'my righteous one'. The natural interpretation of the quotation in its present context, particularly in view of what is to come in the next chapter (to which the *UBS* editors give the simple heading 'Faith'), is that it is through perseverance in faith that the righteous will live. In his earlier admonition, at 6:12, he urged his readers to be 'imitators of those who through faith and patience inherit the promises'. It is perhaps not too much to say that, after his usual fashion, he is now picking up this theme again; the long roll of the 'heroes of faith' in the next chapter will make his point abundantly clear.

39. Meanwhile he rounds off this section with a word of re-assurance, expressing his confidence in them: **we are not of those who shrink back and are destroyed, but of those who have faith and keep their souls.** A more literal rendering might be 'we do not belong to those who shrink back, which results in destruction, but to those of faith, which results in saving of soul' (or better, 'the gaining of life'; the Greek word *psyche* does indeed mean 'soul', but that suggests some 'spiritual or immaterial part of man, held to survive death' (*Concise Oxford Dictionary*), a Platonic rather than a biblical concept (cf. 6:19 above). At Mk 8:35, where the word occurs again, *RSV* translates 'whoever would save *his life* will lose it'; there is not much point in winning a fortune if one does not live to enjoy it!).

As in his earlier admonition, the author shrewdly blends together rebuke and encouragement, giving due recognition to the past achievement of his readers but at the same time warning of the dangers that may lie ahead. Constant harping on faults and short-comings might have defeated his purpose, by inducing a sense of hopelessness, a feeling that there was no point in making any effort, since the standards set were beyond their reach. The extra effort that may make all the difference is more likely to be summoned up when people feel that they have almost reached the goal. After a long climb, one last burst may be enough to reach the summit; but people are not likely to try if they think they are still somewhere on the lower slopes. On the other hand, standards must be set and maintained; there would be no point in lulling his readers into a false complacency. As Paul wrote (Phil. 3:13–14): 'one thing I do, forgetting what lies behind and straining forward to what lies ahead, I press on toward the goal'. That is the attitude our author wishes to inspire in his readers.

This second lengthy admonition echoes some of the themes of the first, but in different wording. In particular his emphasis on faith and endurance leads him to pick up the theme of 6:12, which he goes on to develop and elaborate in the next chapter.

THE HEROES OF FAITH

II:I–40

As is often the case, there is no real break at this point; the chapter and verse divisions merely break up the argument into manageable sections, and serve to facilitate reference. The ground is prepared by the references to faith in the preceding verses, and now our author proceeds to the development of this theme. The chapter begins with what appears to be intended as a definition: **Faith is the assurance of things hoped for, the conviction of things not seen.**

1–2. Like its English equivalent **faith**, the Greek term has a fairly wide range of meaning (cf. *BAG* 662ff. and the literature mentioned there). It can for example refer to the Christian religion (e.g. Gal. 1:23; 6:10), or to a body of doctrine (Jude 3). As Montefiore notes, the verb 'to believe' can range in meaning 'from the act of bare intellectual assent (Jas 2:19) to personal commitment (Jn 1:12)'. Hebrews 4:2 above provides an example of the difference between the mere hearing of the message and its reception in faith. The important point is however that in the New Testament the chief significance of the word is not in terms of a body of propositions to be intellectually accepted; the primary reference is not to a system of doctrine. Broadly speaking, we can distinguish two main meanings, with various possible sub-divisions under each; the first relates in general to 'that which causes trust and faith' (*BAG*), in other words faithfulness, reliability. We have had examples of the cognate adjective 'faithful' in this sense at 2:17; 3:2, 5 above. The second and more common sense is that of '*trust, confidence, faith* in the active sense' (*BAG* 2). In the synoptic gospels, Jesus looks for faith in those who seek his help, wants them to trust him, have confidence in him. The story of the Calming of the Storm (Mk 4:35–41), often regarded as merely a miracle story, provides an interesting example, not only in Jesus' question to the disciples 'Have you no faith?' but in the fact that at the height of the storm 'he was in the stern, asleep on the cushion' (v. 38); such was his own trust in God. This faith, it should be added, is no mere transitory trust and confidence; the thought quite readily passes over into that of continuing fidelity and endurance. Commenting on the Habakkuk verse quoted above, Sir George Adam Smith wrote, many years ago, 'In face of experience that baffles faith, the duty of Israel is patience in loyalty to God' (*The Book of the Twelve Prophets* II, London [1928], p. 143).

The problem in this verse lies in the word rendered **assurance**. The Greek word (*hypostasis*) has already occurred at 1:3, where it presents no problem and clearly refers to the reality of the divine nature, and also at 3:14, where the phrase 'our first confidence' is literally 'the beginning of the *hypostasis*'. Many commentators are prepared to accept a shift from the objective sense of 'reality' at 1:3 to a subjective sense of 'confidence, assurance' at 3:14 and here, but Köster (*TDNT* VIII, p. 585ff.) argues that the latter view is no longer tenable. *Hypostasis* in the present verse stands in parallel with *elenchos*, which refers to proof rather than to inner conviction; the cognate verb relates to exposure, reproof, censure, for example by cross-examination in a law-court. In Köster's view, 'faith is the reality of what is hoped for in exactly the sense in which Jesus is called the *character* of the reality of the transcendent God in 1:3. The one formulation is as paradoxical as the other to the degree that the presence of the divine reality is found in the one case in the obedience of a suffering and dying man (cf. Heb. 5:7) and in the other in the faith of the community' (*op. cit.*, p. 588). *Hypostasis* 'always denotes the "reality" of God which stands contrasted with the corruptible, shadowy, and merely prototypical character of the world but which is paradoxically present in Jesus and is the possession of the community as faith' (*ib.* pp. 588f.). It should be added that Köster observes in a footnote (p. 586) that the subjective understanding 'dominates English exposition'. This may however be a case in which we should not distinguish too rigidly between the 'objective' and the 'subjective' meanings. Long ago Marcus Dods wrote: 'Substantially the words mean that faith gives to things future, which as yet are only hoped for, all the reality of actual present existence; and irresistibly convinces us of the reality of things unseen and brings us into their presence. Things future and things unseen must become certainties to the mind if a balanced life is to be lived' (*Expositor's Greek Testament ad loc.*).

The **things hoped for** must presumably include the fulfilment of

God's promises, but the reference to **things not seen** introduces another aspect, the invisible realities of the heavenly world. The tension between the 'already' and the 'not yet' is characteristic of some parts of the New Testament, and there is something of that here: the readers already have the hope and the assurance, but the full realisation of the promise is yet to come; they can see the visible realities of this earthly world, but the invisible realities of the heavenly world have yet to be revealed. What they can see even now is the faith shown by others, which demonstrates that they lived not for the things of this world but for hoped for and invisible realities. It is because of this that **the men of old received divine approval** (lit. 'were testified to'; the word occurs at 7:8, 17 above and in verses 4, 5 and 39 of the present chapter in the sense of someone having witness borne to them, while the active 'bears witness' appears at 10:15); commentators regularly refer to the 'fathers' of 1:1. They are the men of old (lit. 'elders') of this verse.

The rest of the chapter consists of a series of brief statements, some with a short explanatory comment, all introduced by a programmatic **by faith**. The first group consists of seven items (verses 3–12), followed by an interlude (13–16) which anticipates the concluding verses of the chapter; then follows a second group (17–31) of eleven items, after which our author cuts short his list and confines himself to a more generalising summary (32–38).

3. The first item is not strictly part of the series, but is, in Montefiore's words, 'prerequisite to all the rest'. If the world originated from a fortuitous concatenation of atoms, without any real meaning or purpose to our human life, that would almost inevitably lead to one attitude and way of life; belief in a doctrine of creation leads to quite another. But this is a matter of faith and not of scientific proof: **by faith we understand that the world** (lit. 'the aeons') **was created by the word of God**. The obvious reference is of course to the Creation story in Genesis, but we may recall also Ps. 33:6, 9; 2 Pet. 3:5. The word rendered **created** is not the usual term but one which means to set in order or put to rights (e.g. it is used at Mark 1:19 of the disciples 'mending' their nets); moreover **word** here is not *logos* but another term also used at 1:3 and 6:5 above; we should not think of the pre-existent Word of the Johannine prologue. The last clause **so that what is seen was made out of things which do not appear** could, in terms of the Greek word order, be translated 'so that the visible did not come into being out of the phenomenal', but this is less likely (cf. *NEB*: the visible came forth from the invisible). The verse is sometimes claimed as a proof-text for a doctrine of *creatio ex nihilo*, but this is not stated in so many words; rather the (superior) invisible world is the source and origin of the (inferior) visible realm.

4. It is often said that God is no respecter of persons (Ac. 10:34; cf. Rom. 2:11; Eph. 6:9; Col. 3:25); he shows no partiality. If he accepted Abel's sacrifice rather than Cain's (Gen. 4:3–7), there must be some reason, although Genesis did not explain it. Later interpretation held that Abel's sacrifice was accepted because he was righteous and Cain wicked (e.g. 1 Jn 3:12); or animal sacrifice was more acceptable than the fruits of the earth. Philo (*de Sac. A. et C.* 52) makes Cain guilty of a double fault, in that he made his offering only 'in course of time', and merely 'of the fruits', not of the firstfruits (for comparison cf. Williamson p. 323). For our author it is Abel's faith that makes the difference, and through it **he received approval as righteous.** In Gen. 4:10 the Lord says 'The voice of your brother's blood is crying to me from the ground', probably meant as a cry for vengeance; here however the meaning seems to be that **through his faith he is still speaking,** as the first in a chain of witnesses.

5–6. According to Gen. 5:24, 'Enoch walked with God; and he was not, for God took him'. LXX modifies this to read that Enoch 'was well-pleasing to God; and he was not found, because God translated him', and our author follows this to make two points: first, **Enoch was taken up** (the LXX verb rendered 'translated' above), which is explained by the addition **so that he should not see death;** and second, that **he was attested as having pleased God.** Now according to our author **without faith it is impossible to please him,** therefore it was by faith that Enoch pleased God, and by faith that he was taken up. Verse 6 adds an explanatory comment: **whoever would draw near to God must believe that he exists and that he rewards those who seek him.** Mere belief in the existence of God is not enough: it could be belief in a god remote and unconcerned, indifferent to human sorrows and to human sins alike. On the contrary, this is a God who acts, who has made himself known through the prophets and through his Son (cf. 1:1–2), and who is able to reward those who seek him. Reference was made above to Jas. 2:19, which deserves quotation here: 'You believe that God is one; you do well. Even the demons believe—and shudder'. Faith is more than a bare intellectual assent.

In the Old Testament, Enoch is one of three figures who are reported not to have died a normal death, the others being Elijah (2 Kg. 2:11) and Moses (Dt. 34:5–6, which says he died but the place of his burial remained unknown; cf. also Jude 9). Enoch became a popular figure in literature and legend, especially in apocalyptic works (e.g. the Book of Enoch, 2 Enoch and 3 Enoch). Our author however takes no account of any of this, but confines himself to the narrative in Genesis (cf. also Ecclus. 44:16; Wis. 4:10).

7. The third example is Noah, who follows Enoch in Ecclus. 44:17. **Being warned by God concerning events as yet unseen, he took heed and constructed an ark** (see Gen. 6:13–7:1). He thus provides 'an excellent instance of faith as the proving of what is not seen (cf. 11:1)' (Montefiore). His faith, his acceptance of the warning, led to **the saving of his household** when a doomed humanity was overwhelmed in the Flood (Gen. 7:21–24). As to the statement that **he condemned the world**, 'the conduct of one person, since it sets a standard, can result in the condemnation before God of another person whose conduct is inferior' (*BAG* 412a, listing Wis. 4:16; Mt. 12:41f.; Lk. 11:31f.; Rom. 2:27 and the present verse). Earlier references to **the world** (4:3; 9:26; 10:5) are neutral, but here and in verse 38 below the phrase recalls the usage, frequent in the Johannine literature, in terms of society organised in hostility to God. In Gen. 6:9 'Noah was a righteous man, blameless in his generation', even before his obedience to God's warning; in Gen. 7:1 however the words 'I have seen that you are righteous before me in this generation', follow the statement that Noah 'did all that God commanded him', and it may be that our author has this in mind when he speaks of Noah becoming **an heir of the righteousness which comes by faith**. In any case, as the preceding examples show, faith and righteousness are closely connected. The phrase **the righteousness which comes by faith** is reminiscent of some Pauline phrases (e.g. Rom. 4:13; 9:30; 10:6; Gal. 5:5), but before conclusions are drawn on the basis of similarity in English versions it should be noted that in the Greek the formulation is different; we also need to ask if this righteousness which comes by faith is exactly what Paul has in mind (cf. e.g. Bultmann, *Theology* II, p. 167, who notes that only here does it refer to 'the substance of salvation' (for Paul see esp. I, pp. 270ff.); cf. also Schrenk in *TDNT* II, pp. 199f.).

8–12. As Moffatt notes, 'the faith of Abraham, as might be expected, receives more attention than that of any other'. As the founding father of the people of Israel he is a natural candidate for inclusion; moreover, his faith is expressly attested in Genesis (15:6: he believed the Lord; and he reckoned it to him as righteousness). In the following verses three points are made, and a fourth is added in verses 17–19, after the 'interlude' in verses 13–16. The first point is his obedience **when he was called to go out** from the land of Haran (Gen. 12:1–4). It is not actually said there that Abraham did not know **where he was to go**, but it is a natural inference; it is only when he has reached Canaan (Gen. 12:5–7) that the Lord says to him 'To your descendants I will give this land'. The faith of Abraham is not actually mentioned until Gen. 15:6, quoted above, but again is a natural inference: his acceptance of the call was an act of faith. Incidentally, as Manson notes (p. 77), 'Hebrews and Stephen (Ac. 8:2–7) alike start from Genesis 12 for their exposition of Abraham's faith, not like St Paul from Gen. 15:6'. If verse 8 shows faith issuing in obedience, verse 9 illustrates faith as perseverance and endurance: **he sojourned in the land of promise, as in a foreign land**. Abraham was literally 'a stranger and sojourner' (Gen. 23:4; cf. verse 13 below and 1 Pet. 2:11) with no fixed abode, and no property in the land until he bought the cave of Machpelah to serve as a family burying ground (Gen. 23:3–20). According to Gen. 21:5 Abraham was a hundred years old when Isaac was born, according to 25:26 Isaac was sixty at the birth of Jacob; since Abraham lived a hundred and seventy-five years (Gen. 25:7), all three could have travelled together. More important from our author's point of view is the fact that Isaac and Jacob also received the divine promise (Gen. 26:3; 28:13): they were heirs with Abraham of the same promise. Despite his reference to the land of promise, our author now goes beyond the Old Testament and affirms that Abraham's real goal was not any mere earthly inheritance, but **the city which has foundations, whose builder and maker is God**. Verse 16 below speaks of 'a better country, that is, a heavenly one', 12:22 of 'Mount Zion', 'the city of the living God, the heavenly Jerusalem'. Here again there are similarities with Philo (e.g. *Leg. All.* III.83; *Mig. Ab.* 43f), but for one thing our author does not allegorise so completely as Philo; and for another the idea of a new or heavenly Jerusalem was widely spread in Jewish expectation (cf. Schürer II. pp. 529f.; for the New Testament, see Gal. 4:26; Rev. 3:12; 21:2, 10), and therefore need not have been derived from Philo. In *Praem. et Poen.* 150 Philo remarks that observers looking at cities razed to their foundations will doubt that they were ever inhabited; here in contrast is a city with foundations, permanent and lasting. The word translated **maker**, which occurs only here in the New Testament, was later used by the gnostics to describe the inferior creator of the universe, the Demiurge; but it goes back at least to Plato, and there is no need to think of gnostic influence here—rather the gnostics are using for their own purposes a term which Philo and others could use quite happily for the supreme God and Creator. The difference is that the gnostics in their repudiation of this world and all that belongs to it also degraded its creator.

The following verse presents something of a problem, although it is glossed over in English versions: **by faith Sarah herself received**

power to conceive, even when she was past the age, since she
considered him faithful who had promised. Verse 12 immediately
returns to Abraham. The sudden introduction of Sarah into a
passage relating to Abraham is not in itself a difficulty—she was
after all his wife; but to say she received power to conceive by faith
is at variance with Gen. 18:12-15, where she laughs the very idea
to scorn. Moreover the phrase rendered 'conceive' is literally 'for
the depositing of seed', not for its reception; it refers to the father's
part in procreation, not the mother's. There are no personal
pronouns in the second part of the verse, and a third person singular
verb could be used either with a masculine or a feminine subject.
If the reference to Sarah were omitted, the verse could be a further
point relating to the faith of Abraham: even beyond the age (as noted
above, he was a hundred when Isaac was born) he received power
to deposit seed, because he believed God's promise. This would
agree with Gen. 15:6, where it is Abraham's faith in the promise of
a son of his own that is reckoned to him as righteousness. It is not
however necessary to excise the reference to Sarah, although it could
have been a gloss. Two alternatives have been suggested: first, to
read the relevant words in the dative, i.e. 'along with Sarah'; or
secondly to take them as a parenthetic circumstantial clause (cf.
Black, *An Aramaic Approach*, Oxford [1967], pp. 83–89; the *UBS*
Greek New Testament prints the words within dashes as a parenthesis). This would yield the reading: by faith – Sarah herself being
barren—he received power for the depositing of seed, even when
he was past the age. The whole of this section would then refer to
Abraham. Verse 12 echoes the promise of Gen. 15:5–6 and 22:17–
18.

   13–16. Verses 13–16, as already noted, form a kind of interlude
which in some respects anticipates the final verses of the chapter.
At first sight it seems to interrupt the sequence of the section about
Abraham, who is again the subject in verse 17; but this is no mere
interpolation. These verses take up and develop some points in the
preceding verses, particularly the thought of promise and that of
the city which has foundations. Strictly Enoch did not die (see verse
5), and there are no promises in the stories of Abel and Enoch in
the Old Testament; but our author is thinking primarily of
Abraham, Isaac and Jacob. Abraham did not see his descendants
multiply 'as the stars of heaven' (Gen. 15:5; for Isaac and Jacob see
26:3–4; 28:14), nor did any of them take possession of the land of
promise: they **all died in faith, not having received what was
promised**. This might seem in conflict with 6:15, where Abraham
'having patiently endured, obtained the promise'; but 'promise'
there is in the singular, and could be understood as referring simply

to the birth of Isaac. In the present verse 'what was promised' is in
the plural (lit. 'the promises'). What the patriarchs were given was
a promise and a vision, which they welcomed gladly, remote though
the fulfilment might be. They therefore lived and died **in faith**
(here not the recurring dative of the preceding sequence, but a
prepositional phrase; it is a stylistic device, with no real difference
in meaning, but sets this paragraph in some sense apart from those
which precede and those which follow). Moreover they **acknowledged that they were strangers and exiles on the earth.** The
phrase **strangers and exiles** (or 'sojourners') is familiar from the Old
Testament (cf. Gen. 23:4; 47:9; 1 Chr. 29:15; Ps. 39:12; also 1 Pet.
2:11; at Eph. 2:12, 19 the readers are said to be no longer alienated
and strangers, but that is a different context), but by adding **on the
earth** our author gives it a new turn, which he at once explains:
**people who speak thus make it clear that they are seeking a
homeland.** If they had been thinking of the land they left, they
could have gone back (verse 15), so that was not their true home;
nor was it the land of Canaan, as was already indicated at 4:8 above.
As it is, they desire a better country, that is, a heavenly one. For
our author, the nomadic life of the patriarchs shows them on a
quest, for a true homeland; their death without seeing the fulfilment
of the promise shows that this homeland is not of this world. The
reward of their faith is briefly stated in the closing words of the
section: **therefore God is not ashamed to be called their God** (cf.
Exod. 3:6, 15; 4:5; often echoed in the New Testament), **for he
has prepared for them a city.** Later it will become clear that the
readers are in the same situation: 'here we have no lasting city, but
we seek the city that is to come' (13:14). Like Israel in the wilderness, the patriarchs are types of something that is yet to be (on
typology in Hebrews, see Goppelt, *TYPOS*, ET Grand Rapids
[1982], pp. 161–178). Barrett notes that 'Philo allegorizes the *OT*
material about travelling and pilgrimage, but the result is markedly
different from Hebrews' (*Dodd Festschrift* p. 377; cf. the whole
discussion of 'The Pilgrim's Progress', pp. 373–383): 'Philo's allegorical pilgrimage of the soul can be paralleled in the philosophers,
who also think of man as imprisoned for the space of his earthly life
within conditions which are essentially alien to him; the pilgrimage
described in Hebrews is different. Expressed in *OT* language, it
is in fact drawn from a fresh understanding of the eschatological
circumstances of the people of God' (p. 378). The readers are
already God's house (3:6), the people of God, but in the words of
Käsemann's title, they are *das wandernde Gottesvolk*, the wandering
people of God, a pilgrim people. Hence the repeated emphasis upon
holding fast to confidence and conviction and to faith. The promise

is sure, guaranteed by God himself (6:17–18), but the readers have
need of hope and confidence, of faith and endurance, to persevere
to the end; to take a modern example, the faith and courage to write
an exposition of Hebrews in a Nazi prison cell.

17–19. Verse 17 returns to Abraham, resuming the sequence of
examples introduced by the programmatic **by faith**. The reference
is to the supreme test of Abraham's faith, recorded in Gen. 22:1–
14 and frequently alluded to in Jewish literature, although not in
detail as here (cf. Wis. 10:5; Ecclus. 44:20; 1 Mac. 2:52; for the
New Testament cf. Jas 2:21): the 'binding' of Isaac. Isaac was not
actually Abraham's **only son** (there was also Ishmael, Gen. 16:15),
but he was the only one through whom the promises of Gen 17:16,
19 could be fulfilled (verse 18 here actually quotes Gen. 21:12). To
offer him up in sacrifice therefore meant the end of Abraham's
hopes of posterity from a son of his own by Sarah. Nevertheless he
was ready to offer up his only son (lit. 'was offering up', cf. Gen.
22:10). In Genesis this is presented simply as a matter of Abraham's
faith and obedience, and Isaac is saved by divine intervention, but
our author places his own interpretation upon it: **he considered
that God was able to raise men even from the dead.** This attributes
to Abraham a belief in resurrection, which is anachronistic: the
earliest clear statements of the belief in the Old Testament appear
at Isa. 29:19 and Dan. 12:2 (the miracles of Elijah (1 Kg. 17:17ff.)
and Elisha (2 Kg. 4:18ff.) are rather a different matter; cf. on 11:35;
13:20 below). The plain meaning of the text of Genesis is that
Abraham expected to return with Isaac (Gen. 22:5), that he believed
that God would somehow resolve the problem (Gen. 22:8), and that
his faith was justified: **hence, figuratively speaking** (lit. 'in a
parable') **he did receive him back.** Later patristic writers saw the
sacrifice of Isaac as a type of the sacrifice of Jesus (e.g. Barn. 7:3),
and the germ of that idea could be seen in Rom. 8:32 (which seems
to echo Gen. 22:16 LXX), but there is nothing of that here (but cf.
also Jn 3:16, which likewise has the *monogenes*, translated 'only son'
in verse 17 above).

20–22. The next three figures are dealt with very briefly, in a
single sentence each. Nothing is said of Jacob's supplanting of Esau
(Gen. 27); it is merely recorded that **Isaac invoked future blessings
on Jacob and Esau.** Again, there is no reference to Jacob's crossing
of his hands when he blessed Ephraim and Manasseh (Gen. 48; the
bowing in worship over the head of his staff comes from the LXX
text of Gen. 47:31, where the Hebrew reads 'bowed himself on the
head of his bed'); it is only said that he **blessed each of the sons
of Joseph.** Finally **Joseph, at the end of his life, made mention
of the exodus of the Israelites and gave directions concerning his**

burial (Gen. 50:24–25; cf. Exod. 13:19). The point for our author
is that in each case the person concerned is looking to the future,
to things hoped for, things not seen (cf. verse 1); they therefore
belong to his roll of the heroes of faith.

23–28. Verse 23 introduces a sequence of episodes from the life
of Moses, the greatest figure of the old dispensation. The first
actually relates to the faith of his parents, who **hid** him **for three
months** (Exod. 2:2), despite **the king's edict** (Exod. 1:22). All our
author says is that **they saw that the child was beautiful**, but
presumably he has more than this in mind (Josephus, for example,
speaks of a revelation given to Moses' father in a dream, *Ant.*
II. 210–216). In any case, their readiness to save the child's life in
defiance of the royal decree, at whatever cost to themselves, displays
a courage which adds another facet to the manifold variety of our
author's conception of what faith is and what it involves. According
to Exodus (2:5–10), Moses was brought up as the son of Pharaoh's
daughter, but it is not there stated in so many words that **when he
was grown up** he refused the title (Josephus (*Ant.* II. 232ff.) has a
tale of the child Moses dashing to the ground a diadem placed on
his head by the king); it is merely said that 'he went out to his people
and looked upon their burdens', but his slaying of the Egyptian
(Exod. 2:11–12) places him firmly on the side of his people and may
be said to justify our author's claim that he chose **rather to share
ill-treatment with the people of God**. His position at the royal
court afforded opportunity for wealth and pleasure, but it would
have been the transitory pleasure of this world; moreover it would
have involved rejection of the destiny appointed for him, an act of
apostasy: hence the reference to enjoying **the fleeting pleasures of
sin**. Another occurrence of the word translated 'fleeting' is at 2
C. 4:18, which is relevant to this whole context: the things that are
seen are transient, but the things that are unseen are eternal. Verse
26 then makes the point in different terms: **he considered abuse
suffered for the Christ** (lit. 'the reproach of Christ') **greater wealth
than the treasures of Egypt, for he looked to the reward**. Reference
is made at 2:2 to the retribution due for any transgression or
disobedience under the old dispensation; at 10:35 the readers are
urged not to throw away their confidence 'which has a great reward'
(the same Greek word); a cognate noun is used at 11:6, which speaks
of God as a rewarder of those that seek him. In none of these cases
is the precise nature of the reward specified but it is now clear that
it cannot belong to this present world; it must belong to the things
hoped for, the things not seen. Egypt was a land of wealth and
splendour, but the 'reproach of Christ' outweighs all the treasures of
Egypt (cf. Phil 3:7–8). The problem here lies in the words translated

abuse suffered for the Christ: in the first place, a literal translation
suggests not abuse suffered for the sake of Christ, but abuse which
he suffered (cf. *NEB*: the stigma that rests on God's Anointed).
The word rendered 'abuse' has already occurred, in the plural, at
10:33, and a similar phrase appears at 13:13, but these are both
slightly different. Secondly there is the difficulty of a reference to
Christ, who lived centuries later, in the context of a passage relating
to Moses. Attempts have been made to resolve the difficulty by
suggesting that the words are proleptic: Moses chose the suffering
that was later to be the lot of Christ, and hence is a 'type' of Christ;
or that we must think of the pre-existent Jesus as in some sense
present with the Old Testament people of God; but such interpretations are difficult for modern readers, and it may be that they
approach the problem from the wrong end. There are echoes here
of Ps. 89:51 LXX, where the 'anointed' is a defeated and humiliated
king. *RSV* here (verse 50) has 'thy servant', but LXX has the plural,
which suggests the inclusion of the people as well, as indeed do
earlier references to breach in the walls and defeat in battle. The
phrase 'the Lord's Anointed' thus refers to the people of God as
well as to their king. There is therefore something to be said for
the *NEB* rendering (quoted above) here in Hebrews. Naturally,
given the use of Christ (the Anointed *par excellence*) as a title of
Jesus, it was easy to see all earlier references as applying to him, or
prefiguring him; but it may be important to see how the development took place, instead of simply jumping to conclusions on the
basis of similarities. That people did so in time past does not necessarily justify our doing so today.

Verse 27 presents a further problem, that of identifying the
occasion our author has in mind. At Exod. 2:15 Pharaoh sought to
kill Moses, but Moses fled to the land of Midian: 'any attempt to
harmonise this with the words of our author . . . is special pleading'
(Montefiore). On the other hand, to identify the occasion with the
Exodus (Exod. 12:51) involves an inversion of the chronological
order (the Passover, mentioned in verse 28, preceded the departure
from Egypt); moreover both Pharaoh and the Egyptians are there
'urgent with the people, to send them out of the land in haste' (Exod.
12:31, 33). Now the Hebrew of Exod. 2:15 says unambiguously that
Moses fled, but LXX says that he withdrew or departed from the
presence of Pharaoh, and Philo uses the LXX version to claim that
this was not a flight but a strategic withdrawal (*Leg. All.* iii.14).
Moreover, the only reference to Moses' fear in the context concerns
not fear of Pharaoh but fear arising from the discovery that the
slaying of the Egyptian had become known (Exod. 2:14). Following
LXX version, but using a different verb, our author claims that

Moses **left Egypt** not because he was afraid of the king's anger but by faith, **for he endured as seeing him who is invisible**. Attempts have been made to link this last clause with such passages as Exod. 33:11 or 20–23 or the story of the burning bush (Exod. 3:2ff.; note verse 6b), but none of these is strictly relevant: this passage is concerned with Moses' *faith*. Williamson (p. 475) gets the point exactly: 'the Writer of Hebrews meant that Moses was without fear of the king of Egypt's wrath because although he could not at present see God he was absolutely sure of His existence (cf. 11:6) and he believed that one day he would be rewarded by Him for his faith' (cf. pp. 469–480 on the parallels and similarities between Philo and Heb. 11:23ff.). The instructions for **the Passover** (verse 28) are given to Moses at Exod. 12:3–13, and Moses' obedience follows in verses 21–28 (the intervening verses relate to the feast of unleavened bread). English translations of this verse in Hebrews commonly make it a simple statement of fact: **he kept the Passover and sprinkled the blood, so that the Destroyer of the first-born might not touch them**. There is however a change of tense in the Greek, which may convey a slightly different nuance: literally, 'he has made the Passover and the sprinkling of the blood'. The point then would be not just that Moses celebrated the first Passover, but that he instituted the celebration which was continued annually down the centuries, in accordance with Exod. 12:14. The word rendered 'made' has a variety of meanings (at 3:2 above, for example, it is translated 'appointed'), so that reference to the institution seems to be possible; but according to Westcott, while the Greek phrase is 'not unfrequent' for the observance of Passover, it is not used for the institution. The *NEB* rendering of the last clause 'so that the destroying angel might not touch the first-born of Israel' construes the text differently: according to *BAG* the verb takes a genitive of its object (so at 12:20 below), but it can also take the accusative. The question is then whether 'the first-born' is the object of the participle translated 'the destroyer' or of the main verb 'touch'. The translation 'so that the Destroyer might not touch their first-born' certainly appears more appropriate, while the participle could have been derived from Exod. 12:23 LXX, where it has no object. At 1 C. 5:7 the Passover is the 'type' of Christ's sacrifice, but our author makes no use of this, possibly as Bruce suggests to avoid detracting from the correspondence earlier drawn between the death of Jesus and the annual sacrifice on the Day of Atonement.

29. Earlier in the chapter, four points were made with regard to the faith of Abraham (verses 8–12, 17–19), then Isaac, Jacob and Joseph were briefly mentioned, a single sentence being devoted to each. Similarly here, after four points relating to the faith of Moses (although the first strictly refers to the faith of his parents), our author briefly mentions three episodes from the Exodus and the entrance into Canaan. Moses was of course involved in the crossing of **the Red Sea** (Exod. 14:21–31), but he is not specifically mentioned here. It may be worth recalling an earlier passage in the Exodus chapter, when the people were in great fear and cried out to the Lord; 'and Moses said to the people, Fear not, stand firm and see the salvation of the Lord' (Exod. 14:13). At the end of the chapter it is recorded that 'they believed in the Lord and in his servant Moses' (Exod. 14:31). The people's faith consisted in their willingness to go forward, and by making the venture they received the proof of its efficacy. It is not stated that the fate of the Egyptians was due to their lack of faith, although some commentators draw this conclusion. As enemies of the people and of the God of Israel, they were certainly 'unbelievers', but our author may have seen their drowning only as the penalty for a rash and foolhardy venture. Perhaps significantly, nothing is said of the following period, down to the arrival in Canaan: at 3:7ff. the writer has stigmatised the unbelief and disobedience of the wilderness generation. His admonitions there warn against the danger of 'an evil, unbelieving heart' (3:12; cf. 4:1, 11). Now he is urging positively the importance of faith.

30. The story of **the walls of Jericho** is recorded in Joshua 6:1–21. We might have expected some reference to Joshua himself, as Moses' successor and the leader of the march into the Promised Land, but he has already been mentioned, rather negatively, at 4:8 above: the 'rest' to which he led the people was not the true rest, only an earthly prefiguration. Here the emphasis lies on the faith of the people, their willingness to carry out instructions that might well have seemed absurd and inept in the face of a fortified city. But again they were to prove the efficacy of faith and obedience.

31. The final example in this list is that of Rahab, who in Josh. 2:1–21 not only gives **friendly welcome to the spies** but in verses 9ff. actually declares her faith in the God of Israel. As a result, she **did not perish with those who were disobedient**, but was safely brought out after the capture of the city (Josh. 6:22–25). Rahab also appears in the genealogy of Jesus at Matt. 1:5, and as one of two examples of justification by works in Jas 2:25, the other being Abraham's binding of Isaac (Jas 2:21ff.).

32. At this point the author cuts short his list: **time would fail me**! Instead he first adds a string of names, four from the book of Judges, two from Samuel and Kings, with a general reference to the prophets, and then summarises the experiences of past heroes of faith. Incidentally, the word rendered **to tell** is a *masculine* participle (lit. 'in telling'), which would seem to rule out a woman author. The four names from Judges are not in the order in which their exploits are narrated in that book: **Gideon** with a force of three hundred men won a victory against the Midianites, who were 'like locusts for multitude' (Jg. 7:7ff.), while **Barak** led ten thousand men from the tribes of Naphtali and Zebulun against the army of Sisera (Jg. 4:4ff.); the single-handed exploits of **Samson** against the Philistines are recorded in Jg. 13–16, and **Jephthah** was victorious over the Ammonites (Jg. 11). It must be said that not all of them are altogether good examples of faith, since Gideon required some convincing (Jg. 6:36–40), and Barak would only agree to go if Deborah the prophetess went with him (Jg. 4:8–10). We might have expected some reference to Deborah herself, or to Jael, 'most blessed of women' (Jg. 5:24), or to Jephthah's daughter for her unquestioning acceptance of her father's vow (Jg. 11:34–40); but our author is merely singling out a few notable warriors from the early history of Israel. Moreover it is recorded that the Spirit of the Lord came upon three of them: Gideon (Jg. 6:34), Samson (15:14) and Jephthah (11:29), and evidence of their faith and courage and endurance is not lacking in their stories. The placing of **Samuel** after David, against the chronological order, is readily explained by our author's wish to associate Samuel with **the prophets** (he is expressly described as a prophet in 1 Sam. 3:20; 2 Chr. 35:18; Ac. 3:24). **David** is the one king mentioned, probably as the king *par excellence*, to whose reign the people looked back as to a golden age; we need only recall the frequency of references to the throne or the house of David in later literature, and the prominence in Messianic hopes and expectations of a king of David's line. Some of his successors fell sadly short of the ideal he represents. He too was endowed with the Spirit of the Lord (1 Sam. 16:13).

33–34. The next two verses list the achievements of these heroes (and others) in nine terse clauses, which fall naturally into three triplets. That they **conquered kingdoms** is evidenced by the victories mentioned above, and in particular by the conquests of David. The enforcing of **justice** was part of the task of government, and hence the responsibility of the 'judges', although it is more often their martial prowess that is mentioned in the book of Judges; Samuel 'judged Israel all the days of his life' (1 Sam. 7:15), while David 'administered justice and equity to all his people' (2 Sam. 8:15). Several of those listed **received promises** of one kind or another (e.g. Gideon, Jg. 7:7, 9), but we may recall especially the promise made through Nathan to David (2 Sam. 7:8–16). At first sight this seems to conflict with verse 39 below, where it is said that 'all these . . . did not receive what was promised'; but, for one thing, a different verb is used in the Greek, and for another there appears to be a subtle distinction in the writer's use of the word **promise**. It is employed five times in the singular: at 4:1 of the promise of entering God's rest; at 6:17 of heirs of the promise; at 9:15 of the promise of eternal inheritance; at 10:36 of the hope that the readers may attain to the promise; and finally at 11:39. In all these cases it seems to refer to the ultimate eschatological promise of 'the saints' everlasting rest'. The only exceptions are at 6:15, where Abraham, 'having patiently endured, received the promise', presumably in the birth of Isaac, and in the reference to 'the land of promise' at 11:9; but as 4:8 has already shown, this land is not the 'true' rest. The word is used in the plural at 6:12 of those who inherit the promises, who (as in the present chapter) are models to be imitated; at 7:6 of Abraham who had the promises (cf. also 11:17); and in the present verse. This suggests a reference to promises of various kinds, which might or might not be fulfilled in the lifetime of their recipients (cf. 11:13), as distinct from the promise of the eternal inheritance. The only other occurrence of the plural is at 8:6, where the new covenant is said to be 'enacted on better promises'. An alternative interpretation would be that those who received the promises had promises made to them, but did not always see their fulfilment. At any rate there is no ground for accusing our author of inconsistency.

The second triplet relates to cases of personal deliverance: both Samson (Jg. 14:5-9) and David (1 Sam. 17:34-37) are reported to have slain **lions**, but the most immediate reference in the first clause is to Dan. 6:22, where the angel of God 'shut the lions' mouths'. The words **quenched raging fire** also recall Daniel, where three young men are delivered unscathed from 'the burning fiery furnace' (Dan. 3:13-27). Specific references for those who **escaped the edge of the sword** are more difficult to find in these precise words, but many a warrior must have been close to death in battle. At Exod. 18:4 the name of one of Moses' sons is explained in the words 'the God of my father was my help, and delivered me from the sword of Pharaoh'; both Elijah (1 Kg. 19:2, 10) and Elisha (2 Kg. 6:31f.) were under threat, while David twice escaped Saul's spear (1 Sam. 18:11; 19:10-11). The words may be reasonably taken to signify the danger of sudden and violent death, particularly at the hands of an enemy.

In the third triplet **strength out of weakness** recalls the last exploit of Samson (Jg. 16:17-30), but also perhaps the story of David and Goliath (1 Sam. 17); there were however several who 'out of weakness were made strong' (*AV*). Similarly the clauses **became mighty in war, put foreign armies to flight** would be appropriate to several of those listed in earlier verses. The words translated 'foreign armies' (lit. armies of aliens) are both frequent in I Maccabees (e.g. 2:7; 3:15,17) for the Gentile persecutors of Israel and their hosts, and it may be that the author is no longer confining himself to those he has listed above. According to Moffatt, 'the last three clauses are best illustrated by the story of the Maccabean struggle'. Since he used the Greek Old Testament, the author could have been familiar with I Maccabees.

35. There are two cases in the Old Testament in which **women received their dead by resurrection**, the stories of Elijah and the widow of Zarephath (I Kg. 17:17–24) and Elisha and the Shunammite (2 Kg. 4:18–37). From deeds and achievements our author now passes on to the sufferings endured by some of the heroes. **Tortured** is perhaps an understatement: the victim was lashed to a frame, the *tympanon* ('drum'), and beaten. Since **scourging** is mentioned separately below, it may have been more like breaking on the wheel. At any rate the aged Eleazar died from the blows (2 Macc. 6:18–31). The word translated **mocking** appears in the following chapter of 2 Maccabees (7:7), in the story of the seven sons and their mothers; *NEB* here translates 'brutality'. The victim often had to suffer mockery as the case of Jesus shows (cf. Mt. 20:19; 27:29, 31, 41 and parallels, where the cognate verb is used), but the passage in 2 Maccabees suggests that in the present context something more is meant. Certainly Eleazar and the seven brothers refused **to accept release**, and some of the brothers expressly affirmed their hope of resurrection. **That they might rise again to a better life** is literally 'that they might attain a better resurrection', which probably refers to resurrection to eternal life in contrast to the resuscitation to earthly life mentioned in the first part of this verse; the adjective 'better' frequently has in Hebrews associations with the heavenly realm: a better hope (7:19), a better covenant (7:22; 8:6), a better and abiding possession (10:34), a better country (11:16).

36. If the **others** who **suffered mocking and scourging, and even chains and imprisonment** are to be taken as different from the Maccabean martyrs, as the 'others' suggests, we may think of Micaiah (I Kg. 22:26–27; 2 Chr. 18:23–27) and particularly Jeremiah (Jer. 20:2; 37:15; 38:6; for mocking, cf. 20:7ff.). The translation 'even chains and imprisonment' suggests that this is an even greater trial, but the Greek is not necessarily intensive; it could mean 'and also'. Prolonged imprisonment under the conditions Jeremiah had to suffer (Jer. 38:6–13) could however have entailed great hardship. The readers knew that from the experience of some of their number (cf. 10:32–34 above).

37-38. Stoned refers to the normal Jewish method of execution (cf. Exod. 19:13, quoted at 12:20 below; Num. 15:35-36; Dt. 13:10; at Jn 10:31ff. the Jews are on the point of stoning Jesus). We naturally think of the stoning of Stephen (Ac. 7:58), but our author shows no knowledge of Acts and in any case draws his examples from the Old Testament, not from recent history. The case he has in mind is probably that of Zechariah, son of Jehoiada the priest (2 Chr. 24:21; Mt. 23:25 appears to confuse him with the prophet), or perhaps Naboth (1 Kg. 21:8-14). To be **sawn in two** was the fate of the prophet Isaiah (Asc. Is. 5; the book in its present form contains Christian elements, but the martyrdom is a Jewish composition which as Hebrews shows was already known in the first century AD). At this point many manuscripts add 'they were tempted', which is scarcely appropriate in this context. Either it is due to scribal error (many of the letters are also in the word rendered 'sawn in two') or it is a corruption of a more appropriate word (more than a dozen conjectures are listed in Metzger, *Textual Commentary*, pp. 674f.). As for those killed **with the sword**, we may recall Elijah's lament (1 Kg. 19:10, 14; but at verse 1 it is Elijah who has slain the prophets of Baal. Cf. however 18:4, 13); or there is the prophet Uriah, slain with the sword by Jehoiakim (Jer. 26:20-23). The word rendered **skins of sheep** is used in LXX of Elijah's mantle (1 Kg. 19:13, 19), later inherited by Elisha (2 Kg. 2:13), but the whole description could apply to many others, like those who, wanting to maintain their religion, 'went down to the wilds to live there' (1 Macc. 2:29) and were massacred when they refused to defend themselves on the Sabbath. The picture is one of the hardships and privations endured by those who took to the mountains and the deserts, living in caves and holes in the ground, rather than surrender their faith. Of these **the world**, society organised in hostility to God (cf. v. 7 above), **was not worthy**. Their example was to be followed by anchorites and hermits in the early days of monasticism, but that was to escape the enticements of the world, not to avoid the surrender of faith.

39-40. The modern reader, on coming to the final verses of this chapter, is almost bound to feel a certain sense of unfairness, of injustice: **all these, though well attested by their faith, did not receive what was promised, since God had foreseen something better for us.** Why should the present generation be so privileged? What is the situation, the present condition, of those heroes of bygone ages? Are they confined to some limbo to await the final consummation? This however is to raise questions with which our author is not concerned, and to which he gives no answer: moreover it is to mistake his purpose. Once again the chapter divisions may be misleading: it is not without reason that preachers selecting a lesson of manageable compass frequently begin at verse 32 and go on to include the first two verses of the following chapter. The whole aim and purpose of the letter is to stimulate and encourage the readers, in what was evidently a time of stress and anxiety, and to dismiss the effort of the men of bygone ages as fruitless and even futile would have had precisely the opposite effect. As it is, the readers have a better hope (7:19), a better covenant, enacted on the basis of better promises (8:6); but they have not yet attained the goal and have yet to complete their course (12:1). There is a place for them in the purpose of God, but they have need of endurance (10:36). The men of the past have not carried off the trophies so that nothing remains: they did not obtain the ultimate promise, because that purpose of God includes not only the people of the past but the present generation also: **that apart from us they should not be made perfect.** The readers indeed do have an advantage over the people of past ages, in that 'for them the unseen truth which God will one day enact is no longer entirely unseen; it has been manifested in Jesus' (Barrett, *Dodd Festschrift*, p. 382; cf. also Peterson's discussion, *Hebrews and Perfection*, p. 156ff.). 'The exemplars of faith . . . persevered without seeing anything like the fulfilment of God's promises that Christians have experienced. In every respect, then, Christians have greater grounds for not growing weary or faint-hearted in their pilgrimage towards "the city which is to come" ' (Peterson, p. 158). The men of old are not rejected or devalued; they have completed their course and are 'commemorated for their faith' (*NEB*), but the purpose of God involves the later generation also.

Looking back over the chapter as a whole, we can now see that it is an expansion, elaboration and exposition of the opening verse. The heroes are not merely so many examples or illustrations of faith; they serve to bring out the manifold richness and variety of what faith means in our author's view. Reading some English versions (*AV* the substance of things hoped for; *RSV* the assurance of things hoped for; *NEB* gives substance to our hopes) one may be inclined to recall the words of Jesus about the faith which moves mountains (Mt. 17:20; 21:21; Mk 11:23; cf. Lk. 17:6), but that is a figurative expression for the overcoming of difficulties, and not to be taken too literally. Faith is not a magic wand that produces the desired result without effort and without more ado. For all the miracles attributed to disciples and apostles, none of them is reported to have tried to move Mt Hermon by faith alone, nor would modern Christians try it with Snowdon or Ben Nevis, still less Mt Everest! But there have been many, in various fields of life, who have had faith in the quality of a product, in the justice of a cause, in the significance of some discovery or invention, and have persevered despite all obstacles and hindrances until they reached a successful conclusion. Faith is the basis of hope, for without it there is nothing to look for, no incentive to effort; but it involves also a steady and persistent probing into the unknown, a testing and proving of what is not yet seen or assured. The concise brevity of the opening verse presents problems for the translator, as we have seen, because a simple literal rendering could suggest associations which simply are not literally true; but the rest of the chapter serves to make its meaning clear. Faith is trust and confidence, inspires hope and expectation; but it also involves steadfastness, courage and endurance.

DISCIPLINE AND ENDURANCE

12:1–11

1–2. As already indicated, there is no real break in the continuity of thought; our author now proceeds to point the moral and apply the lesson of what has just been said: **Therefore, since we are surrounded by so great a cloud of witnesses, let us also lay aside every weight**. The modern reader naturally thinks of some great arena, an Olympic stadium for example, with the champions of past years looking down as their successors contend for the mastery. The athletic imagery is certainly present in the context, in the reference to **the race that is set before us**, but to press this unduly could be misleading: the primary meaning of the word translated **witnesses** describes not just a spectator, an onlooker, but one 'who can or should testify to anything'. It is in fact the word from which our English word 'martyr' is derived (cf. *BAG* 494 and the literature there). The witnesses are those who have themselves borne witness, and been attested for their faith (11:39 uses the cognate verb). That they now look down from the stands, as it were, comes from the imagery of the context, not from the word itself. In 4 Macc. 17:13–14, where the stories of Eleazar and the seven brothers are summarised in terms of a contest, with Antiochus as their antagonist, and 'the world and all mankind looked on', a completely different Greek verb is used. The **weight** is obviously anything that might prove a handicap or hindrance, and is immediately amplified by the words **and sin which clings so closely**. This last clause translates a Greek adjective which occurs only here, and several meanings have been suggested, but obviously it refers to something that prevents the athlete from doing himself full justice. The *NEB* margin 'which all too readily distracts us' renders a very similar word, but this is poorly attested in the manuscripts. In Greek mythology, Atalanta was defeated by a suitor who dropped golden apples to distract her, but that is the kind of allusion more likely to occur to a later age; our author's examples are consistently biblical. The word rendered **lay aside** is used at Rom. 13:12 of 'casting off' the works of darkness, at Jas 1:21 of 'putting away' all filthiness and rank growth of wickedness, at 1 Pet. 2:1 of putting away malice, guile, insincerity, envy and slander. It is often used in a context of baptismal renunciation (cf. Selwyn, *The First Epistle of Peter*, London [1955], pp. 393ff.; Best, *1 Peter*, p. 96), but there is no need to import a baptismal reference here; the imagery comes again from the context: sin is like some long, flowing garment that would impede free movement. The words **let us run with perseverance** are a reminder that this is no short sprint, but a test of endurance: the cognate verb is used at 10:32 above, and in verses 3 and 7 below, the noun at 10:36. This word-group incidentally provides a link with the passage in 4 Maccabees mentioned above, as does the following clause **looking to Jesus the pioneer and perfecter of our faith**. At 4 Macc. 17:10 the suggested epitaph for the Maccabean martyrs includes the words 'They vindicated our nation, looking towards God and enduring the tortures even unto death'. In the present case, however, the thought is not so much of looking in hope and expectation of vindication as of looking to the supreme exemplar, the **pioneer** (the word was already used at 2:10), the forerunner (6:20), the one 'on whom faith depends from start to finish' (*NEB*). *RSV* here inserts a possessive pronoun, reading **our faith**, but this is not in the Greek: Jesus is the pioneer and perfecter of faith absolutely. Here it is appropriate to look back at some earlier passages: 2:10 speaks of the pioneer of salvation being made perfect through suffering; 5:8–9 says that although he was a Son, he learned obedience through what he suffered, and being made perfect he became the source of eternal salvation to all who obey him; 7:8 contrasts the earthly high priests with a Son made perfect for ever. This perfection was attained through struggle, through faithful endurance, as we are reminded in the following words of the present verse, **who . . . endured the cross, despising the shame**. There are therefore grounds for seeing here a reference to the exercise of faith by Christ himself: 'because Christ has given faith "a perfect basis by his high-priestly work", his faith, and what it achieved both for himself and for others, became *a greater incentive for faith on our part than the faith of OT saints*. His faith is thus "qualitatively" and not just "quantitatively" greater than theirs' (Peterson, p. 173 (italics original); see his discussion of the passage, pp. 168ff.). The words **for the joy that was set before him** could be taken to mean 'in place of the joy that was open to him' (*NEB* margin), which would provide a further link with the Philippians hymn (Phil. 2:6–11), and would also seem to be more consistent with 5:7. Most commentators however take the preposition to mean 'for the sake of' (Moffatt: 'to secure'), the sense in which it is used at 12:16 below. For Westcott, 'the joy was that of the work of redemption accomplished through self-sacrifice'; or we may think more generally of the eschatological joy of exaltation and enthrone-ment, but as Bruce remarks, recalling the Farewell Discourse in the Fourth Gospel, this joy 'is not something for Himself alone, but something to be shared with those for whom He died as sacrifice and lives as high priest'. The final words of the verse once again echo Ps. 110:1 (cf. 1:3, 13; 8:1; 10:12). It should be added that here again the name of Jesus comes at the end, in the climactic and emphatic position: lit. 'looking to the pioneer and perfecter of faith—Jesus'.

3–4. At 3:1 the readers were invited to consider the apostle and high priest of their confession, Jesus. Now our author invites them to consider him again, using a different Greek verb which has associations of analogy or comparison: **consider him who endured from sinners such hostility against himself, so that you may not grow weary or faint-hearted**. The word rendered **hostility** was used at 6:16 and 7:7 above in the sense of dispute or contradiction, but here it has more the force of 'speaking against' or even 'reviling' (the cognate verb is used at Ac. 28:22: with regard to this sect, we know that everywhere it is spoken against). The obvious allusion is to the events of the Passion story: the example of Jesus in the face of hostility and mockery should be their inspiration. As it is, in their **struggle against sin** they **have not yet resisted to the point of shedding their blood**. These words are often taken as an argu-ment against a late date, on the ground that they could not have been addressed to the Roman community after the Neronian persecution. For *the community* that could be true, but it is not the only possible interpretation: the meaning could be that they have not 'resisted unto blood' as others of their number did, or in view of the immediate context that they have not resisted as Jesus did, in his enduring of the cross. At all events, opposition and hostility are only to be expected; as the story of the Pauline mission in Acts shows, Christians were often exposed to attack. The words rendered **grow weary or faint-hearted** are used by Aristotle (*Rhet.* 3.9) of an athlete flagging and exhausted, so that the imagery of the arena is continued at least to this point; in verse 4 some scholars have thought of martyrdom (cf. Phil. 2:8, 30: unto death), others of mortal combat (cf. 2 Macc. 13:14), others again of boxing, which involved gloves spiked with metal and therefore liable to draw blood. This last suggestion would continue the imagery of the arena further: Spicq ([1977], p. 201) notes that as in 1 C. 9:24–26 the metaphor of boxing immediately follows that of the race-track. Bruce however thinks that in the light of 11:35–38 'actual martyrdom seems much more probable'. This would only extend the range of possible interpretations noted above.

5–11. Ancient manuscripts did not have our modern conventions in regard to punctuation, so that sometimes it is possible to divide sentences in various ways, or convey a different nuance through a difference in punctuation. Here *RSV* takes the first part of verse 5 as a question, followed by a quotation of Prov. 3:11–12. *NEB* makes it more of an accusation: You have forgotten. The author can be stern in his rebuke, as we have seen, but he can also adopt a more conciliatory tone, and this may be the case here. The word translated **exhortation** has already appeared at 6:18 in the sense of 'encouragement', and will occur again at 13:22 in the author's own description of the letter, 'my word of exhortation', or perhaps better 'of encouragement'. In the quotation, our author follows LXX, as does Philo (*de cong. quaer.* 177; see Williamson, pp. 573–575), although there are differences of detail between Philo and Hebrews. The main difference between LXX and the Hebrew text is in the fourth line, where the Hebrew reads 'as a father the son in whom he delights'. The change can be explained by a misreading of the Hebrew. Other variations between the text as printed in the Old Testament and the quotation here illustrate the differences which can arise between a text translated direct and a text translated at second hand, through the medium of another language, but in this case are not serious. **'Lose courage'** is one of the verbs used in verse 3 above, 'so that you may not grow weary or faint-hearted'.

To understand this passage fully, we must remember that in the ancient world a father's word was law within the family, his authority absolute. **Discipline** and punishment were a normal part of the bringing up of children, and some fathers could be very strict. The quotation indicates two ways in which a son might react, both wrong: he might reject or despise the discipline, **'regard'** it **'lightly'**, and continue to follow his own rebellious ways; or he might break down in self-pity, and abandon any effort. The true course is to accept the discipline, endure the punishment, in the knowledge that it is ultimately for good. 'The patient acceptance of reproof is rewarded by the deepening awareness of one's filial relation to God who is the author of all disaster and whose purpose it serves' (J. C. Rylaarsdam, in *The New Peake Commentary* par. 393i (p. 446)). This observation, from a commentary on the book of Proverbs itself, might serve as a summary of our author's understanding of the quotation, which he proceeds to develop in verses 7–11. **It is for discipline that you have to endure** (lit. are enduring): the word discipline is the Greek *paideia*, which means '*upbringing, training, instruction*, in our lit. chiefly as it is attained by *discipline, correction*' (*BAG* 603ab; see also Bertram in *TDNT* V 596ff; for Heb. 12 see pp. 621ff.). The very fact that they are subjected to discipline is proof that **God is treating you as sons** (even the Son had to learn obedience through suffering (5:8), and they are being treated in the same way). If they were **left without discipline**, they would be **illegitimate children**, in whose upbringing the father had no interest. Verse 9 introduces another argument, in our author's favourite form, comparing the discipline of earthly fathers with that of God: **they disciplined us for a short time at their pleasure**, yet **we** nonetheless **respected them. Shall we not much more be subject to the Father of spirits? . . . he disciplines us for our good, that we may share his holiness**. Verse 11 then rounds off the argument of this section: **for the moment all discipline seems painful rather than pleasant**—nobody enjoys being punished! But **later it yields the peaceful fruit of righteousness to those who have been trained by it,** (cf. the 'harvest of righteousness' in Jas 3:18). We might also compare Paul's words at Rom. 8:18: 'the sufferings of this present time are not worth comparing with the glory that is to be revealed to us'. Trial and temptation, discipline and suffering, may be hard indeed to endure, but if there is a purpose to it—and our author is convinced there is—then they can be endured, not in a stoic indifference but triumphantly.

One phrase calls for some special comment: **the Father of spirits**. The word 'spirit', in Greek as in English, has a wide range of meaning (cf. *BAG* 674b–678b; *TDNT* VI 332ff; for Hebrews see 445f.). In Hebrews it is used of the angels as 'ministering spirits' at 1:7, 14; of the Holy Spirit at for example 2:4; 3:7; 10:15; of the spirit in man at 4:12; at verse 23 below it refers to the spirits of the departed. A similar phrase 'the Lord of spirits' occurs in the Parables of Enoch (104 times in 34 chapters; see Black, *The Book of Enoch*, Leiden [1985], pp. 189ff.), where it is probably an 'interpretative version' of the Old Testament title 'the Lord of hosts' (so Black); there is a parallel in 2 Macc. 3:24, 'the ruler of spirits'. We may also recall the doctrine of the two spirits in *1QS* 3.13–4.26 (cf. A. R. C. Leaney, *The Rule of Qumran and its Meaning*, London [1966], pp. 143ff.). These passages might seem to suggest that the

spirits here are celestial powers (so *BAG* 675, n. 4b), but for one
thing the date of the Parables of Enoch (Enoch 37–71) is disputed;
for another, none of these passages speaks of God as 'Father' of
spirits: he is Lord or Ruler, or in the Qumran text their creator.
The phrase in Hebrews appears to be as unique as it is unexpected.
Now the verse draws a contrast between earthly fathers (i.e. fathers
'after the flesh') and the Father of spirits, and it is natural to think
of the familiar contrast of flesh and spirit. There are therefore
grounds for the *NEB* translation 'our spiritual father'. We may
compare Rev. 22:6, which speaks of 'the God of the spirits of the
prophets'. There may be an echo of Num. 16:22; 27:16, 'the God
of the spirits of all flesh', where LXX has not 'of all flesh' but
'and all flesh', thus separating the two. Our author, having already
mentioned fathers 'after the flesh', simply chooses the first part of
the description, substituting 'Father' for 'god' to suit his contrast.

   The suffering of the righteous has been a problem at least from
the book of Job onwards, and not only in the biblical realm (cf. the
articles Evil, Suffering and Theodicy in *A New Dictionary of Christian Theology*, ed. Richardson and Bowden, London [1983]). A
merely simplistic view which sees in misfortune the punishment for
wrongdoing, in well-being and prosperity the reward for being and
doing good, is quite inadequate, for it simply is not true to the facts
of life: it is all too often the wicked who prosper, the innocent who
suffer. Our author's idea of suffering as a discipline, intended to
promote the ultimate good of the sufferer, may be useful up to a
point, but we have to recognise its limitations. To adopt the imagery
with which our author began this chapter, an athlete has to undergo
gruelling training in order to reach peak fitness. It is not however
a complete answer in a modern world, where television and the
newspapers bring home to us the suffering of the innocent victims
of earthquake, famine or flood: how can a righteous, caring and
loving God allow such things to happen? Some part of it may be
due to over-exploitation of the soil, the destruction of forests, failure
to make proper use of resources, with due regard for conservation,
and so on; but human error and misjudgment do not account for
volcanic eruptions and other disasters. It should however be noted
that our author is not trying to 'justify the ways of God to men'.
He is not concerned with the problems of theodicy. He is dealing
with a particular situation, the details of which we unfortunately do
not know, writing to people anxious and fearful as to what the
future may hold, striving to stimulate and encourage them to steadfastness and endurance. This comes out in the practical admonition
of the following verses, which might well have been included as the

climax to this section. In the situation facing the readers, the thought
of suffering as discipline could be helpful and encouraging; at least
it was so in our author's opinion. It may also be helpful to us in
facing personal problems and difficulties; but to preach endurance
to the redundant and unemployed, to the victims of natural disaster,
is no answer. Some practical steps to assist must be taken first, but
the problems of theodicy remain to tax our minds.

Reference has been made at various points above to the problems
of Christology, and to the fact that our author, naturally enough,
provides no answer to questions which were only to be raised in a
later age. What is now clear, despite all the difficulties which later
Christological thinking may present for the modern reader, is the
absolute centrality of Jesus for Christian faith. He is the pioneer
and perfecter of our faith, the one 'on whom faith depends from
start to finish' (11:2). The great salvation was 'declared at first by
the Lord, and attested to us by those who heard him' (2:3). The
letter begins with the exalted figure of a Son, in whom God 'in these
last days' has spoken. At 2:9 it becomes clear that this Son is Jesus,
and in the following verses it is made evident that this pioneer of
salvation is to become perfect through suffering (2:10; cf. 5:8), and
further that he is fully human, 'made like his brethren in every
respect' (2:17; cf. 4:15). He can therefore officiate as a true high
priest in the service of God, sinless and holy as befits his office, yet
understanding and sympathetic to his weaker brethren. The 'chapter
of priesthood' makes it clear that his ministry is fulfilled not in any
earthly sanctuary but in the true sanctuary in heaven, and that he
has offered once and for all the sacrifice necessary to priesthood, in
the giving of himself: he 'endured the cross, despising the shame'.
The reference to 'the joy that was set before him' should not be
taken to mean that he endured the cross in order to obtain the joy,
which would reduce it to a business transaction; he attained the joy
that was destined for him as a result of his endurance. As a result
of his devotion the readers are in better case: they now have a hope
that is set before them, almost within their grasp (6:18). Indeed,
they are accorded the signal honour of being summoned to display
the same kind of devotion in their own trials and tribulations, with
the added assurance which the example and the triumph of Jesus
can bring for their encouragement.

FURTHER ADMONITION

12:12–17

12–13. As at some earlier points, it is difficult to know whether verses 12–13 should be taken as the climax and culmination of what has gone before (so for example Montefiore, *NEB*, the *UBS* Greek New Testament) or as the beginning of a new paragraph (so *RSV*). There is certainly no break in the continuity of thought: **Therefore, in the light of all that has been said, lift your drooping hands and strengthen your weak knees.** This quotes Isa. 35:3 (cf. also Ecclus. 25:23), which may be significant if Dodd is correct in thinking that particular verses quoted were intended as pointers to the whole context (*According to the Scriptures*, p. 126): the passage continues 'Say to those who are of a fearful heart, "Be strong, fear not!" '. A modern analogy might be that of a drill-sergeant with a squad of raw recruits, exhorting them to square their shoulders, throw out their chests, and swing their arms in the regulation manner; regiments with a high level of discipline are renowned for their prowess on the field of battle. The author however is reverting to the imagery of the stadium. **Make straight paths for your feet** echoes Prov. 4:26, where the preceding verse runs 'Let your eyes look directly forward, and your gaze be straight before you'. We may recall also Isa. 40:3, quoted at Mk 1:3 par., but both the word **paths** and the imagery are different: there the thought is of the building of a highway, of preparation, here of a track direct towards the goal. In Proverbs the next verse runs 'Do not swerve to the right or to the left'. The final clause of verse 13 is difficult: **so that what is lame may not be put out of joint but rather be healed.** The first verb could mean 'be turned aside', continuing the imagery, but the reference to healing is then perplexing. It is better taken in a medical sense, of a limb put out of joint. *NEB* resolves the problem by making a new sentence: 'Then the disabled limb will not be put out of joint, but regain its former powers'.

14–17. The author now abandons his athletic imagery, and resorts to straightforward admonition. **Strive for peace with all men** recalls Paul's words at Rom. 12:18, and could be taken as referring to all men generally; but in the Greek verses 14–16 are a single sentence (lit. 'Strive . . . seeing to it'), and this suggests that the reference is to peace within the community. It is possible that 'what is lame' in verse 12 is an oblique reference to some members of the community who were in danger of falling away (cf. 10:25); there have been indications earlier (e.g. 4:1, 11) that only some were affected, but all must **see to it that no one fail to obtain the grace**

of God. The **holiness** they are to strive for is not any sanctimonious and self-conscious piety, but consecration to the service of God; the word picks up another word from the same root in verse 10 above, where the purpose of discipline is said to be 'that we may share his holiness'. The best definition is indeed to recall such verses as Lev. 20:26: 'You shall be holy to me; for I the Lord am holy' (cf. Lev. 11:44–45). Without such holiness **no one will see the Lord**, for according to a widespread belief 'like is known by like'. 'To see the Lord' is common in Philo for that vision of the Divine which is 'the rare reward of those who can purify themselves from the sensuous' (Moffatt, referring to Kennedy, *Philo's Contribution to Religion*, London [1919], pp. 192ff.; it may be worthy of note that the first lecture in K. E. Kirk's *The Vision of God* (London [1939]) is headed 'The Vision of God and the Problem of Discipline'). For Philo, however, 'God is clearly manifested only to him who has put off mortal things and had recourse to the incorporeal soul' (Drummond, *Philo Judaeus*, London [1888], II.6); here, as the following verses show, the primary qualification is ethical. The differences may be subtle and difficult to formulate, but they are nonetheless present.

The word translated **See to it** is used at I Pet. 5:2 of exercising oversight (*RSV* margin); it is cognate with the noun from which the English 'bishop' is derived. Here the charge is laid on the whole community. Three points are mentioned, the first of which has already been noted: **that no one fail to obtain the grace of God**. This repeats a word used at 4:1 above, and means to be excluded from God's favour, as were the wilderness generation because of their unbelief. In the second, the **'root of bitterness'** echoes Dt. 29:18, which in LXX speaks of 'a root sprouting up in gall and bitterness' in the context of a warning against apostasy to serve other gods. **Cause trouble** contains all the letters of 'in gall' in Greek, in a different order, and is a variant in some LXX manuscripts. **The many** recalls the frequent occurrence of the Hebrew equivalent in the Qumran texts for the community as a whole; we may also recall the saying that 'a little leaven leavens the whole lump' (cf. I C. 5:6; Gal. 5:9). Finally there is a warning against anyone becoming **immoral or irreligious**, and the example of Esau is introduced to point the moral: **afterward, when he desired to inherit the blessing, he was rejected** (cf. Gen. 27:30–40). In keeping with our author's 'rigorist' position, **he found no chance to repent** (cf. 6:4–6 above). It is not actually said in Genesis that Esau was immoral, but the view that he was is expressed in the book of Jubilees (25.1ff.), in Philo (cf. Williamson, pp. 263–267) and in rabbinic tradition. According to Gen. 36:2, Esau married

Canaanite wives (the names differ at Gen. 26:34), and such marriages are expressly forbidden at Dt. 7:1–7, precisely because of the danger of idolatry. Moreover the Greek word for 'immorality' was often figuratively used for apostasy and idolatry: in Jg. 2:17 it is said that the people 'played the harlot after other gods', and the imagery is common in the prophets (cf. for example Jer. 2:20; Ezek. 16:15ff.; Hos. 4:15; 9:1; in the *Exegesis on the Soul* from Nag Hammadi, a catena of such passages is used to present the myth of the fall of the soul, which is parallel to the gnostic myth of the fall of Sophia, but this comes from a later date). Since the word 'immoral' is clearly used in a literal sense at 13:4 below, it should probably be taken literally here, but the context suggests that the associations with apostasy and idolatry are present in the background. Another possibility would be to separate the two adjectives and take the reference to Esau with the second only (so *NEB*: no immoral person, no one worldly-minded like Esau). This would certainly simplify the verse, and allow us to take 'immoral' in its literal sense; but it is not the most natural way to understand the Greek. At all events the main point of the passage is abundantly clear: it is vital that no member should be found wanting, and the responsibility for the holiness of the community rests upon all.

THE HOPE THAT LIES BEFORE US

12:18–24

18–21. In two earlier passages of extended admonition (5:11—6:12; 10:19–39) our author has blended encouragement and rebuke, sternness and conciliation, and so he does again here. Following the warning in verses 12–17, he now points to the present condition of his readers, the status they now enjoy, which they, or some of them, are in danger of losing. The heading above deliberately echoes 6:18: the readers have a hope set before them, almost within their grasp; but first they must run the race that lies before them (12:1), looking to Jesus, who has now entered into the joy that was set before him (12:2). Once again the point is made by a comparison of the old covenant and the new: **You have not come to what may be touched, a blazing fire, and darkness, and gloom, and a tempest.** Some manuscripts add 'a mountain' to the first phrase, but this word occurs at two different places, which is often a sign of interpolation, and it may be a (perfectly correct) gloss. On the other hand, to take the phrase as qualifying 'fire' (so *NEB*: the palpable, blazing fire) is difficult: one does not handle fire without grave

danger! A better interpretation is to take both participles as referring
to the same thing, but not to the fire, although all three words are
in the dative (a Greek dative can mean 'with' as well as 'to'). This
would yield the translation 'You have not come to what can be
touched, to what blazes with fire, to darkness, gloom and tempest'.
This resolves the problems, and matches the description in Exodus
(see below). The point is that fire, darkness, gloom and tempest are
all tangible or visible things of this world, in contrast with the
heavenly realities mentioned below. **What may be touched** is a
general statement, expanded and clarified in what follows. **You have
come** suggests arrival, which is too strong: they have not yet reached
Mt Zion (verse 22); but the word can also mean 'approach', 'draw
near', and this is the sense required. At Exod. 19:17 it is said that
the people 'took their stand at the foot of the mountain', at 20:21
that they 'stood afar off, while Moses drew near'. Exod. 19:16
mentions thunders and lightnings, a thick cloud, and 'a very loud
trumpet blast', while verse 18 says Mt Sinai 'was wrapped in smoke,
because the Lord descended upon it in fire'. There is an even closer
parallel in Dt. 4:11-12 (cf. 5:22), from which our author has drawn
some of the words he uses: darkness, tempest, the sound of words;
but here there is no reference to the trumpet. **A voice whose words
made the hearers entreat** is literally 'a voice (or sound) of words,
the hearers of which entreated'. This comes from the description of
the people's reaction at Dt. 5:23-27. As that reaction shows, even
the old covenant was given in awe-inspiring circumstances. **The
order** which **they could not endure** is contained in Exod. 19:12-
13; so holy was the mountain that any trespass upon it entailed the
utmost danger. Montefiore recalls the death of Uzzah at 2 Sam.
6:6f.; we may perhaps add the story of the burning bush (Exod.
3:1-6) and the strictures which hedged about the high priest's
entrance into the Holy of Holies. In the ancient world, the holy was
quite literally *mysterium tremendum*. **Indeed, so terrifying was the
sight that Moses said, 'I tremble with fear'** (lit. 'I am terrified and
trembling'). There is nothing to correspond to this in the Exodus
theophany at Sinai, and the closest parallel is in Dt. 9:19, from
which the first words are quoted; but that is in fear at the Lord's
anger over the golden calf. At Ac. 7:32 Stephen is reported as saying
'Moses trembled and did not dare to look'; but that is in connection
with the burning bush. Without the aid of chapter and verse
divisions, and concordances, ancient writers had to rely on their
memories, and it is not uncommon for material from different
sources to be combined, nor is it surprising that this should happen.
We may recall Gregory's comment on Justin Martyr's quotations
from the Gospels: 'Justin quotes from memory. He sometimes

quotes much at random. He adds to one book words from another.
He combines two or three passages into one unwittingly . . .' (*Canon
and Text of the New Testament*, Edinburgh [1907], p. 96).

22–24. In contrast, the readers **have come to Mount Zion and
to the city of the living God, the heavenly Jerusalem**. Once again,
as in verse 18, they have not yet actually arrived, but they have
drawn near; they have the hope, the promise, the assurance, but
they have still to endure. What is important, however, is not the
degree of their proximity; it is the contrast in the goal of their
journey. Zion is one of the hills on which Jerusalem is built. It was
the site of a Jebusite stronghold which David captured (2 Sam. 5:7)
and made his capital; hence it became known as the city of David.
The name is often used as a synonym for Jerusalem, especially in
the poetic books of the Old Testament. With the installation of the
ark of God in the city (2 Sam. 6:2ff.), and later the building of
Solomon's temple (1 Kg. 5–8), it became also the religious centre
of Israel, 'the city which the Lord has chosen out of all the tribes
of Israel' (1 Kg. 14:21). Solomon in his prayer of dedication (1 Kg.
7:27ff.) acknowledges that even the heavens cannot contain God,
'much less this house that I have built', and it is not difficult to
understand the development in certain circles of the idea of a heavenly Jerusalem (cf. Rev. 3:12; 14:1; 21:2. But where Revelation
speaks of the new Jerusalem coming down, Hebrews appears to
think of the readers going up into it. For comparison between Heb.
12:18–24 and Qumran, see Gaertner, *The Temple and the Community*,
pp. 88–99).

In the following lines there is again a difference in punctuation
(cf. *RSV* margin) arising from the absence of punctuation marks in
the original manuscripts; indeed, no fewer than five different
patterns of punctuation have been suggested for just six Greek words
(Peterson, p. 161; cf. pp. 160ff. for discussion of this passage). The
word rendered **in festal gathering** may be taken with what precedes,
relating to **innumerable angels** (lit. myriads of angels), as in the
RSV text, or co-ordinated with the following words (so *RSV*
margin, *NEB*, the *UBS* Greek New Testament). In the first case,
the word 'describes the angelic hosts thronging with glad worship
round the living God' (Moffatt); in the second it seems to separate
'the general assembly and church of the first-born' (*AV*) from the
angels just mentioned. The latter phrase, especially with the
addition **who are enrolled in heaven**, would seem to refer to men
and women, the saints whose names are written in the Lamb's book
of life (Rev. 21:27); but in that case, why the reference to **the spirits
of just men made perfect** below? Attempts have been made to
resolve this problem by identifying the one group with the heroes

of Old Testament times, the other with Christian saints and martyrs, but without any very conspicuous success. For one thing, which group is which?

The key to the solution of some rather complex problems would appear to lie along the lines of Peterson's suggestion (p. 162) that 'the vision in 12:22–24 is of *the ultimate, completed company of the people of God, membership of which is now enjoyed by faith*' (italics original). 'In coming to Christ, who is in the midst of this heavenly assembly as mediator of the New Covenant (verse 24), men and women become members by faith, with the promise of one day enjoying the full rights of citizenship in the heavenly city, as the inheritance of the first-born'. '*The relationship with God that believers may now enjoy, by virtue of Christ's finished work, involves as its implied end the transfer of believers to the heavenly city*' (p. 166; italics original). **The assembly of the first-born** is then not a further description of the angels, as some would have it, but refers, as one would naturally expect, to men and women (in the other occurrence of the word rendered **assembly,** at 2:12 ('congregation'), it stands in parallelism with 'brethren' in the previous line, and again naturally refers to people). The use of two different expressions for the same group of people (**the assembly of the first-born** and **the spirits of just men made perfect**) is explained by the intervening reference to **a judge who is God of all.** This heavenly assembly is 'in some sense met for scrutiny or judgment' (Peterson, p. 162). **The spirits of just men made perfect** 'will refer to the saints of all ages as those who have been perfected by the work of Christ' (*ib.* 164). At 10:14 above it is said that he 'has perfected for all time those who are sanctified', and it was noted there that 'sanctified' is a present participle, implying a process that is still going on. The people of God thus includes both those who have completed their course (the spirits of just men made perfect) and those who still have a race before them, but who as 'enrolled in heaven' already belong to that people. As Gaertner puts it (*op. cit.,* p. 97), 'Christians are "holy", and as such live in fellowship with the "holy ones", the saints in heaven'.

Verse 24 then forms a climax, with its reference to **Jesus, the mediator of a new covenant.** Where **the blood of Abel** cried out for vengeance (Gen. 4:10f.), that of Christ **speaks more graciously:** 'It speaks of acceptance and forgiveness, perpetually available to those who draw near to God through Christ (cf. 7:25; 4:16). It speaks of the opening of the heavenly sanctuary for immediate encounter with God (10:19ff.) and as a hope to be grasped for the future (6:18–20)' (Peterson, p. 165). 'The assurance that believers have been perfected by the one sacrifice of Christ (10:14; 12:23) and that Christ's blood continually avails for the forgiveness of sins (12:24) means that Christians on the march to the heavenly city have the greatest encouragement to hold fast the confession of their hope without wavering' (*ib.* p. 166). The Coptic Gospel of Thomas incidentally contains a logion (82) known also to Origen (in *Jerem. hom.* XX.3; cf. Puech in Hennecke-Schneemelcher, *NT Apocrypha* I. 303; Jeremias, *Unknown Sayings of Jesus*, ET London [1964], p. 66ff.), which may also be relevant in this connection: 'He that is near me is near the fire; he that is far from me is far from the kingdom'. Jeremias (p. 72) interprets the fire as 'the fire of testing, of tribulation, of suffering . . . through which every follower of Jesus must pass'. The second half of the logion contains the alternative: 'If we refuse to follow Jesus we are shut out of the kingdom of God. The fire is only a way through—to the glory of God!'

FINAL WARNING

12:25–29

The contrast in the preceding section leads naturally into a final and urgent warning: **See that you do not refuse him who is speaking. For if they did not escape when they refused him who warned them on earth, much less shall we escape if we reject him who warns from heaven.** A link is provided by the reference to **him who is speaking,** which picks up the verb 'that speaks' in verse 24 (both are participles, although in different cases). The verb **see** is not the one used at verse 15 above but another of the Greek words for seeing, which occurs eight times in Hebrews; perhaps significantly, the only other case where it appears in this construction, in a prohibition (see that . . . not), is in the warning at 3:12 ('take care') in the context of the rejection of the wilderness generation. It is clearly the same kind of argument that is intended here (cf. also 2:1–3; 10:28–29): if rejection of an earthly warning proved disastrous, how much more (our author's familiar *qal wā-hōmer* formula) will rejection of a heavenly warning! **Refused** is the word used at verse 19 above of the people's entreaty that no further messages should be spoken to them. Strictly speaking, Exod. 20:19 and Dt. 5:24–27 do not mention rejection, but rather an entreaty born of terror; but the Exodus story contains ample evidence of the people rejecting God's commands and suffering for their disobedience. The Greek word order would make it more natural to translate 'they did not escape on earth' or 'when on earth they

refused him who warned them', but the sense obviously requires a
contrast between an earthly warning and a heavenly one.

The general sense of the verse is clear enough, but there has been
debate over one point of detail. The three references to 'him' have
been variously understood: a) as referring to God, who is now
addressing his call to the readers, as of old he spoke to Israel on
Sinai (but God's word at Sinai came from heaven, the passages
mentioned above do not speak of rejection, and it was Moses whose
word was rejected; this view would however lead smoothly into
verse 26); b) as referring to Christ, who as pre-existent spoke under
the old covenant and now as glorified and exalted speaks from
heaven (but the idea of a pre-existent Christ speaking through Old
Testament figures is somewhat difficult, and verse 26 surely refers
to God). Verse 26 is linked with verse 25 by a relative pronoun (lit.
'whose voice then shook the earth'), and this verse clearly refers to
God; the one who warns from heaven, then, must naturally be God,
whether as speaking through Jesus or through some other agency.
The one who warned on earth is most naturally Moses, although
the people later also 'refused' many of the prophets. In verse 24 it
is the sprinkled blood that speaks, but this is the blood of Jesus;
hence the one who is speaking here is naturally Jesus. The swift
changes of subject may be perplexing, but the main point of the
verse is beyond doubt or question.

26–29. At Sinai 'the whole mountain quaked greatly' (Exod.
19:18; cf. Ps. 68:8); earthquake is often a sign of the presence of
God (e.g. Isa. 6:4; Ps. 18:7), although at 1 Kg. 19:11 'the Lord was
not in the earthquake'. Here there is a contrast: **His voice then
shook the earth; but now he has promised, 'Yet once more I will
shake not only the earth but also the heaven'.** At Sinai only the
earth was shaken, so that here something more devastating, of
cosmic dimensions, is in view. Actually Hag. 2:6, which is adapted
here, is really a promise, for after the shaking of heavens and earth
and sea, it goes on to end with 'I will fill this house with splendour'.
Our author this time has selected only the first words, and by
reversing their order and inserting 'not only . . . but also' has made
of it something rather different: a prophecy of the final consummation. This is brought out in the next verse, in which our author
explains: **This phrase, 'Yet once more', indicates the removal of
what is shaken, as of what has been made, in order that what
cannot be shaken may remain.** We may recall the verses quoted
from Ps. 102 at 1:10–12 above: heaven and earth belong to the
created order, as the work of God's hands, **what has been made.**
What cannot be shaken is then explained in verse 28: **Therefore
let us be grateful for receiving a kingdom that cannot be shaken,**

and thus let us offer to God acceptable worship, with reverence and awe. Here again **receiving** is a present participle, indicating a process that is still going on; as Montefiore notes, 'if the kingdom had actually been received, there would have been no need of this final exhortation'. The word rendered **reverence** has already appeared, at 5:7, where as noted above it presents something of a problem, since it would seem to be contradicted by the facts. Its use here of the proper attitude towards God, in reverence and awe, may be taken to confirm the translation 'godly fear' at 5:7. The real question at that point concerns the meaning of the words 'was heard'. The cognate verb is used at 11:7 ('took heed'): Noah showed the same reverence and godly fear when he obeyed and built the ark.

Earthquake is among the portents associated with the Day of the Lord, like the 'blood and fire and columns of smoke' of Jl 2:30 (cf. Ac. 2:19); in the following chapter of Joel (3:15f.) the sun and moon are darkened and the stars withdraw their light, the Lord roars from Zion and the heavens and the earth shake—but the passage ends with a promise: the Lord is a refuge to his people (cf. also Isa. 13:13). In 2 Pet. (3:7ff.) the heavens and earth that now exist have been stored up for fire, being kept for the day of judgment. The day of the Lord will come like a thief (verse 10), 'and then the heavens will pass away with a loud noise . . . and the earth and the works that are upon it will be burned up'. Yet despite the universal conflagration the author looks forward in hope: 'But according to his promise we wait for new heavens and a new earth in which righteousness dwells' (cf. also Rev. 6:12ff.; 16:18f.; and especially 21:1–4). The point in these and similar passages is that while created things may be shaken, or even pass away, there remain some things not shaken. At Mk 13:31 Jesus says, 'Heaven and earth will pass away, but my words will not pass away'. For all their expectation of cosmic catastrophe at the end of time, these writers still had a conviction of something more permanent and lasting; if they thought in terms of renewal, a new heaven and a new earth, it was still God who made all things new. The **kingdom that cannot be shaken** is then naturally the kingdom of God, a concept central to the teaching of Jesus in the Gospels (cf. for example Perrin, *The Kingdom of God in the Teaching of Jesus*, London [1963]; id. *Rediscovering the Teaching of Jesus*, London [1967]), but less common in the epistles, where it usually refers to the future destiny of the faithful (e.g. 1 C. 6:9, 10; 15:50; Gal. 5:21; 1 Th. 2:12; 2 Th. 1:5; 2 Tim. 4:18; it will be noted that several of these references are set, as here, in a context of fidelity and endurance. At 2 C. 5:1 Paul uses a different image for the same idea: if our earthly tent is destroyed, we have from God 'a house not made with hands, eternal in the heavens').

The reference in the preceding paragraph to a universal conflagration may recall the Stoic idea of the return of the soul to the primal fire from which it came, which in turn is a reminder that such ideas, with the contrast between what is transitory and what is permanent, were widely spread in the ancient world. If there is an Alexandrian background to the letter, then such ideas could be reflected here, as they are in Philo (cf. Williams, *The Immovable Race*, Leiden [1985], pp. 14f. and the index of references to Philo), but it is certain that the primary influence on our author is to be sought in the Old Testament (cf. Williams, pp. 8ff., and for Heb. 12:25–28 *ib.* 17f.): at Ps. 46:5f. the city of God 'shall not be moved', though kingdoms totter and the earth melt. In LXX (Ps. 45:6–7) the word used with reference both to the city and to the earth is the verb translated 'shaken' in our present passage. There is, as it happens, a whole group of words (e.g. unshakeable, immovable, immutable, unchanging) which could also be taken into consideration, and it is evident that there was some measure of cross-fertilization between biblical ideas and those of Greek philosophy. The designation with which Williams is concerned occurs in five of the Nag Hammadi texts, and apparently nowhere else in ancient literature; belonging to this 'immovable race' means 'membership in the ideal Human family, for which therefore all humans are potential candidates' (Williams, p. 184). It would be dangerous to claim Hebrews as the source of this conception, in view of the abundant parallel material, but the definition Williams gives could also serve for the status of the readers in our author's view. The necessary qualification, which must not be forgotten, is that they are still potential candidates. Their status is not something on which they can presume, to be taken for granted. On the contrary, as the logion quoted above from the Gospel of Thomas suggests (see at verse 24), their situation is still precarious: **for our God is a consuming fire**. This echoes Dt. 4:24 (cf. Isa. 33:14; Mal. 3:2; there are numerous passages in which the wrath of God is described in terms of fire): God is merciful and gracious, long-suffering and full of compassion, but not to be trifled with. The proper attitude is one of worship, with reverence and awe.

This chapter forms the climax and culmination of the main body of the letter, containing the author's final and urgent admonition to his readers. At the very beginning he had written of 'these last days' (1:2), at 10:25 of 'the Day drawing near'; the readers have already tasted the heavenly gift, become partakers of the Holy Spirit, tasted the goodness of the word of God and the powers of the age to come (6:4f.). Now they have come to Mount Zion, to the heavenly Jerusalem (12:22), the race that is set before them has now to be run (12:2). If we knew more of the background to the letter, the situation facing the readers, we might find a special relevance in this approach, but unfortunately there is but little to guide us. They have already suffered (10:32–34), but not to the point of shedding blood (12:4), which would certainly fit in with a date just before the Neronian persecution; but as indicated in the Introduction such a date cannot be affirmed with any degree of confidence. The use of argument based firmly on Old Testament material suggests a Jewish-Christian author writing to Jewish-Christian readers, but this too is by no means certain: the author may be a Jewish Christian, but it is not so clear that his readers were. The Greek Old Testament was the Bible of the early Church when there was as yet no New Testament to set alongside the Old, so that it was the natural basis for any such argument, for Gentile as well as for Jewish Christians. More to the point, it was Gentile Christians who later preserved the letter, so that evidently they found it meaningful in their own changing situations; and this in turn points to the abiding significance of this letter, for all ages. Much of it is in the language and thought-forms of a bygone age, using an imagery that is foreign to the modern world, so that it requires interpretation and elucidation for a proper understanding; but trials and tribulations, doubts and questionings, obstacles and hindrances, are in various ways part of our common lot. Now one of the things our author does for his readers—in all ages—is to place things in perspective: trials that may seem too much to bear take on a new appearance when we realise that others have already endured them, that there is meaning and purpose to these tribulations, however hard it may be to see it. Hughes at one point (*Hebrews and Hermeneutics*, p. 131) speaks of a 'serious erosion' of Christian faith: 'the tendency on the part of the readers is in fact not toward a faith-commitment, but in the opposite direction. It is more accurate to say that the letter is written from faith to incipient unbelief than from faith to faith'. It is precisely here that the letter has a message for every generation, including our own: without the faith to persevere, it is not possible to reach the goal.

PRACTICAL ADMONITIONS

13:1-6

At an earlier point (see comment on 2:1-4) it was noted as one of
the differences between Paul and Hebrews that whereas Paul tends
to deal with theological questions first and then turn to ethical
admonition, our author interweaves his admonitions with his theological exposition. This can now be seen to require some qualification. It is true enough that our author introduces admonitions into
his exposition, but these admonitions are directly related to that
exposition: they are admonitions to faith and courage and endurance, to perseverance, not practical admonitions for the conduct
of life. The present chapter in fact provides a better parallel to
Rom. 12:1ff. than the admonitions in the main body of the letter.
This also serves to explain why the letter continues, in what some
have seen as a kind of appendix or postscript, after the main argument has been completed: the author is following a more or less
established pattern. It has sometimes been argued that the style and
content are so different that this chapter must be assigned to a
different hand, but the suggestions offered are not such as to inspire
much confidence: some anonymous later editor converting a homily
into an epistle (if he added a postscript, why did he not add a
superscription at the beginning?); deliberate imitation of Paul's style
to secure acceptance of the book as Pauline; or that this is a fragment
of Paul's 'severe letter' to Corinth. As Bruce puts it, 'These theories
can be given no higher status than that of curiosities of literary
criticism'. In point of fact. as Michel and others have noted, there
are links between this chapter and the main body of the letter. This
is not a later addition, but an integral part of the whole.

The author makes no attempt to cover the whole range of Christian ethics, but simply sets out certain 'basic Christian social duties'
(Montefiore). Michel sees here four pairs of injunctions: i) brotherly
love and hospitality (1-2); ii) care for prisoners and the ill-treated
(3); iii) respect for marriage (4); iv) avoidance of covetousness,
contentment with what one has (5). Each pair has a brief justification
attached, although it must be said that the second (in verse 3) has
a different form from the others, while the last is both longer and
includes a quotation.

1-2. Brotherly love was one of the cardinal virtues in primitive
Christianity (cf. Rom. 12:10; 1 Th. 4:9; 1 Pet. 1:22; 2 Pet. 1:7),
and was to become one of the distinctive characteristics of the early
Church. It is not quite the same as the love which Jesus advocates
in the Synoptics, since that embraces even enemies; but obviously

those who are called upon to love even enemies may be expected to show at least the same love to one another. Jesus widened and universalised the commandment of Lev. 19:18 by giving a new meaning to the word 'neighbour' (cf. esp. Lk. 10:29–37), but in the epistles and in the Johannine literature (cf. Jn 13:34; 15:12, 17; 1 Jn 3:11, 14, 23) the emphasis is more on love within the Christian community ('the brethren', 'one another'). The readers have already shown such love (6:10), but 10:24–25 above suggests that some may have needed this injunction: their love for one another must **continue** and develop. One practical way of expressing this love was in **hospitality**, which in Harnack's words 'was repeatedly inculcated on the faithful' (*Expansion of Christianity*, ET London [1904], I. p. 220 and note 1; cf. Rom. 12:13; 1 Pet. 4:9). **Strangers** here refers in the first instance to fellow-Christians on a journey: inns in the ancient world were sometimes of doubtful reputation, and charges could be high, so that travellers would be glad of the hospitality of fellow-Christians. This was in fact an obligation both for Jews and for Christians; that the hospitality was sometimes abused is shown by Didache 12: the guest is to stay no more than two or three days, and if he wishes to settle down he is to work for his bread. The justification here appended may recall Mt. 25: 31ff.; but it is more likely that our author as usual is thinking of Old Testament examples (cf. Gen. 18:1–8; 19:1–3).

3. The admonition in verse 3 again reflects back to the main body of the letter: in their struggle in 'the former days' the readers 'had compassion on the prisoners' (10:34), and were themselves 'publicly exposed to abuse and affliction'. This expression of Christian love is also to be continued, but as noted above the justification appended is different in form: instead of a clause connected by 'for', it is woven into the two injunctions (lit. remember the prisoners as bound with them, the ill-treated as being yourselves in the body). It is a question of solidarity: as Paul writes at 1 C. 12:26, 'if one member suffers, all suffer together (for later Christian practice in care for prisoners, cf. Harnack, *op. cit.* I. pp. 201ff.). **In the body** refers simply to ordinary human existence; had our author wished to utilise the Pauline conception of the Body of Christ he would have made it clear.

4. In verse 4 there is no verb in the main clause, and it could be taken as a statement (so *AV*: Marriage is honourable; cf. *NEB*, which however continues 'let us all keep it so'), but in this context it is more probably a further injunction, and one the more necessary in an environment noted for sexual promiscuity. There is no sign here of any tendency to repudiate **marriage** (cf. 1 Tim. 4:3), or of the ascetic concern for chastity even within the marriage bond which

marks some of the apocryphal Acts or the Pseudo-Titus epistle (see
Hennecke-Schneemelcher, *NT Apocrypha* II). Marriage is accepted
(in Judaism it was regarded 'not only as the normal state, but as a
divine ordinance': Moore, *Judaism*, II. p. 119); the concern is that
it should be **held in honour among all**. Defilement of **the marriage
bed** most obviously refers to adultery, as the following warning
confirms. **Immoral** echoes the word used of Esau at 12:16 above.
The two words **immoral and adulterous** are not synonymous, the
first being more general and referring to sexual sins of any kind,
while the second refers specifically to infidelity to the marriage vow.
These words also appear together, with other terms, in Paul's list
of those who will not inherit the kingdom of God (1 C. 6:9–10).
The 'justification' here is more a solemn warning, in which the
Greek word order suggests a different emphasis: they will be
judged—by God himself (cf. also Gal. 5:19, 21; Eph. 5:5).

5–6. According to 1 Tim. 6:10, the **love of money** is the root of
all evils; at 1 Tim. 3:3 one of the qualities required in a bishop is
that he should be no lover of money (the word used here, in its only
other occurrence in the New Testament). One possible translation of
1 Th. 4:6 is 'that no man defraud his brother in business' (*RSV*
margin), and this as here follows closely after a warning against
immorality. Covetousness is condemned as far back as the
Decalogue (Exod. 20:17), and there it relates not only to a neighbour's possessions but also to his wife. The association of covetousness and sexual sins is thus of very long standing. In the Sermon
on the Mount, Jesus warns against storing up treasures on earth,
and shortly afterwards speaks against anxiety over food and drink
and clothing (Mt. 6:19–21, 25–26, 31–33). Our author of course did
not have Matthew's Gospel, but he stands in the same tradition.
The admonition **be content with what you have** corresponds with
a fairly widespread attitude in the ancient world: several schools of
philosophy urged the reduction of wants to a minimum (at 1
Tim. 6:6 the Greek word rendered 'contentment', cognate with the
verb used here, was a Stoic watch-word, 'self-sufficiency'). What is
distinctive at this point, and not derived from philosophical thought,
is the motivation: **for he has said, 'I will never fail you nor forsake
you'**. This contentment is not the result of any philosophical theory;
it is grounded in trust in God's promise. Here again we may recall
the teaching of Jesus (cf. also Mt. 7:11 and similar passages). The
quotation is an adaptation of Dt. 31:8 (cf. Dt. 31:6; Jos. 1:5. In
RSV the Joshua verse seems closer, but the Greek formulation is
different; it can be dangerous to argue from similarities in English
translations). Verse 6 then presents the appropriate response in
words drawn from Ps. 118:6.

As noted above, the author makes no attempt to deal with the whole range of Christian ethics, but he does set out some basic principles which are fundamental to a right Christian attitude, and from which other principles might develop. Moreover, these principles are just such as would promote the cohesion of a community: brotherly love, concern for those less fortunate, mutual trust and fidelity, contentment with what one has rather than a constant striving after riches. If a group is to survive, its members must be able to trust one another to the full, with no lingering suspicion that the other may be more concerned for his own advantage or his own desires. The solidarity and the survival of the community depend on the mutual trust and fidelity of the members, and they in their turn may place their trust in the promises of God. Even in these few verses, a number of links with the main body of the letter have been noted, and the final assurance in verse 5 may serve to confirm that this chapter is indeed an integral part of the work. From the beginning our author has been concerned to stimulate and encourage his readers, to assure them that their trust in the promises of God is well-founded, and this he does again here.

FURTHER ADMONITION, AND A WARNING

13:7–16

7–8. Verse 6 with its quotation of Ps. 118 forms a convenient point at which to pause and begin a fresh paragraph, but as so often before there is no real break in the continuity. Following the general admonitions of the first six verses, our author now bids his readers: **Remember your leaders, those who spoke to you the word of God; consider the outcome of their life, and imitate their faith.** At 2:3 above it was said that salvation was declared at first by the Lord, and attested to us by those who heard him. The first transmitters of the Gospel were of course those who heard Jesus himself, i.e. his disciples, but in the Greek at that point there is no object to 'heard', and while the addition of 'him' is very natural, it is by no means the only possible interpretation: the words could refer to those who heard *the message*, the whole chain of witnesses from the first disciples down to the **leaders** mentioned here. The word employed to describe them is not one of the terms later used for church office, like 'bishop' and 'presbyter', but one used of high officials (e.g. Ac. 7:10: 'governor') and military commanders, and in some papyri of religious leaders (*BAG* 343b); at Ac. 15:22 it is used of 'leading men' among the brethren. This suggests a still

fairly primitive form of church organisation. Here the most likely
reference is to the founders of the community, but the recurrence
of the word at verses 17 and 24 below suggests that some of them
are still alive. The only other occurrence in the New Testament of
the word translated **outcome** is at 1 C. 10:13, where it means 'a
way of escape'; at Wis. 2:17 it means 'the end of life', and many
have taken it so in the present verse, but it can also mean the
outcome or result of an event (cf. Wis. 8:8; 11:14), and this seems
the most probable meaning here. It is not indicated that these
leaders suffered martyrdom (12:4 might tell against that). What is
meant is that the readers should consider the effect of faith in the
quality of their lives, and so **imitate their faith**. The readers are
being given examples not only from the distant past, as in chapter
11, but also from their own more recent history.

This motif of imitation provides another link with the main body
of the letter (cf. 6:12), and is common in Paul (cf. Best, *Thessalonians*, p. 76): at 1 Th. 1:6 Paul says his readers 'became imitators of
us and of the Lord' (cf. also 2:14); at 2 Th. 3:7–9 he says he earned
his own living so as not to be a burden 'to give you in our conduct
an example to imitate'; at 1 C. 4:16 he urges the Corinthians 'be
imitators of me', at 11:1 'be imitators of me, as I am of Christ'. It
is worthy of note that in some of these cases there is reference to
tribulation in the context: at 1 C. 4:9 Paul speaks of the apostles as
'like men sentenced to death . . . a spectacle to the world', which
would fit very well with the imagery of 12:1–2 above. In the light
of this, verse 8 is not so sudden and unexpected as it might seem
at first sight. In fact, if we had to choose a single verse to sum up
the main point and theme of the letter, this might well be that verse:
Jesus Christ is the same yesterday and today and for ever. The
great high priest exalted in the heavens is not a different person
from the Jesus who 'partook of the same nature' (2:14), 'endured
the cross, despising the shame' (12:2), 'learned obedience through
what he suffered' (5:8); he is the same yesterday and today, and for
all time. We have not a high priest unable to sympathise with
our weakness, but one who has himself suffered, and therefore
understands to the full what it means (4:15; cf. 2:18). We therefore
have all the greater cause for confidence.

9. Reference to Jesus as the constant and abiding object of faith
leads naturally enough into a warning against false doctrine: **Do not
be led astray by diverse and strange teachings**. The verb here
means to be carried away, and is used at Jude 12 of clouds driven
by the wind (the 'clouds' in that instance, are people given to false
doctrine). A similar metaphor, of drifting away, was used at 2:1
above. We may also recall Eph. 4:14, where a different compound

is used ('carried about'); in some manuscripts this form is substituted here. These teachings are **diverse**, manifold, varied, in contrast with the unity of authentic Christian teaching (Westcott makes a relevant but all too often forgotten point: 'The faith of the Christian is in a Person and not in doctrines about Him'); they are also **strange** or foreign, possibly as coming from outside (cf. Ac. 17:18, where some call Paul 'a preacher of foreign divinities'). What these teachings were we do not know for certain, but they were alien to Christianity. The one clue comes in the following words: **for it is well that the heart be strengthened by grace, not by foods, which have not benefited their adherents.** **Grace** here obviously refers to the grace of God, already mentioned several times in the letter (cf. 2:9; 4:16; 12:15 and the final benediction at 13:25; 10:25 speaks of the Spirit of grace; at 12:28 the word has its other meaning of thankfulness: 'Let us be grateful'). The problem is: what is meant by **foods**? The natural tendency is to think of Jewish food laws, but these were in the main restrictive, specifying foods which were *not* to be eaten; what appears to be meant here is the eating of some kind of food as a means to salvation. The same objection applies to any interpretation in terms of ascetic practice (cf. 1 Tim. 4:3; Col. 2:16, 21ff.). T. W. Manson, who suggested that the letter was written by Apollos to the churches of the Lycus valley (*Studies in the Gospels and Epistles*, Manchester [1962]), aptly paraphrases by speaking of 'a dietary discipline that was of no real advantage to those who submitted to it' (p. 254), but then goes on to speak of 'Jewish food laws or pagan mystical asceticism'; others have thought of some form of incipient *gnosis* or gnosticism, 'perhaps with Essene or quasi-Essene affinities' (Bruce). Paul in 1 Corinthians has quite a lot to say about food sacrificed to idols, but if that is what our author had in mind, why did he not say so? Another suggestion is that the reference is to some false interpretation of the Lord's Supper as a sacrificial meal (e.g. Moffatt). The very variety of the interpretations shows the complexity of the problem. Now at 1 C. 8:8 Paul says quite bluntly that 'food will not commend us to God', at Rom. 14:17 that 'the kingdom of God does not mean food and drink'; such things are quite simply irrelevant. At 9:10 above, the only other occurrence of the word **foods** in the letter, there is reference in the context to 'regulations for the body imposed until the time of reformation'. All such things are no longer of any importance; what matters now, as the whole letter has sought to emphasise, is faith, loyalty, perseverance. As the next verse shows, Christians have a better altar. **Their adherents** is literally 'those who walk in them', the one occurrence in this letter of the 'decidedly

Pauline' use of the word (*BAG* 649a) with reference to conduct or way of life.

10–12. At verse 10 our author reverts to the imagery of the Day of Atonement which he used in the main body of the letter. It was the rule that the flesh of some sacrifices should be eaten by the priests in the sanctuary (e.g. Lev. 6:26; 10:16ff.), but the Atonement ritual was an exception: the victims were to be carried outside the camp and burned (Lev. 16:27, cf. 6:30). Our author makes use of this point in the following verses. The most obvious and natural interpretation (of verse 10) is that **we** Christians **have an altar** in the heavenly sanctuary **from which those who serve the tent**, i.e. the earthly tabernacle, **have no right to eat**. The difficulty with this is that **an altar** would seem to imply continuing sacrifice, and our author has repeatedly said above (e.g. 9:12, 28; 10:10, 12) that Christ's sacrifice was offered once and for all. Accordingly some commentators (e.g. Moffatt, see above) take **those who serve the tent** to refer not to the priests and Levites of the old dispensation but to worshippers generally, in particular Christians. 'The Christian sacrifice, on which all our relationship to God depends, is not one that involves or allows any connexion with a meal' (Moffatt). This would fit in with the interpretation of 'foods' in verse 9 as referring to a false understanding of the Lord's Supper as a sacrificial meal, and would also provide a smooth transition to the following verse. Incidentally, it is worthy of note that the author makes no reference to the Lord's Supper, even where one might have been expected: is this precisely because it had become open to misunderstanding? On the other hand, the verse on this interpretation is cryptic, to say the least; the Holy Table does not seem to be called an altar until much later (cf. Westcott's Additional Note, pp. 455ff.), and the 'foods' in verse 9 appear to be rejected as irrelevant. It would therefore seem better to treat the verse as a contrast: we too have an altar, and a sacrifice, but it is a sacrifice already complete, once and for all, and in this those who cling to the old dispensation have no part. Verse 11 summarises the procedure on the Day of Atonement, as stated in Lev. 16:27: **the bodies of the animals . . . are burned outside the camp**. Verse 12 then draws a parallel: **so Jesus also suffered outside the gate in order to sanctify the people through his own blood**. It is not actually stated in the Gospels that Jesus was crucified outside Jerusalem: Mark speaks of him being led out (Mk 15:20), but that could be merely from the judgment hall; Matthew (27:31) and Luke (23:26) speak of him being led away; the closest is Jn 19:20, which says the place where Jesus was crucified was 'near the city', and therefore outside it. It was however normal for executions to take place **outside the camp** (cf.

Lev. 24:14, 23; Num. 15:36) or **outside the gate** (Dt. 22:24); at Lk. 4:29 the people of Nazareth put Jesus out of the town, intending to throw him over the cliff, at Ac. 7:58 Stephen is cast out of the city and stoned. In the body of the letter our author has already made the point that Jesus entered the Holy place 'taking not the blood of goats and calves but his own blood' (9:11-14), and that his offering is effective to cleanse and sanctify his people (9:14; 10:10, 14, 29). The old ordinances however had to be continually repeated, and had at best a limited validity (cf. 9:6-10; 10:1-4). Now a further contrast emerges: the bodies of the animals were burned outside the camp, but Jesus lives, a priest for ever, seated at the right hand of the throne of God.

13-14. Verse 13 then draws a conclusion: **Therefore let us go forth to him outside the camp, bearing abuse for him.** This last phrase means literally 'bearing his reproach', which recalls the phrase used of Moses at 11:26, 'the reproach of Christ' (*RSV*: abuse suffered for Christ). *NEB* there renders 'the stigma that rests on God's Anointed', and here 'bearing the stigma that he bore'. The readers have already suffered **abuse** (the same word in the plural), indeed have been made a public spectacle (10:33; *NEB*: abused and tormented to make a public show. Cf. 1 C. 4:9, quoted at verses 7-8 above), and it may be that the prospect of some recurrence is a part of the anxiety to which this letter is directed. If so, they are now given assurance that their sufferings are meaningful, part of a greater purpose. The same attitude to suffering appears at several points in 1 Pet. (e.g. 1:6-9; 2:15-16, 21-24; 3:15-18). Col. 1:24 even speaks of completing what is lacking in Christ's afflictions for the sake of his body, the church. Christ himself has pioneered the way, and they are now called upon to follow, to **go forth to him outside the camp.** This means abandoning the security of defensive walls, a venture into the unknown; but others have gone before. At 11:10 it was said that Abraham looked forward to the city whose builder and maker is God (cf. 11:16; 12:22). Now this note is struck again, in verse 14: **For here we have no lasting city, but we seek the city which is to come.** There is no need to think of Jerusalem, or to raise questions as to why the author does not refer to its destruction if it has already taken place; as at many points already, he shows no interest in contemporary or recent history—the nearest he comes is in his reference to 'your leaders' at verse 7 above. His concern is with the pilgrimage on which his readers are engaged, the pilgrimage of life with its joys and sorrows, its trials and tribulations and its triumphs. He is only too well aware of the transitory character of life: **here we have no lasting city.** His gaze is fixed on **the city which is to come**, and it is to this that he seeks to direct his readers. They have achieved much already, and received much; they have the promise, the hope, the assurance. Now they must **go forth**, in faith and confidence.

15–16. At 10:8 above our author interpreted Ps. 40:6–8 as signifying the abolition of animal sacrifice in favour of obedience, in particular the obedience of Christ: his single offering is effective for all time (10:14). Where sins have already been forgiven, there is no need for further sin offerings (10:18). In this our author, as already noted, stands in the tradition of the prophets, who are frequently critical of reliance on the sacrificial system (e.g. Hos. 6:6; Mic. 6:6–8): true religion is not a matter of outward ceremony, however lavish the offering. It is a response in gratitude and thanksgiving to the grace and love of God, and a dedication to a matching way of life: **Through him then let us continually offer up a sacrifice of praise to God, that is, the fruit of lips that acknowledge his name. Do not neglect to do good and to share what you have, for such sacrifices are pleasing to God. Through him** refers back to Jesus (verses 12–13) as the mediator of Christian prayer and thanksgiving; it is a common New Testament formula, especially in the context of thanksgiving and glorification (cf. Rom. 1:8; 7:25; 16:27; 2 C. 1:20; Col. 3:17; 1 Pet. 4:11; Jude 25; 1 Pet. 2:5 speaks, in terms similar to our present verse, of offering 'spiritual sacrifices acceptable to God through Jesus Christ'). The phrase **a sacrifice of praise** occurs in the LXX version of Lev. 7:12 (7:2 LXX), but here it is immediately re-interpreted by words drawn from Hos. 14:2 LXX. *RSV* there follows LXX, with the Hebrew reading in the margin; cf. *NEB*: 'we will pay our vows with cattle from our pens'. Here again it is the LXX reading that suits our author's needs. The thought of thanksgiving as a sacrifice is already present in Ps. 50:13–14, 23 (cf. Ps. 141:2). The words **the fruit of the lips** also appear at Isa. 57:18, but not in LXX; we may compare *1QS* IX.4, where Leaney translates 'the offering of the lips' (*The Rule of Qumran*, pp. 210, 224f.; but many of his references relate only to 'lips'). Vermes here translates 'prayer rightly offered' (*The Dead Sea Scrolls in English*, p. 87), but has 'the fruit of the lips' at *1QH* I.28 (*ib.* 152). The sect repudiated the Jerusalem temple and its sacrifices as polluted, and regarded itself as set apart to make atonement, a new temple with new and spiritual sacrifices. As Gaertner notes (*The Temple and the Community*, p. 86f.), the resemblance is striking, but there are also important differences: the sect *replaced* the temple sacrifices with its own rites, which were regarded as atoning, and it would seem that they looked forward to a restored temple with a purified cultus and a valid priesthood. Hebrews is more radical: there is but one atoning sacrifice, which has already been offered; the 'spiritual' sacrifices

here are not atoning, but 'no more than expressions of the moral
obligations of the new life' (Gaertner). This appears in the way in
which our author goes on immediately to speak of **doing good** and
sharing what one has. **To share what you have** is a paraphrase of
a word variously rendered as communion, fellowship, participation,
sharing. This is its only occurrence in Hebrews, but a cognate verb
is used at 2:14 of 'the children' sharing in flesh and blood, a cognate
adjective at 10:33 of the readers as partners of those ill-treated. The
noun itself is used at Ac. 2:42 in the sense of 'fellowship' (cf. 1
C. 1:9; Phil. 1:5), at Rom. 15:26 of a contribution to the poor of
the saints of Jerusalem, at 1 C. 10:16 of participation or communion
in the body and blood of Christ, at 2 C. 13:13 of the fellowship of
the Holy Spirit (cf. Phil. 2:1); it is thus a word rich in meaning,
and not easily to be rendered by any one English word.

As with the first six verses of the chapter, what might at first
appear to be a string of more or less disconnected injunctions and
statements proves, on closer examination, to be more tightly integrated. From general admonition, but such as would be vital to the
well-being of the community, the author passes to the assurance
contained in the quotation at verse 5, with its response in the
following verse. He then bids his readers to remember their leaders,
and specifically to remember and imitate their faith. This leads to
a programmatic statement of the core and heart of that faith (verse
8) and this in turn to a brief warning against false teaching. The
reference to foods (verse 9) seems to recall the fact that the flesh of
animals offered in sacrifice was the portion of the priests and this
leads to a further point: we have an altar, but the sacrifice offered
on it is already complete, and needs no repetition. It is parallel to
the Atonement ritual, and there the priests had no right to eat. The
bodies of the victims were burned outside the camp, and this is now
linked with the fact that Jesus suffered outside the gate. This leads
to the exhortation 'Let us go forth to him outside the camp', to
venture forward into the unknown, which again is explained by
verse 14: here we have no abiding city. Finally the last two verses
of the section sum up the only offering that remains for the readers
to bring to God, the sacrifice of praise, the fruit of lips that confess
his name, the life and conduct befitting those who know, in Paul's
words, that they are 'bought with a price' (1 C. 6:20; 7:23). Christian conduct springs from the experience of deliverance, and is not
undertaken in order to win it. At Rom. 12:1 Paul uses similar
language when he appeals to his readers to 'present your bodies as
a living sacrifice, holy and acceptable to God, which is your spiritual
worship ('acceptable' is an adjective cognate with the verb used

here). The thread of the argument may be difficult for us to grasp, but it is none the less present. Moreover, this section offers further links with the main body of the letter.

RESPECT FOR LEADERSHIP

13:17–19

17. At verse 7 above the readers are urged to remember their **leaders,** which in view of the context some have taken to refer to leaders now departed ('those who spoke', 'the outcome of their lives'). As noted there, however, this is not the only possible interpretation, and both here and at verse 24 the reference is beyond doubt or question to leaders who are still alive. 'Remember' in verse 7 certainly suggests the past, but Gal. 2:10 ('that we should remember the poor') and Col. 4:18 ('remember my fetters') show that this is not inevitably the case. The main point is that we have no firm basis for taking the word rendered 'outcome' in verse 7 as meaning their death, still less for assuming that it refers to martyrdom. Verse 7 *could* refer to past leaders, or to leaders some of whom are now deceased; verses 17 and 24 refer to leaders in the present. The readers are urged to **obey** them, and **submit to them,** and a reason is given: **for they are keeping watch over your souls, as men who will have to give account.** A similar admonition to 'the younger' at 1 Pet. 5:5 is preceded by four verses of admonition to the 'elders', while the responsibility of 'teachers' is underlined in Jas 3:1. The Pastoral epistles show how seriously the responsibilities of leadership were taken in the early Church. **Keeping watch** is a verb meaning to keep awake or be on the alert, and hence figuratively to guard or care for, like a shepherd watching over his sheep. **Over your souls** is a literal rendering, perhaps over-literal, since the word 'soul' is all too often understood in Platonic rather than in biblical fashion (cf. on 5:19. 10:39 above); *NEB* has 'they are tireless in their concern for you'. The leaders will have **to give account** of their stewardship, so the readers are urged **Let them do this joyfully, and not sadly, for that would be of no advantage to you.** The last clause is a classic understatement! The point is that authority in the Church is not a matter of domination: rulers in other fields may lord it over those entrusted to their charge (cf. Mk 10:42; Luke 22:25), but here the leaders are faithful to their task, and are to be given due respect and support.

18–19. The next two verses ask for the readers' prayers (cf. Col. 4:3; 1 Th. 5:25). Verse 18 uses the first person plural, while

verse 19 changes to the singular. Some commentators take the plural
as 'purely literary' (so e.g. Bruce. cf. 5:11; 6:1, 11), in which case
both verses refer to the author himself. The first person plural
however may vary in its reference, even within a single document:
it may be 'literary', or it may include both author and readers,
perhaps within a still wider group (cf. the 'we' in verse 10 above),
or again it may distinguish a group including the author from those
who are addressed. The same problem arises in some other books,
for example in 1 Jn (see Dodd, *The Johannine Epistles*, London
[1946], pp. 9ff.). Since it follows so closely on the reference to the
leaders in verse 17, it is at least possible that the author himself is
one of their number, although he is apparently for some reason
(temporarily?) separated from the community. This is of course
conjectural, but it would help to explain his evident knowledge of
the situation of his readers. In that case verse 24 would refer to
those leaders who are still among them. Here it is well to remember
how little we actually know for certain about the organisation of the
early Church. There were itinerant evangelists like Paul (although
we have but scant record of any others), who moved from town to
town, and Paul certainly maintained contact with the churches he
founded, as his letters show; but did others? There would also
be local leaders, probably chosen among the leading men of the
community, those senior in age (hence 'elders'), or the earliest
converts, but beyond such general statements we cannot safely go.
The Didache (ch. 11) reveals that itinerant teachers were becoming
something of a problem, and could introduce false doctrine (cf. the
warning against schism at 4.3), and also shows the beginnings of a
more structured organisation (ch. 15). What the situation was in
the community to which our letter is addressed we simply do not
know.

If the 'we' of verse 18 includes other leaders of the community, the
author is **sure that we have a clear conscience**: the responsibility of
verse 17 is being duly discharged. If it is 'purely literary', then his
own conscience is clear (cf. Ac. 23:1; 24:16; Rom. 9:1; 2 C. 1:12)
and his concern is **to act honorably in all things**. The word
conscience appears in the main body of the letter at 9:9, 14; 10:2,
22, but if a link were intended the 'we' in **we have a clear
conscience** would presumably require to include the readers, and
this would entail a sudden and unexpected change of reference. It
seems more natural to relate the clear conscience to the responsibility
of verse 17. Verse 19 is unambiguous: **I urge you the more earnestly
to do this in order that I may be restored to you the sooner.** Here
for the first time (apart from 11:32) the author speaks in his own
person. The only uncertainty relates to the word **restored**, which

is used at Mt. 12:13 par. of healing (cf. also Mk 8:25) but can also be employed for the restoration of the temple to the Jews (2 Macc. 11:25) or the return of hostages (2 Macc. 12:25). There are thus several possibilities: imprisonment seems unlikely in view of verse 22, since the author appears to be a free agent, but he could have been on a journey, or he might have been ill. At all events he was certainly a leader in the Church in the wider sense, and no stranger to this community.

BENEDICTION AND FINAL GREETINGS

13:20–25

20. Similar benedictions and doxologies are common at or near the end of New Testament letters (cf. Rom. 15:33; 16:25–27; 1 C. 16:23; 2 C. 13:14; Gal. 6:18; Eph. 6:23–24; Phil. 4:23; Col. 4:18; 1 Th. 5:28; 2 Th. 3:18; 1 Pet. 5:14; 2 Pet. 3:18; Jude 24–25. The varying position of the doxology in Romans is one of the factors which have led scholars to raise questions about the last two chapters of that letter; cf. Metzger, *Textual Commentary*, pp. 533ff.). This is one of the more extended forms (cf. Cuming, *NTS* 22 [1976], pp. 110ff.); some are no longer than the brief final benediction in verse 25 below. The title **the God of peace** is common in the Corpus Paulinum (Rom. 15:33; 16:20; 2 C. 13:11; Phil. 4:9; 1 Th. 5:23; cf. 1 C. 16:33; 2 Th. 3:16). The benediction of 1 Th. 5:23 followed by the final grace in verse 25 presents the closest parallel to the present passage, but cf. also 1 Pet. 5:10–11, 14). Since the readers are urged at 12:14 to strive for **peace** with all men, and at 13:17 to submit to their leaders, the use of this title has been thought to relate to divisions and dissensions within the community, which need to be overcome; but there is no indication that the community was beset by the kind of dissension with which Paul had to deal in Corinth. Moreover the word **peace** frequently corresponds to the Hebrew *shalom* (cf. Paul's characteristic expansion of the epistolary greeting: 'grace and peace'), and it may well be that the associations are rather with well-being, with salvation, which would be specially appropriate in such a letter as this (cf. *BAG* 227b). In the following clause, **who brought again** (or: brought up, cf. Rom. 10:7; the compound can have either force) **from the dead our Lord Jesus, the great shepherd of the sheep, by the blood of the eternal covenant,** the translation follows normal English word order, but in the Greek, as on several previous occasions, **our Lord Jesus** comes in the emphatic position at the end. This is the one reference in the entire letter to the resurrection of Jesus (6:2 is general, 11:19 explicitly figurative); our author lays his emphasis on the exaltation, in the light of his exegesis of Ps. 110. He never uses the verbs 'to raise up' or 'awaken', or the noun 'resurrection', in connection with Jesus, and at 11:35 appears to distinguish between the resurrection by which women received their dead again (actually a restoration to *earthly* life, cf. 11:19) and a 'better' resurrection. The form of the present clause is based on Isa. 63:11 LXX, which reads *shepherd* in the singular, and thus identifies him with Moses, mentioned in the immediate context. The title **the great shepherd of the sheep** of course recalls the Good Shepherd of Jn 10:1–16, but the imagery goes back to the Old Testament and is so widespread in the New that there is no need to postulate influence from John (cf. Best in *NTS* 16 [1969–70], p. 97): it is used of God at Isa. 40:11 and Ps. 23:1 (this would make transference to Jesus easy when the title Lord was applied to him) and of leaders like Moses (see above), Joshua (Num. 27:17) and David (Ezek. 34:22f; at the first mention of David, in 1 Sam. 16:11, he was 'keeping the sheep'); for the New Testament cf. Mk 14:27 par. (from Zech. 13:7); 1 Pet. 2:25; 5:4. It may have a particular appropriateness here, in that reference has just been made in verse 17 to the leaders 'watching over' the community (cf. 1 Pet. 5:1–3): they are not like the shepherds who incur the condemnation of the prophets (cf. Isa. 56:11; Jer. 23:1ff.; Ezek. 34:2ff.)! The phrase **the blood of the covenant** comes from Zech. 9:11, **the eternal** (or everlasting) **covenant** from Isa. 55:3; Jer. 32:40; Ezek. 37:26. Our author has had much to say in the main body of the letter about a new covenant, including an extended quotation from the preceding chapter of Jeremiah, some of which is echoed in the immediate context of Jer. 32:40. This verse thus draws several threads together, and by introducing the theme of the resurrection of Jesus provides a crown and culmination to all that has gone before: God has proved his faithfulness.

21. Verse 21 continues (still in the same sentence) with a prayer: **the God of peace . . . equip you with everything good that you may do his will, working in you that which is pleasing in his sight, through Jesus Christ; to whom be glory for ever and ever. Amen**. As noted above, this follows a pattern also found at 1 Th. 5:23 and 1 Pet. 5:10–11 (in the latter case, note the *RSV* margin: some manuscripts have an optative form instead of the future). **Equip** is a word already used at 10:5 ('prepared') and 11:3 ('created'); it means to put in order or into condition, e.g. at Mk 1:19 of attending to nets, hence to prepare or make complete. *RSV* takes the following preposition as meaning 'with', *AV* and *NEB* as meaning 'in'. Both senses are possible, but *AV* and *NEB* are perhaps too strong in translating the verb 'make you perfect': Greek has a different verb for this, which has already been used nine times in the letter (cf. Peterson, p. 279 n. 1). *AV* certainly ('in every good work'), and *NEB* possibly ('in all goodness'), follows an inferior text: 'work' is not in the earliest manuscripts, and Metzger (p. 676) calls it 'an obvious homiletic gloss'. The point here is not their being made perfect, but their being equipped **to do his will** (cf. 10:36 above; the author says there that they have need of endurance to do God's will, but they are not left entirely to their own devices). For **pleasing in his sight** cf. 11:5, 6; 12:28; 13:16, all of which translate forms from the same root as the word used here. The marginal reading 'working in us' is actually more strongly supported in the manuscripts; the difference is only in a single letter, and confusion one way or the other is very common. Here the 'you' just above would make the change both easy and natural. If we read 'us', then the author is joining himself with his readers (cf. *NEB*: 'may he make of us what he would have us be'). **To whom** could refer to **Jesus Christ** immediately before (cf. 2 Tim. 4:18; 2 Pet. 3:18), but probably refers to God, who is the main subject of the whole sentence (Westcott, p. 466f. lists sixteen New Testament doxologies, three of which are directly addressed to Christ, eleven to God; the two doubtful cases are the present verse and 1 Pet. 4:11, where in their commentaries Selwyn for example takes the one view and Best the other).

22. At verse 22 the author betrays some apprehension as to the reception of his letter: **I appeal to you, brethren, bear with my word of exhortation, for I have written to you briefly.** It is in fact these last four verses that convert the homily into a letter: the benediction of verses 20–21 and the following Amen effectively close the work. There is no reason to separate chapter 13 from the main body, to which it constantly refers, nor is there ground for regarding the **briefly** here as referring to this chapter alone. At 5:11 above our author wrote that he had much to say, while at 11:32 he clearly and deliberately cuts things short. His apprehension obviously stems from the length of his work, but considering all that he has put into it, it is not unduly long. Many commentators have observed that it could be read aloud in an hour. The only true criterion here is not the length of a work but its contents, and in that respect this book must claim a high place. It is not in fact so long as Romans or 1 Corinthians, and distinctly shorter than Acts (though that is not a letter); it is however some three times the length of 1 Peter, whose author also claims to write 'briefly' (1 Pet. 5:12). The word rendered **exhortation** has already been used at 6:18 in the sense of 'encouragement', at 12:5 in that of 'exhortation'; it is probably the former that

is most appropriate here, and as already noted this is a quite admir-

able description of the book. The word also occurs at Ac. 4:36

in the explanation of Barnabas' name, and the whole phrase at
Ac. 13:15.

23. Verse 23 then adds a piece of information for his readers:
**You should understand that our brother Timothy has been
released, with whom I shall see you if he comes soon**. The natural
inference from this translation is that Timothy has been in prison,
for whatever cause, and has now been set free, but this is not the
only possibility: at Ac. 15:30 the same verb is translated 'when they
were sent off', i.e. had taken their departure, been seen on their
way, while at Ac. 28:25 it is said of the Jews at Rome that 'as
they disagreed among themselves, they departed' (cf. *NEB* at both
points). In neither of these cases is there any question of imprisonment, so that it is possible here that the news is that Timothy has
already set out to meet the author. The readers of course would
know what was meant, but this is one of those cases in which our
information fails us. The only **Timothy** mentioned in the New
Testament is Paul's co-worker, and it is practically certain that he
is the person intended here. Beyond that, there is little that we can
say. Is it authentic, or a piece of window-dressing to suggest Pauline
authorship? If authentic, the letter would have to fall within
Timothy's lifetime, at a stage when he was still capable of under-
taking a possibly lengthy journey; but when was he born, and when
did he die? We simply do not know (cf. Introd., p. 5). Obviously
there is scope here for speculation and conjecture, but if we indulge
we must remember that such speculation is nothing more than
guesswork.

24. Verse 24 then brings comprehensive greetings: **Greet all your
leaders and all the saints**. There is no singling out of any one group
rather than another; the letter and its greetings are sent to all. If
there were divisions within the community, this could be a way of
promoting unity and harmony; but there are other possibilities, for
example that any separation was not doctrinal, but due simply to
the fact that some members were separated by distance. We do not
know the circumstances, but in a large city some members might
have some distance to walk to the place of meeting; or again the
community might consist of a number of house-churches, each with
its leader, and our author's concern might be that all these groups
should share his message, and his greetings. Here once more we are
reduced to speculation. Finally, **those who come from Italy send
you greetings**. This is most probably some group originating from
Italy, who if the letter was sent to Rome have asked for their

greetings to be included (cf. Introd., p. 9). Paul similarly sends
greetings from the churches in Asia to Corinth (1 C. 16:19), while
1 Peter more cryptically includes greetings from 'her who dwells in
Babylon, chosen like you' (5:13 *NEB*; commonly taken as a cipher
for the church in Rome).

25. The final **Grace be with all of you** is identical with that in
Titus 3:15, although *RSV* there has 'Grace be with you all'. Even
so short a sentence can give scope for translation variants! Similar
formulae appear at the end of all the letters in the Pauline corpus
(but not of other letters), ranging from the simple 'Grace be with
you' of Col. 4:18; 1 Tim. 6:21; 2 Tim. 4:22 to the trinitarian
formula of 2 C. 13:14. In the major epistles Paul usually has 'the
grace of our Lord Jesus' (1 C. 16:23) or 'our Lord Jesus Christ'; at
the end he has simply 'with you' in 1 C. and at 1 Th. 5:28, 'with
you all' at Rom. 16:20; 2 Th. 2:18, and 'with your spirit' at
Gal. 6:18 and Phil. 4:23. There are however manuscript variations
in Romans. Ephesians stands apart by itself.

However much one may have laboured with a text, however
careful and thorough the preliminary work and preparation, the
writing of a commentary poses continually new problems as the task
proceeds. Links previously unobserved, nuances hitherto over-
looked, call for attention, and for the modification and adjustment
of earlier judgments. It is a voyage of exploration, with new vistas
constantly opening up, new questions arising in changing situations.

Detailed examination of the letter has yielded but little in the way
of answers to the questions raised in the Introduction, and this is
not unexpected: had the answers been there, they would have been
noted long ago. It is, however, a question whether the problems of
introduction are so vitally important. It would certainly be useful if
we knew the date and destination, and particularly the situation
to which the letter is addressed: these might help us to a better
understanding, clarify some obscurities, and make some allusions
plain. It would be interesting to know the identity of the author,
but it is not after all so vital: the significance of a book does not
depend on the name on the title page. Otherwise an unknown author
might find it even more difficult to get into print! It is the quality
of a work that matters. Hence the questions of introduction are far
less important than the content of the author's message, what he is
trying to say to his readers.

The content of Hebrews could certainly be relevant to several
situations: for Jewish Christians tempted to relapse into Judaism,
as in the traditional theory; for Jewish Christians and others in a
period of tension and uncertainty, whether around the time of the

Neronian persecution or later in the period of the Jamnia reconstruction; or for Gentile Christians, or Christians generally, as Moffatt
and others have argued. We do not know; but what is significant is
the fact that it could be relevant to so many different situations,
and evidently was felt to be relevant long after the time of its
composition by those (predominantly Gentile) Christians who
preserved it and handed it down. The background, the imagery,
the method of argument may all be strange and alien for us today,
when a burnt offering is for many not a religious offering but a
culinary disaster, yet when we understand the author's aim and
purpose his work has meaning and significance, and relevance, even
for our vastly different modern world. This is a book with a message,
of encouragement, inspiration, hope, assurance. Whatever their situation, temptation to relapse, failure of courage, loss of nerve, waning
enthusiasm, the readers needed stimulus, encouragement, reassurance, and this our author provides by demonstrating that there is
purpose and meaning to it all. Looking back across the centuries of
Old Testament history, he builds up an impressive case, with
numerous examples of faith and perseverance on the one hand, and
the dangers of doubt and unbelief, apostasy and faintheartedness
on the other. With close on two thousand years of Christian history
behind us, we of today have even greater incentive to heed his
words.

One notable feature is the resemblance his work shows to the
basic pattern of the Philippians hymn, without the kenotic element
('emptied himself', Phil. 2:7) or the note of humiliation ('humbled
himself', Phil. 2:8). There is the exalted pre-existent figure of the
prologue (cf. Phil. 2:6), then at 2:14ff. the emphasis on the
humanity of Jesus (in even stronger terms than in Philippians), at
5:8 the reference to obedience (cf. Phil. 2:8), at 4:14 and throughout
the latter part of the letter the exalted figure of the great high
priest who has passed through the heavens (cf. Phil. 2:9). It would
however be dangerous to draw hasty conclusions regarding possible
dependence, since the resemblance is one of basic pattern and there
are differences both of emphasis and of detail. For example, the
emphasis of Hebrews is more upon the great high priest exalted in
the heavens: while there are several references to the suffering or
the sacrifice of Jesus, the cross is specifically mentioned only once
(12:2) and so is the resurrection of Jesus (13:20). That in itself is
enough to suggest that the letter is not by Paul (cf. 1 C. 1:23; 2:2),
although Paul actually does not specifically mention the cross in
Romans.

A special interest attaches to the Christology of the letter, particularly at a time when problems of Christology have attracted wide-

spread attention. The first point to be made is that our author wrote long before the controversies which ultimately led to the Nicene and Chalcedonian creeds: we cannot expect to find in his work the answers to questions that were not raised until long after his time. It is a question rather of observing what position he adopts, what statements he makes, in other words of seeing what developments have taken place, how far Christological thinking has advanced, even at this comparatively early stage in the history of Christianity. As already noted above, he begins in his prologue with the exalted figure of a Son, as yet unnamed, a figure of cosmic significance, God's agent in the creation of the world, upholding the universe by his word of power. After the demonstration of his superiority to the angels, it emerges at 2:9 that this Son is Jesus, and at 4:14 he is given the full title Jesus the Son of God. This, incidentally, is closely associated with the title of great high priest, already introduced at 2:17 and at least hinted at in the prologue, a title which will figure largely in later parts of the letter. For all these exalted titles, the main emphasis in the early chapters is on the humanity of Jesus, on his being made perfect through suffering; he had to be like his brethren in every respect, that he might become a merciful and faithful high priest in the service of God. From chapter 5 on, the emphasis shifts to the high priest in the heavenly sanctuary, into which Jesus has gone as a forerunner on our behalf (6:20), having offered once for all the only necessary and effective sacrifice for sins (cf. e.g. 9:12, 26; 10:10, 12). It is clear enough that the exalted figure of the prologue, the human Jesus and the great high priest in the heavenly sanctuary are one and the same—in the words of 13:8, Jesus Christ is the same yesterday and today and for ever—but while it is easy to understand the transition from the second stage to the third (he has passed through the heavens (4:14), been brought again from the dead by God (13:20), entered in as our forerunner (6:20) by virtue of his resurrection and in consequence of his obedience), our author nowhere explains the relation of the first stage to the second, how the exalted Son was made like his brethren, or whether in the days of his flesh he retained any of the powers and attributes of his pre-existent state. If anything, 5:7ff. might suggest that he did not. But these were questions that were to exercise the minds of later generations; our concern is with what our author actually says.

His purpose was to stimulate and encourage, to lift up drooping hands and strengthen weak knees (cf. 12:12), to inspire hope and confidence and assurance. We have no record of the success of his efforts so far as the community he addressed is concerned, but his work has proved its value down the ages. Those who preserved it, and eventually received it into the New Testament canon, were wise in their generation. We in our own day have need to give ear to his message.

INDEX OF MODERN AUTHORS

GENERAL INDEX